AMERICA'S COVERED BRIDGES

PRACTICAL CROSSINGS—NOSTALGIC ICONS

Terry E. Miller and Ronald G. Knapp

Photography by A. Chester Ong

TUTTLE Publishing

Tokyo | Rutland, Vermont | Singapore

DEDICATION

Terry's father, Max T. Miller (1916–2009) of Dover, Ohio, provided the initial stimulus for investigating America's covered bridges. The authors and photographer hereby dedicate this book to the memory of Max T. Miller.

Published by Tuttle Publishing, an imprint of Periplus Editions (HK) Ltd

www.tuttlepublishing.com

ISBN 978-0-8048-4265-5

Distributed by

North America, Latin America & Europe
Tuttle Publishing
364 Innovation Drive
North Clarendon, VT 05759-9436 USA
Tel: 1 (802) 773-8930
Fax: 1 (802) 773-6993
info@tuttlepublishing.com
www.tuttlepublishing.com

Japan
Tuttle Publishing
Yaekari Building, 3rd Floor
5-4-12 Osaki
Shinagawa-ku
Tokyo 141-0032
Tel: (81) 3 5437-0171
Fax: (81) 3 5437-0755
sales@tuttle.co.jp
www.tuttle.co.jp

Asia Pacific
Berkeley Books Pte Ltd
61 Tai Seng Avenue, #02-12
Singapore 534167
Tel: (65) 6280-1330
Fax: (65) 6280-6290
inquiries@periplus.com.sg
www.periplus.com

15 14 13   10 9 8 7 6 5 4 3 2 1

Printed in Singapore   1311TW

Front cover Spanning scenic Loyalsock Creek at Forksville (population 147) in Sullivan County in Pennsylvania's northeast, the Forksville Bridge is one of the state's most attractive covered bridges. Because it carries the relatively heavy traffic of Bridge Street going to and from SR 154, the state has hidden I-beams beneath the deck for safety and forestall replacement on the grounds of its official "inadequate" rating. The bridge was designed and constructed in the 1850s by Sadler Rogers, who created bridges large and small in the area. When yet a young man, he built a scale model of the rugged Burr truss that supports this 153-foot span. Although most of present-day Sullivan County (population under 7,000) is heavily forested, during the nineteenth century the hills and mountains were denuded by lumbermen, and vast quantities of hemlock logs were sent by raft down Loyalsock Creek under this bridge to the local tanneries. (A. Chester Ong, 2012)

Back cover One of ten remaining covered bridges in California, the Bridgeport Bridge dates to 1862 (page 244). With the demise of New York's Blenheim Bridge in 2011, this striking single-span Howe truss bridge with a clear span of 210 feet now has the greatest span of any bridge in the United States.

Front flap Hillsgrove, a hamlet nestled in Sullivan County, Pennsylvania's Appalachian uplands, illustrates well the ephemeral character of timber bridges: the need for bridges to carry pedestrians, carriages, and railways; technological change and the replacement of materials; and the role of covered bridges in the "industrialization" of once heavily wooded areas. Constructed by Sadler Rogers in the 1850s, the wooden bridge on the left led directly into the settlement, while the taller railroad bridge brought timber-laden railcars to the odoriferous and polluting tannery, an industry that began in 1870 and lasted in Hillsgrove until 1924. As engines became larger, rail traffic increased, the industry flourished, and the wooden covered railway bridge was replaced by a "modern" iron truss bridge. Because tannin extracted from the bark of the bountiful hemlock trees in the area was used to produce leather from hides, a boom in population benefited this area. By 1890, 805 people inhabited Hillsgrove, but with the man-made development of acetone to replace tannin there was the following decline: 1900, 686; 1920, 273, and by 1930, 50 persons left. At the beginning of the twenty-first century, with a year-round population of about 70, the hamlet and surrounding area entice countless visitors to enjoy its reforested hillslopes, clean water, and fresh air. Branded as Pennsylvania's Endless Mountains, locals take great pride in the three surviving covered bridges at Forksville, Hillsgrove, and Sonestown even as others are only recalled in memory and faded photographs. (Sullivan County Historical Society's Museum)

Spine The Schofield Ford or Twining Ford Bridge, which was originally completed in early 1874 in Bucks County, Pennsylvania (page 205), was burned by arsonists in 1991 and completely rebuilt in 1997 by local volunteers. Today, it offers passage across the picturesque Neshaminy Creek in Tyler State Park. A stone pier supports the bridge, which likely was constructed as a single span utilizing the Town lattice truss. (A. Chester Ong, 2010)

Page 1 Blacksmith Shop Bridge, New Hampshire (page 171). (A. Chester Ong, 2010)

Page 2 Knight's Ferry Bridge, California (page 248). (A. Chester Ong, 2012)

Page 5 Twining Ford Bridge, Pennsylvania (page 205). (A. Chester Ong, 2010)

Pages 6–7 Ashuelot or Upper Village Bridge, New Hampshire (page 166). (A. Chester Ong, 2010)

Front endpaper The longest historical covered bridge in the United States, the Cornish-Windsor Bridge (page 172), crosses the Connecticut River between New Hampshire and Vermont. On a heavily traveled route with a ten-ton load limit, the bridge carries two-way traffic day and night. In addition to ongoing maintenance to its Town lattice truss, extensive repairs have been carried out periodically since it was constructed in 1866. (A. Chester Ong, 2010)

Back endpaper Thomas Wilson's painting of Eagle Mills in Rennsselaer County, New York, depicting the village around 1845, places a two-lane covered bridge at its center, flanked by large mill- or factory-type structures along with a wooden mill building next to the dam. Today, a cider mill sits next to the dam and an undersized covered two-lane pedestrian bridge crosses Poesten Kill nearby. The main part of the village is seen in the distance. (Colonial Williamsburg Foundation, Abby Aldrich Rockefeller Folk Art Museum)

contents

Preface

Anyone who collects books on covered bridges and watches those bookshelves increasingly sag could legitimately ask, why yet another book on covered bridges? Granted, there are a lot of books.

Only a few combine history, technical aspects, and a survey of existing bridges, the exemplary models being the works of Richard Sanders Allen, whose *Covered Bridges of the Northeast*, his first book, appeared in 1957. Allen thoroughly researched covered bridge history and technology as well as visited and photographed hundreds of bridges for a set of books that continued until 1970. Most books since then have been limited to states or regions. Joseph D. Conwill's *Covered Bridges Across North America* (2004) is an exception.

Many books on any bridge lover's shelf are essentially photographic anthologies with captions. More recent ones are in full color and make for pleasurable reading. The earliest books devoted to covered bridges include two published in 1931: Clara E. Wagemann's *Covered Bridges of New England* and Rosalie Well's *Covered Bridges in America*. The first is replete with drawings and etchings as well as a readable narrative focusing on the social and economic conditions. The second is a fascinating photographic anthology of black and white images. Both include many covered bridges now long gone. It is significant that Wagemann's 1931 book and its revision in 1952 were published in Rutland, VT, by Tuttle, a venerable printing and antiquarian publishing house whose history dates to 1832. In the more than half century since 1948 when the renamed Tuttle Publishing Company was formed, the firm has become the leading publisher of books on Asia. We are grateful that Tuttle is publishing our book, which echoes their pioneering interest in the subject.

Increasing in number are books devoted to the technical aspects of covered bridges, especially bridge trusses. Thomas E. Walczak's *Built in America: Covered Bridges: A Close-up Look* (2011) is especially valuable, including as it does numerous drawings from the HAER (Historic American Engineering Record) archive. Related to these are books concerned with timber framing and restoration, such as David Fischetti's *Structural Investigation of Historic Buildings: A Case Study Guide to Preservation Technology for Buildings, Bridges, Towers, and Mills* (2009).

What is our claim for more shelf space? While much information on covered bridges is already in print, there is a need for a broader humanistic approach to the covered bridge that includes both historical and technical information as well as a reappraisal of the *place* of the covered bridge in American culture. We have organized this study into broadly conceived "perspectives": the covered bridge as a utilitarian object, as indicator of technological ingenuity and progress, as obsolete nuisance, and as a nostalgic icon and symbol of the past. When covered bridges first came to widespread notice in the 1950s, they were still plentiful but being rapidly lost. It was important to catalogue them and begin to understand their history. Sixty years on, our perceptions of covered bridges have changed drastically. While few are now being lost, we are confronted with a new challenge—how to "renovate" without destroying. Today's engineers and timber framers are highly skilled in (re)constructing covered bridges, but more and more "authentic" historical bridges are sadly being lost to replication. We address this matter head on.

So who is qualified to write such a book? Since covered bridges have no consistent place in academia, we cannot expect any particular group of scholars to step up to the plate. It is also true that today there is a dedicated coterie of covered bridge "enthusiasts," people who spend goodly amounts of time and money "chasing" covered bridges, as Paul Parrott put it in the title of his 2005 *Chasing Covered Bridges and How to Find Them*. While some enthusiasts do contribute articles to publications, no one has been inclined to take on the daunting task of making sense of covered bridge history and technology on a North American scale. Indeed, it could be asked if anyone is capable of taking on such a challenge. While constantly aware that we "do not know everything," we also understand that "if not us, then who?"

Primary author, Terry E. Miller, is a retired professor of Ethnomusicology, a field devoted to the study of music around the world, at Kent State University in Ohio. His work over the past forty plus years has focused on the music of Mainland Southeast Asia, primarily Thailand and Laos, while having a second major interest in orally transmitted psalm and hymn singing spanning the British Isles, North America, and the English-speaking West Indies, and a third interest in Chinese music. It is reasonable to ask, how is an ethnomusicologist qualified to write on covered bridges?

Miller was born and raised in Dover, Ohio, a town of about 10,000 in east-central Ohio. His interest in covered bridges developed because his late father, Max T. Miller (1916–2009), purchased a Leica M-2 camera in 1951 and decided to shoot pictures of a few of the known covered bridges in nearby counties, especially Harrison and Coshocton. His home county, Tuscarawas, had lost its last covered bridge by 1947, long before anyone in the Miller family was aware of such structures. At age eight, the author began appearing in his father's photographs, though having little appreciation of the significance of covered bridges.

One experience, however, did leave an indelible impression: walking through the 400-foot Conesville Bridge spanning the Muskingum River south of Coshocton, whose overwhelming width and height dwarfed the young boy. He also vividly recalls meeting the by-then long retired "Mad Marshall" Jacobs, once a notorious steeplejack and "flag pole sitter."

In 1956, Miller's father began systematically photographing the covered bridges of Ohio, and in 1959 expanded into Pennsylvania. By 1962, however, coinciding with the younger Miller's acquisition of a driver's license, his father had lost interest, leaving the zeal for covered bridges to his son. Since then, Miller has continued visiting, measuring, and researching nearly 1,000 covered bridges, most in the United States, but including four in Switzerland, around fifty in Canada, and over forty in the People's Republic of China. During his years of college and graduate study (1963–75), including two years in the military (1968–70), covered bridge research sometimes had to wait, but in 1966 he managed to draft his first book, *The Covered Bridges of Tuscarawas County, Ohio*, which was self-published in 1975 but had been researched in the early 1960s. He also escaped from his studies at the College of Wooster (Ohio) during 1966–7 to research the covered bridges of Coshocton County, which was published in 2009 as *The Covered Bridges of Coshocton County, Ohio: A History*. Spanning this time, he also published numerous short articles in several covered bridge magazines, built a number of balsa wood scale models of particular bridges, and around 1960 won a "superior" in a state-wide science fair for a study of covered bridge trusses that included scale models.

Ronald G. Knapp also is a retired professor, but of Cultural and Historical Geography, at the State University of New York at New Paltz. Over the past forty plus years through some twenty books, numerous articles, and many lectures throughout the world, he has analyzed, celebrated, and promoted an understanding of China's architectural heritage. In recent years, his research and writings have broadened to include the Chinese diaspora in Southeast Asia and America's covered bridges.

Born in Pittsburgh, Knapp saw his first covered bridge in the early 1950s in the counties north towards Erie as he visited an old farm owned by a family member. No photographs were taken and memories are only hazy. In 1955, his family moved to south Florida, a state without historic covered bridges but with many folly bridges built more for decoration than function. When he moved to New York in 1968 to begin his college teaching career, he found that the college was just four miles from the bypassed Perrine's Covered Bridge, the second oldest in the state. His Historical Geography course often focused on the evolution of transportation in the local region. These tentative forays pale in comparison with Terry Miller's ongoing and extensive investigation of covered bridges throughout North America during the same decades.

Knapp's wide-ranging field work throughout rural China documenting vernacular architecture led to researching and photographing old bridges, including increasing numbers of covered bridges. While several articles and a small 1993 book on Chinese bridges were published, it was not until 2005 as a participant in a Chinese conference devoted to newly discovered covered bridges that his focus began to change seriously. It was fortunate that accomplished photographer, A. Chester Ong,

attended the conference with him. After traveling nearly twenty times together to remote areas of China and Southeast Asia, they have collaborated on four award-winning books. In 2008, they published the first comprehensive book in English about Chinese bridges, among the least known and understood of China's many wonders. *Chinese Bridges: Living Architecture from China's Past* was listed as an Outstanding Academic Title for 2009 by *Choice* magazine. This book is the model we have used as we have written and illustrated *America's Covered Bridges: Practical Crossings—Nostalgic Icons*.

It was purely by chance that in early 2005 Miller unexpectedly learned of the existence of Chinese covered bridges while traveling to a music conference in Fujian Province, China. Later that year, he was able to visit two Chinese counties to see China's marvelous *langqiao* ("corridor bridges"), but it was not until 2007 that he met Knapp and Ong at the 2nd International Conference on Chinese Lounge [Covered] Bridges in Shouning County, Fujian Province, China.

Miller visited Knapp at his home in New York in 2008, and they spent two days visiting covered bridges there. While traveling, Knapp proposed that the two write a comprehensive book on American covered bridges, with Chester Ong's gorgeous photography taking center stage.

Since late summer 2010, the three have managed ten bridge shooting trips covering selected areas of the United States and Canada in pursuit of this goal.

This book has no intention of being "everything about covered bridges" or "the last word" on the subject even as its heft suggests significant comprehensiveness. We see the book, instead, as a reconsideration of the subject and offer a few new ways to view these utilitarian objects that have now become nostalgic icons. We provide also enough information about research resources to make this book and its associated website a starting point for further work by a new generation of bridge scholars.

Opposite from left Eight-year-old Terry E. Miller dwarfed by the massive 400-foot-long bridge over the Muskingum River at Conesville, Ohio. (Max T. Miller, 1953)

The co-author's father, Max Miller, began photographing bridges in 1953 and involved his entire family on this 1960 vacation in Lancaster County, Pennsylvania. (Max T. Miller, 1960)

Below from left Co-author Ronald G. Knapp with photographer Chester A. Ong at a village bridge in China's Shouning County. (Terry E. Miller, 2007)

Co-authors Miller (left) and Knapp (center) with photographer Ong (right) at Grafton County, New Hampshire's Swiftwater Bridge. (Sara Stone Miller, 2010)

Ong, Knapp, and Sara Stone Miller pause for lunch at Covered Bridge Pizza, North Kingsville, Ohio, inside a portion of Ashtabula County's former Eagleville Bridge. (Terry E. Miller, 2011)

New Perspectives on North America's Covered Bridges

Just think about it: you can still drive over (or, more properly, through) an all-wood covered bridge constructed as many as 180 years ago before bridge builders had even explained mathematically how bridges work. Over these years, the American covered bridge has passed through a series of phases, from its beginning as a common utilitarian river crossing to become a principal icon for an imagined, romanticized, and nostalgic past. As our perceptions have changed, so have our attitudes towards everything that affects the life of covered bridges, including "progress," preservation, and re-imagination. While most Americans living east of the Mississippi or in the Northwest probably have seen a covered bridge, few besides a small body of enthusiasts have given them much thought. When examined in greater detail, covered bridges tell us much about our history, attitudes, ideas of progress, and sense of self. We seek to reflect about these matters in this book.

For those who simply enjoy visiting covered bridges, the rural or village setting, the rocky creek, or the chance to take some photographs of one's children throwing stones into the water are sufficient attractions. For dedicated "covered bridge lovers," however, there is much more to discuss and even debate. At one end of the spectrum are purists who desire that the bridges remain in their original condition, but at the other end are people who accept all manner of "preservation," reconstruction, and alteration. The point where push comes to shove is in compiling the National Society for the Preservation of Covered Bridges' *World Guide to Covered Bridges*, the edition of 2009 being the seventh (going back to 1956) and the official list of sanctioned covered bridges. Earlier editions began attracting controversy when they started listing some of the newly built covered bridges found on housing estates, private property, and in parks. These disagreements were a major reason why it took twenty years (1989–2009) to compile the latest edition, which now differentiates "authentic" covered bridges from ones deemed less authentic. In spite of the apparent agreement in the guide, not everyone is satisfied, and some argue for delisting of certain of the sanctioned bridges or adding ones that were omitted.

What is a Covered Bridge?

Defining a "covered bridge" would not strike most people as anything controversial. Is it not simply a bridge with a roof? But the discussion can raise hackles when questions of authenticity arise. For many years, the major divide was between those who accepted newly built, often undersized "fake" bridges and those who rejected them, at least with respect to including them in the *World Guide* or featuring them in *Covered Bridge Topics*, the National Society's periodical. Today, the rapidly growing number of replicas—newly built copies—of original authentic bridges, where the original structure was either lost through arson, flood, or tornado or merely torn down and replaced by a new bridge using between a few and no original truss members, is creating new challenges. Resolving these questions turns on one fundamental question: how do we define a "covered bridge"?

If the descriptor—"covered"—defines the type, then any bridge with a roof and siding merits inclusion. But there are alternate ways to define the type as well. Some use the material as the critical element: the bridge must be all wood or a combination of wood and metal with wood dominating. According to this definition, then, stone arch bridges with wooden covers, often found in China, would not satisfy the criteria and would be excluded. For example, the now famous "Japanese Covered Bridge" in Hoi An, Vietnam, well known to thousands of Western tourists flocking to this UNESCO World Heritage City, does not qualify for inclusion since it is a pair of two small brick arches flanking a center span built on a stone slab, this base then covered with a small Buddhist temple.

Perhaps the most stringent definition is based on structure. To be "authentic," the bridge must have a functional load-supporting truss system of some sort. As a consequence, "stringer bridges," which have simple beams for support, do not qualify. Similarly, simple bridges having non-functioning simulated trusses also would not qualify. But excluding stringer bridges requires inconvenient exclusions because, here and there modest, homemade covered bridges have long been

Left The Chua Cau (Pagoda Bridge) in Hoi An, Vietnam, usually called in English the "Japanese Covered Bridge," has multiple stone arches and a wooden covered walkway along with a small temple over the water behind the bridge and entered from it. Built in the early seventeenth century by Japanese craftsmen who resided in Hoi An, the bridge is now an important part of this UNESCO World Heritage City. (Terry E. Miller, 2009)

Above from left A late example of the Paddleford truss, built in 1890, the Saco River Bridge sits within the town of Conway, New Hampshire, and remains open to traffic. (A. Chester Ong, 2010)

Although built late in the nineteenth century (1898), the Oakalla Bridge in Putnam County, Indiana, is a classic Burr truss typical of bridges built eighty or more years earlier. (A. Chester Ong, 2011)

Both to enhance the county's long-running covered bridge festival and to provide a practical crossing, County Engineer John Smolen built the State Road Bridge in 1983 in Ashtabula County, Ohio, using a traditional Town lattice truss. (Terry E. Miller, 2006)

One of Smolen's many "neo-traditional" bridges, the Caine Road Bridge, built in 1986 in Ashtabula County, Ohio, combines wood and steel to form a new version of the Pratt truss. (Terry E. Miller, 2009)

included in the "canon" of genuine entries, the *World Guide*. Delisting them after many decades will upset some.

Considering structure as the key factor also raises the question of which trusses are authentic. Some of the recently built "neo-traditional covered bridges," such as Ashtabula County, Ohio's State Road Bridge (35-04-58), built in 1983, make use of traditional trusses (in this case a Town lattice). But Ashtabula County has also constructed other new bridges using variants of the more modern Pratt truss (typical of metal bridges), such as the Caine Road Bridge constructed in 1986 and the Smolen-Gulf Bridge constructed in 2008. The Pratt truss is atypical among historical bridges, though not unprecedented.

Additionally, if having a "functional" truss is a requirement, then what about authentic bridges that have been reinforced to the point that the trusses, while present, no longer bear the load or merely support themselves and not the deck? When supports are added, these, rather than the trusses, support the bridge. Additional steel I-beams hidden beneath the deck to fully support the bridge render the trusses

non-functional. By that standard, the 1894 Meems Bottom Bridge in Shenandoah County, Virginia, which was partially burned but could be saved and reopened supported by I-beams, would no longer qualify. The 1852 "double-barrel" bridge at Philippi, West Virginia, made famous as a battle site during the Civil War, is now a modern concrete and steel bridge housed over by the original trusses and roof and would also not qualify.

Less satisfactory is a definition that privileges age and date of construction. It is agreed that the "golden age" of covered bridges was the nineteenth century, but basing authenticity on age creates more problems than it solves. Virtually all of Oregon's bridges were not only built after 1900 but continued to be built routinely into the 1950s. The same holds true for Québec and New Brunswick in Canada, where many bridges (all in New Brunswick) were built after 1900 and as late as the 1950s. Using date of construction as the determinant would also eliminate from consideration all newly cloned bridges, authentic in construction, but mostly built after 1990.

Ascertaining original intention is a difficult criterion. If the reason for building the covered bridge is purely pragmatic and functional, that is, as the best solution based on questions of efficiency and cost, then the bridge is arguably authentic regardless of age, truss, or material. Ashtabula County, Ohio's Smolen-Gulf Bridge, dedicated in 2008 with Pratt trusses measuring 613 feet (making it the longest covered bridge in the United States, *if* accepted as authentic), was considered an appropriate choice by its builder, John Smolen. But do we wish to accept or reject this bridge based on the question of whether wood construction was cheaper than concrete and steel? And can we be sure that tourism was not a major factor in a county which features its covered bridges in an annual festival?

Building "covered" bridges for reasons of nostalgia or ambiance, especially with tourists in mind, would seem to exclude them based on the question of intention. This criterion makes it difficult to accept most of the new bridges, many of which might fail on other criteria as well. For example, the covered steel truss bridge in Ohio's Mohican State Park, built for atmosphere rather than function, fails on several counts, including date, material, and intention. But can we be sure of the intention for (re)building Madison County, Iowa's Cedar/Casper Bridge, whose original was burned by arsonists in 2002? When the county cloned the bridge in 2004 using its original plans, was it because this was the best solution for crossing Cedar Creek or because Madison County wished to maintain all examples of its greatest tourist draw—its covered bridges—based on the success of Robert James Waller's novel, *The Bridges of Madison County*, and the movie of the same name?

We could ask, what is the purpose for list making, such as the *World Guide*? What do readers (including those of this book) want to know? If the purpose is to list and discuss every known covered bridge in the land regardless of its attributes, multiple volumes might be required. If the list's purpose is to identify only the strictly historical bridges, then it will be a rather slender volume. Would readers like to know about clones such as Kentucky's Bennett Mill Bridge and the out-of-whole-cloth Town lattice State Road Bridge in Ohio's Ashtabula County?

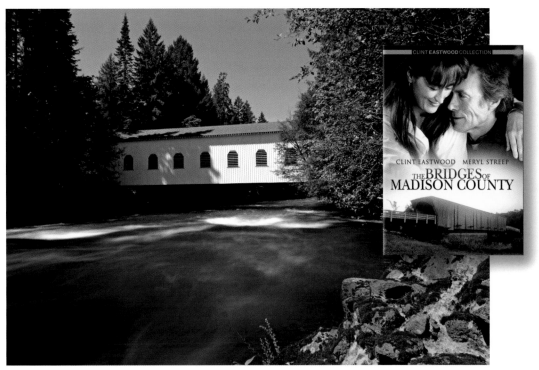

Left Constructed in 1966 and the fourth bridge at this site since 1890, Lane County, Oregon's Belknap Bridge spans the scenic McKenzie River. Although a typical Oregon Howe truss crossing, its late date of construction is slightly past the years when such covered bridges were still normal in Oregon, and Lane County's reputation for bridges likely influenced the decision on replacement after its predecessor flooded out in 1964. (A. Chester Ong, 2012)

Inset Meryl Streep, a war bride named Francesca Johnson, and Clint Eastwood, a National Geographic photographer named Robert Kinkaid, with Madison County, Iowa's Roseman Bridge. The 1995 film *The Bridges of Madison County* was adapted from Iowa author Robert James Waller's 1992 novel of the same name. For the film, county officials agreed to "age" the bridge to make it appear more rustic than its modern upkeep did. A Broadway musical based on the story will open in 2014. (Warner Brothers)

Below from left Eberly's Mill Bridge, built in 1846 of Burr truss construction, is typical of Lancaster County, Pennsylvania. Though retaining a high density of Amish who continue using their horse-drawn buggies, as seen here, the county's spectacular growth has altered its countryside from rural to suburban, forcing the Amish to live within urban development and congestion. (A. Chester Ong, 2011)

This three-span Howe truss deck railroad bridge crossed the Allegheny River at Foxburg on the western edge of Clarion County, which is north of Pittsburgh. Approached on both banks by long, curving trestles, the upper deck carried trains and the inside deck appears to have carried wagons, while a pedestrian walkway runs outside the trusses. Such structures came about in response to America's growing industrialization. (Smithsonian Institution)

The last remaining covered canal aqueduct in the United States, Metamora, Indiana's Duck Creek Aqueduct, was built in 1847 to replace an 1842 predecessor destroyed in a flood. Sixty feet long and of Burr truss construction, it carried the Whitewater

Canal over Duck Creek for only a brief period. The 76-mile-long canal, built between 1836 and 1847, was so heavily damaged again by flooding in 1847 that little of it remained open. After falling into disrepair, the state restored the bridge in 1946, and today it carries tourists seeing the village of Metamora from a newly built canal boat. (A. Chester Ong, 2011)

The Juniata Division of the Pennsylvania Canal—actually a system—was opened in 1832. Starting from Duncan's Island on the Susquehanna River, the canal crossed the Juniata River through a 600-foot multi-span Burr truss-covered aqueduct with interior towpaths. This canal branch, with 86 locks and 25 aqueducts, never made a profit, and the right of way was eventually sold to the Pennsylvania Railroad. (Pennsylvania Canal Society)

Built in 1838 by John Hough to cross the Scioto River, the Circleville Aqueduct was the longest covered aqueduct on the Ohio and Erie Canal. After the canal ceased operation in 1878, the bridge served as an ice skating rink in the winter and as a dance hall at other times until it burned under mysterious circumstances in 1915. (Miriam Wood Collection)

Should they also know about the same county's newest bridge, the gigantic Smolen-Gulf Bridge? I think most do. Further, should they know about Parke County, Indiana's newly rebuilt Bridgeton Bridge whose burned original was central to the county's covered bridge festival?

Ultimately, it is up to the editors of publications listing covered bridges to set standards for inclusion. The World Guide is more problematic in that changes in policy could wreak havoc on each edition if new editors make major changes such as including or excluding all those "fake" bridges we love to hate. Designating a bridge with an official number (state-county-bridge) lends it legitimacy. Once a number has been assigned to a bridge, you cannot eliminate that listing or replace it without creating a certain amount of chaos.

We favor distinguishing "classic" historical bridges from those which are less so. But we also recognize that a full discussion of the covered bridge in America (including Canada) cannot take place without the inclusion of bridges that have been modified or even reconstructed. In many cases, the World Guide adds #2 to the bridge's number. Indeed, let that be the thread that unifies the narrative: our changing perspectives on the covered bridge.

Bridge Basics

Covered bridges are essentially wooden (or mostly wooden) trusses that carry a roadway over a body of water. While most such bridges today carry (or carried in the past) vehicular traffic, many similar bridges also carried railroads. Less common were aqueducts designed to carry a canal and canal boats.

When the roadway passes between trusses whose base is level with the roadway, engineers call this a "through" bridge. When the roadway passes above the trusses, engineers call this a "deck" bridge. Because covered bridges by definition have a roof, all covered bridges are "through" bridges, but a great many wooden through truss bridges, especially those built for railroads, were left uncovered. Deck bridges could be covered in that the sides were protected with siding, but just as many were left open. Some deck bridges, sided or not, carried vehicular traffic, but the majority carried railroads.

Through bridges have the advantage of being higher over the water, and deck bridges, because the trusses are below grade, tend to be closer to the water and therefore more vulnerable to floods and ice jams. Aqueducts could be either through or deck, covered or uncovered. Some through aqueducts were fully covered. Through aqueducts, however, were necessarily quite wide to allow for towpaths on each side of the trough. Not surprisingly, the majority of aqueducts were deck trusses with the trough running between the upper portions of the trusses.

In addition to full-sized bridges and aqueducts, there are also "pony" truss bridges. Some are simply low trusses in an otherwise normal covered bridge, while others are boxed and lack a roof.

Bridge trusses had to be placed on some kind of foundation. Where stone was plentiful, these foundations consisted of large rectangular blocks laid without mortar. Where stone was difficult to obtain, builders often used heavy wooden posts, but foundations of wood naturally deteriorated quickly. The foundations on each bank of the river or stream are called "abutments," while supports built between them in the river are called "piers."

In most cases, the builders preferred to build the roadway right to the bridge entrance, sometimes held in place by stone parapets or retaining walls. In other cases, builders constructed free-standing abutments at the water's edge and away from the higher river bank, requiring open wooden approaches.

Sometimes these approaches were supported by simple wooden trusses, either open or boxed in. While this solution provided the river a wider space during flooding, it made entering the bridge more dangerous for vehicles, and open wooden approaches naturally rotted quickly too. Open approaches are common in the American South and Midwest, especially Illinois and Iowa.

How the Book is Organized

The era of the covered bridge in North America spans slightly over two centuries. Chapter One views them both historically and as common sense, logical solutions to the problem of getting people, animals, and goods across rivers. They were simply bridges—utilitarian, functional, commonplace—although sometimes later recognized as engineering marvels or seen as aesthetically pleasing masterpieces.

During the first half century or so, roughly to 1850, bridge builders worked from their experience in constructing other kinds of wooden

Above Like many bridges in the Illinois-Iowa-Kansas area, where streams are muddy and lack defined banks, Sangamon County, Illinois's Glenarm Bridge sits on four metal cylinders filled with concrete, with short open approaches to the bridge. (Terry E. Miller, 1968)

Left A buggy emerges from an old and long-forgotten bridge over the Yocona River in Lafayette County, Mississippi, in the early 1900s. The Town lattice design was preferred in most parts of the South. (Lafayette County, Mississippi Genealogy and History Network)

Opposite In Bartow County, Georgia, travelers crossing the Lowry or Euharlee Creek Bridge first had to cross a wide flood plain on an open approach. While necessary, such structures were subject to rapid deterioration because of exposure to the elements. (A. Chester Ong, 2011)

framed structures, especially houses, barns, churches, and mills. Although bridge building became a mathematically informed science during the second half of the century, with the appearance of several "treatises" and textbooks on bridge building, many local builders continued to work within local traditions based on an experientially learned body of knowledge passed down from elder to younger. Indeed, some local builders were illiterate, yet could construct wooden bridges capable of carrying heavy traffic for many years.

Chapter Two traces the history and development of bridge design. At first using only the materials at hand—mainly timber but small pieces of iron hardware as well—bridge builders developed an increasing array of structural patterns—called "trusses"—which offered greater and greater flexibility, strength, and efficiency. Hundreds of bridge trusses were devised, many of them receiving patents, though practically speaking only about a dozen came into common use.

Chapter Three addresses a question that has long perplexed bridge enthusiasts: exactly how were covered bridges erected? After exploring several theories that have been proposed, we examine a body of evidence comprised of bridge treatises, personal reminiscences, and vintage photographs. We suspect that the answers have been difficult to come by because the methodology of bridge construction was simply taken for granted.

Chapter Four traces the fate of the covered bridge into modern times. As befell the canals and water-powered mills that developed during the same period as the covered bridge, new technology gradually

rendered the covered bridge obsolete. As bridge building became an engineering science and foundries produced ever greater amounts of iron in ever larger pieces, wooden bridges gave way to metal bridges. As wood was giving way to metal, bridge building transitioned through a period of "combination" bridges in the 1870s to the 1890s, some being open, some covered. Oddly, though, the building of covered bridges did not end with the development of iron bridges. At the beginning of the twentieth century, when wooden bridges were mostly obsolete in New England, the Middle Atlantic States, and parts of the Midwest, two other areas began building covered bridges in great numbers—the American Northwest, especially Oregon, and the Canadian provinces of Québec and New Brunswick. Both areas were remote from iron foundries and steel mills in regions where wood was more plentiful. The American South, for similar reasons, continued building covered bridges into the 1930s.

This chapter also considers the period when covered bridges became, in most areas at least, obsolete, if not nuisances and impediments to progress. If covered bridges were well maintained, they remained capable of carrying most traffic, but increasing vehicle size and heavier loads created problems. Large trucks now carried freight, buses became heavier and larger, and farmers had tractors pulling larger and larger pieces of farm equipment over country roads. Another major change was the increasing use of school buses, especially when many small rural schools consolidated. To most people, especially those living nearby, covered bridges were considered simply old, obsolete, and "dangerous."

While New Englanders generally valued their covered bridges as links to the past, elsewhere many people viewed them negatively. "Progressive" county officials pledged to replace them with nondescript, generic concrete and steel bridges fit for the modern times. In some areas, where officials were slow to discard the old bridges, local citizens forced the process by burning bridges. Although arson is a felony crime, relatively few of the culprits were caught, often on account of local politics where who you are trumps what you did. Throughout this time, floods, ice, windstorms, and other natural calamities also took a heavy toll, as they had been doing since the advent of bridge building. However, whereas in the nineteenth century when a bridge was lost to nature and would likely be replaced with a similar bridge, by this time the replacements were always modern.

Chapter Five examines covered bridges during our present time period, the late twentieth and early twenty-first centuries. With the elimination of most bridges vulnerable to nature or deemed nuisances, covered bridges have become much rarer than even just thirty years ago. But, as the covered bridge became increasingly associated with notions of "a simpler past" and attained the status of nostalgic icon, a number of counties around the United States discovered that covered bridges could draw thousands of tourists for festivals, bringing economic benefits to many, especially in places like Parke County, Indiana, which otherwise have little industry or economic activity.

By now, most covered bridges are well over a hundred years old, some up to 150 years, and fewer and fewer of them are up to carrying normal traffic. Whereas in the previous period, officials "progressed" by replacing the old bridges with modern ones, in this period every effort is made to keep the bridge "in some form" while still making engineering progress. In some cases, old bridges were bypassed and then became the responsibility of a park board or other entity as they sat in splendid retirement. Sometimes, however, the land and bridge reverted to the property owner, which unfortunately sometimes led to abandonment and deterioration. In many more cases, bridges were moved into parks, sometimes over water, sometimes not.

The greatest challenge currently to covered bridge aficionados is what is denoted as "restoration" or "reconstruction." These terms mean different things to different people. The most conservative processes involve replacement of only the "bad" timbers, but defining "bad" is the issue. Traditional timber framers seek to keep all but the worst timbers in order to preserve the historical integrity of the bridge. Many "modern" engineers find little of the old wood to be serviceable. The question then becomes, at what point has a bridge's historical integrity been compromised—with 40 percent new timber, 60 percent, or 80 percent? In quite a few cases, engineers simply replicated the old bridge using 100 percent new materials. When replacing a bridge that had been burned or destroyed, there is no choice. But when an historic bridge that remains in serviceable condition is simply dismantled and a replacement out of whole cloth put in its place, covered bridge lovers tend to become vexed.

Chapter 6 features fifty-five exemplary covered bridges in the United States and Canada, each with photos and an essay. Some are inimitable and exceptional, others are more typical. Each has something unique to offer: a colorful story, unusual construction, a special environment, or an object lesson. They are intended as a sampling rather than a "canon" of exceptional bridges.

Below With its open approaches removed, the 1858 Waldo or Riddle's Mill Bridge in Talladega County, Alabama, isolated on tall stone pier-abutments, has been inaccessible perhaps since being condemned in the 1960s. Luckily, it survived the Civil War when a Union Army unit called Wilson's Raiders crossed in April 1865. Several attempts to refurbish the bridge and develop a park have failed. (A. Chester Ong, 2011)

chapter one

THE BIRTH OF THE NORTH AMERICAN COVERED BRIDGE

taken from the North-East-Side
on the 5th of October 1872.

UTILITARIAN CROSSINGS FOR A NEW CONTINENT

Although they are commonly called "covered bridges," the essence of such bridges is what lies beneath and is protected by the roofing and siding. The full name would more accurately be "covered wooden trussed bridges" because the last two elements—the trusses and their material, wood—are essential. While the enveloping roof and siding are critical to the survival of a trussed wooden bridge, they no more define it than our own skin, also critical to our survival, defines us as a human being. Consequently, in order to pursue a full understanding of covered bridge history and development in the United States and Canada, it is necessary to consider *all* wooden bridges, whether covered, uncovered, partially covered, or even those blending wood and iron.

Covered bridges as defined above are not unique to North America. Historically speaking, the covered bridges of central Europe and southern China have much longer histories than those considered here, but the North American (hereafter "American") covered bridge appears not only to have developed independently of these older traditions but along a radically different path.

What makes this so is not the phenomenon of having covers but the nature of the wooden trusses that supported the bridges. Indeed, Chinese covered bridges (*langqiao*, meaning "corridor bridge") have no trusses in the conventional sense, their support being provided beneath the deck and built to accommodate only pedestrians, animals, and small carts (Knapp, 2008). European bridges appear to have originated during medieval times, only developing into vehicular bridges after several hundred years. Their truss systems are mostly unlike those that were developed in the United States. From the beginning, American covered bridges, on the other hand, were intended for vehicular traffic such as wagons, as well as for pedestrians and animals, yet in time they came to include use by even railroad trains and canal boats. Several European countries are known to have built wooden rail bridges but mostly under American influence, while China never had covered bridges carrying trains or boats. While wooden truss bridges, covered or uncovered, did not originate in the United States, the designs that emerged of such bridges were uniquely American.

Above The Santiao Bridge in Taishun County, Zhejiang Province, People's Republic of China, straddles a rock-strewn chasm. It was built in 1843 on the site of nearby older bridges that helped link the stone-lined footpaths in this remote area. (A. Chester Ong, 2007)

Right Seen from beneath, the Santiao Bridge is lifted by major and minor timbers that are woven together to raise the structure some 10 meters above the streambed. (A. Chester Ong, 2007)

It is commonplace to describe "the past" as simple, uncluttered, and stress-free. We are inclined to idealize the eighteenth and nineteenth centuries as slower paced and more personal, and believe that the absence of distractions such as telephones, audio systems, computers, and traffic congestion made life more relaxing and peaceful. The European immigrants who arrived at various places on the eastern coast of North America in ever greater numbers during the seventeenth century were confronted with a relatively pristine natural environment but had enormous challenges ahead of them. Except for Indian trails, there were no roads through the vast forests or over the mountains. Even in 1837, when English civil engineer David Stevenson traveled throughout the eastern United States and published his *Sketch of the Civil Engineering of North America*, the American road system was deplorable. Writes Stevenson: "Road-making is a branch of engineering which has been very little cultivated in America, . . . direct[ing] their

whole attention to the construction of canals, as being much better adapted to supply their wants." And also: "The roads throughout the United States and Canada, are, from these causes not very numerous, and most of those by which I travelled were in so neglected and wretched a condition, as hardly to deserve the name of highways, being quite unfit for any vehicle but an American stage, and any pilot but an American driver. In many parts of the country, the operation of cutting a track through the forests of a sufficient width to allow vehicles to pass each other, is all that has been done towards the formation of a road" (1859: 131–2). Besides the mountains and endless forest, there were rivers and streams of all sizes, from the mighty Delaware River to minor rivulets. With or without roads, travelers had only two ways to cross these waterways: by fording or by ferry.

Even as late as 1797, famed American portrait painter Charles Willson Peale warned: "Easy and safe passages over the waters of the United States are much wanted—even our post roads are deficient; often the affrighted traveller stops, and surveys the turbulent torrent that hides an unknown bottom, he hesitates—doubts whether to risk a passage or not; at last, by delay grown impatient, he with fear and trembling cautiously moves forward and perhaps arrives in safety on the opposite bank; but alas! Too frequently the rash, or fool-hardy driver, is carried down the stream, and all is lost!" (1797: iii).

Fording was only possible when water levels were low enough and the stream bed solid enough to support hooves or wagon wheels. This could change suddenly after a hard rain, making travel extremely unpredictable.

Since deeper and wider rivers, especially the broad estuaries of the great rivers approaching the sea, could never be forded, toll ferries appeared when individual proprietors found it possible for them to be economically viable. When the water level was too high, too low, too swift, or the river was frozen, ferry services usually ceased operation, leading citizens to wish for a better solution—a bridge.

Peale also commented on this matter: "Legislatures, and you men of influence in the counties of each State! Turn your attention to this important object—shorten the distance to market for the sale of the product of your lands. I offer you a cheap and easy mode of building Bridges, the principles of which are so simple, and the mechanism so easy, that any ingenious man may execute them" (p. iii).

Even then, of course, humankind already had long and extensive experience building bridges. European immigrants to America knew bridges from home and had doubtless crossed many in their lifetime. But standing there on the wooded shore of one of America's wild and hitherto unbridged rivers, they had to determine for themselves how to get people, animals, and freight across safely. Some of the pioneers knew stone masonry and wood joinery from the "old

Right The old Miller Ferry crossed Alabama's Tallapoosa River before a covered bridge was built. Its peaceful appearance belies an exceptionally violent battle fought here on March 26, 1814 when troops under General Andrew Jackson fought the Red Stick tribe of the Creek in a war for control of much of the South. Jackson's troops, aided by a rival tribe, killed nearly 800 of the 1,000 Red Stick warriors, a tragic event memorialized in a national park. (Horseshoe Bend National Military Park)

country," principally parts of the British Isles or one of the German-speaking areas of central Europe. Few, however, had experience building bridges.

Looking about, they had only two materials at hand: stone and timber. Europeans, particularly those from the British Isles, knew stone to be an effective material for building bridges, but such structures were costly and time-consuming to build. There were too few skilled stone masons and builders to cross more than a few of the smaller streams, and crossing major rivers was out of the question. While true that stone bridges predominated in the British Isles, Britain had mostly small streams and modest rivers to cross.

More abundant and more easily worked was wood from America's vast forests, which were filled with old growth trees of every kind. Perhaps a few of the German speakers had seen wooden bridges in central Europe, particularly in what are now Germany, Austria, and Switzerland, but if any were experienced bridge builders, we do not know their names. Thus, the settled immigrants in the British colonies, soon to become the United States of America, had to use their own ingenuity to solve the most pressing problem that blocked transportation: learning how to build bridges.

Among them were skilled wood joiners with experience building mills, barns, and houses. Sawmills were already well established. Builders understood how to create strong frameworks of beams and how to span distances, especially for roofs. Small foundries could make nails, bolts, and straps of iron. Stone masons could build abutments and piers for bridges using patterns similar to those in houses and mills. However, bridge builders found that wooden beams alone are neither long enough nor strong enough to span more than a limited distance, requiring in most cases a series of stone piers, and the techniques for building such structures within the moving waters of a mighty river were as yet unknown.

How much American bridge builders knew about wooden bridge building in central Europe remains uncertain, but the solutions that developed in the young United States suggest Yankee ingenuity rather than a continuing tradition. If there was an American timber framing tradition, it relied on fundamental principles rather than wholly learned bridge patterns. The two principles that form the basis of virtually all bridge solutions that emerged in America are, one, the rigidity of the triangle, and two, the strength of the arch. Beyond these, there was only trial and error, experience, and common sense since scientific analysis of stress in bridge design was unknown until the middle of the nineteenth century. In fact, Civil Engineering as a named field offering training in bridge design and construction developed long after that.

An understanding of what came to be the "American covered bridge" requires, first, an understanding of the basic solution to the stream-crossing challenge—the bridge truss. Builders realized that by joining timbers into patterns consisting of little more than triangles or by creating continuous arches they could build structures rigid enough and strong enough to span great distances, eliminating the need for extra stone piers, which were obstructions to the flow of the rivers and to navigation. Although some small iron fasteners and straps were available, most of the joinery required only wooden dowels, called trunnels ("treenails").

Builders came to find endlessly creative ways of combining timbers into individually named trusses based on the triangle principle, whether combined with an arch or not. Moreover, being entrepreneurs they sought to protect as well as capitalize on their designs through the newly developed patent system, which promised an inventor a fee for the use of his design. As was typical of what many identify as the "American spirit," designs proliferated, some becoming wildly successful, others having little or no application, and some appearing downright whimsical. What came to be called the "American covered bridge" initially was simply a "bridge," and the story of the American *covered* bridge is essentially one of innovations in framing trusses.

The United States conducted its first census in 1790, ascertaining that there were slightly fewer than four million people living in what had recently been thirteen colonies, plus the districts of Kentucky, Maine, Vermont, and Tennessee. All but around 200,000 citizens were classified as "rural," for America's cities were then mere towns compared to what they would become. In 1790, New York City had but 33,131 people, Philadelphia only 28,522, and Boston a mere 18,320. Even with immigration, the US population would not exceed 100 million until the 1920 census. What this tells us is that relatively few people had to perform the tasks required to build the new nation, including its bridges.

Thus, the self-appointed, amateur "civil engineers" who took it upon themselves to solve the river crossing problem were forced to improvise based on common sense and experience. Having no known direct knowledge of Germanic timber bridges, they had at their disposal few documents that might provide clues. One of these was the writings of Italian architect Andrea Palladio (1508–80), the person most responsible for codifying classical architecture and designing numerous significant buildings and churches that now characterize the Italian Renaissance style. His *I quattro libri dell'architettura* [The Four Books of Architecture] was first published in 1570 and came to be known to the English-speaking world after an illustrated translation was published in London in 1738. In this document, Palladio described both in words and drawings four proposed wooden bridges, only one of which is known to have been built. All were simple trusses based on two of the most fundamental patterns, the kingpost and the queenpost, which are described in the next chapter. None was capable of spanning more than about 50–60 feet, however. While we can document the possible availability of Palladio's drawings to American builders, there is no way of knowing whether they actually replicated his basic designs into their own bridges.

Two Swiss bridges and their intricate structures were known to potential engineers in places like Philadelphia and New York because numerous travelers had provided detailed diagrams, some published in the United States. The first was the immense two-span covered bridge at Schaffhausen, Switzerland, built by Hans Ulrich Grubenmann between 1756 and 1758. Originally intended to be a single span of 364 feet, the city elders insisted on two more modest but unequal spans measuring 193 and 171 feet respectively, each supported by an elaborate system of overlapping queenposts plus a system of struts reinforcing the ends. The second

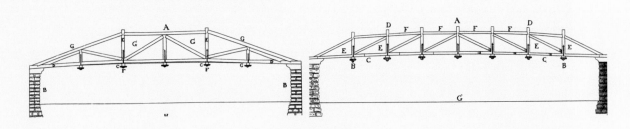

bridge was built in the 1760s by members of the Grubenmann family at Wettingen over the Limmat near Baden. Its 200-foot span was supported by a massive seven-layered, iron-banded, laminated arch nearly seven feet thick attached to the frame. Although not typical of American bridges then or later, at least one of eminent American builder Theodore Burr's massive bridges, the multi-span bridge crossing the Delaware at Trenton, which took three years to build (1804–6), closely resembles the Wettingen bridge. Engravings of both Swiss bridges clearly showed them to have been covered with roofs. From references in several documents, we know that a few Americans knew the European tradition of covering wooden bridges for protection.

Although there is the possibility that America's self-made bridge builders could have known the work of Palladio and the Grubenmann families, there is no known direct evidence to connect them to those specific designs or bridges. What is so remarkable about the nation's first generation of bridge engineers is that they not only, as it were, had to "reinvent the wheel" but did it with an unparalleled boldness bordering on the brazen. Civil engineering historian Lee H. Nelson's concise but definitive study, *The Colossus of 1812: An American Engineering Superlative* (1990), focuses on the work of four exemplary early builders and their bridges: Charles Willson Peale (1741–1827), Timothy Palmer (1751–1821), Theodore Burr (1771–1822), and Lewis Wernwag (1769–1843).

Among the first problems encountered by early bridge builders was that many of the young American towns needing bridges sat beside broad tidal rivers which often flowed deep. Some were more than a thousand feet wide, others even half a mile, and in one case, the Susquehanna in central Pennsylvania, more than a mile wide at some points. All were major impediments to transportation, trade, and urban expansion. Frances Manwaring Caulkins' *History of Norwich, Connecticut* sums it up well: ". . . roads could

(a) PLAN OF FLOOR

(b) SECTION   Center Line

(c)   (d)

not have been opened and rendered safe for traveling in any direction without spanning a multitude of small streams with some kind of stone-work, or with timber and plank, and these perhaps the next spring flood would sweep away. Consequently the work of building and repairing bridges was always beginning, ever going on, and never completed" (1874: 343).

Until the French developed deep-water caisson technology during the nineteenth century, builders of multiple-span bridges had to contend with the difficult task of placing stone piers mid river, sometimes utilizing simple coffer dams, which were temporary enclosures within a stream. It was not until 1872 that James B. Eads, the builder of the Brooklyn Bridge, took out his path-breaking patent for a watertight caisson structure that greatly facilitated the construction of deep-water bridge piers. Until then, builders were only able to construct piers in relatively shallow rivers and consequently were forced into creating (or at least imagining) grandiose spans for other situations. Some early builders proposed and even built some of the most daring bridges in American history.

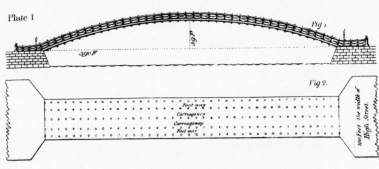

To get an idea of their boldness, consider New York "architect and landscape gardener" Thomas Pope, who patented in 1807 his "Flying Pendent Lever Bridge," a rainbow-like "grand parabolic arc," which is described in detail in the last 50 pages of his 288-page *A Treatise on Bridge Architecture* published in New York in 1811. That same year he came to Philadelphia and exhibited a model of half of such a bridge which was, by his account, some 50 feet long and weighed 10 tons (1811: 23).

During this time, Pope proposed to build several bridges, but only that for the Lancaster-Schuylkill or Upper Ferry, the future location of a bridge by Wernwag, has survived. Presumably using a plan like his "Flying Pendent Lever Bridge," he proposed a single span of 432 feet, 46 feet above the water, and estimated to cost $50,000 exclusive of the abutments and covering. That the city fathers ignored the proposal suggests sane leadership on their part. In a footnote in his book, Pope also noted that the specifications printed there were for a single span of 1,800 feet with a "versed sine" (arch rise) of 223 feet over the East River in New York. However mad his idea seems, Pope must be credited with being the most flamboyant bridge designer in American bridge history.

Not far behind was noted portrait painter Charles Willson Peale, who in his 1797 *An Essay on Building Wooden Bridges* proposed to span the Schuylkill at Market Street with a 390-foot laminated arch bridge rising 39 feet at the center. This rise, however, would have created an horrendous burden on the teams pulling the loads over this unwieldy structure. Pope and Peale wished to attempt such feats because building piers in the deep river was then impossible.

Peale's drawings for a giant laminated wooden arch bridge show he planned to leave it uncovered. Peale was aware of the option of covering the structure, because he mentioned that bridges with covering already existed. Writes Peale: "It has been advised to make roofs to cover Bridges, and some are so constructed in America; but I conceive this to be a very unnecessary expence [sic], for if the Bridge is not wholly [sic] kept from the wet by such covering, then instead of being a benefit, the roof becomes a disadvantage, by hindering the sun and air from drying and carrying off the moisture; and moreover such high and large surfaces for the wind to act upon, would require a great addition of width in such Bridges. Yet I must acknowledge if ever such coverings are necessary, it must be in the old construction of wooden Bridges with numerous mortices [sic], which are so many deep receptacles for holding water; and it is here that they have their points of bearing, for the support of such arches are only at certain distances, and hence for the maintaining of such constructions, they are obliged to be composed of an immense weight of timber" (1797: 13–14).

Taking Peale at his word, then two things are clear: first, that wooden truss bridges with siding and roofing were in existence at least by 1797 (and probably some years earlier since he wrote this in 1797), and second, that their covering was of no significance other than as a utility. Our current obsession with *covered* bridges might have struck Peale as odd because he was concerned only with bridges—bridges necessarily built of wood and necessarily protected, either with pitch or weatherboarding. It goes without saying that the covering now thought to be so nostalgic and romantic had no such meanings in early America.

Peale's observation also suggests that the type of bridge then being covered had some sort of truss because the covering protected the mortise and tenon joinery. Timbers had to be joined because they had to bear stresses both from their own weight as well as from live loads. Therefore, the main reason to cover a wooden bridge was to protect its stress-bearing trusses pinned together with mortises. Since transportation priorities probably dictated that the first bridges would span the most obstructive waterways, therefore these must have been substantial.

Ever since the publication of Richard Sanders Allen's *Covered Bridges of the Middle Atlantic States* (1959), students of covered bridges have accepted his assertion that the first covered bridge in the United States was Timothy Palmer's "Permanent Bridge" of 1801–5, which Owen Biddle covered with roof and siding only after completion of the trusses in early 1805. But Allen's book also hid an apparent secret in full sight on page 2, that the idea of a covered bridge had been recognized as early as 1787, some eighteen years earlier. The first issue of *The Columbian Magazine*, published in January 1787, included a detailed drawing of a proposed bridge by an anonymous builder, presumably to cross the Schuylkill in four spans. The cutaway drawing clearly shows what was later called a "multiple kingpost truss" with

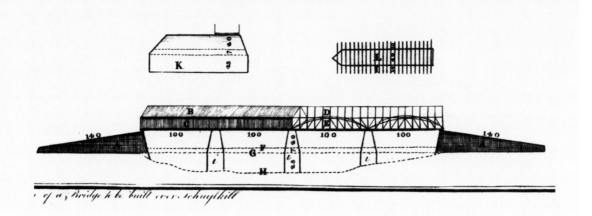

additional arches that appear to rest on the lower chords and not into the abutments and piers.

Indeed, this is exactly what was later known as a Burr truss or Burr arch after Theodore Burr. Since Burr would have been only sixteen at the time, it is highly unlikely he had anything to do with it, and besides, he was being raised in distant Torrington, Connecticut. Both roof and siding are clearly visible. Granted, there is no evidence that this exact bridge was ever built, but clearly builders already envisioned the type of bridge that became typical only twenty or so years later. The most likely reason for its not having been built is that masons had no way to build the three stone piers in the river's deep waters.

Earliest Documented Wooden Bridges

The "covered bridge," including Palmer's "Permanent Bridge" of 1805, of course did not just appear out of the blue. It developed within the historical context of American bridge building, and the act of covering a bridge was simply an option chosen more and more when builders wearied of having to rebuild bridges every few years because they kept rotting and collapsing, wisely giving in to common sense. Builders resisted covering their work because some believed it trapped moisture inside or provided too much wind resistance, while others thought a cover denied the public the opportunity to be awestruck by the magnificence of their work. While true that Palmer's great bridge over the Schuylkill was the first *documented* covered bridge, it was but one of Palmer's many engineering feats. And feats they were. But Palmer was not alone. The first generation of American bridge builders included some of the boldest bridge designers and builders in American engineering history. This Hall of Fame must include at least these additional names: Colonel Enoch Hale (1743–80), Moody Spofford (1744–1828), Jacob Spofford (1755–1812), Timothy Palmer (1751–1821), William Weston (1763–1833), John Templeman, Samuel Carr, Theodore Burr (1771–1822), Lemuel Cox (1736–1806), James Finley (1756–1828), and Samuel Sewall Jr (1724–1815).

One can hardly speak of a road system during the colonial period, the sparsely populated cities being connected with an uncertain system of dirt/mud roads, sometimes "paved" with corduroy (logs), many of them

private turnpikes. If bridges crossed any of the many streams and rivers, they had to have been simple structures little noted in written documents. Some that were noted were built by Lemuel Cox who, with Samuel Sewall Jr, built several pile and trestle bridges before the Revolutionary War. Their "Great Bridge" or "Sewall's Bridge," some 270 feet long, built in 1761, crossed the York River in what is now York, Maine.

After the war, Cox built a toll bridge 1,503 feet long linking Boston and Charlestown, which opened on June 17, 1786. The next year he built another over the Mystic River north of Cambridge, Massachusetts. His greatest pile and trestle structure, however, bridged the Charles River at West Newton with a structure 3,483 feet long and 40 feet wide that was carried on 180 wooden trestles (Allen, 1991: 11–14). Most of these included a drawspan to allow boats to pass. Caulkins' *History*

of Norwich, Connecticut, quoted earlier, details the innumerable bridges built in that area, few of which lasted longer than two or three years: "These early bridges, being supported mainly by heaps of stones, and studs driven into the bed of the river, could offer but slight resistance to the crushing piles of ice that came down with the released waters in the time of floods" (1874: 350).

Most bridge historians credit Revolutionary War hero Colonel Enoch Hale with constructing the nation's first substantial bridge. Built in 1785, it crossed the Connecticut River far to the north of Boston and Philadelphia, at Bellow's Falls, Vermont, where the river is narrowed by dramatic rock outcroppings. Here was a critical crossing point where the usual solution, a ferry, was not feasible. Although it was an open wooden structure, Hale's crossing lasted an amazing fifty-five years, until 1840, when it was replaced by a substantial covered bridge, by then a typical solution. Hale's Bellow's Falls crossing consisted of massive beams placed vertically at key points on the rocky out-croppings, with a flat deck above supported by heavy wooden corbels running at 45 degrees from the vertical posts to the deck beams and forming what appears as a simple triangular "arch." Considering the limited construction technology of the day, it is a wonder that mere men could place such heavy timbers within a dangerous river bed and complete such a long-lasting structure (Litwin, 1964: 13).

A possible "missing link" in American bridge history is the "Leffingwell Bridge," named after the nearest landowner. According to Frances Manwaring Caulkins, writing originally in 1845, and quoting a newspaper

article from June 20, 1764: "Leffingwell's Bridge over Shetucket river at Norwich Landing [Connecticut] is completed. It is 124 feet in length and 28 feet above the water. Nothing is placed between the abutments, but the bridge is supported by Geometry work above, and calculated to bear a weight of 500 tons [*sic*]. The work is by Mr. John Bliss, one of the most curious mechanics of the age. The bridge was raised in two days and no one hurt. The former bridge [Edgerton's bridge] was 28 days in raising" (1874: 348).

Caulkins continues: "This bridge retained its position, and the proprietor was allowed a portion of the toll for fourteen years. But in 1777 it was much injured by floods, and the town having purchased Leffingwell's remaining interest, united with Preston in petitioning the Legislature (May session, 1778) for leave to raise money by lottery for the erection of a new bridge. The petition was granted" (p. 348).

"Geometry bridge" suggests the use of a truss. Considering that Palladio's work had been known after its translation into English was published in 1738, it is entirely possible that builders here and there were constructing at least modest spans, almost certainly not covered. Indeed, Caulkins later refers to a bridge standing in 1813 as "the Geometry Bridge at Chelsea" (p. 349).

The Faith Trumbull Chapter of the Daughters of the American Revolution (DAR) in Norwich possesses a large-scale wooden model of uncertain age that purports to depict the old bridge. If this is accurate, then we can be sure a "geometry bridge" was an open double polygonal arch with posts forming four panels. While polygonal arch covered bridges exist in Germany and Switzerland, they are generally more complex, suggesting that Bliss either knew something of such precedents or independently invented it. Otherwise, the Leffingwell Bridge appears to be an isolated, one-of-a-kind design.

Between Hale's brave span of 1785 and Palmer's fully covered "Permanent Bridge" in 1805, a mere twenty years, American bridge technology made tremendous strides thanks to a small group of incredibly savvy, bold, and self-taught "bridge carpenters." All of the documented bridges, because they spanned major rivers, required extensive amounts of cut and sawed timber, thousands of tons of massive stone blocks, and hundreds of men, horses, and their necessarily simple tools. Additionally, every project had to be initiated with private capital because the governments of the time were not yet in the business of building roads and bridges. Risking great amounts of money to construct bridges over dangerous and wild rivers that routinely flooded with both water and ice floes each year, these early entrepreneurs appear to have lost out more often than they succeeded. In those days, investing in a bridge company was no sure way to safeguard one's assets or increase one's equity, and thus the bridge building business developed slowly.

Right from top The Connecticut River, running between Vermont and New Hampshire, passes through an especially rugged gorge at Bellow's Falls, Vermont. In 1785, Colonel Enoch Hale managed to construct a beam bridge supported by angle braces here that lasted until 1840, though no photographs of it are known. (NSPCB Archives, R. S. Allen Collection)

This scale model, believed to be John Bliss's 1764 "Geometry Bridge," also called Leffingwell's Bridge, over the Shetucket River at Norwich, Connecticut, is kept at the Faith Trumbull Chapter of the Daughters of the American Revolution (DAR) house in Norwich. (Gerald Dyck)

At least six major bridges were constructed over Massachusetts' Merrimack River between 1792 and 1795. Three men were chiefly responsible: Moody Spofford, Jacob Spofford, and Timothy Palmer, all living in nearby towns. Of these, Palmer, of Newburyport, became the most famous, though he is said to have learned his skills from the Spoffords. Together with Jacob Spofford, Palmer first designed and built the Deer Island Bridge between Newbury and Salisbury Point, also known as the Essex Merrimack Bridge, in 1792, only seven years after Hale's corbel-supported bridge at Bellow's Falls. The Essex Merrimack Bridge Company was authorized on May 30, 1791, and their charter granted on January 9, 1792. Amazingly, the bridge opened in late November (one source gives November 26, another November 20) of that same year. Two historians, Laura Woodside Watkins and Richard Sanders Allen, have written brief histories of the bridge, Allen's 1996 study contradicting Watkins' 1961 one on several points.

The Essex Bridge crossed the river in two segments separated by Deer Island. According to an engraving and plate description published in *The Massachusetts Magazine* in May 1793, the bridge's length was 1,030 feet in total. The northern segment, connecting Salisbury Point to the island, consisted of three short trestle spans, one of them a 40-foot draw, between what were likely piers of wood cribbing, completed with a trussed span of 113 feet to the island. The southern portion was mainly a trussed span of 160 feet. The engraving contradicts the description in several ways, showing the shorter trussed span with ten panels and the longer one with eight, and also not mentioning the long approach on the Newburyport side shown in the engraving. According to the drawings, the multiple kingpost trusses have arched upper and lower chords with either corbels or arches reinforcing the bridge from beneath. If accurate, the engraving suggests that Palmer had followed the basic principles of Palladio's designs, especially that of his bridge over the Brenta River at Bassano, Italy, "at the foot of the Alps" (1738: 67–8). In December 1792, only a month after the bridge's opening, *The Massachusetts Magazine* noted "The arch is deemed the *largest on the continent*. The whole work contains more than 6000 tons of timber. Mr. Timothy Palmer, an ingenious house wright of Newburyport, has received a medal, for the best construction of an arch."

By 1810 the southern span had deteriorated to the point that it was torn down and replaced by a novel chain suspension bridge based on the patent design of Judge James Finley of Pennsylvania and built by John Templeman of Georgetown, Maryland (now District of Columbia), and Palmer's close associate, Samuel Carr. The north span, covered around 1810, survived until 1882. A photograph in the R. S. Allen archives shows this remaining span as a fully covered double-lane structure with one or more arches beneath the trusses and deck.

In 1793, two major bridges were built, but the first of them, the Middlesex-Merrimack Bridge at Lowell, Massachusetts, also called the Pawtucket Bridge, consisted of three open flat-deck spans, the eastern two braced with corbels and the longer western span supported by an arch placed beneath the deck. The designer and builder may have been Col. Loammi Baldwin (1745–1807). Reports say that it was "rebuilt" in 1795 and again in 1805.

The second was the Andover Bridge over the Merrimack built by Timothy Palmer and Moody Spofford, reportedly for 3,998 pounds, but there are no known illustrations. It was described as having three spans with wooden piers, the center span being 110 feet. Considering who built it and the length, we would assume it to have been another arched truss bridge. As in so many other cases, nature was unkind to Andover's citizens, for the main span collapsed eight years later, on August 28, 1801, under the weight of a livestock drive. Asa Town replaced it with a bridge of three framed

Top Published by Ebenezer Turrell Andrews and Isaiah Thomas in *The Massachusetts Magazine* in 1793, "Newbury Bridge over Merrimack River" clearly shows Timothy Palmer's Deer Island Bridge between Salisbury Point and Newbury constructed as open trusses in 1792. The left span was 113 feet long plus open trestle spans, and the right span was 160 feet, both using arch-reinforced trusses. The north span (left) was covered in 1810 and survived until 1882 while the south span (right) was replaced in 1810 by a chain suspension bridge. (Boston Athenaeum)

Above A view from the shore of Palmer's Newbury Bridge long after being covered, showing part of the trestle and drawbridge approach. (NSPCB Archives, R. S. Allen Collection)

arches, but an ice jam destroyed most of the bridge in 1807, and the crossing was not rebuilt until some thirty years afterwards.

The following year, 1794, saw the construction of two more remarkable bridges. The lesser known Piscataqua Bridge, seven miles north of Portsmouth, New Hampshire, consisted of a hundred short spans on pile and trestle piers but having a "stupendous arc" span of 244 feet over the navigable channel of Great Bay. Considering that the builders included Timothy Palmer, we can surmise that the arched span resembled those built earlier, but its length, if correct, would be remarkable and unprecedented. If correct, then Palmer's span approached the bold dimensions of some bridges proposed but not built by Pope and Peale.

The bridge from Haverhill to Bradford, Massachusetts, over the Merrimack is probably the best understood of Palmer's great bridges since it lasted until 1875 when it finally had to be demolished. Although there are numerous photos of the structure taken long after it had been covered, according to Timothy Dwight, President of Yale University and author of *Travels in New-England and New-York* (1821–2) who visited the bridge twice, in 1796 and 1812, the bridge underwent considerable "rebuilding" or "remodeling" in 1808 and 1825, the earlier one supervised by Palmer himself. Because the piers were so massive, each containing 4,500 tons of stone, it is unlikely the remodeling changed the span lengths, each of the three being 182 feet. In addition, the bridge was double lane, each lane being 15.5 feet wide, and the arch, located beneath the trusses, rose 8 feet. Wright related that Palmer, along with co-builder Moody Spofford, first demonstrated the bridge's strength with a 10-foot model that allegedly held eleven men weighing together 1,600 pounds. Between the Bradford shore and the third span stood a 30-foot drawbridge. Dwight reports that decay had set in by 1812 on his second visit, and that the arches had been removed. Since he does not mention the bridge as now covered, we presume that covering came later, perhaps as late as 1825. Surviving photos, however, show that the arches had been restored and an uncovered walkway added. That Palmer and Spofford could have built such a magnificent bridge with such great spans in 1794 demonstrates how advanced bridge building had become by that time.

Although there are photographs of the Rocks Village Bridge over the Merrimack between West Newbury and East Haverhill, these include the 1828 Town lattice replacements for two of the original six built by Palmer and Moody Spofford in 1795 and partially rebuilt by them around 1812. The original bridge, which opened on November 26, 1795 and was described as the "longest on the river," is said to have been nearly 1,000 feet long with six arched trusses. Palmer's rebuilding, around 1812, only survived until 1818 when ice and high water destroyed part of it. The crossing then remained incomplete for ten years.

Although Palmer's early bridges all crossed the Merrimack River in Massachusetts, his fame spread, and in 1796 he was commissioned to build what was later known as the Chain Bridge over the Potomac River two miles above Georgetown at Little Falls. Chartered in 1794, the company hired Palmer and Jacob Spofford to build a multi-span bridge with a roadway that ascended and descended over each arched truss span. The longest was described as being 130 feet long with two additional spans that were shorter. Benjamin Henry Latrobe (1764–1820), a traveler from England, said it had been "framed in New England of white pine & brought hither by water," suggesting that it was prefabricated, probably in Massachusetts, and shipped by water (1905). After its opening in 1797, it is said that George Washington routinely crossed it on the way to Mount Vernon. A critical French visitor wrote that it was "disgusting in its heaviness, having an immense quantity of timber

Right from top In 1794, Palmer and Moody Spofford built this great bridge from Haverhill to Bradford, Massachusetts, over the Merrimack River. Each of its three spans was 182 feet long, over 30 feet wide, plus a short drawspan that allowed ships to pass. This photograph, taken during demolition in 1875, shows something of its structure. (NSPCB Archives, R. S. Allen Collection)

Left uncovered until about 1825, the Haverhill Bridge received its open walkway on one side at a later date. (NSPCB Archives, R. S. Allen Collection)

A view of Palmer and Spofford's Haverhill Bridge in the winter when the bridge's floor would have been paved with snow to allow sleighs to pass. (NSPCB Archives, R. S. Allen Collection)

and iron wasted on it" (La Rochefoucauld-Liancourt and Neuman, 1799). Not knowing that the bridge had already decayed and collapsed in 1804, Palmer wrote in 1806 that "the bridge I built over the Potomac at Georgetown in 1796 is not safe for heavy teams to pass over" (quoted in Peters, 1815). The Georgetown Bridge Company, owner of the crossing, duplicated the original, but only six months later a spring freshet destroyed the bridge. The third bridge, a chain suspension bridge, which gave the crossing its name, was built by James Finley (1756–1828) of Pennsylvania and John Templeman of Georgetown in 1807–8.

Although more and more bridges were being built by this time, two stand out. One was a two-span arched bridge built uncovered by Captain Boynton between May 5 and November 21, 1797 over the Kennebec River at Augusta, Maine, for $27,000. The eastern span collapsed on June 23, 1816, but a new bridge was not built until 1818 when the western span was also replaced. The second bridge, the Lansingburgh-Waterford Union Bridge, a 800-foot-long four-span bridge over the Hudson River in New York State, is the first known work of Theodore Burr (see further discussion below). If Palmer was bold, Burr was brazen, for each arched span was around 200 feet long, with 18-foot-high arches, and two roadways. Opened on December 3, 1804, this was the first bridge over the Hudson and remained uncovered until 1814. When it burned on July 10, 1909, it was then the oldest wooden trussed bridge in the country.

By 1804, then, several builders had brought the science of wooden bridge construction to a surprisingly sophisticated level with many remarkable bridges and daringly long spans. None of them is known to have been covered with roof and siding, Peale's assertion notwithstanding. Clearly, though, builders knew about covering bridges, but there was not yet general agreement on the benefits. None could deny, however, that in spite of tight joints, paint, or pitch, these glorious

arches and trusses deteriorated if left open to the elements. The next step would lead to the creation of the first *documented* covered bridge in the United States.

Bridge historian Francis E. Griggs Jr's concluding remark on the significance of Timothy Palmer's Permanent Bridge in Philadelphia, the country's first known covered bridge, sounds a bit hyperbolic, but within the historical context up to that point, he is likely correct: ". . . there is no doubt that Palmer had designed and built one of the most significant bridges in the world and maybe the most advanced wooden bridge ever" (2009: 516). Additionally, thanks to its location and the attention it garnered both in the United States and Europe, there is voluminous documentation, including diagrams, paintings, letters, and contracts, but alas, no photographs. Palmer, however, who later partially rebuilt and covered his 1792 Salisbury span over the Merrimack in 1807, wrote in a letter: "Last summer, I rebuilt one of the Arches; the span of which is 113 ft and is on the same principle with your Bridge" (Griggs, 2009: 513). Since there are photos of this bridge, we can more easily picture the much longer but more artistically finished Permanent Bridge.

Boston and Philadelphia were doubtless the two most important cities in the English Colonies at the time of the Revolution. During the revolutionary period, Philadelphia was the site for the signing of the Declaration of Independence, the writing of the Constitution, and the convening of the Continental Congresses. Following American independence, which was declared on July 4, 1776, and the final surrender of the British to General George Washington at Yorktown on October 19, 1781, Philadelphia continued to play a critical role as the seat of new national government, and from 1790 to 1800 it served as the temporary capital of the young United States while Washington, DC, was being built. In spite of a deadly outbreak of yellow fever, the city prospered, but its growth and communication with all points east were stymied by the Schuylkill River

Above Originally built in 1795 by Palmer and Moody Spofford, the Rocks Village Bridge over the Merrimack, nearly 1,000 feet in length, lost two spans to a flood in 1818, these not being replaced until 1828. In this photo of the successor spans—none, apparently, the originals—an open turning bridge allows a sailing ship to pass. (NSPCB Archives, George B. Pease Collection)

and the limitations of the ferry service first established in 1723. A movement to build a bridge on High Street, later called Market Street, began in 1750, but for numerous reasons—financial, technological, and political—only succeeded fifty-five years later when Palmer's Permanent Bridge opened on January 1, 1805.

During this period, the best architectural and engineering minds of the city proposed numerous solutions. The first plan, submitted in 1767, was for a wooden bridge in a single arch some 400 feet in length and 47 feet above the water, but that proved unrealistic.

Two years later, on January 31, 1769, a Philadelphia architect named Robert Smith proposed building at least one wooden arched span, ". . . well covered to secure it from the Weather" (Griggs, 2009: 507). Though his proposal was ignored by the city assembly, it was the first known mention of covering a bridge in the colonies and foreshadowed Palmer's Permanent Bridge. Another pioneering proposal appeared in 1774 when Thomas Gilpin of Philadelphia proposed building a suspension bridge with chains 400 feet long over the main channel approached by 300-foot-long abutments from each shore. Politician Thomas Paine, a man of many interests—both common and necessary in that day—proposed in 1786 both wooden and iron bridges, even building a 13-foot-long model of the iron bridge which he offered to Benjamin Franklin, who displayed it in his garden. The following year, Paine took that model to France, hoping for approval from the most highly respected bridge engineers in the world. Paine's knowledge of iron bridges is all the more amazing considering that iron bridge technology had only just been introduced in England, first in a couple of obscure minor bridges and then prominently in Abraham Darby III's amazing cast-iron bridge built over the River Severn in Coalbrookdale, England, between 1779 and 1781, only five years earlier. Because this was only possible due to the availability of iron from Darby's nearby foundry, Paine's idea for anything comparable in the United States was not yet feasible. Indeed, the city did not seriously consider Paine's iron span because of concerns about its cost, the difficulty of procuring materials, and whether the abutments could withstand the weight.

In 1787, a plan with a drawing published in *The Columbian Magazine* (discussed earlier in this chapter) for a four-span wooden covered bridge with arches and a truss was likely a reworking of Smith's 1767 plan. Who offered this proposal is unclear since Smith had died in 1777. Finally, two visionaries offered unrealistic plans for gigantic single spans, Frenchman Godofres Du Jareau in 1796 for a 300–400 foot wooden arch, and Charles Willson Peale's own single arch, also discussed earlier. It is fair to say that rationality prevailed in most of these cases. Smith's proposal for a wooden arched truss bridge, however, was the most realistic, but the main drawback was the impossibility of building the necessary piers in such deep water.

The term "permanent bridge," in reference to the bridge Palmer eventually built on Market Street in Philadelphia, strikes some as odd, since clearly no bridge is ever permanent. The term derived from the desire to build a long-lasting solution to crossing the Schuylkill in contrast to earlier temporary solutions, and proposals, such as a military pontoon bridge, a floating log bridge, or a low stone bridge only passable in low water. Because this river, like most in the eastern United States, was prone to flooding and massive ice jams that swept all before them, even some of the more practical solutions that involved approaches restricting the river's flow could not be considered. A complete history of the project appeared in 1806 that permits us not just to know the facts of Palmer's bridge but, through the inclusion of numerous letters and other documents to hear the arguments for and against various aspects, especially the matter of covering the bridge. Originally a report written in 1806 titled "A Statistical Account of the Schuylkill Permanent Bridge, Communicated to the Philadelphia Society of Agriculture, 1806," it was reprinted in 1815 in the *Memoirs of the Philadelphia Society for Promoting Agriculture*, Vol. 1.

Though the solution was not yet clear, Judge Richard Peters convinced the state legislature and governor to pass an "act for incorporating a Company for erecting a Permanent Bridge over the river Schuylkill, at or near the City of Philadelphia" on March 16, 1798, with Peters elected as President (Peters, 1815: 19–21). The Company offered 15,000 shares at $10 each for a total capitalization of $150,000, plus another 7,500 shares for unforeseen problems. Although still holding many unsold shares, the directors began searching for an affordable plan. Those proposed included one by William Weston, a British stone mason and engineer, who offered to build a series of stone arches. Another by Benjamin H. Latrobe, also of England, proposed a brickwork arch bridge. Still without a plan, the company hired a contractor to begin building the eastern abutment on October 18, 1800. Thanks to Weston's advanced knowledge of hydraulics and coffer dams, the company decided to proceed with a pier in the shallower eastern channel, still hoping they might be able to bridge the western portion of the river (and the deeper channel) with a single span. Although challenging, the workers completed it during the fall of 1801. Judge Peters later wrote: "We know that no iron superstructure of such a span had been erected. We sent for Mr. Timothy Palmer, of Newbury Port, a celebrated practical wooden bridge architect. He viewed our site, and gave us an excellent plan of a wooden super-structure. But he pointedly reprobated the idea of even a wooden arch extending farther than between the position of our intended piers, to wit, 187 ft. He had at the Piscataway bridge, erected an arch of 244 feet; but he repeatedly declared, that wherever might be suggested by theorists, he would not advise, nor would he ever again attempt extending an arch, even to our distance, where such a heavy transportation was consistently proceeding" (1815: 71). There being no way to span the channel from the eastern pier to the western shore without an intervening pier, Weston and his masons proceeded to construct one in the deepest water— around 40 feet—beginning (oddly) on Christmas Day, 1802 and finishing it during the spring of 1803. Peters later wrote of this problem: "I have never in the course of my experience, or reading, heard of a pier founded in such a depth of water, on irregular rock, affording little or no support to the piles" (1815: 44).

Even though the piers were in place, Palmer, assisted by Mr Carr and other experienced workmen, only began building the superstructure in 1804, and although they expected the project to proceed quickly, in fact it took nearly a year to complete. But Palmer's bridge, now benefitting from more than ten years of experience/ experiments in New England, was to be his *magnum opus*, a judgment accepted by observers at the time as well as the many travelers who later passed through the bridge and wrote glowing accounts of its great beauty.

The "Statistical Account" of 1806 summarizes the bridge's dimensions: total bridge length was 550 feet, consisting of three spans, the outer two of which had clear spans of 150 feet each and the middle span an amazing 194 feet 10 inches. Adding the abutments and wing walls, the bridge covered 1,300 feet. The width was 42 feet, with an interior clearance of 13 feet for each of two lanes plus footways 5 feet wide on each side separated from the carriageway by "turned posts and chains." The three trusses (two outer, one separating the roadways) each consisted of double arches rising from the masonry walls to the lower chords beneath the roadway plus slightly curved lower and upper chords rising 8 feet in a continuous arc (and avoiding the rise and fall of each span encountered in Palmer's earlier bridges). The arches of the outer spans rose 10 feet while that of the middle span rose 12. The kingposts were not only radial but extended below the lower chords to the arches, as was also true of the braces. Each of the shorter spans had eight panels while the center span had ten. While the report says the carriage-way was 31 feet above the water, we are uncertain whether that was at the base or apex of the arches. In all, the bridge required 22,000 perches of stone—each equivalent to 24.75 cubic feet—and 1,500,000 board feet of timber. Its total cost came to nearly $300,000, a huge sum in those days.

Although the bridge opened on January 1, 1805, it remained unfinished in some ways and also uncovered. Judge Peters, though President, had been forced to accept the wishes of the Board in leaving the structure exposed to the weather. Some believed that covering it would cause water to be retained and prohibit drying, though Peters and Palmer believed that sealing the timbers with paint or some form of pitch would prohibit the timbers from becoming seasoned. Others feared

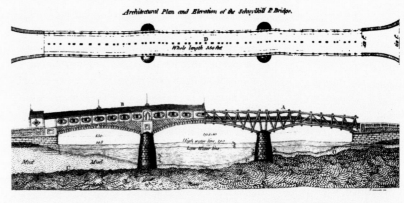

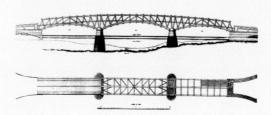

Above Philadelphia's Market Street crossing of the Schuylkill challenged engineers for many years because they could not build stone piers. (Peters, 1815)

Left A clear rendering of both truss and deck structures of Palmer's Permanent Bridge over the Schuylkill River on Philadelphia's Market Street. (Weale, 1843; reproduced in Nelson, 1990: 14)

Above British-born painter William Russell Birch (1755–1834) arrived in Philadelphia in 1794, ten years before Palmer's Permanent Bridge was completed. His paint-ing of the uncovered bridge must have been done early in 1805 because by the end of the year Owen Biddle had roofed and sided the structure, creating America's first documented "covered bridge." (Encore Editions)

Left Birch's etching, shown in the foreground along the shore and reproduced here, reveals the bridge after it was covered. (American Philosophical Society)

that siding would play havoc with windstorms and cause the bridge to be blown from its foundations. Peters, apparently aware of Smith's earlier advocacy of covering in 1769, had already sounded out Palmer on the matter of a roof and siding, for his letter to the Board of June 11, 1805, originally printed in the *US Gazette* in 1805 and included in the "Statistical Report" of 1806, its reprinting in 1815, and again in *The American Farmer* for November 16, 1821, quotes a letter he received from Timothy Palmer written on December 10, 1804. Although Palmer's earlier bridges were not covered at the time of construction, Palmer indicated an understanding of its benefits. Palmer wrote: ". . . relative to the durability of timber bridges, without being covered sides and top, I answer, from the experience that I have had in New-England and Maryland—that they will not last for more than ten or twelve years, to be safe for heavy carriages to pass over." After citing problems with the open bridges he had built earlier, he concluded: "And it is sincerely my opinion, that the Schuylkill bridge will last 30 and perhaps 40 years, if well covered" (1815: 48).

In Judge Peters' letter to the board, he made the following argument. "From the time of the first idea of a wooden superstructure, I have never wavered in my opinion of the indispensable necessity *of the cover*." Pointing out that covering the exposed timbers with paint, some other coating, or even with lead sheets leads to cracking, rotting, and feculation, he asserted that "Nothing has been proved so effectual, as cover-ing the whole of a frame, constructed of large timber, with a roof; and, at the sides, excluding rain, without preventing an uninterrupted circulation of air" (1815: 46). Aware of the famous Schaaffhaǔsen [also spelled Schauffhausen and Schaffhausen] bridge in Switzerland, he wrote: "It had been by its cover, effectually preserved from decay for thirty-eight years, and was perfectly sound, at the time the French [by Napoleon's troops in 1799] destroyed it" (p. 47). He then quotes Palmer's letter at length. Peters had earlier assumed the Board would agree to a cover and had already sketched plans for it, three of them submitted individually by Mr Dorsey, Mr Traquair, and Mr Owen Biddle.

At last the board relented and agreed to proceed, based on Peters' estimate of $8,000. But first Peters also had to argue for the work being done immediately because some thought the wood might better age in the open for a year or so. Owen Biddle, one of the young nation's premier builders and author of a handbook entitled *The Young Carpenter's Assistant; or A System of Architecture Adapted to the Style of Building in the United States*, published in 1805, completed the work within the year. Wrote Peters: "It was executed with singular fidelity and credit, by Mr. Owen Biddle, an ingenious carpenter and architect of Philadelphia. . . ." (p. 27). Indeed, Biddle's work gave the bridge an elegant appearance, with the lower arched portion not just painted to look like a stone arch with stone blocks

above but with stone dust embedded into the paint. The upper portion consisted of vertical colonnades and twenty-two windows with shutters on each side.

The builders also carried out two other apparent innovations. For protection, they installed lightning rods along the roof, a technology whose invention is attributed to Benjamin Franklin in 1749 following his (in)famous experiment with a kite and a key. Later, to keep the decking boards from being worn, they installed planks lengthwise to carry the wheels of most carriages and wagons in addition to planks along the trusses to keep vehicles from damaging them. Peters also requested that William Rush, a prominent Philadelphia sculptor, be commissioned to create pediments at each end, the eastern one celebrating commerce and the western one agriculture. Finally, the company had "a pyramidical Pedestal, surmounted with four Dials, for the benefit of passengers," which was an obelisk, erected at the eastern end celebrating those who erected the bridge, listing its vital statistics, and telling the story of the heroic efforts to erect the two piers (pp. 77–80).

Covered Bridges for a New Nation

Judge Richard Peters, President of the Board that built the Permanent Bridge, the first *documented* covered bridge in the United States, had not created the idea of preserving a wooden superstructure with roof and siding, but he appears to have been the first to persuade builders to actually cover a bridge. The Permanent Bridge is not just well documented but was seen and noted by virtually all of the many travelers who later published descriptions of their travels around Philadelphia. Although an iconic structure and the most perfect of Palmer's many bridges, the Permanent Bridge had to be replaced in 1850, by which time bridge technology had advanced dramatically. By then, a bridge capable of carrying railroad trains as well as pedestrians and carriages was required, but building covered bridges such as this first had to become routine.

As noted earlier, Charles Willson Peale, writing in 1797, alleged that there were already covered bridges in the United States: "It has been advised to make roofs to cover Bridges, and some are so constructed in America." But there is no known documentation of any actual bridges so covered. Peale's statement implies that somewhere, perhaps in some smaller towns far from the cities, there were a few covered spans lurking. But it must be borne in mind that we are attempting to reconstruct a complete jigsaw puzzle with only a small percentage of the pieces. There is a likelihood that wooden trusses had developed as early as the 1760s. We know that the *idea* of covering bridges was known, both from Robert Smith's statement in 1769 and the drawing in *The Columbian Magazine* from 1787. These ideas cannot have come from nowhere. It was also difficult for any one writer to know about distant areas, and in those days "distant" could have been a mere thirty miles

depending on the existence of passable roads. There is ample documentation of the great bridges of the period, but it is unlikely that *every* bridge was noted.

The populations of New England and Pennsylvania were very limited and infrastructure barely existed. Even in 1837, as described earlier by Englishman Robert Stevenson, America's road system was deplorable, though New England's was somewhat better. Nonetheless, before 1800, even in New England the road system was minimal. Neither federal nor state governments were building infrastructure at the time. Bridges, like roads, had to be built by private investors who contributed capital towards an enterprise that hopefully would pay a dividend through the tolls collected. Because there would be no incentive for a company to build a modest bridge on a back road—since users there could easily avoid tolls by crossing the stream in the usual way, by fording—the principal bridges being built were over major bodies of water and often of dramatic dimensions. It seems likely that most, if not all, of these larger bridges have been documented. Indeed, most were by Timothy Palmer himself, who affirms that none of his earlier bridges were covered (though some were retrofitted with covers after 1805). How would Peale know there were covered bridges elsewhere? Unless he had seen them with his own eyes, we must ask where were they? Possibly he had seen the drawing in *The Columbian Magazine* of January 1787. Perhaps he had heard of covered bridges in Europe and thought they were in the United States. However authoritative his statement may sound, there is no corroborating evidence. Thus, Palmer's 1805 Permanent Bridge retains the title of "first covered bridge" until there is hard evidence showing otherwise.

This milestone, however, important as it is, privileges the least significant of Palmer's innovations. Everything else about this bridge and the ones preceding it built by Palmer and the two Spoffords demonstrate the real progress made in American bridge design: the development of deep-water pier construction, the rapid evolution of timber bridge trusses, and the ability to construct massive spans of exceptional length and strength. After this, successive builders created ever more innovations in truss design, and America's first professional engineers developed the science of stress analysis, making bridges ever more rational and efficient. Their story will be told in Chapter 2.

More Remarkable Bridges: Theodore Burr and Lewis Wernwag

After knowledge of Palmer's Permanent Bridge spread, the idea of covering a wooden truss bridge to protect it from the weather was no longer considered odd or controversial. Covered bridges soon became the norm and continued to be so until the building of timber truss bridges was phased out during the late nineteenth and early twentieth centuries. The essence of covered bridges, then, is what the roofs and siding protect— trusses and other construction features. This vast subject will be treated systematically in Chapter 2.

Timothy Palmer, although having achieved near perfection in Philadelphia, built at least one more bridge before his death in 1821, the three-span 490-foot bridge over the Delaware between Easton, Pennsylvania, and Phillipsburg, New Jersey. Theodore Cooper visited this bridge in the 1880s and reported: "This bridge, after eighty-four years' service, is still in use and about five-sixths of the original timber is in good condition. It has always been covered in from the weather" (1889: 8). His Plate V includes a drawing of the truss, demonstrating that it was a virtual copy of the Permanent Bridge. Photos show that he even copied the painted-on stone arch bridge effect for the lower portion along with a similar series of windows above (Allen, 1959: 52). This was possibly America's second *documented* covered bridge.

Overlapping Palmer's time, however, was the next up-and-coming bridge builder, Theodore Burr (1771–1822), whose short life included some of the most ambitious and daring bridge projects ever attempted in the United States. Though he was born in Torringford, Connecticut, Burr's major bridges spanned rivers in New York, Pennsylvania, and Maryland. The son of a millwright, he moved to Oxford, New York, in 1792 to continue his father's craft. Thus, his earliest work included a local grist mill, a dam, and an open bridge over the Chenango River in Oxford, a small village located midway between Binghamton and Utica. Successful as a builder, between 1809 and 1811 he built for himself a large Federal-style house in Oxford which,

years later and with two added wings, became the Oxford Memorial Library and is now the home of the Theodore Burr Covered Bridge Archive. Burr's many bridge building activities, however, necessarily kept him from enjoying his grand home.

Fortunately, a number of original letters written in Burr's hand survive, giving us a first-hand impression of the man. Hubertis M. Cummings' authoritative article published in 1956 in *Pennsylvania History* offers the best summary of his work. Since Burr moved with his young bride, Asenath Cook, to Oxford just as Palmer was beginning to build innovative bridges in Massachusetts, it is doubtful that Burr ever saw them. With skills in mill construction but little bridge experience, Burr nonetheless boldly entered the bridge building business. Between his 1800 debut in building the bridge in Oxford and 1808, he constructed at least seven more bridges, none known to have been covered at the time of construction. The first of these was a 400-foot "drawbridge" over Catskill Creek at Catskill in 1802 followed by a 330-foot bridge at Canajoharie over the Mohawk River. Of these we know little, but clearly Burr's early bridges exhibited an experimental spirit. Where Palmer created and perfected a specific pattern combining truss and arch, Burr tried out completely original structures in his Mohawk and Trenton bridges as well as used a more conventional truss-arch pattern in other bridges, the latter becoming the foundation of what we now know as the "Burr truss."

Because of its longevity, we know much about the Lansingburgh-Waterford Union Bridge in New York State, built in 1804. With a length of 800 feet, it was the first bridge across the Hudson River. Consisting of four two-lane spans, each a different length ranging between 154 and 180 feet, its level roadway passed through triple trusses of X panels and massive arches, each of the latter having eight layers of wood bolted together. Had Burr covered it initially, he might have beaten Palmer for the distinction of "first covered bridge," but his massive arches were left exposed until 1814. Because the bridge lasted until it burned in 1909, there are numerous photos. Compared to others he built, this was fairly "conventional."

Far more experimental was Burr's next project, the five-span bridge over the Delaware at Trenton, New Jersey, with two spans measuring 203 feet each, one at 198 feet, one at 186 feet, and the last at 161 feet, these said to be "clear" spans. Thus, the bridge's total length was well over 1,000 feet. Cooper, who also visited this long-lasting bridge, originally built between 1804 and 1806, described its construction: "Each span had five arched ribs, formed of white pine plank, from thirty-five to fifty feet in length and 4 inches thick, repeated one over the other, breaking joints, until they formed a depth of 32 inches. . . . The roadway was suspended from the arch ribs by vertical chains. The arch was counter-braced by diagonal braces, formed of two sticks 6 x 10 inches spiked to the lower chord and secured to the arch above by iron straps" (1889: 8–9).

Although the bridge lasted until 1875 when it was replaced by one made of iron, it had undergone various renovations in 1832, 1848 (to carry trains), and 1869. Cooper includes a clear drawing of the structure, including the flared ribs out 50 feet from the abutments and piers designed to provide bracing against the wind. Never covered in the conventional sense, Burr's successful experiment had a partial roof over the top that followed the contours of the arches.

Clockwise from top Bold to the point of brazen, Theodore Burr's 1,000-foot crossing of the Delaware between Trenton, New Jersey, and Morrisville, Pennsylvania, was unprecedented in design and only partially covered. (NSPCB Archives, R. S. Allen Collection)

Burr and Palmer were contemporaries, but Burr succeeded in building bridges with level roadways when Palmer's were arched. The Lansingburgh-Waterford Union Bridge over the Hudson used Burr's usual design, having a panel truss with both braces and counterbraces, along with laminated arches. (NSPCB Archives, R. S. Allen Collection)

Carrying both carriages and light rail, Burr's Lansingburgh-Waterford Union Bridge crossed the Hudson River in four spans of varying length, totaling 800 feet. Built open in 1804, it was not covered until 1814 but lasted until 1909 when it burned. (NSPCB Archives, R. S. Allen Collection)

Old Bridge, Waterford, N. Y.
GEORGE MICHON, Publisher, Waterford, N.Y.

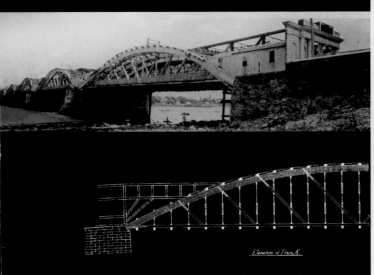

THE MOHAWK BRIDGE.
Showing Construction.

Burr's next project, aptly described by Cooper as "a curiosity," demonstrates both Burr's originality and his daredevil nature. According to Cooper, Burr's first attempt to bridge the Mohawk River in 1808 between Schenectady and Scotia, New York, resulted in disaster when one of the two spans, each apparently 450 feet long, either collapsed or was swept away. His second attempt, according to the contract quoted by Cooper, placed the bridge at the same site but with additional piers. A double-lane bridge tightly covered under roof and batten siding at some point, it was an experimental wooden suspension bridge. Says Cooper: "The curved ribs are formed of eight 4 x 11-inch planks spiked or bolted together" (1889: 9). Cooper's drawing, copied from that attached to the contract seen by him, shows an undulating wooden "chord" rising like an arch above the piers and sweeping to the deck level between, in the manner of a suspension bridge. While chain suspension bridges were already well established, it is doubtful anyone had tried to use laminated wooden "cables" in extreme tension. Additional bracing, both vertical and diagonal (the latter from the piers), could not maintain stability. According to an old photo, engineers had tried to reinforce the bridge with additional bracing (Mohr, 1957b: 5). By 1828, six years after Burr's death, the spans were sagging dreadfully and had to be shored up with new piers between the original ones. Though it looked

like a wet blanket stretched over supports and must have given passengers seasickness as they rose and fell over each span, this bizarre-looking crossing lasted until 1873. Though it served sixty-five years, it was clearly a design failure from the start.

Perhaps recognizing that the Mohawk River plan had flaws, his next project was a three-span bridge over the Schoharie River at Esperance, first contracted in 1809 but not completed until January 12, 1812. An interior photo of this last Burr bridge to survive (until 1930) shows a double-lane bridge with three trusses. The downstream photo clearly shows that Burr had constructed three spans with gently curved arches below the roadway, a feature standard in Palmer's bridges. The truss, however, bears no resemblance to Burr's later design, having as it does double panels that resemble half-sized kingpost trusses. Such trusses were probably intended to strengthen the arches, which likely bore most of the weight.

Following his work in New York State, Burr was lured to Pennsylvania eventually to build four superlative bridges over the mighty Susquehanna and a fifth over the same river in Maryland. While all but one were conventional covered bridges, using some form of what had come to be known as the "Burr truss," none was of modest proportions, not surprising considering that the Susquehanna is, as some joke, "a mile wide and an inch deep." The various bridge companies began applying for state approval in 1807. As each was approved, contracts were drawn up with builder Burr, all of which are discussed in Cummings' 1956 article, which also includes a photo of a small wooden bridge model probably made by Burr himself and now preserved by the Pennsylvania Historical and Museum Commission. Between late February 1812 and 1815, Burr completed the five bridges in Pennsylvania, and before 1818 the sixth one in Maryland. From north to south, each was remarkable.

Above top left Burr's Delaware River crossing, connecting Morrisville, Pennsylvania, to Trenton, New Jersey, was one of the most noted bridges of its time, 1806–75. (NSPCB Archives, R. S. Allen Collection)

Above center left Theodore Cooper provided detailed drawings of Burr's experimental design at Trenton, New Jersey. The gigantic arches supported a combination of vertical iron chains and diagonal wooden beams to secure the deck, with only a partial roof over the arches. (Cooper, 1889; reproduced in Nelson, 1990: 17)

Above Originally built uncovered, then covered, the wooden suspension design of the Mohawk bridge required additional piers by 1828. This photo, taken during its dismantling in 1873, allows us to see its deteriorated trusses. (NSPCB Archives, R. S. Allen Collection)

Left Far less successful was Burr's Delaware River bridge between Schenectady and Scotia, New York, built in 1808 in four spans following a failed attempt to cross the river in two spans. (NSPCB Archives, R. S. Allen Collection)

1. Perhaps the most modest of Burr's bridges, and the least known, is the multi-span bridge over the North Branch of the Susquehanna between Nescopeck Falls and Berwick, southwest of Wilkes-Barre.

2. The bridge between Northumberland and Sunbury also crossed the North Branch near its confluence with the West Branch and was separated into two portions of three spans each by an island. According to the contract, there were two carriageways, each 11 feet 6 inches wide with a 4-foot-wide footway between. In the contract, the bridge had to be roofed with shingles and sided.

3. The bridge at Harrisburg, like that at Northumberland, was divided by an island and in total consisted of twelve 210-foot spans in two segments of six each. Begun in 1812 and completed in 1817, the eastern portion survived until 1902 and the western until 1903. It was the western portion, however, which caught everyone's attention because the roadway gently rose and fell with the gigantic arches that were embedded into the abutments and piers far below the deck. Because of this feature, the bridge was widely known as the Camelback Bridge.

4. Although Burr is credited with designing the bridge between Columbia and Wrightsville, the contractors were Jonathan Walcott, Henry Slaymaker, and Samuel Slaymaker. It is hard to imagine how much stone and timber went into constructing a bridge consisting of twenty-six spans of 200 feet each, for a total of 5,690 feet, more than a mile in length and the longest covered bridge ever built. At that time, Pennsylvania was still covered with primeval forest and timber was easily and cheaply available. By the end of the century, however, with the expansion of the tanbark industry and the proliferation of tanneries dependent on a steady supply of hemlock bark and fuel, the building of tens of thousands of wooden houses in towns throughout the east, and countless mills and covered bridges built, including several replacements for Burr's original crossing, Pennsylvania's once magnificent hills and mountains had become denuded.

5. If Columbia-Wrightsville was grandiose in proportions, the McCall's Ferry Bridge, farther south where the river is squeezed through its narrowest point, was stunning for both its span length and the radically innovative manner of its construction. The river, racing between hills that brought about weather more turbulent than normal, had a deep narrow channel along with a shallow area in York County. At low water, that portion was exposed, and building a pier at this point was simple. The remaining distance to the Lancaster County shore, however, was 360 feet, and no one had built a successful span of this magnitude before. Theodore Burr, nonetheless contracted to do just that. But with the river bottom 100 feet below the bridge deck, there was no way to erect scaffolding. Burr decided to build his scaffolding on floats instead, and the arch was built standing vertically along the river shore on the floats, whose ropes had to be adjusted continuously to compensate for the changing water levels. The arch was ready by December 7, 1814, but the river gave them problems by freezing and creating masses of ice, threatening to destroy the greatest wooden arch ever constructed. Always a quick thinker, Burr directed the arch to be cut into two halves and one

of them eventually placed on rollers and moved out onto the ice which workers had smoothed flat. Over a significant amount of time and with the efforts of hundreds of local residents called out to help, they managed to turn the arch halves into line and hoist them onto the pier and abutment, then lock them back together. Considering the weight of the arch and the extreme weather conditions, this was a superhuman feat. During January and February, his crew was able to complete what Cummings called "a feat of engineering hitherto unparalleled in America," building two arched truss spans, one 376 feet long with a clear span of 360

Left Burr's Susquehanna River bridge at Harrisburg consisted of twelve spans, each 210 feet long. It was divided into two bridges by an island, each segment comprising six spans. (Rathmell, 1963: 4)

Below The western portion was more noted than the eastern portion because of its distinctive shape, giving rise to its nickname, the "Camelback Bridge." (NSPCB Archives, R. S. Allen Collection)

Bottom upper left Each span of Burr's "Camelback Bridge" at Harrisburg, Pennsylvania, was 210 feet long, equal to the "longest single-span covered bridge" at Blenheim, New York, that stood until 2011. Typical of Burr's bridges, the truss portions had both braces and counterbraces, but the massive three-piece arches caused the rise and fall in the deck that gave rise to the "camelback" moniker. (Dauphin County Historical Society, Pennsylvania)

Bottom lower left The third Columbia-Wrightsville bridge over the Susquehanna River in Pennsylvania was a Howe truss rail bridge in twenty-seven spans built in 1868 and destroyed by a tornado in 1896. The first was designed by Theodore Burr, built by others in 1812, and then destroyed by ice in 1832. The second was finished in 1834 and burned by Union troops during the Civil War. (NSPCB Archives, R. S. Allen Collection)

Bottom right The "camelback" segment in the west totaled 1,260 feet in six spans, somewhat shorter than today's "World's Longest Covered Bridge" at Hartland, New Brunswick. (Terry E. Miller Collection)

feet 4 inches, the other having a span of 247 feet, all the arches having been raised on floating falsework (Cummings, 1956: 482). With a width of 32 feet, the bridge provided ample passage for the many farm products of the area that needed to go to markets in Philadelphia and other points east, since this was the only bridge from Columbia-Wrightsville near Harrisburg to south of the Maryland border.

Shortly after completing the bridge, Burr wrote a letter on February 26, 1815, to his friend, fellow bridge builder Reuben Field of Waterford, New York, detailing how the bridge was built. This is probably the most detailed historical description of bridge building known and helps us appreciate just how overwhelming this task was (Burr, 1815). In the letter, Burr exclaims: "This arch is, without doubt, the greatest in the world. . . . The altitude or rise of the arch is thirty-one feet. The arch is double and the two segments are combined by kingposts seven feet in length between the shoulders, and are united to the arch by lock-work. Between the kingposts are truss braces and counteracting braces. The arch stands firm and remarkably easy, without the least struggling in any part of the work." As detailed as this account is, it leaves many questions unanswered. If the bridge is 32 feet wide, as Burr writes, then it suggests two lanes. Burr writes of the raising of only one arch. Before proposing a solution, readers need to know that Burr's triumph was short-lived. On March 3, 1818, while Burr was still working on the Susquehanna bridge at Rock Run, Maryland, the natural forces of water and ice ripped the McCall's Ferry Bridge from its foundations and smashed it against the rocks along the river. Even to this day, there is no crossing at McCall's Ferry. But there is a clue. Burr's otherwise little known and short-lived bridge over the Mohawk at Canajoharie, New York, built in 1806, was described as a single arch

of 330 feet. In June, 1808, Anne M. H. Hyde de Neuville painted "Incomplete Bridge, Palatine" of the remains of one end of the bridge. It shows two trusses, each with the arch as the lower chord and reinforced with a framework of posts and cross bracing. Assuming that the McCall's Ferry Bridge was similar, we can surmise that Burr had the entire framework built on the floating falsework, cut the bracing between the trusses, and moved each separately over the ice onto the stonework. Burr was unchallenged on his genius and daring.

6. Burr's final bridge over the Susquehanna was between Rock Run and Port Deposit, villages halfway between Conowingo and today's I95 in Maryland and whose former tollhouse is in what is now Susquehanna State Park. The bridge, consisting of eighteen spans, each 200 feet, with eight from the western shore to the first island, two to the second island, and eight from that to the eastern shore for a total length of 4,170 feet, was completed in 1818. Beginning in 1823, it suffered a series of calamities. First, on January 1, the eastern half was set on fire from a spark generated when a sleigh rail scraped a nail head. Lewis Wernwag, Burr's greatest contemporary (though Burr had already died the year before), rebuilt the damaged spans. Another fire in 1828, now on the western side, required the rebuilding of six spans, again by Wernwag, which he completed by September, 1831. The bridge's final disabling came on October 27, 1854, when a herd of cattle coming from Port Deposit collapsed or damaged four spans. At this point, officials decided to abandon the bridge. On February 11, 1857, an ice floe administered the *coup de grace*, bringing down much of what remained.

The last four years of Burr's life were ones of misery and stress. There are unconfirmed reports that he may have built some modest bridges and might have been in

Below Built in 1806 and already having collapsed by the time this painting was made in 1808, Burr's bridge over the Mohawk River at Canajoharie, New York, at 330 feet was as daring as it was unsuccessful. "Incomplete Bridge, Palatine, New York" by Baroness Anne-Marguerite-Henriette Hyde de Neuville (c. 1761–1849) (watercolor and graphite on paper), 1808. (Acc. #1953.211, Collection of The New-York Historical Society)

the middle of a project in Pennsylvania when he died. Though he was a bold, innovative, and ambitious bridge builder, he was far less skilled in managing money, for coordinating the construction of and payments for multiple bridges simultaneously necessitated a small army of accountants. Just as ice so often bunched up and destroyed covered bridges, mounting debts and competing demands for cash flow brought Burr's otherwise glorious life to an early end. All that is known is that Burr died in Middletown, Pennsylvania, in November 1822. Nothing is known of the cause of death or the whereabouts of his burial. Of all of America's many bridge builders, Theodore Burr stood out as the unrivaled leader, but, like his mighty McCall's Ferry Bridge, his fame was short-lived and he left the scene suddenly. Most builders after Burr were less visionary and more reasonable, though one more daring bridge builder requires inclusion.

He was Lewis Wernwag (1769–1843), born in Riedlingen, Wurttemberg (Germany). Coming from a millwright tradition, he immigrated to Philadelphia in 1786, likely to escape military conscription and the endless conflicts in central Europe. There he began erecting mills and making mill wheels. Though without training in bridge design, he built an open draw-span bridge over Neshaminy Creek around 1810 on the Frankford-Bristol Turnpike just northeast of Philadelphia, the design of which is thought to be shown in an engraving from around 1815 by Enoch G. Gridley. This was apparently his only preparation for designing and constructing one of the most daring bridges actually built in the United States. Because the records of the construction of this grand bridge over the Schuylkill, officially the Lancaster-Schuylkill Bridge but also known as the Upper Ferry Bridge or the Fairmount Bridge, are extant, engineering historian Lee H. Nelson could write a detailed history which recognizes the bridge by the name Wernwag dubbed it: *The Colossus of 1812: An American Engineering Superlative* (1990). Thirty-one years earlier, Richard Sanders Allen had featured the bridge in his *Covered Bridges of the Middle Atlantic States* (1959) and provided a color reproduction of the painting by Thomas Birch as the frontispiece.

Even though Palmer's Permanent Bridge crossed the river nearby, a group of businessmen proposed a second crossing on January 30, 1811 and called for proposals. At first, only two proposals came in, an implausible one by the visionary Thomas Pope, and two designs—now lost—by architect Robert Mills, one uncovered, one covered. Only later did Wernwag step forward with a design for a triple-arched structure reinforced with a truss with an unprecedented clear span of 340 feet with two lanes. On December 5, 1811, the company contracted with Wernwag based on the believability of his presentation and the use of a well-constructed scale model to build the bridge. Wernwag demonstrated great wisdom in anticipating a number of problems and designing solutions, especially the problem of rot

developing between members: "This Bridge has a superiority of any other, having near 100 feet span [*sic*], more than any in Europe or America. The dry rot is entirely prevented by the timber being sawed through the heart, for the discovery of any defect & kept apart by iron links & screw bolts, without mortice or tennon, except the king posts & truss ties. No part of the timber comes in contact with each other, & can be screwed tight at any time when the timber shrinks. Any piece of the timber can be taken out & replaced if required without injury to the Superstructure" (quoted in Nelson, 1990: 21).

Wernwag's design is known to such an extent that it could be reproduced today. The main structural element was a series of massive wooden arches, each composed of six members joined in pairs to create three arches. Because of his concern for dry rot, Wernwag designed an ingenious iron bracket, two per panel, that separated the members and yet preserved their working in union. The arches together acted as the lower chord. Above it were panels having double 6 x 12 inch kingposts and each made rigid with braces and counterbraces, apparently of equal size. There were systems of iron bars, rods, and clamps, including ones that anchored the entire bridge diagonally back into the abutment

From top Lewis Wernwag's Colossus, opened on January 7, 1813, was 340 feet long in a single span, the longest such bridge at that time. While it could have served many more years, arsonists destroyed the structure in just twenty minutes in 1843. (Yale University Art Gallery)

"A View of Fairmount and the Water-Works, c. 1837" (watercolor, pencil and gouache) was painted by John Rubens Smith from the perspective of a hotel verandah looking towards Wernwag's monumental Colossus. It clearly shows the bridge within the context of human life at the time in a city that was still quite compact. (Bridgeman Art Library)

Wernwag designed a bridge primarily supported by three compound arches that doubled as lower chords with an upper chord that, while curved, was non-parallel. These were made rigid with posts and braces. (US Patent Office)

Above William Strickland's painting, "A View of a Bridge over the Schuylkill River" (oil on canvas), actually shows America's two most important bridges of the time, Palmer's Permanent Bridge in the foreground and Wernwag's Colossus upriver in the distance. Although part of Philadelphia's city streets, the surroundings indicate how much open countryside remained. (Bridgeman Art Library)

walls, throughout the structure. Lateral bracing was anchored to what he called iron "boxes" placed on the tops of the kingposts. The upper chord did not run parallel to the arches, having a flatter curve, giving the bridge a flared shape, with the middle narrower than the ends. Overall, the design was as sophisticated as any ever proposed in the United States or Europe, and the ease with which Wernwag completed the construction was also amazing.

The bridge, which was not covered at first, was officially opened on January 7, 1813. As related years later by John Wernwag, Lewis Wernwag's son, there was great apprehension that when the scaffolding was removed, the bridge would fall. Wernwag famously brought the nervous company managers to the bridge before the ceremony, who asked, "Well, Lewis, do you think our bridge will stand the test today?" Wernwag answered, "Yes, gentlemen, it will" (quoted in Nelson, 1990: 24–5). He then showed them that he had removed the blocks between the bridge and scaffolding the day before, and the bridge was already supporting itself. It was not until March 13 that the company agreed to "roof and finish" the bridge with a shingled roof and ten windows with shutters at a cost of about $90,000.

Although Wernwag's record for building the longest single-span wooden bridge fell to Burr's short-lived McCall's Ferry Bridge in 1814, nature was kinder to the "Colossus of Fairmount" than to the McCall's Ferry structure, destroyed by flood waters only three years later. A hurricane that struck Philadelphia on September 3, 1821 tore off the roof and siding of the Colossus. But just four years before Wernwag's passing, in 1843, arsonists accomplished what nature had failed to do: by setting fire to the bridge and causing it to fall into the river within only twenty minutes. The crossing remained without a bridge for four years, until Charles Ellett Jr built an innovative suspension bridge using woven wire rope.

Having begun his bridge building career with his capstone achievement, Wernwag could devote himself to less ambitious projects. As related by Richard Sanders Allen: "From then on, Wernwag practically had to fight off agents from bridge companies. Usually they would offer a big block of stock in their infant organizations, but sometimes there was cash on the barrelhead. The now famous inventor chose only the best offers, and the next few years found him building bridges across the Delaware at New Hope, over the Schuylkill at Reading, and spanning the Susquehanna at Wilkes-Barre. Out in Pittsburgh in 1816, he erected that growing city's first bridges across the Allegheny and the Monongahela" (1959: 16).

Of these, one in particular stands out, the bridge over the Delaware River at New Hope, Pennsylvania, which was built between 1813 and 1814. The six spans of 175 feet each, for a total of 1,050 feet, were constructed using an innovative truss designed by Wernwag and apparently not used again. As was typical in that day, the bridge was 32 feet wide, with two carriageways and flanking pedestrian walkways. According to an engraving that showed this design, along with that of the Colossus and a swing bridge, the structure consisted of a laminated or multi-sectioned arch resting on the lower chords at each end, and a panel truss of wooden kingposts and iron rods apparently in tension, because they are placed diagonally from the center towards the ends—the reverse of the wooden braces found in more usual trusses. There appear to be numerous iron separators and clamps similar to those he proposed for and used on the Colossus.

After this, Wernwag became involved in a number of industrial projects, but the business practices of the day made such investing risky, and Wernwag's involvement in what came to be the Phoenix Works, a large mill making iron implements, came to naught, when, as a result of the war of 1812, the firm went bankrupt. He also invested in a lumber mill at Conowingo, Maryland, which manufactured pre-cut timbers for trestle bridges in Tidewater Virginia, and there he built a ten-span covered bridge over the Susquehanna to facilitate customers crossing to his mill. When Burr's Port Deposit Bridge was heavily damaged by fire in 1823 and 1828, Wernwag was called in each time to rebuild the lost spans. Finally, in 1824, he moved to Harpers Ferry, Virginia (now West Virginia), where he purchased an island in the Shenandoah near its junction with the Potomac. Emory Kemp sums up his career: "In 1824 he purchased the Isle of Virginius at Harpers Ferry, Virginia . . . and there established a manufacturing center. This move to Virginia brought him into contact with the Baltimore and Ohio Railroad (or B&O), for which he built bridges, the most notable being a Y-shaped bridge over the Potomac at Harpers Ferry [1842]. Ironically, one of Wernwag's smallest structures was to become famous as a result of John Brown's raid in 1859—the engine house at Harpers Ferry that sheltered Brown and his men during the abortive raid" (2005: 11).

As with Burr and Palmer, none of Wernwag's bridges have survived, though the engine house remains as part of the Harpers Ferry National Historical Park. Where Burr's truss design became a dominant one, those used by Palmer and Wernwag are only echoed faintly in a few bridges surviving today. Many continue to call Burr trusses with flared (radial or fanlike) posts a Wernwag truss, but this pattern is not a patented feature. Many builders in addition to Lewis Wernwag used such a variation.

Following Independence in 1776 and the end of the Revolutionary War with the Treaty of Paris in 1783, the people of the young United States were energized to develop their vast land at almost any cost. With a relatively small population and little educational infrastructure, the citizenry had risen to the needs and martialed a degree of creativity and boldness unimaginable in old Europe. What was later called "American optimism" led self-taught craftsmen with little or no training in bridge design not just to construct grandiose bridges in astoundingly difficult circumstances but to also imagine solutions that were unlikely to have been conceived in Europe at that time. And they accomplished this at a time before the advanced technologies of material, design, and construction equipment had sufficiently developed. It is difficult for us, used to seeing powerful cranes capable of lifting virtually anything, including whole bridges, to imagine how mere mortals using little more than horses, ropes, pulleys, and simple derricks could span some of America's widest and most treacherous rivers. We try to understand the bravery of men who could create coffer dams in deep water with little technology, and then descend into them, somehow building piers of multi-ton blocks of stone, knowing that if the dam gave way, they were instantly gone.

Below Because it straddled the boundary between the Union and the Confederacy, Confederate Brigadier General Joseph Johnson burned the Harpers Ferry bridge on June 14, 1861. Its temporary replacements, all built by the B&O Railroad, were destroyed three more times by war and five times by flooding during the war period alone. (*Harper's Weekly*, 1861)

Bottom Designed by Lewis Wernwag and built by Benjamin H. Latrobe II (1806–78) for the B&O Railroad in 1837, the great bridge over the Potomac near its confluence with the Shenandoah River at Harpers Ferry, Virginia, added a "Y" branch in 1839 to eliminate a curve. The bridge became famous when John Brown crossed the bridge in 1859 to raid the armory. (NSPCB Archives, R. S. Allen Collection)

The Diffusion of Covered Bridges Throughout North America

By the 1820s, knowledge of American timber bridge truss technology was not just spreading to a rapidly growing corps of young builders but over an increasingly wide geographic area. Palmer and Burr had evolved designs based on the fundamental principles of triangle and arch framed in wood, but Wernwag experimented both with design and materials, increasingly using elaborate iron elements such as spacers that separated pieces of his arches to prevent dry rot. Timber truss bridges thus evolved rapidly in the hands of the first generation of builders from 1792 to the 1820s. The idea of covering them, though discussed as early as 1769, became a documented reality only in 1805 with Palmer's celebrated Permanent Bridge. After that, "covered timber truss bridges" became the norm. The earliest bridges had been built where the population was concentrated, from Massachusetts south to Maryland and New Jersey and in eastern New York and Pennsylvania. Movement to the west and much of the south was obstructed by the Appalachian Mountain range. In mountainous or hilly regions, towns were founded along rivers because these provided transportation, power, and water supplies, though sometimes also ice jams and floods. The same held true as explorers and pioneer families explored the territories to the west and south, establishing towns in areas formerly occupied by the native peoples who were mostly forced off their lands, either into reservations or migration to the barren lands farther west.

Westward expansion naturally pushed past Pittsburgh into Ohio, then Indiana and Kentucky, and on to Indiana, Illinois, and Missouri. Towards the south, people migrated into the Appalachians, including what became West Virginia, western Virginia, the Carolinas,

and then Georgia, Alabama, and Mississippi. As they settled in these newly populated areas, they encountered the same problems earlier generations had struggled with in New England and the Middle Atlantic states: vast roadless forests, unbridged rivers, and mountain terrain. As was true earlier in the east, there were no "bridge engineers" per se among them, that science not yet having developed in the young United States, but many were experienced in building homes, mills, and churches, and they too—though perhaps having learned something from the examples set by Palmer, Burr, and Wernwag—set about teaching themselves to build bridges. The covered bridge became the norm, though generally on a more modest scale.

Throughout the rest of the nineteenth and well into the twentieth century, timber truss covered bridges proliferated throughout the eastern half and to a lesser degree in the western half of the contiguous forty-eight states. Covered bridges were also constructed in Hawaii in the late nineteenth century and in Alaska during the first decades of the twentieth. Over time, they became

PITTSBURGH.
PENNSYLVANIA.
1902.

merely "normal," as newsworthy as concrete and steel highway deck bridges are today. Until the advent of iron bridge technology, especially after the Civil War, there were few alternatives: open wooden bridges, pony truss bridges, stone arch bridges, and simple stone culverts.

We can never know just how many covered bridges were built in the United States (and later in Canada as well), but two individuals, Bill Caswell and Trish Kane, are seeking to do just that. Still a "work in progress," their website, www.lostbridges.org, seeks to list every covered bridge that exists now or existed in the past in the United States and Canada. As of April, 2012, they had listed 12,895, but certainly this inventory is incomplete. Some states, such as Ohio, have been thoroughly researched while others have not, which likely skews the data. Nonetheless, we can gain some indication of relative numbers of bridges and their ages from the website. The data show a clear pattern of covered bridge building concentrations and document a chronological expansion of the phenomenon. They also provide some indication of how few remain today.

The old patterns continued. Private companies built turnpike (toll) roads connecting towns and cities as well as into the wilderness, but increasingly the United States Government became involved. In 1811, Congress authorized the building of the "National Road" from Cumberland, Maryland, across West Virginia, Pennsylvania, Ohio, Indiana, and Illinois, terminating at St. Louis, Missouri. By 1818, the road had reached Wheeling, but in 1837, resulting from a "panic," funding ceased, leaving the road completed only to Vandalia, Illinois. In addition to using Scottish engineer John Loudon McAdam's technique of constructing roads using pebbles instead of stone blocks or bricks pressed into the soil, the so-called "macadam roads," designers began to construct handsome stone arch bridges. These included the seemingly mysterious "S Bridges," mostly in Ohio, so-called because of curves at each end necessary to approach a bridge built perpendicular to the creek. The builders of the National Road, as well as builders of other turnpikes connecting to it, also built

Left from top By 1902, Pittsburgh had at least a dozen bridges over its two rivers, only one being covered. When the covered Union Bridge was built in 1875, Pittsburgh already had its first iron suspension bridge, which was built in 1859 by John Roebling, the German-born engineer who later built the Brooklyn Bridge. The covered bridge, too close to the water, was a nuisance well before it was damaged in the flood of 1907 and replaced. (Library of Congress)

Spanning the Allegheny River at Pittsburgh's "Point," where it joined the Monongahela River to form the Ohio River, the Union Bridge was the first at this location, having been built in 1875 to carry pedestrians, carriages, and the trolley. (Thomas and Katherine Detre Library and Archives, Senator John Heinz History Center)

Pittsburgh's Union Bridge consisted of five spans supported by especially powerful Howe trusses with triple rods reinforced with massive laminated arches. Such a structure was needed to support such a wide bridge with long spans and heavy traffic. (Carnegie Museum of Art, Pittsburgh; Gift of the Carnegie Library of Pittsburgh)

The first, and perhaps the only covered bridge over the Ohio River, connected Wheeling's island over the west channel to Bridgeport, Ohio, on the National Road. Designed by Lewis Wernwag, the bridge, consisting of three double-lane spans using doubled Burr trusses, was constructed from 1833 to 1836 (some say 1837) by Noah Zane. It was not replaced until 1893. (NSPCB Archives, R. S. Allen Collection)

covered bridges, with most of them being double lane. Urban bridges also usually had at least one pedestrian sidewalk as part of the bridge. Perhaps the longest crossed part of the Ohio River from Wheeling Island to Bridgeport, Ohio, on the National Road and was a three-span Burr truss structure designed by Lewis Wernwag in 1836. Although nearly burning down in 1883, the bridge survived until 1893 when it was replaced with an iron bridge. Other covered bridges on the National Road and associated turnpikes were among the earliest bridges built in Ohio and Indiana.

The heaviest concentrations of covered bridges, according to Caswell and Kane's research, were in Pennsylvania, Ohio, and Indiana, though West Virginia and Kentucky appear to have had a great many as well. To illustrate, they have documented 2,068 bridges in Pennsylvania, 4,761 in Ohio, and 598 in Indiana (so far), the earliest in Ohio being 1819 and in Indiana 1831.

Beyond Indiana the numbers fall dramatically, and the earliest bridges appear later: 168 for Illinois from the later 1830s, 54 in Missouri from the 1850s, 96 in Iowa from the 1860s. To the north, the numbers fall dramatically: Michigan only 46 from the 1840s, Wisconsin 35 from the 1850s, and Minnesota only 13 from the 1860s.

Going south the numbers tend to decline. Florida is not known to have had any covered bridges. West Virginia had 255 from the 1830s, Kentucky 838 from the 1830s, and Virginia 104 from the same period. Although North Carolina documents only 135 bridges, one is dated to 1818 and South Carolina only 44 but to the 1820s. Interestingly, Georgia and Alabama document 180 and 117 bridge respectively, both from the 1830s, while Tennessee and Mississippi had far fewer, 34 and 12 respectively, from the 1840s.

Once you cross the Mississippi River, there were few covered bridges until you reach the west coast: California had 98 from the 1850s onwards and Oregon 720 from the 1860s. Between Mississippi and California, the few documented bridges were mostly for railroads: 4 in Arkansas after 1840, 8 in Texas after 1850, 13 in Kansas after 1859, 7 in Nebraska after 1879, and a few scattered bridges, mostly on rail lines, in Wyoming, Arizona, and Washington, all from around the turn of the century. Ten states are not known to have had any, including Florida, Louisiana, Oklahoma, the Dakotas, New Mexico, Colorado, Utah, Montana, and Idaho. Surprisingly, however, Alaska had 7 from the 1920s and Hawaii is known to have had at least 2.

Closely related are thousands of open wooden trussed rail bridges built and rebuilt over the decades, virtually all using the Howe truss with its adjustable iron rod verticals. They were built open so as not to capture the smoke and hot ashes from the steam locomotives, but because they were open, they rarely lasted longer than ten years. Although few in number,

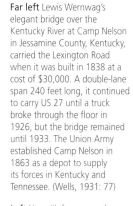

Far left Lewis Wernwag's elegant bridge over the Kentucky River at Camp Nelson in Jessamine County, Kentucky, carried the Lexington Road when it was built in 1838 at a cost of $30,000. A double-lane span 240 feet long, it continued to carry US 27 until a truck broke through the floor in 1926, but the bridge remained until 1933. The Union Army established Camp Nelson in 1863 as a depot to supply its forces in Kentucky and Tennessee. (Wells, 1931: 77)

Left Hawaii's few covered bridges, all gone now, were not quite comparable to those on the mainland. This open-sided kingpost bridge, apparently going uphill near Hilo, photographed around 1880 may have been a footbridge. (Hawaii State Archives)

Left Alaska had perhaps a dozen or so bridges, all of the Western Howe design built after 1900. These "twin bridges" were on the Seward-Anchorage Road in south central Alaska and were removed before 1959. (Alaska State Library)

Left Spanning Salt Creek at the north entrance to Indiana's Brown County State Park, the Ramp Creek Bridge was originally built in 1838 just south of Fincastle in Putnam County on what became US 231. This bridge, built by Henry Wolf and Chilion Johnson, is both Indiana's oldest and its only "double-barrel" bridge. It was moved here in 1932. (A. Chester Ong, 2011)

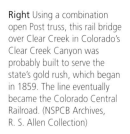

Above This historical photo taken in the early 1870s shows Obadiah Wilcox's 1813 highway bridge over the Sacandaga River near Hadley in Saratoga County, New York. Behind it is a four-span open deck Howe truss bridge carrying the Adirondack Railroad's first engine, the General MacPherson. The rail bridge was built in 1870 but by 1905 all spans had been replaced. (NSPCB Archives, R. S. Allen Collection)

there were here and there covered aqueducts on the canal systems that developed throughout the Middle Atlantic and Midwestern states in the first half of the nineteenth century. Today, fully covered rail bridges only survive in New England, but in the past they were relatively common in the Midwest and even as far west as Washington State. What percentage of the total number of bridges survives? While it is possible to compute these based on the number of known bridges divided into the number of surviving bridges, the results vary wildly, from 1.5 percent in Kentucky to 23 percent in Washington. For most states where such bridges started early and were built in profusion, the number is in the 2–8 percent range.

Covered bridges in Canada were mainly built in New Brunswick and Québec. Where Québec began building such bridges in the 1850s and has 1,035 documented crossings, of which 86 survive, and New Brunswick had 454, all built after 1900, with 63 surviving, Ontario had only 11, with 1 surviving today. Oddly, Nova Scotia is credited with 13, with the earliest going back to 1835, but none survive. Far to the west there were perhaps 6 wooden rail bridges, some covered or partially covered, and 1 semi-covered span survives to this day in British Columbia. Today, there are 151 covered/semi-covered bridges listed for Canada out of a historical total of 1,519, or 10 percent.

Right Using a combination open Post truss, this rail bridge over Clear Creek in Colorado's Clear Creek Canyon was probably built to serve the state's gold rush, which began in 1859. The line eventually became the Colorado Central Railroad. (NSPCB Archives, R. S. Allen Collection)

Left The Boston and Maine Railroad built and owned most of the covered rail bridges in New England. This one at Bennington, New Hampshire, was built in 1877, probably by David Hazelton (1832–1908), chief bridge engineer for the railroad. Until it was destroyed by fire in 1965, it was the oldest remaining covered rail bridge in the United States. (NSPCB Archives, R. S. Allen Collection)

Below The Rouge or Sainte-Agathe Bridge spans the Palmer River over a rocky gorge next to Parc de la chute Sainte-Agathe in Québec, Canada. Built in 1928, it is typical of the province's Town lattice variation. (A. Chester Ong, 2012)

Bottom Typical of the covered bridges in New Brunswick, Canada, the Tynemouth Creek Bridge near St. Martins in Saint John County was built in 1927 using a standardized Howe truss. Because it is near the Bay of Fundy, the area is often shrouded in fog. (A. Chester Ong, 2012)

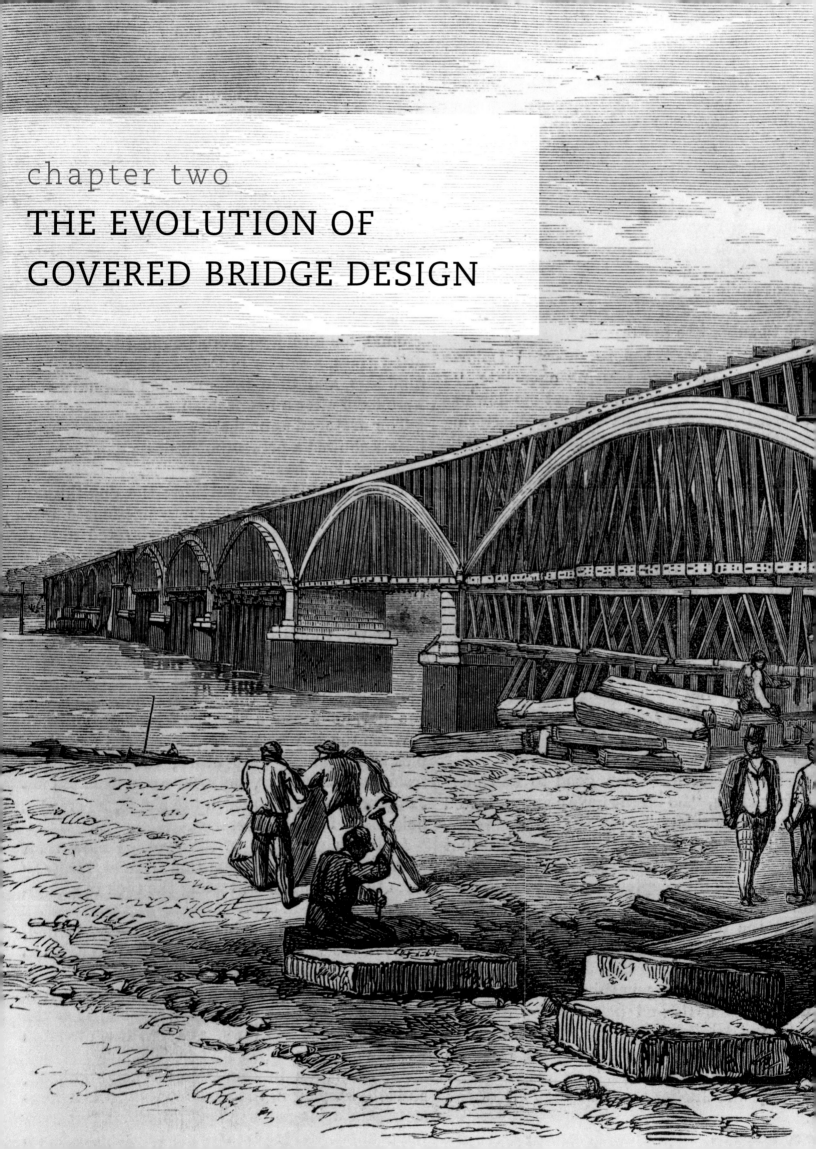

chapter two

THE EVOLUTION OF COVERED BRIDGE DESIGN

THE PLANNING, PREPARATION AND DESIGN OF A COVERED BRIDGE

During the last years of the colonial period and into the first decades of the nineteenth century—roughly from 1760 to 1820—the relatively few men with knowledge of timber framing were called upon to meet unprecedented engineering challenges. None had formal training in civil engineering generally nor bridge construction in particular, and the science of stress analysis in bridge design was still decades away. What they had was common sense, experience, and a bold, creative streak. To that we might add generous doses of bravery and what some might even call "chutzpah." A few, like Thomas Pope, emphasized the "bold, creative streak" over common sense—he proposed to span the East River with a monumental 1,800-foot wooden arch that would join the cities of New York (now Manhattan) and Brooklyn and even mentioned one over the Hudson River—but most men recognized both the limitations of the materials and their own abilities.

The previous chapter documented what is known of the early history of American timber bridge building, introducing many of the key players. The present chapter explores the process of planning the construction of covered timber truss bridges, the builders, and their many truss designs.

BUILDING A COVERED BRIDGE INVOLVES AT LEAST THE FOLLOWING STEPS.

1   Proposing and financing a bridge
2   Engaging builders for both abutments/piers and superstructure
3   Designing all aspects of the structure: abutments, piers, trusses, deck system, lateral bracing, roofing, siding, and roadway
4   Steps in the construction of the foundations and superstructure
5   Maintenance
6   Obsolescence and decline: the changing fate of covered bridges

Proposing and Financing a Bridge

Essentially, there were two ways to get a bridge built, either by private initiative or by a government body. Only gradually during the nineteenth century did governments take on the responsibility for building and maintaining bridges. Before that became common, bridge building was mostly left to private businessmen hoping not just to solve a transportation problem but also to turn a profit from tolls. Although we know little about bridge building before the advent of companies, we find pieces of evidence here and there. Frances Manwaring Caulkins' *History of Norwich, Connecticut* (1874) provides an unusual amount of information on early bridge building: "The earlier bridges were built and kept in order by the inhabitants as highway work. In April, 1717, a petition was presented to the General Assembly 'for assistance in building a cart bridge over Showtucket [Shetucket] at the falls' . . . it is probably that this first bridge over the Shetucket was built in the usual way, by a general turn-out of the inhabitants" (p. 343).

Later, she refers to another incident—to be explored more fully further on because it involved a bridge building accident—and writes: "A large party of the inhabitants had assembled to assist in raising the bridge, which was 20 feet high and about 250 feet in length" (p. 343). If these practices were widespread, this pattern probably prevailed throughout the colonies, reminding us of today's tradition of "barn raisings" among the Amish. Such bridges had to have been simple if ordinary citizens could construct them.

As the century progressed and the growing towns and cities required ever more substantial bridges to allow the transport of goods and mail, and travel for people over the colonies' major rivers, it was necessary to form companies that in turn hired reputable builders, often selected from several competing proposals. After independence, virtually all of the substantial bridges spanning, for example, the Hudson, Merrimack, Schuylkill, Delaware, Mohawk, and Susquehanna rivers, required the formation of companies and approval by the state legislature. Similarly, the legislatures had to approve the formation of companies for canals, turnpikes, and other public improvements. The fact that a bridge company was authorized, however, did not mean the bridge was actually built. The bills included toll rates for passage. Those for the Permanent Bridge in Philadelphia ranged from one cent per foot passenger, riderless horse, or head of cattle to twenty cents per four-wheeled pleasure carriage drawn by four horses to $1.35 for a "carriage of burden" weighing the maximum load allowed of six tons.

Philadelphia's other great bridge, the Lancaster-Schuylkill Bridge, began with an Act of Incorporation approved by the legislature and governor on March 28, 1811, the company beginning with 800 shares at $50 each, for a total of $40,000. By June, the company had elected officers and began advertising for proposals. Eventually, they contracted with Lewis Wernwag to

build a single-span bridge later known as "The Colossus." All of Theodore Burr's bridges were financed and built by companies, though sometimes there was a considerable time delay between formation of the company, its financing, and completion of the project. Indeed, that is precisely the problem encountered by the companies that hired Burr. As he took on more and more projects requiring increasing cash flows to pay for materials and workers, the companies became reluctant to make advance payments because of endless delays and Burr's peripatetic work style. As a result, Burr gradually went bankrupt. Additionally, many other companies went bankrupt when their all too new bridges succumbed to one of the annual spring floods or ice jams, and bridges could not be insured against these "acts of God."

Although government responsibility for building bridges developed slowly, the National Road, started in 1811, was exceptional because of extensive federal investment. Wernwag's bridge over the Ohio River at Wheeling, built in 1818 as a key section of the National Road, was discussed in Chapter 1. When the National Road reached Zanesville, Ohio, in 1830, the federal government was still funding the project, but within

Above left Most early covered bridges were built by entrepreneurs hoping to turn a profit by charging tolls. This necessitated having a toll booth on one end and hiring someone to collect the money. (NSPCB Archives, R. S. Allen Collection)

Above right Although the Cornish-Windsor Bridge spanning the Connecticut River is mostly within New Hampshire and belongs to the Town of Cornish, its earliest toll booth stands on the Windsor, Vermont, side. (A. Chester Ong, 2010)

Below The National Road had to cross two rivers in Zanesville, Ohio, where the Muskingum River meets the Licking River. Pictured is the third Y Bridge, built in 1832. The first, in 1813, was an open trestle, but the second, of 1819, was covered. (Ohio Historical Society Archives)

Above The covered wooden Y Bridge (background) in Zanesville, Ohio, carried the National Road US 40 until 1900 when it was replaced by a concrete bridge. The steel rail bridge in the foreground is no longer in existence either. (Van Tassel, 1901)

Right from top It was customary for county officials to publish a "notice to contractors" when taking bids for a new bridge. This one was published in Coshocton County, Ohio, in 1865, for the Croy's Mill Bridge. (Terry E. Miller Collection)

Companies, hoping to receive invitations to bid on bridges, advertised in newspapers and magazines. T. H. Hamilton of Toledo, Ohio, was still offering Howe truss bridges in 1885 near the end of the wooden truss era. (Kemp, 2005: 28)

As seen in the County Commissioners' Journals from 1874, these are the handwritten bids for both superstructure and masonry of the Jacobsport Bridge in Coshocton County, Ohio. The bridge was bid by the lineal foot and stonework by the perch. (Terry E. Miller Collection)

four years, in 1834, they decided to delegate the funding for the project to the individual states. The most unusual bridge on this route, which later became US 40, was the "Y Bridge" in Zanesville, so-called because it crossed the Muskingum River at its confluence with the Licking River, offering travelers a choice of left or right turns at the center.

The earliest bridge at this site was built by Rufus Scott in 1813, long before the National Road, as a simple trestle bridge. Short-lived, the bridge was damaged by a flood in 1815 and then succumbed to rot, falling into the river in 1818. A second bridge was built in 1819, this time a timber truss bridge with—according to an engraving on a Muskingum Bank of Zanesville five dollar bill—an arch-like shape, suggesting a design akin to those used by Palmer. Built by a private company about which little is known, the bridge continued to serve the now established and increasingly busy National Road. When ice damaged the structure during the winter of 1831, one of the owners, Ebenezer Buckingham, joined his son Catharinus to form a new company. Young Catharinus, only twenty-five, designed a double-lane bridge using multiple kingpost trusses. To overcome concerns about his design, Catharinus built a model, placed 500 pounds on it, then had someone stand on the model as well, thereby winning the contract.

Using newly built piers, construction proceeded during the summer of 1832. On August 20, when young Catharinus was ill with cholera, his father told him that one of the new spans had shifted about six inches. The next day, August 21, while Ebenezer was inspecting the structure, they only realized that the trusses had shifted to the old pier when, according to Norris F. Schneider, "About 3 o'clock the span fell, taking nine men with it. Ebenezer Buckingham and one other man were killed in the fall" (1958: 12). Catharinus successfully completed the bridge, and the company prospered from its relatively expensive tolls. Indeed, by 1849 citizens were complaining about the tolls and the company's 18 percent dividends, but it was not until 1868 that the state and city jointly agreed to purchase the bridge and relieve the citizens of tolls.

Most toll bridges crossed substantial rivers, and travelers were willing to pay the required tolls to avoid hazardous alternatives. In the case of more modest

bridges crossing ordinary streams, the old method of fording might remain an option when water was low, with the result that travelers could avoid tolls. Various patterns developed to get bridges erected. Yet, without a comprehensive history of this aspect of bridge building, we have only anecdotal evidence and a general understanding. These ranged from local initiative with no government involvement to projects that included contributions from local government. There is no consistent pattern. Though all states were divided into counties, the divisions of government below that and their individual responsibilities varied widely. These patterns affected both how bridges came to be erected and how records were kept, the latter being a key source for anyone writing history today. For example, New York State was, and still is, governed by "home rule," a practice in which local governments may pass laws and ordinances peculiar to their own jurisdictions. As a result, bridges in New York State were usually initiated, financed, and built through local efforts, with or without state approval or financing, and often with minimal record keeping. Thus, it was common in New York for a group of local landowners to band together

Bridge Notice.

TO STONE-MASONS AND CARPEN-
TERS.

Sealed Proposals will be received at the Auditor's Office, in Coshocton, until 10 o'clock A. M. October 7, 1865, for the Building of a Buckingham Bridge, across Mill Creek,
At Croy's Mill, in Keene Township.
Specifications at Auditor's office.
By order of Commissioners.
C. H. JOHNSTON, Auditor.
Sept. 12, 1865.

AD GAZETTE. [APRIL 17, 1885.

HOWE'S PATENT TRUSS.

T. H. HAMILTON,
Bridge Builder and General Contractor, - - Toledo, O.

to finance and build—sometimes themselves—a needed bridge. In other states, mostly farther west, such as Ohio, county government came to control and finance bridge projects. In the case of a state like Oregon or the Canadian province of New Brunswick, where most covered bridges were built after the time of their obsolescence in the east, the highway departments were usually in charge and, as a result, imposed standard designs.

Based on research in Ohio, we know that during the earlier nineteenth century the group wishing to build a local bridge might petition the county commissioners for financial assistance in order to erect a "free bridge." In these cases, the county might contribute as little as $100 or perhaps $300 towards the effort, the rest of the money being "subscribed" by members of the bridge committee.

A particularly complex case occurred when the citizens of Coshocton in east-central Ohio sought a bridge over the Walhonding River on Hill Street between Roscoe and Coshocton. Though the Ohio Legislature initially authorized the commissioners to build a free bridge using funds from individual subscribers on February 21, 1833, not enough money was raised, and on March 3, 1834 the state amended the act to allow the county to contribute funds. While the bridge project remained in limbo, the state passed yet another act, on January 27, 1836, allowing the commissioners complete responsibility for erecting that and other bridges: "Bridges to be free and to be double track." To pay for the bridge, they asked for proposals to loan the commissioners between $15,000 and $20,000 (about $375,000 to $500,000 in today's currency), but no one came forward. At that point, the commissioners appointed General Joseph Burns to find the money, and, believing he would be successful, let a contract for the bridge totaling $19,900. When Burns returned from Baltimore empty handed, the commissioners had to take extreme measures, borrowing $10,000 at 7 percent from the estate of a wealthy man in Brownsville,

Pennsylvania, and $10,000 from the Ohio Life Insurance and Trust Company. Because the practice of borrowing money to pay for a "free bridge" seemed risky, the state then passed an amendment allowing for the collection of tolls. We do not know the toll rates or how long tolls were collected, but over the years the county had to pay for many repairs before replacing the Coshocton covered bridge with an iron bridge in 1887.

Engaging builders for stonework and superstructure

As the nineteenth century progressed, county and local governments gradually assumed greater responsibility for public works and were increasingly able to pay for them using tax dollars. But the formal pattern we know today—calling for sealed bids, selecting the lowest bid (that met specifications), inspecting the project upon completion, and paying in full—only developed towards the end of the Civil War (1860–5). After that, at least in counties where full records were kept, the covered bridge building process becomes better known. In areas where local government was responsible for bridge building, record keeping tended to be unsystematic, and over time many documents disappeared. For example, Pennsylvania's county records provide limited information to researchers since many counties have "cleaned house" by throwing out what records there were. In the case of Ohio and Indiana, at least, the county commissioners kept moderately detailed records. Nineteenth-century journals were handwritten by a secretary, and depending on that person's diligence, preserved much or little detail. In counties whose records have been most thoroughly researched, we find the commissioners' journals listing all the bids for both stonework and superstructure, noting to whom the contract was given, and accounting for all (or most) of the payments. What is missing in most cases are the original bids submitted by builders along with any drawings, plans, or specifications they provided.

During the period from about 1865 to the end of the covered bridge era (1890s for most areas but later for

Indiana, the South, and the Far West), officials contracted for two matters, the stonework for the abutments and piers and the wooden superstructure. Stonework was bid by the perch and the wooden superstructure by the lineal foot. One perch of stone was 24.75 cubic feet, equivalent to a unit of blocks, 16.5 feet long, 1.5 feet wide, and 1 foot. Bridge foundations generally used large blocks of cut stone quarried locally, but it was also common in some areas of the country for abutments and piers to be made of flat field stones. Stonework was normally laid up dry, that is, without mortar. These were often built on foundations of wooden piles, though little is known of this aspect (see Chapter 3). In areas where stone was difficult to obtain or too expensive, contractors built the bridges on wooden pilings, often replaced later by metal cylinders filled with cement. This was especially so in areas where creek banks and beds were muddy, thus providing a poor base for stone. Although builders preferred abutments built into the bank on either end, when the creek banks rose only gradually, creating a flood plain, the abutments might be built like piers in the water out from the bank, with open approaches of various lengths and designs. Some bridges, for example many in Georgia, had approaches hundreds of feet long.

Bids for the superstructure usually specified the truss. Whether bidders normally included drawings or blueprints is uncertain; few of these have survived. In the early days of bridge building in New England and Pennsylvania, in the case of major bridges, the builders themselves met with the company directors to make a sales pitch, often enhanced with a sizeable wooden model of their bridge. Most stories concerning such sales practices tell of the builder standing on the model or having several men stand on it to demonstrate its strength. A few of the models survive in museums today but none as large as Thomas Pope's 50-foot-long half model for his "Flying Lever Pendent Bridge." Ithiel Town, however, did not use models to sell his lattice truss; indeed, he challenged their efficacy: "The reason of this difference between large and small spans is evident—it is for the same reason that a model of some modes of building bridges may have considerable strength, and appear to *many* to be good, yet when executed *full size*, will either fall down when the stages are removed, or soon thereafter…. Thus, then, the idea or belief that models are good representations of the strength of bridges when built, is erroneous in the extreme, and leads to sure disappointment and the destruction of property" (1839: 10).

In the case of Ohio, the county commissioners' journals provide little or no information on the bidding process before the Civil War, but afterwards the list of bids was recorded by the secretary. As an example, here are the bids received on November 15, 1867 by the Coshocton County, Ohio, commissioners for a three-span bridge at Warsaw over the Walhonding River.

ABUTMENTS AND TWO PIERS (PER PERCH)

	Stonework	Protection [of the banks]
John Shrake	$6.65	$1.39
John L. Jones	$9.74	$1.99
G. T. Arnold	$7.99	$2.00
Wm. Arnold	$6.99	$1.35
Wm. Moore	$10.55	$1.90
Chas. Mowery	$7.50	$1.50
White & Evans	$10.74	$1.90
Daugherty & Bush	$8.40	$1.15
W. R. Wilson	$10.90	—
Jno. Colhower	$13.35	—
C. H. Johnston	$8.35	$1.60
O. Y. Hillery	$7.97	—
Mat. Johnston	$11.00	$1.50

The bids for the superstructure were mostly for the "Buckingham plan," which means a multiple kingpost design.

SUPERSTRUCTURE (PER LINEAL FOOT, ALL BUCKINGHAM PLAN)

John Shrake		$17.87
J. R. Brown		$16.87
G. J. and J. B. Hagerty		$17.97
C. H. Johnston		$19.75
A. M. Allen	Oak & Poplar	$18.43
Same	Pine	$23.71
Geo. H. Vroom		$19.50
Jacob Gardner		$27.98
Michael Lapp		$18.90
Mat. Johnston		$22.00
C. C. Morrison	Burr 18–20' wide	$18.50
Jno. Hesket		$18.40

Perhaps of greater interest were the bids from June 26, 1877, for another bridge over the Walhonding just east of the village of the same name.

Samuel Mills	Buckingham	$14.00	No plans [inc]
William Morford	Buckingham	$11.25	Plans
Mat Johnston	Buckingham	$12.00	No plans
Mat Johnston	Howe	$14.00	Plans
Smith Bridge Co.	No. 1 Howe	$17.50	Plans
Smith Bridge Co.	No. 2 Howe	$16.19	Plans
Smith Bridge Co.	No. 3 Smith	$15.50	Plans
Black, Borneman Co.	"A" Comb. Truss	$16.00	
Black, Borneman Co.	"B" Howe	$15.25	
Black, Borneman Co.	Howe	$16.00	
Black, Borneman Co.	Howe	$15.50	
Black, Borneman Co.	Howe	$12.25	
J. B. Brown	Comb.	$14.95	
J. and S. Shrake	Howe	$14.85	
S. P. White	Howe	$15.20	

Without any of the plans mentioned, it is difficult to know the exact differences among the trusses noted

or what was meant by "combination truss" other than it combined wood with iron members.

When a bridge was completed, it was customary for officials to inspect the work before authorizing payment. In earlier times when bridges were less common and often sizeable, their opening was noted in the press. After the building of bridges became a routine government duty, such notices were less common unless the bridge were located in the midst of a sizeable town or city. In some cases, community celebrations, ribbon cutting, and first passage by prominent citizens and officials occurred at the opening.

Considering that many early bridges were built over major rivers, that there was then no flood control, it should come as no surprise that the lifespan of a covered bridge in the nineteenth century was often short, anywhere from six months to a few years being numbingly common. Even as county and state governments stabilized their finances through regular taxation, having to replace major bridges repeatedly must have played havoc with their budgets. In a few cases, a county carried insurance against loss, but few companies would be willing to insure a bridge against ice floes and flood. It was maintenance costs, however, that continually chipped away at the budget. Replacing roofs, siding, and perhaps decks, as well as painting, were ongoing requirements. Damaged bridges could sometimes be repaired, even when washed off the abutments into the creek. Take as an example Sandle's Bridge over Wills Creek in southern Coshocton County, Ohio. Originally built in 1879, the 142-foot multiple kingpost truss bridge succumbed to a flood in the early spring of 1884 that also destroyed a nearby bridge that was only months old. Sandle's Bridge was washed off the abutments, but the commissioners paid Michael Lapp $100 to salvage the bridge from the creek (presumably by disassembling it). After taking bids, they contracted with John C. Miller to "rebuild" the bridge for $718 but then decided to raise the abutments, hopefully to keep the rebuilt bridge out of harm's way. For this, they paid Miller $472.42. In addition, they paid Michael Lapp $375 to add two sets of arches, converting the rebuilt Sandle's Bridge into a Burr truss.

Structural Design

A covered bridge is a complex piece of craftsmanship. Ask any of the people who have measured and drawn them for the National Parks Service's Historical American Engineering Record (HAER), a student of Industrial Archaeology, or a county engineer responsible for maintaining one. Considering that bridges can be discussed in detail, down to the shapes of the fasteners and the multitudinous ways to join beams, a full consideration could occupy volumes. Not having that luxury, we must restrict ourselves to the essentials. One of those essentials is truss design, the primary framework for a covered bridge. Indeed, the presence of a *working* truss is one of the defining attributes of an "authentic" covered bridge in the United States and Canada. And when a deteriorating bridge requires support from steel I-beams placed beneath, a topic discussed in Chapter 5, the truss is effectively neutralized. Most covered bridge listings include "truss type," and while it is desirable to reduce this identifier to a single term such as "Burr" or "Howe," in practice there are nearly endless variations in design that add both interest and confusion. Because trusses are paramount and the rest (deck, cross bracing, roofing, siding, etc.) simply functional or decorative—albeit varied and often interesting—we must concentrate on the trusses while summarizing the other aspects.

As mentioned in Chapter 1, two principles underlie virtually all trusses: the rigidity of the triangle and the strength of the arch. Both are timeless, and their

inclusion in truss design, including patented ones, says less about creativity than about the nature of materials. Following the establishment of the United States Patent Office in 1790, builders, architects, engineers, and dreamers had patented over 600 bridge truss designs by the end of the nineteenth century. As civil engineering moved from common sense and experience to science, patents proliferated. Only four bridge patents were issued before 1800, fifteen more to 1820, twelve more to 1840, and twenty-three to 1850. Thus, only fifty-four of the total appeared during the first half century, a period when there were few alternatives to covered timber truss bridges, while the second half century saw a virtual explosion of designs.

Relatively few patented designs were of practical value and had a noticeable effect on American bridge history. Many were endless variations on well-known designs and only earned patents for their minor "improvements." Metal truss patents were rare before 1850 but proliferated during the following decades, rendering wooden truss patents mostly obsolete after 1870. Nonetheless, covered wooden bridges continued to be constructed for practical reasons over a wide area well into the twentieth century, and in a few exceptional areas even past 1950.

Most patent trusses were named for their "assignee," normally the designer himself (alas, no women are known to have designed any timber bridge trusses). But not all trusses were patented. Several much used trusses are generic in their fundamentals but surprisingly varied in execution, including "kingpost," "queenpost," "multiple kingpost," and simple or "tied" arches. These designs are part of the received wisdom and common sense long known to even the least knowledgeable of builders. Even among the relatively few covered bridges remaining, there are also distinctive truss designs that either lack a known designer or were never patented, or both. Considering how under-developed America's transportation and communication systems were during the "golden age" of covered bridges (1805–c. 1920), it comes as no surprise that patent enforcement and consistencies in royalty payments were haphazard matters. Some builders made a lot of money licensing their designs; others made only modest sums or perhaps nothing. When the patent office opened,

inventors were only granted patent rights for fourteen years, with a possible extension of seven years. Without an effective way to police usage, it seems unlikely that many bridge truss inventors profited consistently.

Surviving bridges exemplify approximately twenty truss types, but some classifications are problematic. Other truss types exist in multiple variations. The patent design gives the appearance of being settled, but the execution depended on the individual builder. All trusses are not equally significant, and giving each equal treatment tends to distort their importance. We have subdivided them into three groups according to relative importance.

GROUP I	GROUP II	GROUP II
Kingpost	Childs	Brown
Queenpost	Partridge	Haupt
Multiple Kingpost	Paddleford	McCallum
Simple Arch		Wheeler
Burr		Post
Town Lattice		"Inverted Bowstring"
Long		
Howe		
Smith		

A clear understanding of a bridge design based on stress analysis developed gradually during the nineteenth century, as bridge building moved from the realms of house and mill builders, architects, and dreamers such as Peale and Pope, to the realm of civil engineers and theoreticians. Squire Whipple published his *A Work of Bridge Building: Consisting of Two Essays, The One Elementary and General, The Other Giving Original Plans, and Practical Details for Iron and Wooden Bridges* in 1847, and General Herman Haupt his *General Theory of Bridge Construction* in 1851, both offering mathematically based stress analysis. They understood that their main material, wood, is fibrous and capable of being compressed or stretched without breaking. Naturally, they learned to work with the types

of wood at hand, especially the main varieties of pine, oak, and poplar. Iron, at least as fasteners, rods, and straps, came into limited use from the beginning. Whether they knew of Palladio's work or not, they understood the triangle's role in bridge design, well expressed later by De Volson Wood in his 1876 *Treatise on the Theory of the Construction of Bridges and Roofs*: "The triangle is the only geometrical figure in which the angles cannot be changed without changing the lengths of the sides. . . . Hence, to form a truss which will not distort when partially loaded, the truss-work should form triangular figures" (1883: 70).

Bridge builders also knew about the strength of the arch, and they understood that arches could exert tremendous thrust into the abutments, requiring substantial stonework. Indeed, even Thomas Pope, who's "Flying Pendent Lever Bridge" was an impractically gigantic arch, planned for multistory warehouses as abutments. Builders also understood that trusses must be symmetrical to work properly, each half mirroring the other.

In discussing the many trusses that follow, we are mindful of the challenges of terminology, for the name for a given part may vary from profession to profession. Let us consider several basic parts to virtually every wooden trussed bridge beginning with the terms commonly used by writers of books on covered bridges.

CHORDS The main horizontal beams that frame a given truss are "chords" and more specifically "upper chords" and "lower chords." Some refer to them as "beams," "stringers," "sticks," or in the case of the British, "booms." Lower chords work in tension and upper chords in compression.

POSTS Beams running vertically between the upper and lower chords are commonly referred to as "posts" or "kingposts." Since the kingpost truss has a specific configuration with a single post, applying kingpost to longer trusses seems technically incorrect, but it is customary. Another term for them is "ties." (King)posts work in tension.

BRACES Virtually all writers refer to the diagonal members that incline from the ends towards the center as "braces." Braces work in compression.

COUNTERBRACES As with braces, there is general agreement that counterbraces are diagonals that incline from the center towards the ends. Counterbraces usually work in tension, but they also work in compression in certain situations.

TRUSS A truss is a configuration of timbers acting in both tension and compression that, by remaining rigid, supports both the bridge as a whole and all the loads passing over it. Some refer to a truss as a "girder." Most trusses are based on the triangle principle.

Kingpost Truss

The kingpost truss was found in the roofs of medieval wooden buildings where two diagonal braces inclined to a center post rested on a cross beam spanning the building's interior. De Volson Wood calls it a "braced beam" or "braced tie," and it is described as a "two-panel" truss. As a bridge truss, the kingpost design has been used in multiple variations. For very short spans, it can be low in height, what is called a "pony truss." While some pony kingposts were open approaches, others were boxed in to protect the timbers. Indeed, some covered kingpost bridges appear to be built like pony trusses but surrounded with a higher framework

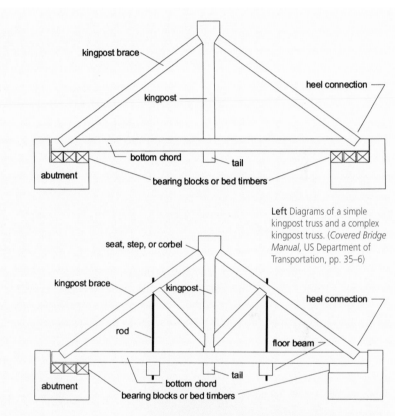

Left Diagrams of a simple kingpost truss and a complex kingpost truss. (*Covered Bridge Manual*, US Department of Transportation, pp. 35–6)

Right A relatively simple kingpost truss in Washington County, Pennsylvania (A. Chester Ong, 2011)

Below A longer than usual kingpost truss in Vermont's Scott Bridge. (A. Chester Ong, 2010)

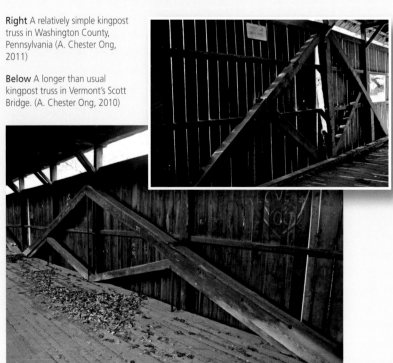

to support a roof and sides, since there is no upper chord. Another common variation uses an iron rod in place of the wooden post, a smart idea considering iron's superior behavior over wood when placed in tension. In slightly longer versions, builders added bracing within the two triangles. Kingpost trusses often have a single lower chord on which rest the center post and the lower ends of the braces, but a few have double chords. These may be secured into notches in the chord with or without additional bolts or straps.

Kingpost truss covered bridges rarely exceed 40 feet in length and thus are only suitable for crossing small streams. In New England, where crossings range from major bridges over the Connecticut River to tiny mountainside streams, kingpost bridges appeared here and there, but generally in hilly regions where only small streams were the norm, such as in southwestern Pennsylvania and parts of eastern Ohio.

Queenpost Truss

Appropriate for longer spans up to a maximum of around 80 feet, the queenpost truss consists of three panels and might be described as the two halves of the kingpost with a horizontal beam between, thus requiring two posts instead of one. Its overall shape explains another common term, the "trapezoidal truss." As with the kingpost, queenposts could be built as open pony trusses or boxed pony trusses, and as fully covered bridges. Although simple queenposts abound, many have additional diagonal bracing within as well as vertical iron rods to provide additional strength. Because the center panel can be disproportionately long, it is normally filled with additional framing, sometimes in the form of an embedded kingpost. The horizontal cross beam of the center panel functions as an upper chord and is therefore in compression. The brace ends might be notched into the lower chord and secured with bolts or straps while the center horizontal

is often mortised into the posts and secured with wooden dowels, called "treenails" (pronounced "trunnels").

Queenpost bridges abound in areas with small streams, but they were most commonly erected in the Middle Atlantic states and parts of the South, especially Virginia, West Virginia, Tennessee, and Kentucky. Boxed pony queenposts were commonly built to cross Midwestern canals as well. However, neither kingpost nor queenpost trusses were appropriate for roads carrying heavy traffic and certainly not for railroads. Related to the queenpost truss are reinforcements in queenpost shape, most commonly added to a Town lattice truss. Most were retrofitted, as seen in Litchfield County, Connecticut's West Cornwall Bridge (see Chapter 6, page 170). A few bridges in Pennsylvania have what appears to be a queenpost reinforcement for a multiple kingpost, but these function like three-section arches because they are anchored into the abutments and bolted to the posts.

Multiple Kingpost

Perhaps inspired by Palladio's designs, perhaps arrived at by common sense reasoning, a multiple kingpost truss is an extension of the kingpost idea into a variable length panel truss. Palmer's earliest truss bridges combined the basic form of the multiple kingpost, albeit with posts that extended below the chords, with arches. We are not aware of any early bridges using the multiple kingpost design alone until Catharinus and Ebenezer Buckingham built Zanesville, Ohio's famous "Y Bridge" in 1831 using this pattern. Because this structure carried the National Road, with its heavy freight wagons and stage coaches, it was unusual for the builders to omit the added strength of arches, and yet the bridge served until 1900. During much of the nineteenth century, Ohio builders denoted this truss as "Buckingham." Although there are multiple kingpost bridges here and there in

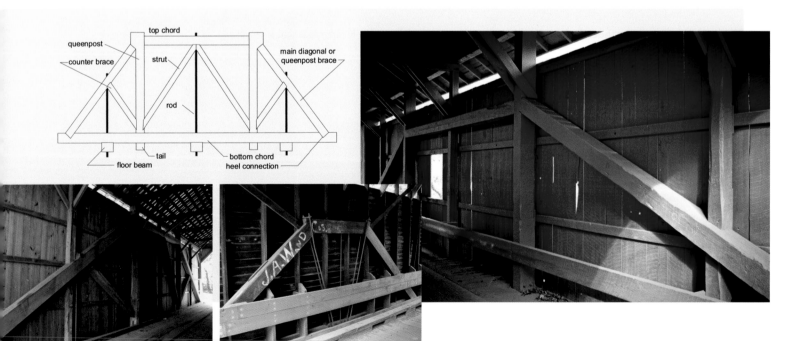

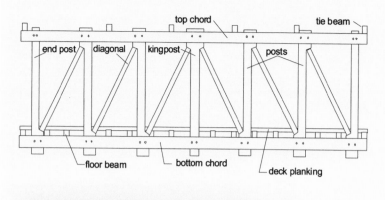

New England and Pennsylvania, the majority seem to have been built in Ohio. New Hampshire, however, offers several examples of the truss with unusually narrow panels, which would give the bridge much added strength. One such example is the Blacksmith Shop Bridge.

Multiple kingpost trusses typically have two lower and upper chords, the posts notched between them and often bolted. Such trusses are capable of carrying spans of 100 feet without difficulty, and although longer spans do exist, the truss's efficiency declines after that point. For additional strength, however, some builders constructed doubled versions with triple chords, double posts, and double braces, even for modest spans. Vinton County, Ohio, still has two such spans, one of them also having a simple plank arch embedded between the truss members but seated on the lower chords.

Two further factors affect all panel trusses, including multiple kingposts. First, panel proportions are important. In general, the greater the height of a truss, the greater its strength. But overly wide panels reverse this advantage. Col. Stephen H. Long described this matter in his 1841 edition of *Description of Col. S. H. Long's Bridges*: "The proper length of a pannel [*sic*] is measured on the string, is about two-thirds the height of the truss frame, the former extending from centre to centre of the posts, and the latter, from centre to centre of the strings of the truss frame" (p. 29). William E. Bell in his 1857 *Carpentry Made Easy* reiterated the point: "The panels of bridges of this kind ought never to be as great in extension as in height between chords; or, in other words, the rise of the braces should always be greater than their run; and practically, it is expensive and inconvenient to extend the panels more than 12 or 14 feet" (p. 102). There are bridges still standing, though barely, with overly long panels. Today, three of Lehigh County, Pennsylvania's bridges exhibit this problem. Two have been heavily reinforced and one is to be torn down and replicated because of its irreparable sag.

The second factor affecting all panel trusses is that the stress is greater towards the ends and less in the middle. As a consequence, there are multiple kingpost bridges with an odd number of panels, the middle either left open or filled with crisscross members in an "X" formation. A few bridges vary the proportions of the panels from the ends to the center for this reason, but it is more common for the panel timbers to decrease in dimensions towards the middle, though there is greater stress on the chords. William E. Bell also commented on this matter: "In all bridges of this kind, the greatest strain upon the braces is at the end of the span; and it will be most proper to use the best and largest pieces of timber for the end braces, and those of inferior quality, if such must be used somewhere, should be placed in the middle" (1857: 102). The chords, however, undergo greater strain at the center and less at the ends.

Simple Arch

Strictly speaking, a bridge supported by nothing more than an arch does not have a truss at all, but because all-wood arches are given to flexing, most simple arch covered bridges also require the stabilization of a frame or simple truss. Engineers have long argued whether a truss combined with an arch produces contradictory support systems, but most see the arch as reinforcing the truss. Theodore Burr, however, used massive arches without trusses in his Trenton-Morrisville Bridge over the Delaware River.

Some of the relatively rare specimens surviving today use laminated arches tied directly to the lower chord at each end, most being in Vermont. The Lincoln Bridge in Windsor County, 136 feet long and built in 1877, is unusual for its length. Its six-layered arch rests on a series of vertical beams, and the floor system is supported by a series of crossed iron rods suspended from the arch. This design has been erroneously called "Pratt with arch." Squire Whipple's 1841 truss is, in fact, an iron arch with X-shaped rod bracing.

A greater number of arch bridges, particularly those found in Germany, Switzerland, and Austria, used arches consisting of a series of straight sections, which is known as a polygonal arch. Each section is fastened to uprights for stability. In the United States, only Giles County, Virginia, has such bridges, all three being rough-looking arches attached to a rectangular frame.

Top Diagram of a multiple kingpost truss. (*Covered Bridge Manual*, US Department of Transportation, p. 38)

Above left A typical Ohio multiple kingpost truss in Fairfield County, Ohio's Hanaway Bridge built in 1901. (A. Chester Ong, 2011)

Above right New Hampshire's Blacksmith Shop Bridge exemplifies a local version of the multiple kingpost truss with unusually narrow panels. (Terry E. Miller, 2010)

Above Vermont's Bower's or Brownsville Bridge, built around 1919, is a rare example of a tied arch truss. (NSPCB Archives, Bill Caswell, 2009)

Right from top Vermont's Lincoln Bridge, built in 1877, combines an extended tied arch with iron rod X bracing, giving rise to an erroneous designation as a "Pratt truss." (NSPCB Archives, Bill Caswell, 2008)

The Link's Farm Bridge in Giles County, Virginia, functions as a simple arch but is built in four straight segments. (Terry E. Miller, 1974)

The Pleasantville Bridge in Berks County, Pennsylvania, built in 1852, is a one-of-a-kind structure using three concentric arches, posts, three chords, and light bracing. (Terry E. Miller, 2010)

Burr Truss

There is the "Burr truss" and then there are the trusses that Theodore Burr actually used. Both of Burr's patents, X662 of February 14, 1806, and X2769 of April 3, 1817, were lost in the disastrous US Patent Office fire of 1836. Only the second was reconstructed, and that was many years after his death in 1822. Thus, we know nothing of the earlier patent and little of the second. By the time of his first patent, he had already constructed at least eight bridges, two of which survived into the era of photography. His Lansingburgh-Waterford Union Bridge built over the Hudson River in 1804 used a truss which resembles what we now call the "Burr truss," but his bridge at Trenton, New Jersey, over the Delaware, built between 1804 and 1806 can only be described as idiosyncratic. Since he applied for his first patent while building the Trenton bridge, we can only guess that his first patent covered that configuration, but we cannot be

sure. The second patent, not surprisingly, is close to what was later recognized as the "Burr truss."

The 1817 reconstructed patent shows an eight-panel multiple kingpost truss with slightly flared posts (radiating outwards) and an arch clearly seated in the abutments. With the exception of the flaring, which has been erroneously attributed to Lewis Wernwag, the drawing depicts what is now a standard Burr truss. Such a truss has two lower chords that sandwich in the posts, but the majority of bridges have a single upper chord, with the post ends mortised and pinned. The single braces are more commonly beveled or notched (also called "dapped") into the sides of the posts, not into the joints, because doing so places stress on the joints which could then become loose and admit moisture, leading to dry rot. Each truss has two parallel arches flanking the truss, these comprised of substantial beams placed end to end. Some were cut from curved-grain wood but others cut to shape from straight-grained wood. The arches are seated beneath the lower chords into well-built abutments and could stand independently of the trusses. They are normally bolted to the posts, but many now have iron rods running from wooden blocks mounted on the arches to the chords; some are original, others added at a later date. Builders had different opinions about whether the arch should be attached to the truss before the falsework was removed or only after the bridge had settled. James Robert Mosse, an English engineer writing about timber bridges in the United States in 1863, wrote: "There are, on the other hand, Engineers in the United States, who do not approve of the arch in combination with the truss [e.g., Herman Haupt]. They hold that a structure composed of two systems, neither of which is strong enough by itself, is defective in principle, and they state it to be very difficult, if not impossible, so to proportion the weight upon each system, as to make each bear its proper share. Practically the best mode of obtaining this combined action, seems to be, [sic] the removal of the scaffolding before the suspension-rods from the arches are secured to the joists, and then by tightening these rods to make the truss rise slightly" (1863: 311).

So what exactly is so original about the "Burr truss" that it deserved a patent? Philadelphia architect Robert Smith had advocated for covering timber bridges as early as 1769, and the diagram published in *The Columbian Magazine* in 1787, possibly the work of Smith, clearly shows a truss design that most readers would now recognize as a "Burr truss." Each of the four spans has a ten-panel multiple kingpost design with an arch. Furthermore, each element was long established in Europe well before 1769, with Palladio being the first known architect to suggest the multiple kingpost design. Most of Timothy Palmer's bridges were somewhat different, however, for their arches started far below the trusses and only ran as high as the lower chords. His posts also extended below the lower chords to the arch and were flared to follow the approximate curve of the structure. While the designs of Palmer and Burr had many differences, both consisted of the same elements. And neither element would seem to deserve a patent.

Burr's earliest bridge for which we have photographs was built before his first patent of 1806, the Lansingburgh-Waterford Union Bridge, discussed in Chapter 1, over the Hudson River opened on December 4, 1804. Left uncovered until 1814, the double-lane bridge underwent numerous repairs and probably reinforcements before its loss to fire on July 10, 1909. Unlike Palmer's bridges, the roadway was level and the chords were horizontal and parallel. Surviving photos show that in most respects it was a Burr truss as we now know it, though certain details distinguish it from the typical pattern (Allen, 1957: 14; Hayner, 1967: 7). The arches consist of at least six layers of timber rather than planks, which resulted in massive arches. In addition to the usual braces, there are counterbraces, some consisting of two pieces divided by the brace, some in pairs sandwiching the braces. Iron rods from the arches support the lower chords. How much was original and how much was added, especially when trolley tracks were added, is difficult to say.

Perhaps Burr's lost first patent resembled the aforementioned bridge. If so, the second patent in 1817 showed a simplification, because the reconstructed drawing omits counterbraces. The Pennsylvania Historical and Museum Commission has a scale model of a two-lane bridge said to have been built by Burr and used in sales pitches (see page 159). The model contradicts the patent drawing and existing bridges: the lower chord appears to be below the roadway with the arch seated into the "abutments" on the same level; the outer trusses appear to have double upper chords because the posts protrude above them; and the center truss rises to the apex of the roof but the arches do not, differing from the Union Bridge of 1804.

Burr and Wernwag

No discussion of the Burr truss is complete without considering its relationship to the so-called Wernwag truss, which some covered bridge historians treat as a distinct truss. Lewis Wernwag is known to have held two patents, but the first one, granted on March 28, 1812, is not available on the Patent Office website and presumably lost. The second, from December 22, 1829, X5760, was also lost but was reconstructed in part. The diagrams depict three distinct types of bridges, the top an arched panel truss apparently with iron rod

Below left Perrine's Bridge just north of New Paltz, New York, was badly deteriorated in 1968, one year before it was restored. First built in 1844, the 154-foot span was again refurbished in 1993. (Klyne Esopus Historical Society Museum)

Below upper Parke County, Indiana's Beeson Bridge, built in 1906 and moved to Billie Creek Village in 1980, has an unusually low arch because of its modest length of 55 feet. (A. Chester Ong, 2011)

Below lower Although Greisemer's Mill Bridge in Berks County, Pennsylvania, is only 140 feet long, the builder in 1868 chose to use double arches for added strength. (A. Chester Ong, 2010)

Bottom from left Barronvale Bridge in Pennsylvania's Somerset County has two unequal spans, the arch of the shorter (foreground) being lower than the other. In addition, it is laminated from planks rather than built of solid beams. (A. Chester Ong, 2011)

The Forksville Bridge in Sullivan County, Pennsylvania, is a classic Burr truss 163 feet long. Note the addition of blocks on the arches to support iron rods connected below the lower chords. (A. Chester Ong, 2012)

The ends of the arches are normally seated into the abutments below the lower chords, as is seen in the Bowser or Osterburg Bridge in Pennsylvania's Bedford County built in 1890. (Terry E. Miller, 2002)

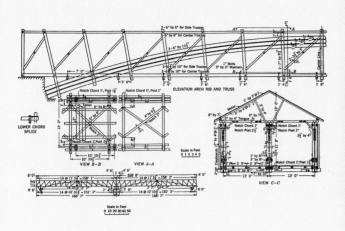

counterbraces only, the lower one an unusual swing bridge, and the middle a drawing of The Colossus in Philadelphia. Like the trusses of Palmer and Burr, Wernwag's design combined a multiple kingpost truss with an arch. As with Burr, Wernwag's design has a level roadway and arches that seat into the abutments well below the lower chords. As in Palmer's bridges, his posts are flared in a fan shape from center to ends, and the posts nearest the end extend below the chords to the arch. We can surmise that Burr exercised little control over his second patent, leaving later builders the freedom to vary it. Wernwag, though the designer or builder of numerous bridges, could not franchise an unpatented design. The practice of flaring the posts, even slightly, seems more a matter of individual preference and common sense than of originality. Because Wernwag's bridges were widespread, even into the West Virginia-Ohio-Maryland areas, it is not surprising that Wernwag contemporaries like West Virginia's Lemuel Chenoweth (1811–87) and Josiah Kidwell built bridges either inspired by Wernwag or using his plans. Many consider the former bridge over the Cheat River on old US 50 (originally the Northwest Turnpike) east of Macomber, West Virginia, to have been the last "genuine" Wernwag truss. Builder Kidwell's two-span double-lane bridge constructed in 1837 was 338 feet long in two spans of 168 feet each. Although the posts and braces were double, there were only two upper and lower chords for the outer trusses, while the middle truss had three. Each truss carried a triple-beamed arch between the braces, which were increasingly flared at the ends and extended below the chords to the arch (Fletcher and Snow, 1934: 372–3). Functionally, it differs little from ordinary Burr trusses, with only the flaring and brace extensions justifying its designation as a Wernwag truss. Retired and bypassed in 1934, this important "state relic" was destroyed on May 23, 1964, by an arsonist, leaving us with no remaining specimens of Wernwag's design.

Later Burr Trusses

Following Burr's death in 1822 and the loss of patent records in 1836, builders were free to interpret the "Burr truss" as they pleased. We could even say that the "Burr truss" had by then gone into the public domain. The truss, with or without some kind of counterbracing, with or without slight flaring, became common throughout New England, New York, West Virginia, and especially Pennsylvania. Oddly, states like Ohio and Kentucky built far fewer Burr trusses, preferring more the later patents, but Indiana builders constructed some of the nation's most classic Burr trusses not only during the later nineteenth but well into the twentieth century. Considering that the Burr truss better exemplifies the most old-fashioned of approaches to bridge construction, it is surprising that so many Indiana builders chose Burr's heavy all-wood design over the more sprightly designer trusses or wood and iron combinations that became widespread after the Civil War.

Town Lattice Truss

None of the early patents held by Pope, Peale, Palmer, or Burr were particularly unique, as all combined the generic multiple kingpost truss with an arch in one way or another. The era of more original trusses, especially ones that brought income to the designer, begins with Ithiel Town's first patent, X3169, granted on January 28, 1820. Where the trusses used by Palmer, Burr, and Wernwag required sophisticated timber framing comprised of large-size beams, Town's truss required only planks and could be assembled—at least Town thought so—by ordinary house carpenters. Town not only benefitted financially from his patents, but bridge builders were still using his designs more than a hundred years later, in the 1930s, in the United States and as late as 1955 in Québec, Canada. Additionally, Town's design was America's first "globalized" bridge patent as it subsequently spread to Europe and even to Palestine.

There was nothing in Ithiel Town's upbringing to suggest he would become one of America's most significant builders and architects. Born into a farming family in Thompson, Connecticut, on October 3, 1784, he moved in with his uncle in Cambridge, Massachusetts at age eight in 1792, began teaching school in 1801 when only seventeen, then apprenticed as a carpenter. It was his association in Boston with prominent architect

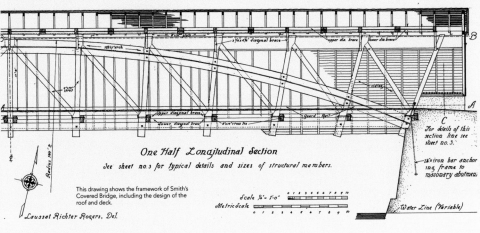

One Half Longitudinal Section

See sheet no.3 for typical details and sizes of structural members.

This drawing shows the framework of Smith's Covered Bridge, including the design of the roof and deck.

Scale ⅛"=1'-0"

Metric scale

Water Line (Variable)

Loussat Richter Rogers, Del.

and author Asher Benjamin (c. 1773–1845) which led Town to establish himself as an independent architect in New Haven where he built Center Church (1812–13) and Trinity Church (1816). Benjamin was an early proponent of codified designs that mimicked Classical, Gothic, and other historical styles.

Town is known to have constructed a few Burr truss bridges in New England early on, but perhaps the possibility of designing even larger buildings in the South lured him there where he evolved his first truss designs. Town's lattice trusses, designed and first built in the South, were as innovative as they were simple. Up to this point, American timber truss bridges were primarily panel trusses consisting of chords, posts, and braces reinforced with one or more arches. Town's lattice was a continuous pattern of overlapping isosceles triangles built from planks, not unlike a garden trellis. Town's first patent of 1820, though lost in the 1836 fire, was easily reconstructed from his pamphlet *A Description of Ithiel Town's Improvement in the Principle, Construction, and Practical Execution of Bridges, for Roads, Railroads, and Aqueducts, whether built entirely of wood, or of cast or wrought iron.* This was first

published in New Haven in 1821, though undoubtedly written while he was living in Fayetteville, North Carolina, and expanded into a second edition in 1839. The patent drawings show a truss with double plank upper and lower chords, overlapping lattice planks, and vertical planks at each end, all intersections pinned with trunnels (wooden dowels, "treenails").

The patent drawings, accompanied by a description in Town's own hand, offer insights into his thinking, first published in a booklet a year later (1821) but quoted here from the second edition: "It has been too much the custom for architects and builders to pile together materials, each according to his own ideas of the scientific principles and practice of Bridge-building, and the result has been, 1st. That nearly as many modes of construction have been adopted as there have been bridges built. 2d. That many have answered no purpose at all, and others but very poorly and for a short time. . ." (1839: 3).

Town then described his plan in detail, referring to six accompanying figures. Figure 2 shows a truss section similar to that of the patent, with single lines of chords, but Figure 1 shows a taller truss with two lines of chords both below and above, a strengthening that may have come from recent experience and a pattern that became prevalent in Town's bridges built throughout North America. He also offered a formula for determining the height of the trusses: approximately one-tenth of the clear span. Thus, a bridge of 100 feet must have trusses at least 10 feet high. For a double-lane bridge, he recommended a center truss reaching the peak of the roof. The lattice members are "composed of sawed plank ten or eleven inches wide, and from three to three and a half inches thick" (p. 4). He recommended white pine or spruce rather than white oak. While recommending three or four trunnels per intersection, he also warned against cutting inserts (or "daps") into the planks where they cross. "String pieces" (chords) are to be similar in dimension to lattice members. Single upper and lower chords are feasible for spans under 130 feet, but longer spans require both primary and secondary chords. Although Town is not known to have built any, he also considered the possibility of a Town lattice in iron, using smaller dimension pieces and a single nut and bolt at each intersection.

Left Ithiel Town's second patent of April 3, 1835, reconstructed following a fire at the Patent Office as 8743X, showing full upper and lower chords and embedded secondary chords. (US Patent Office)

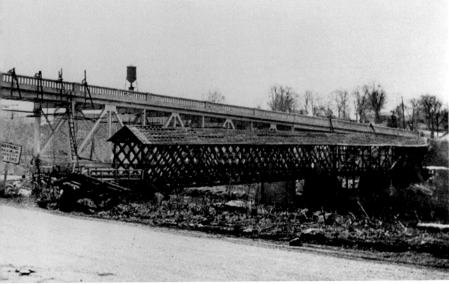

Top The old covered bridge at Central Falls, North Carolina, was being replaced when this photo was taken in 1929 showing a main span with a Town lattice truss without secondary chords and two shorter spans, both queenpost trusses, which were likely uncovered when first built. (Randolph County Public Library, North Carolina)

Above left This two-span bridge linking Bath and Haverhill, New Hampshire, was built in 1829 using Town's lattice with secondary chords. An early set of arches was replaced with massive laminated ones in 1921–2. The bridge was retired in 1999. (A. Chester Ong, 2010)

Above right Virtually all the early rail bridges used the Town lattice truss, but, as in the case of the former rail bridge at Contoocook, New Hampshire, built in 1889, builders normally used high doubled trusses to support the extreme weight of steam locomotives and rolling stock. (A. Chester Ong, 2010)

In a series of twelve points, Town argued in favor of his design. He pointed out that where trusses with arches exert tremendous thrust towards the abutments and piers, requiring substantial and expensive stonework, his trusses have no thrust, only exerting downward pressure. This argument paid off handsomely in the South where many rivers are muddy and allowed builders to use wooden pilings instead of stone. He pointed out that his trusses require no ironwork at all, an advantage in winter, since the iron of the time was brittle and could fail in cold weather. Although minor, he asserted that the lattice trusses themselves provided a base for the siding, saving the expense and weight of a framework. Related to an earlier point, he said that because the trusses exerted no thrust, it was easy to build a drawspan between trussed spans. Though arches could create a problem, where sturdy abutments already existed and the span was long, the trusses could be strengthened with arches. Finally, he claimed that his bridges would cost only half to two-thirds of that of heavy truss bridges, even with added arches.

Town began constructing bridges in North Carolina at least two years before his first patent, building the Yadkin River Bridge (also called Beard's Bridge) in 1818 northeast of Salisbury for Lewis Beard, who had formed a company that would later collect tolls on this $30,000 project. We can only surmise that he perfected his lattice design in this early covered crossing. Town's next project, also built before the patent, from 1819 to 1820, crossed the Cape Fear River at Campbelltown near Fayetteville. Though he erected it on contract for James Seawell, who had obtained state authorization to construct a toll bridge there in 1818, Town later became the principal stockholder and held that position until his death, collecting a substantial income from the tolls. Again, there were no photos made before retreating Confederate troops burned the bridge on March 11, 1865. Its successor, known to be of Town lattice design, was likely similar to the original structure.

Before Town returned to the North in 1825, he designed several more bridges, including a 400-foot structure over the Pee Dee River at Cheraw, South Carolina, and at least designed another over the South Yadkin River in North Carolina which Samuel Lemly, a local contractor, built. After arriving in New York, Town joined Alexander Jackson Davis in 1829 to form one of the first professional architectural firms in the United States. Together they designed several major public buildings, including the Connecticut state capitol (1827–31), the Indiana state capitol (1835), the North Carolina state capitol (1840), the latter not used, as well as the remarkable Potomac Aqueduct over the Potomac River in the nation's capital.

Though Town himself was not a bridge builder, he wisely commissioned agents throughout the states to license use of his patented truss at a cost of $1.00 per lineal foot. Whether De Volson Wood coined the phrase or repeated it from common usage, he later wrote the much quoted quip: "They [Town trusses] may be made by the mile, and cut off by the yard to suit the occasion" (1883: 143). Proof of this assertion can be seen today in Marion County, Iowa, where the Marysville Bridge, built in 1870 as an 81-foot span, was divided in two, one part going to the Marion County Park and the other to the Wilcox Game Preserve, each equally viable. Whenever Town's agents discovered unauthorized bridges, they demanded $2.00 per foot. And the success of his design brought unheard of wealth to Town, even as he continued to perfect his lattice truss design.

Knowing that his original patent was running out and seeing that the country's rapidly expanding rail network needed bridges capable of unprecedented loads, Town rose to the challenge, securing a second patent, X8743, on April 3, 1835. Though given a patent number, it is technically an "amendment" and is marked "A.I." meaning "additional improvement." To offer enough strength to carry locomotives and fully loaded freight cars, Town's improved truss was doubled, using three lines of chords at the bottom and top, double systems of offset latticework, and secondary chords running between them, all again pinned with trunnels. A great many of these massively high and thick truss bridges with or without arches between the lattices were built, especially in New England, and all but two of the surviving rail bridges there use this system. The second edition of Town's promotional pamphlet in 1839, now extended to twelve pages and preceded by a title having 254 words, included testimonials and descriptions of successful rail bridges as well as an early attempt to describe stresses in mathematical terms. After Town died in mid-June 1844, his trusses passed into public domain and came to be freely interpreted by builders in both the United States and Canada through the middle of the twentieth century.

Town's lattice plan proved to be more a powerful concept than an exact plan. With Town's agents no longer harassing copycat builders after 1844, lattice trusses appeared far and wide in numerous variant forms. Individual builders imposed their own ideas, some useful, some less so. One was the "squared-timber lattice" associated with two prominent New England builders, Bela J. Fletcher (1811–77) of Claremont, New Hampshire, and James F. Tasker (1826–1903) of Cornish, New Hampshire. Used in only about a dozen bridges, all built between 1856 and 1869, this variation uses substantial squared timbers notched at their intersection and bolted. Their rationale was to carry longer spans without doubling the trusses (as in rail bridges) or adding arches.

The Town plan came to dominate the deep South, especially Georgia, Alabama, and Mississippi where many streams were muddy and stone abutments would be difficult to obtain or build. Since Town's lattice truss exerted no outward thrust, it was ideal for tubular or trestle foundations. In New England, Town's design was ubiquitous, but with stone foundations readily available, builders there could easily add arches to longer spans. Over time, maintenance departments often strengthened older bridges with arches.

Among the prominent builders of Town's design was the South's most famous builder, Horace King (1807–85), born in South Carolina as a slave of mixed lineage. When King was twenty-three, a house builder named John Godwin (1798–1859) became his master, and, recognizing King's engineering aptitude, sent him north for a formal education. After 1832, when both master and slave moved to Alabama, King began designing and building numerous lengthy Town lattice bridges over the South's major rivers from Georgia to Mississippi. King used some of his earnings to purchase his freedom in 1846. He then established himself in LaGrange, Georgia, in 1850, and continued building both highway and rail bridges until the Civil War disrupted life. Following the war, King was a major contributor to the South's reconstruction, including replacement of some of his own bridges which had been burned by Union troops. All four of his sons continued the bridge building tradition, even passing this skill to some of their sons, the grandchildren of Horace King (Allen, 1970b: 17–18).

Beyond these areas the Town lattice appeared in spotty concentrations. While widely used in New York State, its use in Pennsylvania was mostly limited to the southeastern corner, especially Bucks County, as well as in Indiana County in the central west and Erie County in the northwest. The last location, though, makes sense in that before Ohio's statehood in 1803, this area, along with northeastern Ohio, was part of the Western Reserve and therefore an extension of Connecticut. Not surprisingly, then, most of Ohio's Town bridges are in Ashtabula and Trumbull counties in that corner. The Town idea, however, did not spread much west of Ohio, though it was known in Kentucky. One exception to this is central Iowa, where the majority of surviving bridges have Town lattice trusses. Madison County's six bridges, famous because of a film that featured them, use a lighter-weight variation, with most of them reinforced with queenpost beams and pinned with metal bolts instead of trunnels.

Minnesota's one remaining bridge at Zumbrota, mislabeled as Town, is unrelated and idiosyncratic. The earliest covered bridges in Canada were built in Québec, primarily under the auspices of the Département de la colonisation founded in 1851, the bureau charged with opening up Québec's vast hinterland through the construction of roads and bridges. From the beginning in the 1850s, builders there adopted the Town truss. The vertical posts common in surviving bridges were added to the design. A great number of Town bridges, some exceptionally long, were built routinely until 1955. Oddly, neighboring New Brunswick, though Canada's other covered bridge province, started much later and used Howe trusses almost exclusively.

Top Town's lattice truss was particularly popular in the South. The Euharlee Creek or Lowry Bridge in Bartow County, Georgia, built in 1886, exemplifies the southern tradition. The builder omitted the upper secondary chord. (A. Chester Ong, 2011)

Inset Although Madison County, Iowa's bridges all use the Town lattice truss, the Holliwell Bridge, built in 1880, uses metal fasteners rather than wooden dowels and is reinforced with a flat arch and partial arches at each end. (A. Chester Ong, 2012)

Opposite at bottom, from left Town lattice members in Bucks County, Pennsylvania's Van Sant Bridge, built in 1875. (A. Chester Ong, 2010)

The interior of the West Dummerston Bridge, Vermont, originally built in 1872 and refurbished extensively in 1998. The red streak results from car tail-lights passing through a "time exposure." (A. Chester Ong, 2010)

The Chiselville Bridge in Bennington County, Vermont, one of the highest bridges in the United States, is a classic Town lattice truss with secondary chords. (A. Chester Ong, 2010)

Town's truss was not restricted to use in bridges. Early builders and later engineers who wrote books on timber construction usually included roof trusses as well. Ithiel Town himself adapted his truss to buildings, but because virtually all roof trusses are hidden from view, there is no way of knowing how widespread the idea became. Nonetheless, when Fayetteville, North Carolina's First Presbyterian Church, originally built in 1816, burned in 1831 (along with much of the downtown), Ithiel Town, a resident there until 1825, returned to restore the church, since the brick walls had survived. His 1832 roof trusses, built across the nave and therefore in triangular shape, are scissor-shaped lattices with wooden trunnels. Joseph Conwill noted that the Thomas Bibb House in Huntsville, Alabama, built in 1836 by someone other than Town, used lengthwise lattices in the roof that were reinforced on one side with vertical posts and nailed at the intersections (1996: 3–4). A year earlier, Edwin J. Peck, who is known to have had dealings with Town's architectural firm, Town & Davis, built Madison, Indiana's Second Presbyterian Church (now the John T. Windle Memorial Auditorium), using lattice roof trusses with nailed intersections. Town himself had proposed lattice roof trusses for the North Carolina state capitol building in 1833, but the actual builder eliminated them from the plans.

Perhaps the most interesting manifestation of Town's lattice in a roof was designed by Pennsylvania rail bridge builder Henry Grow (1817–91), who constructed all the bridges on the Philadelphia, Norristown and Germantown Railroad for George G. Whitmore, the line's president, probably in the early 1840s. After being baptized into the Church of Jesus Christ of Latter-day Saints (Mormons) in 1842, Grow moved to Nauvoo, Illinois, in 1843 and then to Utah in 1851 when the church was forced to move following Joseph Smith Jr's assassination. During the following years, Grow built various types of mills and

bridges, including uncovered Town lattice rail bridges over the Provo and Jordan rivers (Dreicer, 2010: 131). His greatest lattice project, however, was in the roof of the Salt Lake [Mormon] Tabernacle, which was constructed between 1864 and 1867. Grow's lattice trusses were 150 feet across and in a series supported the full length of 250 feet. Besides spanning the width, they had to follow the curve of the oval dome, a challenge which continued to vex Grow even as the center of the roof was being shingled. Unlike the roof trusses discussed above, Grow's used mostly trunnels, since nails were scarce in Utah.

Though the usual pattern for technology transfer was from Europe to the young United States, European engineers early on learned of the rapid development of wooden bridges in America, and many engineers made tours of the states, taking home new ideas which were quickly put into practice in a broad range of countries. Town's lattice idea was among those that caught on in Europe. After English engineer David Stevenson toured the United States in 1837 and observed Town's truss, he wrote, ". . . it exerts no lateral thrust, tending to overturn the piers on which it rests. The largest lattice-bridge which I met with, was constructed by Mr Robinson on the Philadelphia and Reading Railroad. It measures 1100 feet in length" (1859: 143–4). Another British engineer, James Robert Mosse, described a number of wooden lattice bridges built for British rail lines: "He [Captain William Scarth Moorsom (1804–1863)] exhibited a sketch, by one of his assistants, of a lattice bridge of 90 feet, or 100 feet span, which had been built under his direction between 1837 and 1840. On the Birmingham and Gloucester Railway he had erected at least a dozen of those bridges. Having left that line, and not being interested in the maintenance of it, he took no trouble to inquire about these bridges till the year 1854, when they had been at least fourteen, or fifteen years in use. He then wrote to

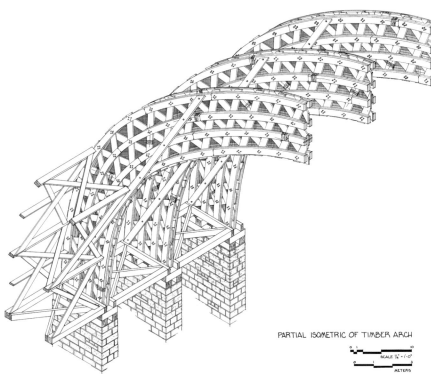

PARTIAL ISOMETRIC OF TIMBER ARCH

SCALE 1/8" = 1'-0"

METERS

the Resident Engineer to know what had been the cost of repairs, and the answer was that the Company had been at no expense, except that of repainting them from time to time. The timber in all those bridges had however been subjected to some preservative process" (1863: 324).

Later Moorsom built at least one lattice bridge in what is now Ireland. His 1864 obituary published in the *Minutes of the Institution of Civil Engineers* includes the following: "The Waterford and Kilkenny Railway [of 1845] presents only two features of interest, one being a station at Kilkenny. . . and the other a viaduct over the River Nore, 285 feet in height and of 200 feet span, constructed in timber, on the lattice principle, the abutments being built of limestone. The cost of the whole was under £10,000, and the work was the largest of the kind in the three kingdoms at the time of its erection (http://www.gracesguide.co.uk/William_Scarth_Moorsom, accessed 9-1-12)".

Gregory K. Dreicer has written extensively on the spread of the Town lattice into Europe both in his doctoral dissertation for Cornell University and his subsequent articles. He noted that: "News of the lattice idea was spread by engineers including French topographical engineer Guillaume-Tell Poussin (1794–1876), Scottish marine engineer David Stevenson (1815–1886), French engineer and economist Michel Chevalier (1806–1879), Austrian mathematics professor and engineer Franz Anton Ritter von Gerstner (1793–1840), and Bavaria-based engineer and theorist Karl Culmann (182–1881). By the late 1830s, engineers had begun to build lattice bridges in France, England, Russia, Austria-Hungary, Prussia, Holland, Ireland, and England" (2010: 129–30).

Just how widely the lattice idea spread is as yet unknown, but there are 1893 photos from what was then Palestine showing an open full-sized all-wood lattice foot and cart bridge over the Jordan River built in 1870 at the location of what is now the Allenby Bridge. The bridge was later burned by the Turks during World War I. (http://www.eretzyisroel.org/~dhershkowitz/pic288a.jpg; accessed 9-1-12) This lengthy structure came complete with latticed doors and a toll booth built over the top of one entrance.

One wonders how the Town lattice could have migrated from the United States to Palestine. It seems likely that some of the British who took control of Palestine from the conquering Egyptians in 1840 but then turned the area over to the Ottoman Turks, remained behind. Considering the relatively wide use of the truss in Europe, including Britain, it would not be surprising that a colonial British engineer could have constructed such a bridge, since large-scale timbers were unavailable and metal was probably difficult to import.

Long Truss

Lt. Col. Stephen Harriman Long (1784–1864) of the United States Engineers was, with Squire Whipple (1804–88), one of the two most influential bridge engineers of the second generation. Long obtained six bridge truss patents and authored a bridge building manual that had not only two American editions but one in German as well. Though his wooden bridge designs are exceptionally sophisticated in their details, he failed to anticipate the coming revolution in bridge design that led to iron replacing wood, that lack of foresight being the major distinction between Long and Whipple.

Born in Hopkinton, New Hampshire, in 1784 but quite unlike the self-taught first generation, Long earned an AB in 1809 and an AM in 1812, both from Dartmouth College. Long joined what would later become the US Corps of Engineers in 1814, achieving the rank of Lieutenant Colonel. Before embarking on his bridge building career, Long had already distinguished himself as an explorer for the US Government, beginning in 1817 with an expedition up the Mississippi River to present-day Minneapolis. Later expeditions reached the Front Range in Colorado and the Canadian border. Longs Peak in Colorado, 14,259 feet high, is named for him. In addition to exploring and bridge building, Long became involved not just in surveying and building the Baltimore and Ohio Railroad but in the design of its steam locomotives, receiving a patent in 1826. Because of his involvement with railroad construction, Long's bridge designs were

Below This unexpected Town lattice footbridge with toll house mounted on the roof, said to have been built around 1870, spanned the Jordan River in Palestine until being burned by the Turks during World War I. After the war this crossing came to be called Allenby Bridge. (Schiller, 1979)

primarily intended for exceptionally heavy loads and are consequently more robust than would be necessary for ordinary road use. Long argued for the Baltimore and Ohio directors to choose his wood designs over the far more expensive stone arch bridges they preferred, but at first they only allowed him to build the "experimental" Jackson Bridge *over* the B&O tracks on the Baltimore-Washington Pike in Baltimore in 1829.

Five of Long's six patents concern the same basic truss design but with refinements in each successive plan. Because the first two were issued before the fire, they had to be reconstructed later and lack printed descriptions, though there are nearly illegible hand-written descriptions. In addition to the patents, in 1836 Long published a 25-page pamphlet titled *Col. Long's Bridges, Together with a Series of Directions to Bridge Builders*, which was expanded to 55 pages and republished in Philadelphia in 1841. This edition also had ten plates showing Long's patent designs to that point, as well as some variations that were not patented. A German edition, published in 1840, was titled *Beschweibung der von dem Oberstlieutenant Long erfundenen hölzernen Brücke.*

Patent X5862 was granted on March 6, 1830, shortly after he built the Jackson Bridge. Patent X9340 was approved on January 23, 1836 and simplifies the first patent, probably for highway use since it is double lane. Patent 1397 of November 7, 1839 returns to the first

patent design but with certain improvements described in detail in the accompanying text. A second patent on the same day, 1398, offers additional refinements to the support system. Patent 5366 of November 13, 1847 takes the original plan to a new level of complexity with additional internal bracing for a double-lane bridge. Long's final patent, 21,203, issued on August 17, 1858, combines all of the above complexities with a wooden inverted "suspension" arch. Most of these designs appear to have been designed for heavy railroad use, and since none of the rail bridges Long built survived into recent times, it is difficult to know which of these designs actually went from the drafting table to the track line. It is also perplexing that none of Long's patents match what we know today—from fewer than a dozen surviving examples—as the Long truss.

Simplified presentations of Long's truss in secondary sources suggest nothing unique enough to justify a patent. These show a symmetrical panel truss with X figures in each panel. Even when we refine the description further, we find little that is new: the Long truss has three upper and lower chords, double posts, double braces, and single counterbraces. Many of Burr's bridges had single counterbraces fitted into the single braces (the "X" element), and many of Wernwag's bridges had triple chords, double posts, and double braces (the "double pattern" element). Would adding counterbraces make that much difference? But Long's original patent was actually more than just an X panel truss. He also included two diagonal corbel braces from the abutments to the second and third posts, knowing that the lower chords are under tension and would benefit from additional support. Also, the four center panels are capped with a low-angled kingpost reinforcement, because the upper chords are under compression and could resist flexing with this addition. With such integrated support, Long suggested that massive timbers were not needed, preferring the use of white pine measuring only 6 x 6 or 7 x 7 inches. The only known bridge with the kingpost frame over the center of the top chord was the Mattawamkeag Bridge between Bangor and Houlton, Maine, constructed by fellow military engineer Capt. Charles Thomas in 1831 (Conwill, 2003: 93)

Joseph Conwill has identified what is likely the most unique feature of Long's trusses, not the overall plan of X panels but the details of how the chords were spliced, how the members were jointed, and—most importantly—the prestressing of the truss that Long recommended. When normal timber truss bridges are subjected to a live load, the bridge deflects slightly as the truss members compress, especially after they have dried out or become worn. Using a simple drawing, Conwill writes: "In the drawing, the upcurved lines at AB and CD represent the original position of the chords before the truss is loaded, and before the counterbraces AF and BF are inserted. The load, G, is added so that the bridge deflects into a level position represented by

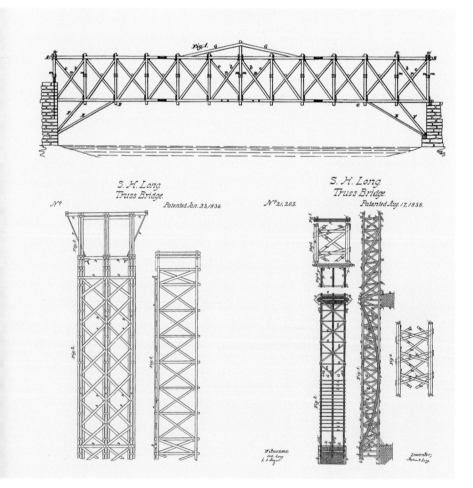

the straight lines at AB and CD. Then counterbraces are inserted and the load is removed. The counterbraces prevent the truss from springing back to its original position. Any load the bridge later carries (up to the original weight of G) will only shift stress from the counterbraces back to the braces EC and ED . . . and this was what made Long's patent original" (2009b: 6).

But Conwill also points out that few of the known Long truss bridges show evidence of this practice. A wedge was supposed to be driven between a tenon at the upper end of the counterbrace and the chord, but in some bridges the wedge is seen at the bottom instead. In others, they are missing altogether. In an earlier essay, Conwill had pointed out problems caused by ignorance of this feature: ". . . even in Long trusses which have the prestress wedges, it appears that their function was forgotten in later years. As timber gradually shrank and crept after construction, the wedges became loose, unless periodically checked and re-driven by maintenance crews . . . but anyone familiar with the condition of our Long trusses by the 1960s can confirm that in many cases the counterbraces were completely loose, and were doing nothing" (2005: 3).

Relatively few Long truss bridges survive today, and they are widely scattered in New Hampshire, Ohio, West Virginia, Indiana, and—until the recent loss of the Blenheim covered bridge—in New York. The latter bridge, built in 1855 by Nichols M. Powers of Vermont over Schoharie Creek at Blenheim, New York, was the most unusual of them, not just because it was double lane but because the center truss reached the roof peak and was reinforced with an embedded arch. Losing Blenheim to Tropical Storm Irene on August 28, 2011, not only deprived us of a splendid example of the Long truss but also the country's longest surviving single-span covered bridge. In West Virginia, both of Jackson County's two bridges are excellent examples of the Long truss, though without the wedging. Hoke's Mill Bridge in Greenbrier County, West Virginia, built in 1899, appears to be a simplified Long truss, probably by a local builder unfamiliar with the fine points of the design. Because Long himself concentrated on rail bridges, none of which survive, the highway versions that survive were by builders who may or may not have understood Long's finer points.

Howe Truss

Although William Howe's life ended prematurely in his forty-ninth year, his bridge truss thrived long after his death, indeed well into the second half of the twentieth century. In spite of the success of Town's lattice and its adaptation over a wide area, Howe's plan came to dominate the timber bridge business, not just throughout the United States but in Canada and parts of Europe as well. Indeed, most covered bridges of Oregon and New Brunswick are Howe designs. In addition American railroad companies built thousands

Above The Allen's Mill or Eldean Bridge in Miami County, Ohio, two spans totaling 224 feet, exemplifies the Long truss. Its "new" appearance resulted from sand blasting during its 2005–6 renovation. (A. Chester Ong, 2011)

Left Jackson County, West Virginia's two bridges are both Long trusses, though the Sarvis Fork Bridge (upper left) is a 2000 replica of the 1889 original and retains the segmented arch of its predecessor. The Staat's Mill Bridge (lower left), an original now moved into a park, well represents a typical Long truss. (Terry E. Miller, 2007)

Left This close-up photo of the Staat's Mill Bridge shows the complex framing where truss members and upper cross bracing join the upper chords. (Terry E. Miller, 2007)

of non-housed Howe bridges on their lines, and the Canadians built at least hundreds of them for both roads and rail lines.

Howe was born in a small home in Spencer, Massachusetts, on May 12, 1803, the eldest of three sons. Perhaps the family had unusually creative genes, because his brother Tyler invented the bedspring and his nephew Elias Howe Jr (1819–90), invented the sewing machine. William began working as a mill-wright and may have developed an innovative roof truss for a church in Brookfield, Massachusetts. Watching the construction of the Western Railway (later the Boston and Albany, begun in 1838) near his home, he took note of the Long trusses being used but had a better idea. The all-wood Long truss used wood in both compression and tension, but knowing that wood is least effective in tension, he thought using adjustable wrought iron rods in place of Long's wooden posts would be an improvement. Howe approached chief construction engineer, George Washington Whistler (1800–49), and was contracted to build a short rail bridge over the Quaboag River at Warren, Massachusetts, in 1838, a photo of which survives but does not reveal the truss design (Allen, 1957: 19). Little is known of a second bridge 75 feet in length at Springfield, Massachusetts, said to have been built by Howe, Whistler, and Howe's brother-in-law, Amasa Stone (1818–83). Because Whistler was evidently impressed with Howe's design, he contracted with Howe and Stone to build a major bridge over the Connecticut River at Springfield, completed between 1840 and 1841. Whistler built a similar bridge over the same river between Windsor Locks and Warehouse Point in 1844.

While the "Howe truss" is well known to all covered bridge enthusiasts—a series of panels having wooden X's and vertical iron rods—Howe's three patents suggest the matter is much more complex. Joseph Conwill's article "Early History of the Howe Truss" in *Covered Bridge Topics* (1977), sorted out what we know of this history, though many questions remain unanswered. Howe's first patent, 1685, was issued July 10, 1840, before he built the bridge over the Connecticut River. The patent drawings include seven figures, Figures 1, 3, 4, and 7 being proposed trusses, the rest showing top views of trusses and a floor system for the first truss. Figure 1, with triple upper and lower chords and a double chord midway, could be understood variously as two Long trusses, one on top of the other, or a simple lattice. While this figure resembles Howe's second patent, the others do not, and none use iron rods. It is also uncertain if any of these were ever used in actual bridges. Howe's second patent, 1711 of August 3, 1840, modified the truss in Figure 1 of the previous patent, substituting iron rods for the quadrupled posts and moving the mid-level chord lower. It also used a "double web" system, where the X diagonals spanned two panels each, as well as overlapped each other (producing the lattice effect). Both bridges over the Connecticut River

used trusses similar to this patent without the secondary chord but with the addition of three diagonal struts from the abutments/piers to the lower chord.

There are no surviving examples of this version in North America, but this design became known in Germany, Austria, Switzerland, and Russia although exactly how is still uncertain. One clue may be that G. W. Whistler, the builder who worked with William Howe, went to Russia where he served as a consultant to Engineers P. P. Melnikov and N. O. Krafft in building Russia's first rail line, the Moscow-Saint Petersburg Railway. Whistler undoubtedly designed and built many of the nine Howe bridges, including one that was 1,800 feet long and another 1,600. (See J. G. James, 1982, reprinted in *Covered Bridge Topics* 56(2): 13 for a list). His work there ended tragically when he contracted cholera and died in 1849 before the line was completed, and because of this he was not given credit. Fletcher and Snow's "A History of the Development of Wooden Bridges" published in 1934 by the American Society of Civil Engineers, includes further discussion by Aksel Andersen who reports that between 1860 and 1875 the Norwegians built Howe truss rail bridges, and the article includes a photo of the Gulfoss Bridge (1934: 384), but the photo is not clear enough to permit complete analysis. Southern Germany, specifically Bavaria, still has two "double web" Howe bridges, a 400-foot two-span deck bridge at Kempten-St. Mang over the Iller River, which was built from 1847 to 1851—now converted to pedestrian use—and a 204-foot two-span bridge over the Rott River at Neuhaus-Mittich built in 1853 and still used by vehicles.

Howe's third patent, 4726 of August 28, 1846, comes closest to what became the "Howe truss." The drawing shows a ten-panel bridge with four upper and lower chords, double iron rods, double braces and single counterbraces, but with the addition of a single arch embedded in the abutments and passing between the braces and struts from the abutment to the upper chord.

In addition, Howe's drawings detail the use of iron bearing blocks around the iron rods to receive the braces and counterbraces as well as smaller iron brackets for the lateral bracing. For Howe, setting a truss's camber was essential, and in his patent he discussed how this could be done, especially by tightening the nuts at the lower ends of the rods. If through shrinkage or wear the timbers became loose, the entire bridge could be tightened to its original specifications by adjusting the nuts. While most exist-ing Howe truss bridges lack the arch, they were quite common in the past for long spans or rail bridges, though usually doubled and built outside the trusses.

Howe's death came only six years after his last patent, and consequently he neither lived to see the success of his bridge truss nor reaped the profits from its marketing. The Howe truss enterprise was carried on by his brother-in-law Amasa Stone, who bought the patent rights in 1842 and thereafter managed the

Below William Howe's second patent,1711 of August 3, 1840, used double webbing and iron rods, and though examples of this were built, it was not a typical Howe truss later. (US Patent Office)

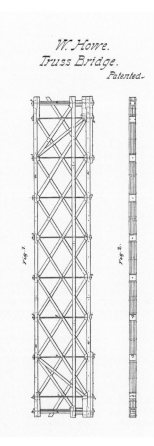

W. Howe.
Truss Bridge.
Patented-

licensing rights to the truss. Stone is better known as a builder of railroads and a major investor in steel mills, especially in the Cleveland, Ohio, area where he settled. Stone, unfortunately, is also remembered for his failures, most notably the Ashtabula, Ohio, railroad disaster. As president of the Cleveland and Erie Railroad, Stone built an innovative all-iron Howe deck bridge with a 150-foot span 70 feet above the Ashtabula River between 1863 and 1865, immediately south of the city and only 300 feet from the station. After performing normally for eleven years, the bridge suddenly collapsed at 7:28 pm on December 29, 1876, during a violent snowstorm with 40 mph winds under the weight of a Lake Shore and Michigan Southern Railway train (the successor company) carrying 159 passengers and crew. Ninety-eight people were killed, many burned beyond recognition, when the wreckage caught fire, and the rest injured. Among the dead was a famed composer of Gospel hymns, Philip P. Bliss (1838–76). A thorough investigation revealed that while the design was sound, the construction was deeply flawed by mismatched structural members, some below specifications, flaws in casting, and possibly different rates of contraction caused by mixing wrought and cast iron. The investigation blamed Stone for the tragedy. That, together with the later failure of several of his mills, led to Stone committing suicide in 1883. Fortunately, Stone was also a generous philanthropist, leaving a significant amount of money to Western Reserve University in Cleveland (now Case-Western Reserve), where his children honored their father's memory by building Amasa Stone Chapel, which was completed in 1911.

In spite of Stone's apparent control of the Howe truss, the design drifted gradually into the public domain as independent builders throughout the United States used it freely, giving rise to what is better described as a "family of Howe trusses." The standard form, with three or four upper and lower chords, doubled rods and braces and single counterbraces seated against angled bearing blocks (usually of iron but sometimes of wood), was one of the first "combination" trusses, that is, a mixture of wood and iron. A great many other trusses, sometimes called "improved Howe trusses," were patented, including Albert Fink's patent 16,728 of March 3, 1857, and patent 104,110 issued to Milo S. Cartter and Hosea B. Cartter of St. Louis on June 14, 1870.

The standard Howe truss dominated railroad bridges throughout the country, at least until the end of the nineteenth century, though they continued to be built well into the twentieth century in places like British Columbia, Canada. A series of publications called the *Annual Report of the Commissioner of Railroads and Telegraphs in Ohio* began in 1867. Some included detailed inspection reports on nearly all rail bridges. The 1886 and 1887 reports list a total of 155 covered rail bridges, but inspectors distinguished three types: 1) fully covered "through" bridges; 2) fully covered "deck" bridges; and 3) individually boxed trusses, some

being "pony" trusses, that is, trusses less than full height. The reports for the years 1882–4 altogether list around 800 timber bridges without roof and siding but otherwise identical to the covered ones. Of these, at least 95 percent were Howe trusses. While the reports noted that covered bridges lasted an average of twenty-eight years while uncovered ones lasted only about eight years, the latter were less prone to fire, since the roof and siding would trap live embers as well as fill passenger cars with smoke. We do not know to what extent this pattern held true in other states, but it can be surmised that tens of thousands of Howe truss rail bridges were built and rebuilt during the second half of the nineteenth century. In retrospect, it now seems incredibly wasteful to have used such massive amounts of prime timber for such ephemeral bridges. Because timber was then readily available and no one worried about the environment, companies and what must have been a virtual army of bridge builders evidently worked throughout the year erecting these prefabricated, industrialized, and quickly constructed timber bridges. In this sense, the Howe truss was the nation's first mass-produced truss and not indicative of any notion of rugged individuality, "folk timber framer," or "romantic crossing."

By the end of the nineteenth century, governments east of the Mississippi were no longer building Howe truss bridges. The transition began in the 1870s when calls for bids typically produced plans for wooden covered bridges, uncovered "combination" bridges, and iron bridges. Though iron bridges were more expensive, their perceived strength and durability finally overcame their increased cost. But the building of wooden Howe trusses did not end west of the Mississippi. California, Oregon, and Washington, all with growing populations and plentiful timber, continued building covered bridges. California, which had built such bridges since at least the 1860s, gradually ceased doing so after 1900, but Oregon and Washington—especially Oregon—built hundreds. Indeed, Oregon's last functional covered

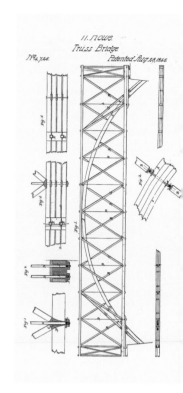

Above William Howe's third patent, 4726 of August 28, 1846, comes closest to what became the typical Howe truss, though with the addition of a wooden arch. (US Patent Office)

Below Amasa Stone's innovative all-iron Howe rail bridge built from 1863 to 1865 over the Ashtabula River in northeastern Ohio was 150 feet long and 70 feet above the water. It collapsed on December 29, 1876, during a ferocious snowstorm, killing 98 of the 159 passengers and crew on the train crossing it at the time. (Jennie Munger Gregory Memorial Museum Collection, Ashtabula, Ohio)

Top from left The Buskirk Bridge between New York's Rensselaer and Washington Counties is a classic Howe truss. It likely retains no material from the 1850 original but consists of timbers replaced over the years, especially in 2005. A. Chester Ong, 2010)

Brown County, Ohio's New Hope Bridge, 170 feet long from 1878, combines a classic Howe truss with a large laminated arch. (A. Chester Ong, 2011)

Above from left The former Ruark or Wimmer Bridge stood in Putnam County, Indiana, until 1968 when county officials stripped and disassembled it but giving photographers a chance to see clearly the parts of a Howe truss. (Terry E. Miller, 1968)

bridges were built as recently as the 1950s. The Howe truss dominated all three, but by this time designers had modified the design to suit modern traffic, including gigantic log trucks. Many of the bridges used a modernized form of the truss having double braces and single counterbraces, along with two or three steel rods (no longer iron), but equally prevalent were trusses with counterbraces present only in the center panels, a variant sometimes called the "Western Howe." In some cases, the vertical rods were placed outside the chords. With so much virgin timber available, builders could construct supersized bridges for loggers, with unusually high trusses consisting of large-scale timbers. Most astounding were the bridges built with single-stick lower chords. Lane County's Pengra Bridge, built in 1938, has chords measuring 16 inches x 18 inches x 126 feet, so long they had to be hand-dressed and hauled to the site on special equipment. In Oregon, the state offered standardized plans, giving its bridges a unity of design not found elsewhere in the United States.

Engineers in New Brunswick, Canada, however, easily equaled Oregon's standardization, where the vast majority of the provinces sixty-three covered bridges are Howe trusses. Most are standard, with counterbraces, though as with Oregon's bridges, the upper chords on each end terminate at the first set of rods, one panel in, giving the frame a trapezoid shape. The oldest surviving covered bridges there are from the beginning of the twentieth century were finished in the late 1950s. New

Brunswick also has a few remaining examples of uncovered bridges on its highways, but although treated with wood preserver, they still deteriorate faster than the covered ones. Some of these, however, use a modified Burr truss design.

Of the many timber trusses designed from the late eighteenth to the end of the nineteenth century, the Howe truss came to be the most widespread and successful. By simply substituting iron rods for the wooden posts found in all other panel trusses, William Howe revolutionized the bridge building business and made the expansion of America's railroad system faster and more economical. From the vantage point of the early twenty-first century, these Howe covered bridges still seem as romantic as any others, but in their time they represented the industrialization and standardization of the bridge industry, replicated by the thousands across the nation and carrying both railroads and motor vehicles across innumerable waterways.

Smith Truss

Among covered bridge builders, Robert W. Smith (1833–98) of Miami County, Ohio, is as significant as were Timothy Palmer, Theodore Burr, and Lewis Wernwag but for completely different reasons. Where that first generation of pioneers had to invent the covered bridge, its structure, and its construction, Smith perfected its standardization and industrialization

Left Technically, the Howe design was a "combination" bridge because it used iron angle pieces to receive the braces and counterbraces at both upper and lower chords, with the rods passing through. Sometimes such bridges used wooden angle pieces, but most were of iron. (A. Chester Ong, 2012)

Left The Beanblossom Bridge, built in 1880 in a remote part of Indiana's Brown County, is an unusual example of a simplified Howe truss using single rods and single braces, similar but unrelated to the typical trusses found in Washington and Oregon. (Terry E. Miller, 2011)

Left from top Typical of bridges using the "Oregon Howe" design, Josephine County's Grave Creek or Sunny Valley Bridge was built in 1920. As is normal, the central panels are in X form while the remaining panels consist only of braces. (A. Chester Ong, 2012)

The Office Bridge in Westfir, Oregon, is not just Oregon's longest covered bridge at 180 feet but is its most heavily built. Constructed in 1944 by the Westfir Lumber Company to carry logging trucks as well as traffic to the company's office (hence, the name), it is unusually high, with triple-braced trusses and a sidewalk. (A. Chester Ong, 2012)

The Lowell Bridge in Lane County, Oregon, is not only the state's widest covered bridge but was not built until 1945. When Dexter Reservoir was built beneath it in 1953, the bridge was raised six feet. Today, it is a museum, allowing visitors to examine the heavily built Oregon Howe trusses in detail. (Terry E. Miller, 2012)

Below from left Not only are most of New Brunswick, Canada's covered bridges Howe trusses but all were built after 1900. This standardized design used both braces and counterbraces in all panels except those at each end, which consisted only of braces. (A. Chester Ong, 2012)

As was the case in the United States, most New Brunswick Howe trusses used iron angle blocks and rods, but some had wooden blocks. (Terry E. Miller, 2012)

as part of a modern urban-based business. Considering that Smith's ideas were not even formulated until the late 1860s, by which time iron bridge technology was rapidly advancing and builders already had at their disposal numerous other successful trusses, it is all the more amazing that Smith's company could build thousands of bridges over little more than two decades, and some of these continue to carry traffic to this day.

Smith's truss appears to be simple—an apparent succession of X's—but it is deceptively sophisticated in its balance of strength and lightness, a kind of "titanium" breakthrough in a world where heavier materials dominated. Fundamentally, Smith simply flared back the posts at a consistent angle from center

to ends and fitted in braces in its simplified form. Such a truss would appear as a series of inverted V's, what many bridge historians later called a Warren truss, after the 1848 British patent obtained by engineers James Warren and Willoughby Monzoni for metal bridges. But what Smith actually patented was a design having two overlapping staggered systems of inverted V's that produce the *appearance* of X's. These X's are therefore not actual panels comparable to those of Howe and Long—which consist of posts/rods, braces, and counterbraces. Understanding this requires a re-examination of Smith's original patent.

Smith's truss was unknown to covered bridge writers until Eldon M. Neff of Springfield, Ohio, published details of Smith's life and work in a 1963 article (pp. 3–4). Neff begins with the migration of Smith's parents from Maryland to Ohio in 1815, the birth of Robert on December 30, 1833, his training as a carpenter, his marriage in 1856, and his move to Tippecanoe City in Miami County (now Tipp City). There was little in his experience to suggest a genius for bridge building except an early innovation in barn roof design. At the age of thirty-four, Smith received his first bridge patent, 66,900, on July 16, 1867, and established a modest bridge building business from his home. Almost immediately, he realized the need to move his rapidly expanding business to an urban center, and this he did via the Miami and Erie Canal to Toledo later in 1867. There his enterprise grew quickly.

According to Neff, "He built 5 in 1867, the year he moved, 22 the next year, and 75 the next, 1869" (p. 4). Neff continues that Smith also developed a "combination" bridge using iron rods in place of diagonal posts capable of supporting railroad stock and was said to be building bridges entirely of iron by 1869. Perhaps based on his experience boating up to Toledo on the canal, he also patented plans for swing and drawbridges. In 1870, Smith reorganized the Smith Bridge Company into a joint stock company with three partners, J. J. Swigert, A. S. Miller, and J. A. Hamilton. Smith was president from 1870 until the firm's liquidation in 1890 when Smith and his partners sold out to the Toledo Bridge Company. Only eleven years later, in 1901, J. P. Morgan bought Toledo Bridge along with twenty-four other bridge companies to form the American Bridge Company, headquartered in what is now known as Ambridge, Pennsylvania, just northwest of Pittsburgh along the Ohio River. Unfortunately, neither of Smith's successors saw fit to preserve the company's records.

Besides Smith's third patent, 155,550 of September 29, 1874, for a rail turntable developed for a Toledo rail yard, Smith received two patents for wooden bridges, the first from 1867 previously mentioned and an "improvement" (97,714) issued on December 7, 1869. As in so many cases, we do not see builders conforming to their own designs, especially when Robert Smith himself had complete control and was free to modify at will. Both patents follow the basic principle of diagonally inclined posts with diagonal braces, but the second patent also adds a "saddled" metal bracket for the X-patterned lateral bracing which became a hallmark of Smith's bridges.

The second study of Smith's truss was published in 1967 by Raymond E. Wilson who, based on Smith's two patents combined with his own observations, classified Smith's trusses into four types, a system that came to permeate the literature (pp. 3–5). As admirable as Wilson's efforts were, his system is problematic for several reasons, including the fact that, as yet, neither he nor anyone else had recognized the Brown and Wheeler trusses, which he rationalized as Smith "variants." Indeed, both Brown's 1857 design and Wheeler's 1870 truss do vaguely resemble Smith's truss. While Brown has no known connection to Smith, Wheeler was a Smith Bridge Company agent in southern Ohio. Thus, we do not follow Wilson's system, finding it necessary to begin anew by looking at the patents and comparing them to surviving specimens.

Looking only at the patent drawing from 1867, with two vertical posts framing a center panel—what Wilson called Type I—is misleading because no bridges with this exact design are known to have been built. It is more important to read his surprisingly brief text. There Smith writes: "The bridge represented is known as a double-truss bridge, as there are *two sets* [italics mine] of posts and braces. Bridges may be made with a single truss, or with three or more, depending upon the strength required." Thus, according to Smith himself, we should classify his trusses into single, double, and triple types, the double being Wilson's Types I, II, and III, and the triple being his Type IV. Wilson had no category for the single truss.

A Smith truss is misleadingly simple when viewed two-dimensionally, but a full understanding requires a three-dimensional view. To this point, all trusses designated "Smith" appear to be a succession of X-patterned "panels," but Smith's X's are not comparable to those of Long and Howe, for example. In the latter trusses, a "panel" consists of two vertical posts (or rods in a Howe), two diagonal braces, and a single diagonal counterbrace. A Smith X consists only of a post and brace (or two posts and braces in the "triple" version). In order to comprehend this, we first need to explore Smith's "single truss," which has until now been designated as "Warren." There are three such bridges remaining, all in Ohio. Two are known to have been built by Smith, but the third has no known relationship to him. The Jasper Road Bridge, originally built by the Smith Bridge Company in Greene County in 1869 and later moved to a private estate just south of Germantown in Montgomery County, consists of six inverted V's (plus a polygonal arch which was likely added). A symmetrical truss, the six members that incline from the center to the ends (three each way) act as posts in tension, and the other members that complete the V shapes act as braces in compression. Although "panel" strictly speaking refers to a rectangular frame, we can consider each inverted V to be a "panel." A second bridge, only 44 feet long consisting of four inverted V's was moved to Carillon Park in Dayton some years ago. Like the Jasper Road Bridge, it is symmetrical but has four posts, two each direction. Both bridges have two lower and two upper chords, and the posts pass through them and are anchored with bolts. The third bridge, called Johnson's Mill or Salt Creek Bridge, is near Norwich in Muskingum County and has no known Smith Bridge Company connections, having been built as an 80-foot open bridge in 1876 by Thomas Fisher, about whom little is known. It was covered in 1879.

Proof that Smith's basic or single truss is a series of inverted V's is seen in a proposal Smith Bridge submitted to the City Council of Chillicothe, Ohio, on June 20, 1872 for a bridge over the Ohio & Erie Canal on Fifth Street. Bidding $10.00 per lineal foot, Smith included a figure showing a 90-foot pony truss in a series of eight inverted V's.

The best way to think of a "double truss" is to understand it to be two single (inverted V) trusses set side by side within triple upper and lower chords, one plane being staggered by half a "panel" in relation to the other. Because of how the members cross, the two-dimensional view produces the illusion of X's but a three-dimensional view reveals it to be two super-imposed inverted V trusses. Smith's first patent fails to

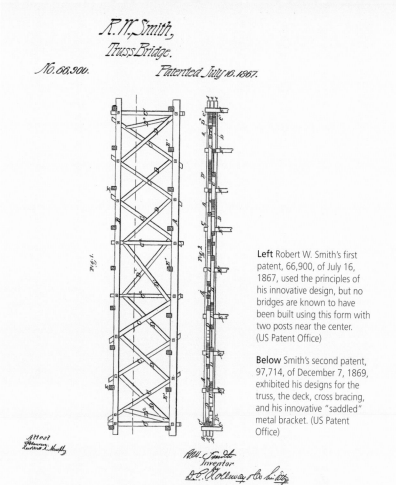

Left Robert W. Smith's first patent, 66,900, of July 16, 1867, used the principles of his innovative design, but no bridges are known to have been built using this form with two posts near the center. (US Patent Office)

Below Smith's second patent, 97,714, of December 7, 1869, exhibited his designs for the truss, the deck, cross bracing, and his innovative "saddled" metal bracket. (US Patent Office)

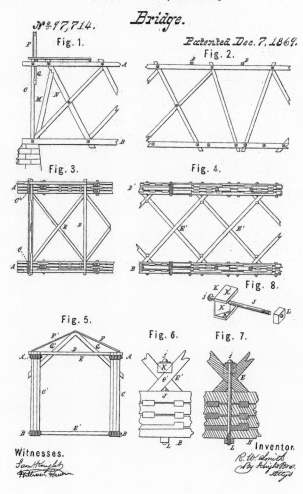

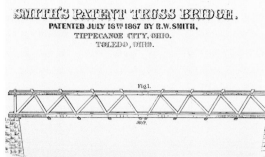

SMITH'S PATENT TRUSS BRIDGE.
PATENTED JULY 16TH 1867 BY R.W. SMITH,
TIPPECANOE CITY, OHIO.
TOLEDO, OHIO.

show this because he included two vertical posts, but this version was quickly abandoned. His second patent, which also shows the "double truss," is symmetrical, the center reduced to two posts in a V formation which are bolted separately within the lower chords. Since load stresses are greater towards the ends, a lightly framed center is reasonable. Such trusses (what Wilson labeled as Type II) were/are relatively uncommon. Using two asymmetrical planes, however, the superimposition could also appear as continuous X's. Understanding how the two planes relate, however, goes beyond the scope of this book. A triple plane truss simply doubles one of the planes of the double version.

Smith's "single truss" has created a thorny problem for students of covered bridges. Because it appears to be a series of inverted V's, it has hitherto been designated as a "Warren truss," but the only recognized Warren truss was designed in England for metal bridges. Writers also mention the American Russell Warren (1783–1860), a Rhode Island architect, as the inventor of a timber version, but we have found no documentation backing this claim. Two of three remaining "Warren truss" bridges are in southwest Ohio and are known to have been built by Smith Bridge. Miriam Wood has documented some thirteen such bridges in Greene County, Ohio, "some by the Smith Bridge Company and some by Henry E. Hebble. E. B. Henderson, . . . built a Warren truss in Washington County in the 1870s" (1993: 37). It appears that the "single truss" was Smith's budget model for modest bridges—the Jasper Road Bridge cost only $6.50 per foot—and because it was not specifically patented could be copied at will by other builders.

Smith was therefore justified in writing in his 1867 patent: "The advantages claimed for this bridge are its strength, owing to the equal distribution of the load; its staunchness following from the mode of bracing; and its lightness and cheapness." While the double and triple designs consist of seemingly independent truss systems superimposed, they are unified by numerous bolts through the chords and truss members wherever they cross. The Smith Bridge Company also preferred white pine, which was inexpensive, lightweight, but strong, a species readily available in Michigan and which could be shipped in bulk to the company factory in Toledo for preparation. Indeed, because the spacing of the truss members in any Smith truss is so complex, with variable angles depending on bridge length, it required skilled workers at the factory to custom cut and assemble each truss before being disassembled and shipped to the bridge site (or nearby) by rail where Smith's workers or those under an agent reassembled the bridge *in situ*.

Another factor in the stability of his bridges was his use of "saddle bolts," an innovation included in the 1869 patent. The X-shaped lateral bracing in most other bridges only stabilized the cross beams above and below. Smith eliminated the need for cross beams in the roof by using expanded X's that crossed each other next to

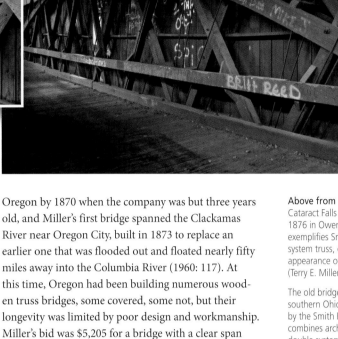

the chords and were held in place by the saddle bolts which also pierced the chord system. Thus, they acted both in tension and compression. Additionally, as with the trusses, the bracing system was built of superimposed V's, so that the timbers crossed over each other and did not require half-cutting.

Not only was Smith's truss light and cheap, it was also quite strong. While most surviving bridges are relatively modest, ranging from about 80 feet to 150 feet, Smith built bridges with surprising dimensions. When, in April 1873, Coshocton County, Ohio's commissioners decided to build two massive bridges over the Muskingum River, one at Morris Ford just south of the county seat, the other at Conesville further south, they received bids for twenty-five designs, eight from the Smith Bridge Company. Their bids included two versions of Smith's patent truss, two "combination" bridges, and four Howe designs ranging in price from $15.10 per foot for a lighter Smith to $19.20 for one of the Howe options. The only bids that were lower were for Buckingham trusses, which would have been too light for such long spans, 184 feet each at Morris and 204 feet each at Conesville. The Smith Bridge Company won both contracts for "triple truss" bridges. Conesville lasted until 1958 when the county burned the structure to make way for a new bridge. To achieve the necessary strength for such long spans, Smith built unusually high trusses. They were also wide enough for vehicles to pass within. Neff's 1963 article also reproduced a photo of a stunning Smith "combination" bridge under construction in West Virginia. This structure, well over 200 feet in a single span, used triple iron rods in place of posts but used wood for the chords and braces.

The Smith Bridge Company was perhaps the most successful covered bridge business enterprise ever created. Smith's business model included exclusive rights to his patented trusses, but he increased his market share by offering a variety of other trusses. He also engaged numerous agents who bid for projects on behalf of the company and could, using their own crews, erect the bridges after the custom-cut parts came to them by rail. The most illustrious of them was Smith's original partner, Albert Stuart Miller, who went first to California, then to Oregon with an exclusive franchise to sell Smith's bridges in the Northwest. Lee H. Nelson writes that Smith's agents had already penetrated

Oregon by 1870 when the company was but three years old, and Miller's first bridge spanned the Clackamas River near Oregon City, built in 1873 to replace an earlier one that was flooded out and floated nearly fifty miles away into the Columbia River (1960: 117). At this time, Oregon had been building numerous wooden truss bridges, some covered, some not, but their longevity was limited by poor design and workmanship. Miller's bid was $5,205 for a bridge with a clear span of 215 feet plus 141 feet of approaches. Because of its lengthy span, the trusses were 22 feet high and the deck 22 feet wide, a giant of a bridge. Although the Smith Bridge Company customarily prefabricated their bridges in Toledo, Ohio, and shipped them by rail to the bridge site, for Oregon this was not possible. Nelson reports: "The larger chords were cut and hewn on the site, with lesser members hauled from Oregon City"

Above from left Indiana's Cataract Falls Bridge, built in 1876 in Owen County, Indiana, exemplifies Smith's double system truss, creating the appearance of X panels. (Terry E. Miller, 2011)

The old bridge at Otway in southern Ohio, built in 1874 by the Smith Bridge Company, combines arches with a double system truss, along with various other forms of reinforcement added by the highway department. (Terry E. Miller, 2011)

Left The Brown Bridge in Ohio's Brown County was built by the Smith Bridge Company in 1878 using Smith's triple system truss. (Terry E. Miller, 2011)

Left When the former Conesville Bridge in Coshocton County, Ohio, was built in 1876 over the Muskingum River, each of its 200 foot spans was supported by unusually high triple-system Smith trusses. (Max T. Miller, 1953)

(p. 115). Although Smith's bridges were durable, unfortunately none have survived to the present, all having been succeeded by "modern" Howe trusses built after the turn of the twentieth century to carry ever larger logging trucks. Smith also had a prominent representative in California, William Henry Gorrill, who arrived in San Francisco in 1869 and soon founded the Pacific Bridge Company in Oakland. His bridge at Paradise Park near Santa Cruz, built in 1872, survives.

The Smith Bridge Company's reach otherwise included only a swath of Midwestern states, in particular Ohio and Indiana, but they also built bridges in Pennsylvania, Kentucky, West Virginia, and possibly Michigan. Such a concentration makes sense considering that their bridges were fabricated in a central location, Toledo, Ohio, and even within these few states there was more than enough business to keep the company thriving for twenty-three years. By 1890, when Toledo Bridge bought Smith out, the covered bridge era was mostly over in the east, Indiana excepted, and the era of iron (and later steel) bridges had fully arrived. As late as Smith was in starting a seemingly obsolete business, his industrial model took full advantage of the last years of covered bridge building, his success enhanced by his company efficiency and prices that undercut iron to a significant degree.

Childs Truss

Horace Childs (1807–?) lived most of his life in and around Henniker, New Hampshire, and is not known to have set foot in Ohio, but the bridge truss he patented on August 12, 1846 (4693) was used for the first and last time only in Ohio and long after Childs' death.

Above Smith's 1869 patent included his distinctive "saddled" brackets that secured the X cross bracing for both roof and deck, here seen in the Otway Bridge in southern Ohio. (A. Chester Ong, 2011)

Right The now bypassed Otway Bridge in Scioto County, Ohio, carried a state highway until retirement. Over the years, the highway department attempted to strengthen the bridge with a variety of rods, arches, and brackets. (A. Chester Ong, 2011)

Right In addition to building Smith's all-wood covered bridges, the company also offered Howe truss and "combination" truss bridges. This massive structure (location unknown) using triple rods in place of slanted braces was being built to carry a rail line. Carrying rail traffic over such a long span required unusually high trusses. (Miriam Wood Collection)

Childs became a prominent builder of both highway and railroad bridges in New England, but his experience and training had been limited to the carpentry trade, which was typical of his day. However, he had the good fortune to be the cousin of Col. Stephen H. Long, one of the country's first "scientific" bridge builders and the designer of various trusses, and, working for Col. Long, built his first bridges around Haverhill, New Hampshire. Evidently, his bridge building activities either ceased or were curtailed following a train accident in the early 1850s near Andover, Massachusetts, that included the death of President-elect Franklin Pierce's son and grave injury to Childs. Even though his patent had been issued before that, there is no evidence that any bridges with the Childs truss were ever built in New England.

Childs truss was not particularly innovative, but he argued that his improvements greatly strengthened the bridge without adding much weight and assured greater stability in the joints. According to the patent drawings, there were to be three upper and lower chords for a multiple kingpost truss in which the braces were mounted against wooden angle blocks at the joints. However, the braces were also secured from angle blocks to the upper and lower chords by long iron screws bored deep into the braces. Additionally, Childs added iron rods secured at both ends with angle blocks and nuts as "counters," and these would act in tension. In 1979, Wayne Perry measured and drew a bridge model at the Henniker Historical Society said to have been made by Horace Childs but without a date (1985: 8–11). Although it has a few characteristics in common with the patent truss, it is otherwise a densely complicated system of vertical posts and a simple lattice with some members reinforced with iron rods.

Today, the Childs truss exists in seven Ohio bridges, one in Delaware County just north of Columbus and six in Preble County on the Indiana state boundary. All were built by the same man, Evrett [sic] S. Sherman (1831–97) of Delaware County. Sherman's father, David, built several bridges in the Delaware County area, all apparently using the Burr truss. Son Evrett was noted as a bridge builder from the 1860s on and in the 1870s ran his bridge building business from Galena where he advertised bridges using Burr, Howe, or "Sherman" trusses. Indeed, Sherman patented a simple design for small open bridges on June 5, 1877 (191,552), combining wood and iron.

Sherman's first known use of the Childs truss was in the Chambers Road Bridge in Delaware County built in 1883 and still standing. Following a massive storm that devastated the roads and bridges of Preble County in May 1887, county engineer Robert Eaton Lowery, a native of Delaware County and possibly a family friend of the Shermans, summoned Sherman to Eaton to construct new bridges. Sherman built fifteen bridges, all using the Childs plan, between 1887 and 1895. Using a patent plan that had now expired, Sherman felt free to make modifications. His bridges have only two lower

and upper chords, omit the long screws that secure the braces, and use increasingly heavy braces towards the ends where the main stresses occur. In bridges having an odd number of panels, the middle panel is left open, and, as in the patent, the middle panels omit the iron counters. David A. Simmons notes that Sherman probably decided to try the Childs patent after the patent expired, though by that time he needed not pay royalties on Howe or Burr either. Simmons writes: "Sherman had read about it [the Childs truss]. In October 1882, a Washington, D.C., patent attorney began a series of illustrated articles in *Engineering News* on truss bridge patents whose period of protection had elapsed, and which were then 'public property'. . . The December 16, 1882 installment included a description and drawing of the 'Childs Bridge.'" Sherman apparently found the design attractive and used it the next year in the Chambers Road Bridge (1991b: 10–11). It is possible that Sherman, knowing how prevalent multiple kingpost trusses were in Ohio, saw Childs' additions as an improvement over the much used design.

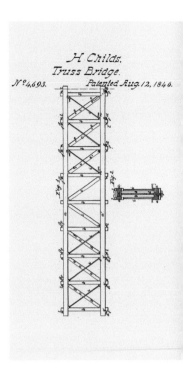

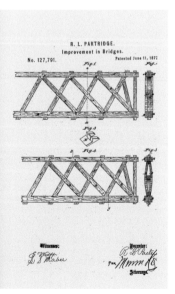

Partridge Truss

By the time they are seventy-seven years old, most people have acquired at least a modicum of common sense. Not Reuben L. Partridge. Union County, Ohio's most famous bridge builder, Partridge was repairing one of his bridges, the Alsaugh Bridge, in 1900 when he fell off, broke his leg, and died from complications on July 17. Born on September 10, 1823, in Wilmington (Essex County), New York, Partridge came to Ohio with his mother after his father died in 1836 to join one of her son's from a previous marriage living in the village of Marysville. There he attended a one-room school, since this part of Ohio was as yet sparsely settled, and there learned various trades, including carpentry. By 1855, Partridge had built his first bridge in Union County and by 1866 was doing this full time, but we do not know what kind of bridges.

David Simmons has traced the Partridge patent through the surviving correspondence between Partridge and the Patent Office. The builder's first application was sent to them in May 1870, touting an all-wood truss in apparent X form with 45 degree posts, 60 degree braces, and special iron foot pieces that provided an angle block for the braces with the post passing through the double chords, thus permitting a reduction of chords to two. Seeing Partridge's truss as too similar to Smith's, the Patent Office rejected the application. The inventor persisted by claiming his was cheaper and of greater "utility" than Smith's, but Ellis Spear, the Examiner, again rejected the application. Partridge tried once more to convince Spear, who in January 1871 wrote to Partridge that his application was "rejected finally" (Simmons, 1991a: 14). Biding his time, Partridge decided to ask the Union County commissioners to affirm that Partridge's "Block Bridge" was "fully as good if not superior to 'Smith's Truss' or any other" because "it can be constructed for less money" (p. 15). Finally, the Patent Office relented and granted 127,791 to Partridge on June 11, 1872.

A patent is only rewarding if others want to use it and pay royalties. As far as is known, only Partridge built bridges using his truss, but he built over 125 of them, all in Union County and a few nearby areas, including Delaware and Fairfield counties. Since some

were built before the patent was issued, as far back as 1868, he had clearly formulated his truss soon after Smith's patent appeared. He is also said to have built a few iron bridges, but most of those were probably built by the Columbus Bridge Company, which he joined in 1886 as company erection superintendent. The still surviving Dietz Bridge near Canal Winchester in Franklin County southeast of Columbus was not only one of his last bridges but perhaps the most impressive of the five that remain (four others in Union County). Built in 1887 by the Columbus Bridge Company, the Dietz Bridge is 134 feet long using a double/triple version of the truss.

As is often true, the patent drawings differ from the extant specimens. Where the double Smith truss required three upper and lower chords, Partridge's design made do with two by requiring the use of his patented iron "foot-piece," an angle block that permitted the post to pass through the chords. The extant bridges have such angle blocks, but they are of wood, not iron. Additionally, the patent does not show the single vertical post used at the center of all surviving bridges. In the lighter version, there are two chords, a single post, and double braces, the former inclined from center to ends at 45 degrees, the latter crossing them at 60 degrees. As in Smith trusses, there is an additional brace at each end in a compressed inverted V shape. Only the Spain Creek Bridge in Union County uses this plan. The other four bridges have three chords, double posts and triple braces.

Partridge used his truss successfully in numerous bridges but only over a small geographical area, and no one else is known to have used his plan (and therefore

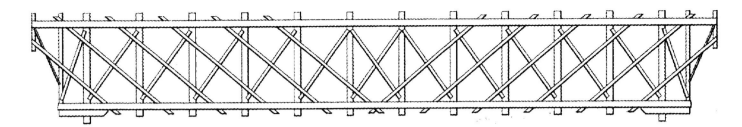

paid royalties). Though his patent clearly infringed on Smith's, Robert Smith probably saw no reason to sue Partridge because he created so little competition, perhaps shutting the Smith Bridge Company out of only one county. Because Partridge remains a historical hero in his home area of Union County, Columbus, artist Curtis Goldstein was commissioned in 2010 to paint a large mural on a public building in downtown Marysville honoring Reuben L. Partridge, the county's most famous bridge builder.

Paddleford Truss

New Hampshire's covered bridges are distinct for many reasons, especially the prevalence of the Paddleford truss. While distinctive and not likely confused with a Long truss, its creator, Peter Paddleford (1785–1859), who was born and died in New Hampshire, never patented his invention, perhaps anticipating charges of infringement from defenders of the Long patent. In fact, Paddleford began by building Long truss bridges but developed a design of his own that departs from Long in numerous ways.

Paddleford, like so many other builders, began his professional work as a millwright but built bridges as well, presumably using existing truss designs, mostly likely Long's. By 1830, the date of Long's first patent, Paddleford was already forty-five years old and by 1835 his son, Philip H. Paddleford, had joined him. Their first bridge using Paddleford's innovations is thought to have been Lyman's Bridge over the Connecticut River built in 1833 and used until it was dismantled in 1930. Considering that Peter retired in 1849 and died ten years later, that his son Philip died in 1871, and that virtually all existing Paddleford truss bridges were built late in the century up to 1890, we can assume that most were built by others, especially Jacob Berry and Charles and Frank Broughton, using Paddleford's plan. Having a patent, while an honor, is only lucrative if others clamor to use it and pay royalties, and that does not seem to have been the case with this truss. All remaining specimens are in New Hampshire except for two in nearby Vermont and five in Maine.

Where Long's bridges had triple chords, double posts and braces, and single counterbraces wedged into the frame to pre-stress the bridge, Paddleford began with a simple multiple kingpost but used triple chords, the inside two together approximating the thickness of the outer one. His distinctive trait was the counterbraces fastened between the two thinner inner chords and

Above Peter Paddleford of New Hampshire never patented his truss, evidently developed in the early 1830s. Now common in New Hampshire and Maine, most Paddleford bridges were built long after the inventor's death in 1859. (Historic American Engineering Record [HAER])

Left from top Spanning the Wild Ammonoosuc River in Grafton County, New Hampshire, the Swiftwater Bridge was built in 1849 using Peter Paddleford's truss. This photo shows where the two spans meet. (A. Chester Ong, 2010)

What differentiated Paddleford's truss from the multiple kingpost was the addition of counterbraces that crossed and were notched into the kingposts both at the top and bottom. (A. Chester Ong, 2010)

Jacob Berry of North Conway, New Hampshire, built the Durgin Bridge over the Cold River in 1869, the fourth on this site, using Paddleford's truss. The laminated arches were added by the Gratons in 1966–7. (Terry E. Miller, 2010)

A gap separates the two Paddleford truss spans of New Hampshire's Swiftwater Bridge, necessary for the overlapping counterbraces. (Terry E. Miller, 2010)

notched into the posts and braces, since they extended past the panel points into each neighboring panel. In Long's bridges, the counterbraces work in compression but in Paddleford's they primarily work in tension, though depending on reaction to a live load they can also work in compression. Thus, Paddleford's truss was much lighter than Long's and yet capable of supporting relatively lengthy spans. On the other hand, Long's truss was designed for railroad bridges and Paddleford's for highway use.

Several factors complicate the history, however. First, there is some evidence that the Lyman Toll Bridge in New Hampshire, built in 1833, had overlapping counterbraces. The Bement Bridge in Merrimack County, built in 1854, allegedly by Col. Long himself, has all the essential features of Paddleford's design and none of Long's, though the counters pass only slightly into neighboring panels. The former Brownsville Bridge in Union County, Indiana (now moved to Columbus, Indiana), a Long in every other way, has counters that pass through the chords. Engineering historians point out that George W. Thayer of Springfield, Massachusetts, patented a truss (4004) on April 16, 1845, that has the overlapping counters along with several other innovations, but Thayer's truss was little used and none survive today. There is also Rowell's Bridge in Merrimack County, built in 1853 by the Childs brothers, that has characteristics of both Long and Paddleford: double posts, double braces, and double overlapping counterbraces on the outsides of the truss, plus an arch which passes within the truss. Many of today's surviving Paddleford truss bridges also have large, laminated arches, but these were added by individual towns as a way of strengthening them long after their original construction.

Brown Truss

Josiah Brown Jr of Buffalo, New York, received patent 17,722 on July 7, 1857 for two versions of a truss that appear to be successions of X's without vertical posts. Nothing is presently known of the inventor, and his truss survives in only two bridges, both in Michigan. (A third example—and the best of the three, White's Bridge in Ionia County—was burned by arsonists on July 7, 2013.) Additionally, it is challenging to match his patent drawings with the actual specimens, one of which matches one of the drawings and one which contradicts both drawings and other known specimens. Brown's patent text indicates that Figures 3, 4, and 5 illustrate how *not* to build a bridge. Brown claims innovation in securing both "braces" and "counter-braces" with bolts in a single crossing point within both upper and lower chords, contrasting this with the allegedly "incorrect" spacing of his predecessors. He mentions George W. Thayer's patent (see above) as flawed in this way, though his Figure 5 illustrating the wrong way would also apply to Peter Paddleford's truss.

Since all diagonals are bolted between the chords, they actually function as "posts" in tension, though *appear* to be either "braces" or "counterbraces." Brown's drawings indicate that two members in each X incline towards the middle and a single member inclines the opposite way. Both White's Bridge in Ionia County, Michigan, and the Ada Bridge in Kent County, closely follow Brown's patent, but the Fallasburg Bridge, also in Kent County, contradicts both. Only White's Bridge, built in 1869, retained the original construction by Jared N. Bresee and Joseph H. Walker in 1869, costing $1,700. The Ada bridge, originally built in 1867 by William Holmes, was destroyed by an arsonist in 1979 and reconstructed with all new material in 1980. The Fallasburg Bridge nearby, also constructed by Bresee in 1871, contradicts both Ada and White's Bridges in two significant ways. First, the beams inclining to the ends are double while those to the center are single, and second, there is no vertical center post. (A few vertical posts elsewhere appear to have been additions because they do not pass through the chords.) If Bresee constructed both bridges, why would one correspond to the patent and the other more or less flip the pattern? Thus, careful observers will note that Fallasburg's trusses are "upside down". We are not aware of the bridge having been partially dismantled at some time and put back incorrectly, but we can offer no other explanation. Apparently, Brown's truss works either way.

Robertson County, Kentucky's lone covered bridge, the Johnson Creek Bridge, is attributed to Kentucky builder Jacob N. Bower in 1874 with an arch added in 1912 by his son Louis. This originally single-span bridge, 114 feet long with a later pier, is listed everywhere as a Smith truss. But in certain ways it also

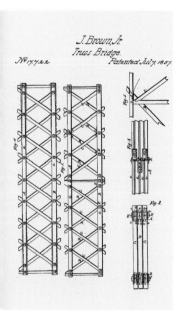

Below Josiah Brown Jr of Buffalo, New York, obtained patent 17,722 on July 7, 1857, for a truss that is only known to have been used in a few bridges in Michigan, two of which remain. (US Patent Office)

resembles a Brown truss but without the center post. Bower could not have known the Brown truss, but most of his known Smith trusses were at variance with the Smith patents, and Johnson Creek is varied to the point that it resembles a Brown truss. Additionally, this specimen is too lightly framed, and that probably explains the attempts to strengthen it with an arch and pier, the latter of which destroys the symmetrical stress arrangements.

Haupt Truss

Pennsylvania born Herman Haupt (1817–1905) lived a long and exceptionally productive life as one of America's premier builders of railroads, tunnels, and bridges. Like his military successor during the Civil War, Daniel C. McCallum, he was one of the most influential and productive bridge builders of his time, but his patented Haupt truss was little more than an engineering footnote. Today, only one modest bridge survives with his truss, and that was built in the remote hills of North Carolina by an independent local builder when Haupt was nearly eighty years old and long retired. A child prodigy, Haupt graduated from West Point in 1835 when he was only fourteen and was immediately commissioned a Second Lieutenant, but less than three months later he resigned to become a civil engineer. Soon working for a railroad company building bridges and tunnels, he also married at age nineteen and in the course of his marriage had seven sons and four daughters. Haupt's only patent was granted when he was twenty-two. For seven years, from 1840 to 1847, Haupt then taught mathematics and engineering at Pennsylvania College (now Gettysburg

College), likely the time when he began writing his ground-breaking 1851 textbook, *General Theory of Bridge Construction*, a highly technical study of stresses in bridge construction with essays on particular bridges he knew. After leaving academia, Haupt returned to building railroads, bridges, and tunnels for various railroads.

In 1862, at the height of the Civil War, Secretary of War Edwin M. Stanton appointed Haupt as chief of a newly created bureau whose charge was constructing and operating military railroads, since the rails had become essential in getting supplies to the troops and bringing wounded soldiers back for treatment. Although only a colonel, Haupt astounded even President Lincoln by rebuilding a temporary structure for the Potomac Creek Bridge in Virginia on the Richmond, Fredericksburg and Potomac Railroad, whose towering three-span deck bridge had been destroyed by retreating Confederate troops. This he did in only nine days in May, 1862, constructing a simple deck supported by some of the highest trestles ever built. The President famously remarked on seeing the structure: "That man Haupt has built a bridge across Potomac Creek about 400 feet long and nearly 100 feet high, over which loaded trains are passing every hour, and upon my word, gentlemen there is nothing in it but beanpoles and cornstalks!" (Allen, 1959: 35–6). After thirteen months, the span was replaced with a more substantial arched lattice deck bridge (see page 107).

Seeing how successful the Confederate Army was in destroying wooden bridges, Haupt copied the "Sesesh" (secessionists) and invented a small "torpedo" in late 1862 capable of bringing down large timber bridges, this described in chilling detail in a manual he himself wrote

Far left White's Bridge in Ionia County, Michigan, was built in 1869 by Jared N. Bresee and Joseph H. Walker for $1,700 using the Brown truss. (Terry E. Miller, 2009)

Upper middle Brown's truss requires four upper and lower chords to receive the truss members, two inclined towards the center and one towards the ends, all bolted. This suggests that these members work in tension, but that is difficult to ascertain. (Terry E. Miller, 2009)

Lower middle Brown's truss patent offered two plans, and the Michigan bridges use the second, with two vertical posts at the center. This photo shows the center posts with a single "brace" intersecting. (Terry E. Miller, 2009)

Upper right This photo shows the center posts where the pairs of center-leaning braces intersect with the upper chords. (Terry E. Miller, 2009)

Lower right Kent County, Michigan's Fallasburg Bridge, also built by Jared N. Bresee in 1871, presents an unusual challenge: its Brown truss is upside down from the norm, with the double braces inclined towards the ends rather than the middle. We can only conclude that when the bridge was restored in either 1945 or 1994, the builders placed the trusses upside down. (Terry E. Miller, 2009)

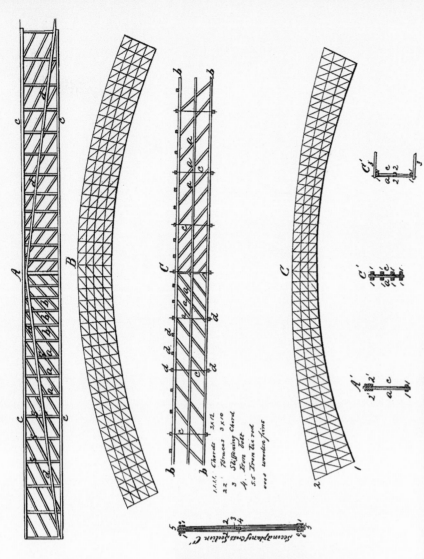

Left Though Herman Haupt later became a prominent Civil War general, his truss patent 1,445 of December 27, 1839 was rarely used. Some followed the patent, as seen in the drawing at far left, while others ignored the diagonal reinforcements. (US Patent Office)

Below North Carolina's only historical covered bridge, the Bunker Hill Bridge near Salem, was built in 1894 or 1895 long after Herman Haupt's death, perhaps from drawings seen in a publication. Its plank trusses dispense with the diagonal reinforcements of the patent. (A. Chester Ong, 2011)

Right Unusually long, the French's Hollow Bridge in Albany County, New York, lacked Haupt's diagonal reinforcements but added laminated arches inside each truss. This photo was taken in 1933 during the bridge's demolition. (NSPCB Archives, Basil Kievit Collection)

Right HAER's drawing of the Haupt truss of North Carolina's Bunker Hill Bridge shows clearly how this relatively simple truss built of planks works. (Historic American Engineering Record [HAER])

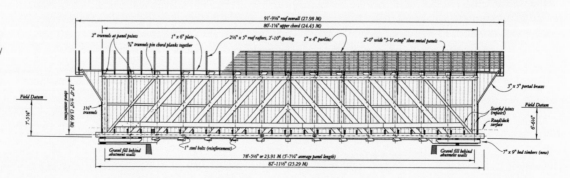

(Allen 1959: 34–5). In September 1862, Haupt was promoted to brigadier general, but after only one year of service in keeping the Union Army's rail lines functioning, he resigned to return to civilian railroad work, succeeded by General Daniel C. McCallum, who continued Haupt's work. Expanding the army's Railway Construction Corps from 300 to 10,000 men, McCallum's unit is said to have "built or rebuilt 641 miles of railroad and 26 *miles* of bridges" (Allen, 1959: 37). As a civilian, Haupt added drilling machines and oil pipelines to his list of inventions. Continuing as a railroad administrator until 1886 when he retired at sixty-nine, he unfortunately lost his fortune over an earlier project, the Hoosac Tunnel in Massachusetts. This five-mile rail tunnel, conceived in 1841 and begun in 1851, turned into a nightmare. Haupt's attempts to complete the tunnel by 1861 came to naught, and the tunnel continued to flummox engineers until 1875. Its final cost was $20,000,000, and Haupt lost much of his fortune fighting battles with the company. Death came of a heart attack at age eighty-eight.

Haupt obtained only a single patent, 1445, on December 27, 1839, but it includes four designs, two of them for curved spans that remind us of the plans of Peale and Pope fifty years earlier. How many of these were actually built is unknown, and the only surviving Haupt truss is at variance with all of them. Haupt, who was quite familiar with rail bridges using Town's lattice design, leveled severe criticism of the design based on his experience, this being the central argument for his patent, which he also called a "Lattice Bridge." Fundamentally, he said that Town's plan consisted of both braces and counterbraces but that the latter failed to work. Haupt's truss essentially eliminated the

counterbraces, keeping only braces while adding a series of vertical posts, for without them nothing would maintain rigidity between chords. One plan includes a bisectional "arch" reinforcement, a feature not found in the surviving specimen.

The Bunker Hill Bridge over Lyle's Creek in Catawba County, North Carolina, was built as an open bridge in 1895 by a local man, Andy L. Ramsour, who covered it in 1900. Why he chose the little-known Haupt patent fifty-six years after its release is unclear, but this area appears to have had a local tradition of building Haupt truss bridges. Town lattice bridges pervaded the South, and the builder must have known them, or perhaps he saw Haupt's patent in a book and thought it easier to build. The structure is modest in dimensions, only 80 feet long and a mere 10 feet wide, built of lightweight planking. The frame consists of double upper and lower chords, fifteen vertical posts (which Haupt called "ties"), and a symmetrical series of twelve braces, each covering two "panels," with an additional half set of braces at the center. Where the braces intersect both the chords and the posts or the posts alone, all are trunneled together. The bridge probably never carried a great deal of traffic and was closed in the late 1940s. Nine years after the bridge was donated to the Catawba County Historical Association in 1985, Arnold Graton, a master timber framer from New Hampshire, restored it, and today the area is parkland.

Some consider Sayre's Bridge in Thetford, Vermont, Orange County, to be a Haupt truss, but it was constructed by an unknown builder, purportedly in 1839. The 129-foot bridge also consists of planks trunneled together wherever they cross, but each brace spans only one narrow panel, making it also appear as a modified multiple kingpost, with an arch likely added later. More likely this is an otherwise unknown local design similar to the great bridge at Bath, New Hampshire.

McCallum Truss

Peter Paddleford had little reason to fear charges of infringement from Lt. Col. Stephen Long . Daniel C. McCallum (1815–78), however, managed to secure two patents which clearly infringed Long's trusses. Born in Johnston, Scotland, McCallum migrated to Rochester, New York, in 1822 with his family, eventually gaining a basic education and learning both carpentry and architecture. Although young and with limited bridge building experience, he received patents for two similar designs (8224 on July 15, 1851 and 16,446 on January 20, 1857), known generally as "McCallum's Inflexible Arched Truss." This he demonstrated to the owners of the New York and Erie Railroad, who had been frustrated with numerous bridge failures resulting from defective designs in both wood and iron. His test bridge at Lanesboro, Pennsylvania, in the hilly northeast of the state was tested with four heavy engines. After that, the rail officials were satisfied, making him General Superintendent in 1855. Three years later, McCallum founded his own company, the McCallum Bridge Company. Richard Sanders Allen writes, "Within seven years there were over a hundred on the line, and their popularity spread from Québec to Missouri, and even to faraway Australia" (1959: 25). Most of these bridges, however, were open wooden trusses. In February 1862, Secretary of War Edwin M. Stanton appointed McCallum Military Director and Superintendent of the Union railroads to succeed Herman Haupt. By war's end, he had been promoted to Major-General. Ironically, McCallum may also have played a role in the destruction of many open and covered bridges insofar as he participated in General Sherman's destructive march from Atlanta to Savannah in late 1864. Following the war, McCallum realized that the world was switching to iron bridges, especially for railroads, his specialty; besides his truss was one of the most complex to erect ever invented. In his fifties, he began devoting some of his time to writing poetry and published many of his poems in 1870, eight years before his death.

McCallum's first patent in 1851 had normal, parallel upper and lower chords, but there was also a slightly curved secondary upper chord which defined the panels. Each panel consisted of double posts, braces, and single counterbraces. Because the stresses are greatest nearer the ends—and that is where most bridges fail, according to McCallum—he added two diagonal struts from the lower chord to the curved upper chord and extended it just beneath the chord to meet the diagonals on the other end—more or less forming a polygonal arch. While much of this looks like a Long truss, a plan which required pre-stressing through the insertion of blocks at the junctions of the

counters, McCallum designed long iron screws which would penetrate the ends of the counters and be adjustable after the span was pre-stressed with a full loading. We do not know if this scheme worked or was even used.

McCallum's second patent of 1857 deleted the parallel upper chord, making the curved secondary chord the actual top. He used four timbers in the lower chord and three in the upper, along with the same double posts, braces, and single counters plus the diagonal struts. Instead of adjustable screws for the ends of the counters, McCallum called for iron plates that were in some way adjustable.

McCallum offered an unusual argument for his curved upper chord. "It is customary to introduce an arch-rib in bridges, and which in ordinary cases, fails to act in unison with the truss, hence there are two systems—the truss proper, and the arch rib. And as it is extremely difficult, if not impossible, so to adjust the two systems, that they shall act in perfect unison, the result must of necessity be a partial failing or yielding of one; before the efficient action of the other can be brought into play. In my bridge a contrary effect is produced: The arched upper chord is a component part of the truss, and so far from its action being independent of the remaining timbers which go to make up the frame, its proper action is essential to the integrity of the truss itself. . . ." (1857 patent)

McCallum's truss not only resembled Long's patent but also 3523 issued to Caleb and Thomas W. Pratt on April 4, 1844. Their patent included two "combination" trusses (wood and iron), one of which had a horizontal wooden lower chord and a curved wooden upper chord separated by wooden posts and iron-rod X's. Superficially they are similar but stress-wise work differently.

McCallum had designed his bridges primarily for railroads, and in that capacity they evidently worked well, but rail bridges were short-lived by nature. Consequently, none survive in the United States. Around 1860, McCallum sold the rights to build his truss to Canadian Robert Graham, whose two-span 180-foot Powerscourt Bridge over the Rivière Châteauguay in Québec's MRC du Haut-Saint-Laurent is the world's only wooden McCallum truss, unusual in a province otherwise dominated by Town lattice bridges. It is also the province's oldest covered bridge. Other than the curved upper chords, it is difficult to distinguish a McCallum from a Long truss.

Wheeler Truss

Isaac Hastings Wheeler (1815–75) was no doubt one of the prominent citizens of a small place, Sciotoville, Ohio, in the state's deep south. Except for Portsmouth along the Ohio River, Scioto County today remains rural and underpopulated. As a bridge builder, Wheeler was a late bloomer, not gaining patent 107,576 until September 20, 1870, when iron bridges had begun

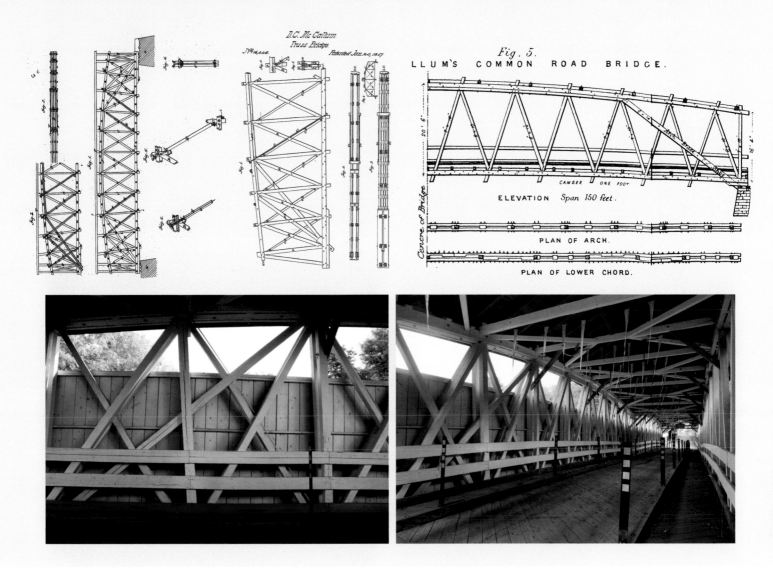

eating away at the timber bridge business. Earlier, he built and operated mills, served as county sheriff from 1844 to 1845 and county commissioner in 1866. In the early 1870s, he became an agent for the rapidly expanding Smith Bridge Company, which had built or would be building numerous bridges in southern Ohio. Although Wheeler claims that his truss was efficient with timber and thereby lighter in weight than most designs, in fact the opposite was true. Furthermore, his design can be seen as a modification of Smith's trusses, but they are much heavier.

It is not known how many Wheeler truss bridges ever existed, but they were certainly restricted to the area around Portsmouth. Today, only one remains, the Bennett Mill Bridge in Greenup County, Kentucky, which was constructed in 1874 to replace an earlier bridge from 1855 built to serve the newly established mill. Whether Wheeler himself built it is uncertain, but there are differences between the patent drawings and the actual bridge. What makes the truss so heavy is the addition of intermediate chords as well as doubled counterbraces matching the double diagonal posts. Smith's truss used double posts and single counters without a center chord. While the patent drawing specifies double lower and intermediate chords and a single upper chord, Bennett's Mill Bridge uses triple chords throughout. The posts (in tension), which

incline towards the ends, pass through all chords and are bolted while the double counterbraces (in compression) are fitted between the lower/upper chord and the middle chord without bolts. The deck's cross bracing uses the same interlocking X's with metal "saddle" brackets found in Smith's bridges.

Bennett's Mill Bridge is, unfortunately, now a replica of the original. In 2000, Kentucky received $600,000 from the Federal Highway Commission to "rehabilitate" the bridge, but after disassembling it, in 2001, the builders replaced at least 85 percent of the timber when the bridge was rebuilt in 2003. The Wheeler truss was unknown to covered bridge researchers until around 1992 both Miriam Wood discovered the truss in the commissioners' journals of Scioto County, Ohio, and Wayne Perry discovered the patent whose drawings then appeared in *Covered Bridge Topics* (Conwill, 1993: 10–11).

Post Truss

Among American bridge builders of the nineteenth century, Simeon S. Post (1805–72) was clearly a leading figure, but because most of his bridges were for railroads, none have survived and he is easily forgotten. We can thank Richard Sanders Allen for a superb article on Post (1995: 5–11), which put Post's life and work in

Top from left Civil War General Daniel C. McCallum's first truss patent, 8,224 of July 15, 1851, was intended for rail bridges, and none of these have survived. (US Patent Office)

McCallum's second patent, 16,446 of January 20, 1857, with its curved upper chord and struts at each end, is basically that seen in the only surviving McCallum truss bridge, at Powerscourt, Québec, Canada. (US Patent Office)

Diagram of a little-known variant of the McCallum truss with end-leaning posts and a reduction in struts. (Tredgold, 1871: Plate XLVI)

Above from left The world's only McCallum truss, built in 1861 by Canadian Robert Graham, is the two-span 180-foot Powerscourt Bridge over the Rivière Châteauguay in Québec's MRC du Haut-Saint-Laurent. (Left upper and lower, A. Chester Ong, 2012)

Fig.1.

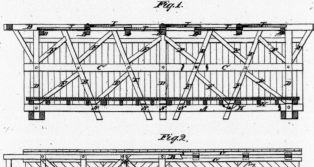

Fig.2.

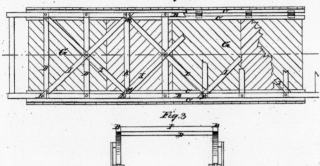

Fig.3.

Witnesses:
Inventor:

Per
Attorney.

Above Isaac H. Wheeler, a bridge builder from Sciotoville in southern Ohio, obtained patent 107,576 on September 20, 1870, for a complex truss requiring lower, middle, and upper chords, with the posts inclined towards the ends and counterbraces in two pieces. (US Patent Office)

Above right Though sources give the Bennett Mill Bridge's erection date as either 1855 or 1875, neither is correct because the State of Kentucky dismantled the original bridge and built a complete replica in 2003. Since the Wheeler truss was only patented in 1870, the 1855 date was always an error, but placing the 1875 date on the bridge now is also misleading. (Terry E. Miller, 2007)

perspective. As a builder of covered bridges, he barely deserves mention, for only one has "survived," Bell's Ford in Jackson County, Indiana, a magnificent two-span crossing 325 feet long built in 1869. After the western span collapsed in February, 1999, during a windstorm, efforts were made to preserve the remaining span, but that too collapsed, on January 2, 2006. Currently, the salvaged parts are in storage pending projected reconstruction on a bicycle trail at Fort Benjamin Harrison State Park in Indianapolis. Nonetheless, Post's "combination" and all-iron trusses were important in the history of the transition from wood to iron.

Post was born in Lebanon, New Hampshire, and like most early bridge builders learned his trade by building houses. After moving to Vermont, where he surveyed for the site of the new capitol building in Montpelier, he became associated with Edwin Ferry Johnson, and

together they began contracting in 1836 for a rail line between Syracuse and Auburn, New York. The rest of Post's professional life was spent working for a string of railroads, often serving as superintendent of construction, but he also devised a parabolic locomotive headlight and designed a system for checking bags. After moving to Jersey City, Post obtained a patent for an all-iron bridge, 38,910, on June 16, 1863, at the height of the Civil War.

Following the war, Post joined with Daniel C. McCallum, the recently retired Civil War general and bridge builder, to form the Atlantic Bridge Works in 1867 in New York City, but this arrangement did not last, and in 1868 Post joined with his nephew Andrew to form the S. S. & A. J. Post Civil Engineers and Bridge Builders firm in Jersey City. Andrew, too, obtained a patent, 81,817, on September 1, 1868 for a wood and metal version of Post's original truss.

The Posts joined with William G. and James Watson in Paterson in 1845, owners of a major foundry that manufactured the metal parts for Post's bridges. After Simeon died in 1872, Andrew attempted to keep the company going, but it went bankrupt in 1876 while three bridges in Brazil were being built.

The combination version was primarily built by two companies associated with Post, McNairy and Claflen Manufacturing Co. of Cleveland and Boomer, Boyington & Co. of Chicago. H. M. Claflen even obtained a patent, 47,395, on April 25, 1865 for a method of splicing the wooden chords. An advertising broadside from 1867 by the Atlantic Bridge Works touts the benefits of the combination version: "In localities where an Iron Bridge may be regarded as too costly, many of its advantages can be secured by a combined Wood and Iron Diagonal Truss, in which the parts subjected to *Compressive Strains* are of Wood, and of Wrought Iron where *Tensile Strains* occur, as in Lower Chords, Suspension Rods, &c. The first cost will not exceed that of a properly-covered and protected Timber Bridge of equivalent strength, while it is nearly as secure against Fire and Wind as if wholly of Iron" (quoted in Allen, 1995: 8).

The partially wood "combination" bridge was widely used, especially for rail lines in the far west, such as on the Colorado Central Railroad (see page 52). Because the rail bridges and most of the highway bridges were open, none have survived.

Bell's Ford Bridge over the East Fork of the White River near Seymour, Indiana, was, until its collapse, the only known covered Post combination truss. Most sources attribute the bridge to Robert Patterson, but William Truax (2011), who helped salvage the bridge parts, writes that McNairy and Claflen of Cleveland built the bridge. Patterson likely erected the bridge using materials fabricated in Cleveland and Chicago. The wooden portion consists of three upper chords, end posts, and a series of posts slightly inclined towards the middle creating the illusion of panels. Their lower ends are seated into a complex pin-connected joint with a shoe on top for the post and a bolt running below to secure the floor beam. All these are joined with four sets of flat iron rods running the length of the bridge as a sort of "lower chord." Each "panel" has one iron rod running diagonally towards the center from the pin-joint to a bracket above the upper chord along with a pair of rods similarly fastened but inclined towards the ends and covering two "panels." Post's advertisement claimed his truss could support a 250-foot span. It is certainly lighter than an all-wood truss, but it lacks a framed truss's rigidity. When the Bell's Ford Bridge collapsed, the truss crumpled into a tangled mess of bent rods and broken timbers. If the span can actually be reassembled, it will be little short of a miracle.

"Inverted Bowstring" Truss

The term "Inverted Bowstring" has long been used to describe the trusses of two covered bridges and one all-metal bridge in Ohio: the Germantown Bridge near Dayton and a pair of bridges in Fairfield County, John

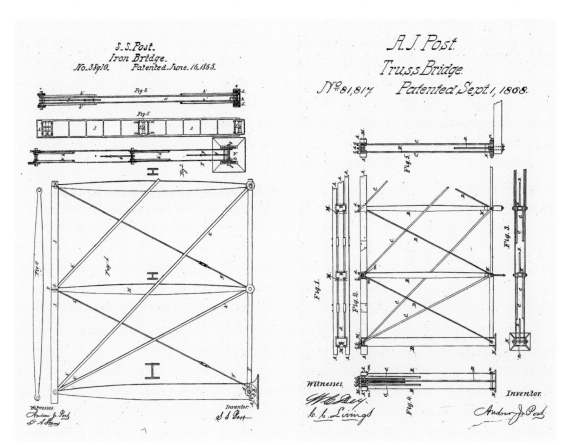

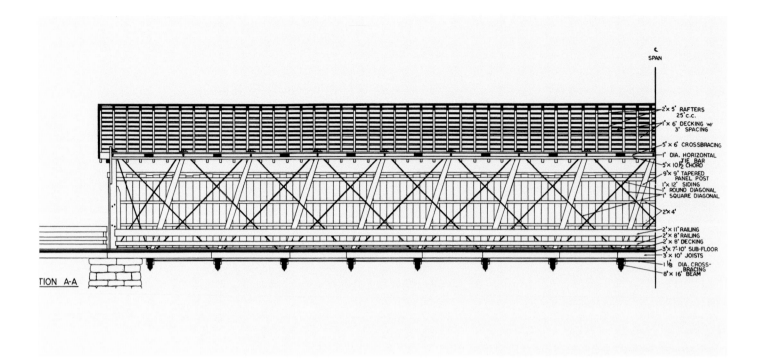

TION A-A

Labels (right side of diagram):
SPAN
2"x 5" RAFTERS 25" c.c.
1" x 6" DECKING w/ 3" SPACING
5" x 6" CROSSBRACING
1" DIA. HORIZONTAL TIE BAR
5"x 10½" CHORD
9"x 9" TAPERED PANEL POST
1"x 12" SIDING
1" ROUND DIAGONAL
1" SQUARE DIAGONAL
2"x 4"
2"x 11" RAILING
2"x 8" RAILING
2"x 8" DECKING
3"x 7"-10' SUB-FLOOR
3"x 10" JOISTS
1⅛" DIA. CROSS-BRACING
8"x 16" BEAM

Above Before its collapse—one span in 1999, the other in 2006—Jackson County, Indiana's Bell's Ford Bridge was the only covered Post truss in the world. Fortunately, HAER had made detailed drawings of the longer surviving span. (Historic American Engineering Record [HAER])

Below The five-span 695-foot road-towpath bridge over the Mohawk River at Cohoes, New York, built in 1872 by Belden & Gale of Syracuse using the "combination" form of the Post truss. (NSPCB Archives, R. S. Allen Collection)

Bright #1 (iron) and John Bright #2 (combination), both of the latter now moved to the Ohio University campus just north of Lancaster. The term "bowstring" properly refers to the string of an archer's bow, but in reference to bridges is primarily associated with iron bridges of the nineteenth century. Structurally, an arch works in compression, creating thrust against the abutments. Inverted, it is no longer an arch but rather becomes a suspension system working in tension. One inventor of such an arrangement referred to it as "catenarian," which is defined by Webster's dictionary as "the curve made by a flexible, uniform chain or cord freely suspended between two fixed points." Thus, perhaps this truss is better called a Catenarian truss. Visually, these trusses resemble, among others, Squire Whipple's patent 2064 of April 24, 1841, but they function on entirely different principles and thus have

nothing to do with any so-called bowstring trusses.

All three Ohio bridges have similar designs but they differ in details and history. Both covered bridges consist of wooden end posts, wooden upper chords, and a segmented "chain" suspension of iron eye-bars stiffened at regular intervals with vertical wooden posts between the chain and the upper chord. These give the illusion of panels filled with iron X bracing. John Bright #2 also has a separate wooden arch flanking each truss and embedded into the abutments, this supporting rods that reinforce the lateral deck beams. Where the eye-bars intersect with the wooden verticals, there are complex iron pinned joints that receive the post, support the deck beam, and bring the iron bars and rods together. There are a number of other patents which resemble these bridges, but none match them.

The bridge that now stands on N. Plum Street over Little Twin Creek in Germantown, Ohio, was originally built on the Germantown-Dayton Pike in 1865 by David H. Morrison and moved to the village in 1911. The bridge, now closed to traffic, was completely wrecked in 1981 when a driver hit a corner post, causing the bridge to fold flat into the creek. Thanks to Germantown's citizens, it was recovered and restored. Morrison (1817–82) of Dayton, an innovative iron and wood bridge builder who eventually formed the Columbia Bridge Works, designed and built several other distinctive bridges, including a three-span covered Burr truss canal aqueduct over the Great Miami River and a four-span all-iron "catenarian" bridge in 1870 in Dayton. Though Morrison is known to have designed the truss seen in Germantown in 1858 (Wood, 1993: 40–1 and Simmons, 1987: 18), he neither patented the truss nor realized the scheme into an actual bridge until 1865. Neither of his patents (20,082 of 1858 or 70,245 of 1867) relate to this bridge.

94 AMERICA'S COVERED BRIDGES

Though closely resembling the trusses of German-town, the John Bright bridges in Fairfield County came quite a bit later from builders with no known relationship to Morrison. Only Miriam Wood has sorted out their histories, and necessarily we summarize her findings here. Both bridges were the work of Prussian immigrant August Borneman (1843–89), who arrived in the United States about 1864 after serving in the Prussian Army. Until 1878, Borneman was closely associated with Fairfield County builder William Black, who built numerous bridges in the area, some as a Smith Bridge Company agent, some for his own company, the Ohio Iron and Bridge Company, and some with Borneman. Black held one patent, 166,960, granted on August 24, 1875 for an all-iron catenarian bridge that vaguely resembles the general form of the Bright bridges.

Borneman and Black formed a partnership in 1877, but the following year Black left the enterprise and in 1879 moved to Urbana, Ohio, to continue building bridges until the early 1890s. Borneman formed the Hocking Valley Bridge Works in 1878, which built numerous bridges of many designs, both covered timber and uncovered iron, throughout Ohio. Borneman's only patent (219,846 of September 23, 1879) is for a small iron bridge on the suspension principle, visually an "inverted queenpost." John Bright #2, the covered combination version, was built over Poplar Creek in 1881 for $13.25 a foot, relatively expensive compared to all-wood trusses. Whether it included the arch is unknown. Just around the corner at Smith's Mill on the same creek stood John Bright #1, an unknown type of combination covered bridge built in 1876 by Black and Borneman. By 1884, it had apparently failed, for Borneman was paid $2,000 (about $22.00 a foot) for a new 90-foot all-iron bridge using a truss otherwise

identical to John Bright #2. Borneman's bridges were distinctive for their all-metal lateral bracing consisting of a metal ring with four metal tension rods forming an X. Borneman's truss also has a striking resemblance to a "Suspension Bridge" patented by Archibald McGuffie of Rochester, New York, 34,311 of February 4, 1862.

While significant differences remain between the McGuffie and Black patents, no other patent truss comes as close to Borneman's solution, but there are also no known connections between the patents. Regrettably, Borneman died of heart failure at age forty-six after only three years of marriage and without children. Hocking Valley Bridge Works was sold to Benjamin F. Dum of Fairfield County, who continued building both covered and metal bridges with his son, H. C. Dum. After the elder Dum went bankrupt in 1907, his sons continued working until 1911 (Wood, 1993: 39–45).

Above Built in 1869, Bell's Ford Bridge in Jackson County, Indiana, was the only known covered Post truss bridge in North America. It combined wooden posts with iron rods working in tension. Both lower and upper connections (the latter having a wooden upper chord) were complex and primarily of metal. (all photos, Terry E. Miller, 1968)

Conclusions

Long before bridge design had become a science, long before there were any trained bridge builders, and long before the technologies of modern construction were available, pioneer craftsmen in New England, New York, and Pennsylvania began solving formidable engineering challenges by spanning the region's largest rivers. Not doing so would have hobbled economic development and expansion in the young United States. With only sketchy knowledge of the timber bridge building traditions of central Europe, where covered bridges were already common, American builders were forced to be as original as they were daring. They had to create technologies for building stone piers in deep or fast-moving rivers, constructing trusses of heavy wooden beams over those waters, and did so in all kinds of weather without the aid of safety equipment. We shall never know how many men were injured, maimed for life, or killed in the building of thousands—perhaps tens of thousands—of timber bridges, the majority of them covered. We can only imagine how many forested hills and mountains were clear-cut to provide the virgin timber that went into the building of massive railroad and highway bridges, some more than a mile long. We cannot estimate how many men sweated in the arduous preparation of bridge timber or how many spent their lives in drudgery quarrying the rock and dressing stone for abutments and piers. We will never know the hardships in the lives of men working and living rough in harsh conditions at bridge sites for months at a time, unprotected from the many diseases common at the time and for which there were usually no effective cures.

When the nineteenth century began, there were relatively few bridge builders and fewer bridge designs. Builders extrapolated from their experiences building barns, mills, and houses. The earliest truss designs were relatively generic: the triangle, the arch, and a garden fence lattice. After Howe successfully combined wood and iron around 1840, truss designs proliferated along with the number of bridge builders, bridge building companies, and advances in metallurgy and construction machinery. Many later truss designers took advantage of the new knowledge being created by civil engineering professors who specialized in stress analysis, people such as Herman Haupt, Daniel C. McCallum, Squire Whipple, and De Volson Wood. Iron designs rapidly proliferated and by 1880 came to dominate bridge engineering. The wooden timber truss, covered or not, was functionally obsolete by the end of the nineteenth century except in areas where timber was so cheap as to defeat the advantages of iron and steel—and when two World Wars created shortages of steel. As a result, some timber covered bridges continued to be built into our own lifetimes. The many old covered bridges still in use, however, were increasingly seen as obsolete technology from the past that required replacement. As a result, the next generation of iron and steel bridges both superseded covered bridges and soon came to replace them.

Right William M. Black of Lancaster, Ohio, obtained patent 166,960 on August 24, 1875 for a design that approximates those of the two John Bright bridges in the same county, but Black's patent is for an all-metal bridge. (US Patent Office)

Right Archibald McGuffie of Rochester, New York, obtained four similar patents between 1861 and 1862. Patent 34,311 of February 4, 1862 approximates those found in Ohio but is probably unrelated. (US Patent Office)

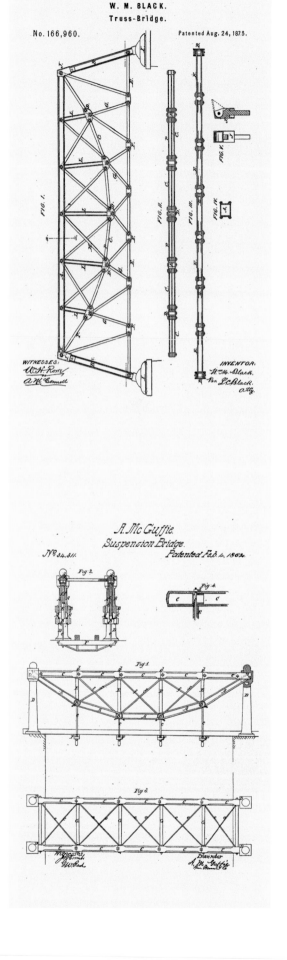

Above The Germantown Bridge in Montgomery County, Ohio, was built in 1865 by David H. Morrison of nearby Dayton. It was moved to its present location in 1911. Following a car accident which completely wrecked the bridge, it was rebuilt in 1981 and closed to traffic. Although similar to the Black and McGuffie patents, the truss combining wood and metal is idiosyncratic otherwise. (A. Chester Ong, 2011)

Left The John Bright #2 Bridge in Fairfield County, Ohio, was originally built in 1881 near an all-metal twin (see Chapter 6, page 225), and both were moved to the Ohio University campus north of Lancaster in 1988. Both were built by local builders August Borneman and William Black, the latter holder of a patent for a truss similar to that of the covered bridge. As with the Germantown Bridge, it is a combination of wood and iron. (Upper left and lower insets, Terry E. Miller, 2011; Center, A. Chester Ong, 2011)

chapter three
FROM PLANNING TO REALITY: ERECTING COVERED BRIDGES

PRAGMATIC SOLUTIONS TO BUILDING COVERED BRIDGES

Considering that covered bridges have existed for nearly 200 years, that numerous builders and civil engineering professors have published books and articles, that photography has existed since before the Civil War, it is surprising how little we know about the process of erecting a covered bridge. Building methods have undoubtedly changed over time as the available technology changed, that building a bridge in 1825 in Massachusetts was different from building one in Oregon or New Brunswick in 1944. What we do know is that the earliest builders, having neither experience nor training, generally developed their own pragmatic solutions by trial and error, which is the subject explored in this chapter.

The first and most formidable challenge for any bridge builder was the necessity of constructing a temporary wooden platform—called "falsework"— to support the structure under construction in deep or fast moving water.

Bridging the Susquehanna River—jokingly described as "a mile wide and an inch deep"—would have been easier than the Schuylkill at Philadelphia where the channel was quite deep. Palmer's Permanent Bridge across the Schuylkill was delayed for years until engineers developed a system for constructing piers using deep coffer dams—temporary enclosures midstream that could be pumped out to create a dry foundation for the stonework. If building piers in deep water was so difficult, how could they place wooden falsework in equally deep water? One possibility was building falsework on the ice. In some areas of the country, this could have been possible since streams might freeze solid. In places like Philadelphia that are farther south and experience milder winters than in New England, this would have been risky. Because most surviving covered bridges are relatively modest in length and often rural, it is easy to forget that so many early bridges were in urban areas, over broad rivers, and were far longer than any in existence today. Thus, pioneers had to solve the most challenging problems first and were not offered a gentle learning curve. Perhaps the reason we can learn so little from early masters like Palmer and Burr is because the process was either obvious to everyone at the time or the builders simply followed what was then "common knowledge." True, Burr wrote a detailed description to a fellow

Right Workers finish a new bridge over Grassy Creek on Straight Shoot Pike in Pendleton County, Kentucky, in 1907. At right is Louis Bower (d. 1936), whose father Jacob (d. 1905 or 1906), a protégé of master builder Lewis Wernwag, started the Bower Bridge Company sometime around the Civil War. At left is a worker named "Charlie." Louis Bower's son "Stock," too young to build bridges, continued the family tradition by repairing them into his old age, completing his last project in 1983. Stock died in 1995 at age ninety. (Robert W. N. Laughlin Collection)

Previous spread Workers build doubled Town lattice trusses reinforced with massive laminated arches for the Maine Central Railroad's bridge over the Passumpsic River in St. Johnsbury, Vermont, in 1905. This bridge lasted until 1927 when it had to be burned to prevent its being washed against the Portland Street Bridge. (Johnson, 1996: 61)

Top Workers erect the falsework before constructing the Gendron Bridge over the Gatineau River near Wakefield, Québec, in 1915. (Archives Nationales du Québec à Québec)

Inset The Stillwater Bridge in Columbia County, Pennsylvania, is 151 feet long and cost $1,124 in 1849, or $7.44 per lineal foot, a cost difficult to imagine in the early twenty-first century. (A. Chester Ong, 2012)

builder of how he erected the McCall's Ferry Bridge over the Susquehanna in 1814, but his detailed letter describes an exceptional method that was likely atypical.

Some Methodological Theories

Let us imagine some of the ways a builder might erect a bridge.

1. Build the bridge as a whole on land and drag it with teams of oxen on rollers over falsework onto the abutments.
2. Build each truss individually, rolling it flat onto the falsework and hoisting it into vertical position with block and tackle.
3. Build the trusses on land nearby or at a central location, such as a factory, mark the parts, disassemble the trusses, and rebuild them on falsework.
4. Custom build the trusses on the falsework.
5. Build truss halves from both abutments in an additive or cantilevered manner using a small crane or derrick that would then meet in the middle.
6. Build complete trusses on land and roll them alongside the abutments on the ice or on boats, then hoist them into place with derricks.
7. Build complete trusses or the entire bridge on land and lift the whole with a crane onto the abutments.

No doubt one could imagine further scenarios. We intend to present the known evidence and allow it to guide us to a conclusion. We do not think it was possible in the past to drag a whole bridge over falsework, although New Hampshire's Milton Graton, "the last of the covered bridge builders," has demonstrated this in recent years. The same is true of building complete trusses and rolling them into position for hoisting. Moving the sheer weight of complete trusses, each perhaps 200 feet long, let alone a complete bridge, seems unlikely considering the technology available in the nineteenth century.

Regarding bridge erection, we have two kinds of evidence: 1) prescriptive and 2) descriptive. Prescriptive evidence is found in a few "how to" bridge building books from the nineteenth century. As time went on, however, fewer of them dealt with practical issues, preferring stress analysis and pages filled with mathematical formulas. Descriptive evidence is more common, primarily observations of bridge construction written into books and articles, builders' mémoires, or as seen in period photographs. Together these provide a reasonably complete picture of the process.

Foundations

Before a superstructure could be built, there had to be foundations. Most early bridges in New England and the Middle Atlantic states, as well as Ohio, Indiana, Michigan, Kentucky, and West Virginia, used stone foundations—abutments on shore and piers mid river—of quarried rock cut into blocks. When readily available, the masons might use fieldstone instead. After about 1910, some foundations began to be constructed of concrete. In much of the South and for the most part in Prairie States like Illinois, Iowa, and Kansas, where

rivers tended to be mud bottomed and rock scarce, the foundations were either wooden bents or metal cylinders filled with concrete. In the Northwest, though rock was readily available, builders preferred to use wooden bents, probably because they were cheaper and faster to build, and timber was plentiful. Bridges in Québec and New Brunswick might have either stone or wooden foundations.

Where the foundations were to be built on bedrock, masons could simply lay the stone after leveling the surface. Piers, because they were usually built within the waterway, required either a temporary coffer dam to expose the river bottom or unusually low water, often the case in late summer and early fall. Unfortunately, we know little about normal coffer dam practice, though Judge Richard Peters described in great detail those used in building the Permanent Bridge in 1804, since they were used to a water depth of about 40 feet.

His description, however, fails to tell us how heavy foundation stones were moved to mid river and lowered into the coffer dam. We suspect they could have been delivered by a boat equipped with a derrick. Derricks capable of lifting stones have a long history in both Europe and Asia reaching back to ancient times. A woodblock print from China shows the construction of the Luoyang Bridge in the twelfth century with a derrick lifting parts for this megalithic bridge (Knapp, 2008: 215). American Thomas Pope published his *Treatise on Bridge Architecture* in 1811 with a proposal to build a "Flying Pendent Lever Bridge" over the Schuylkill River at Philadelphia some 432 feet long. He included a plate showing a cantilevered method of construction using two types of simple cranes (Nelson, 1990: 23).

Where the underlying ground was unstable, consisting of silt or gravel or was waterlogged, builders had to drive wooden piles into the ground to provide a stable base. Pile driving has a long history, at least to

the Roman period when two-man pile drivers called *fistuca* or *festuca* were used in building bridges over the River Rhine. Much of Amsterdam was built on piles. Pile driving machines lifted a heavy object—a log or later a bar of iron—and dropped it onto the end of the log being driven into the ground. Later pile drivers were powered by horses, then steam, and in modern times by gasoline or diesel engines (Webber and Webber, 1991: 14). Where piles would not suffice, masons built a timber crib foundation below the surface, and since it would remain under water, rot was not a problem.

When bents were used as foundations, the vertical timbers had to be driven into the ground. Mr Franklin Derrick (1850–1928), a Wisconsin bridge builder, remembered helping his father build trestle foundations for the Clarence Covered Bridge over the Sugar River southwest of Brodhead, Wisconsin, in 1864: "As a fifteen-year-old boy, I assisted in building it. My father had the contract to supply and drive the heavy piling at each bank upon which the super-structure rests. My immediate business was to keep Old Maje (Old Maje was an old farm horse) going 'round and 'round on the capstan that raised the hammer on the pile driver. 'Old Maje' and I completed our part of the job first, as we necessarily had to do. It was in the early fall of 1864 that the bridge was started" (Derrick, 1928: quoted in http://dianneandpaul.net/DianneGenealogy/d0006/g0000072.html).

In some localities, especially where there was little rock and streams were muddy, bridges were supported on wooden bents, wooden cribbing, or cylindrical metal tubes filled with cement. These were placed beside the stream, but shorter or longer approaches were necessary to cross the flood plain.

Falsework

Let us proceed on the assumption that *most* covered bridges were erected on wooden bents or trestles, what is called "falsework." Bridges built on simple wooden bents with a walkway on top are timeless and found worldwide. Such structures, sometimes seen in classic Chinese landscape paintings, are still found in rural China (Knapp, 2008: 21). They were relatively common in the American Colonies during the eighteenth century before the development of trussed bridges. The most famous of them was built in 1761 by Major Samuel Sewall Jr over the York River at York, Maine, a structure which amazingly remained in use until 1934 but was then unfortunately destroyed. It was 270 feet long and 25 feet wide, and included a drawspan, all built on thirteen "braced bents" consisting of four piles each.

Left When Shearer's Bridge was moved into a park at the edge of Manheim, Pennsylvania, in 1971, officials preserved the distinctive wing walls that are especially common in that state. (A. Chester Ong, 2011)

The wooden bents were first assembled on land, floated to their location, and sunk into the river bed (see Chapter 1, page 31, for photo).

The falsework used to construct wooden truss bridges in the United States was also the poor cousin of railroad trestle structures perfected during the same time. Heavy wooden trestles came to be used widely on rail lines crossing land depressions, swampland, and shallow or overflow water. During the Civil War, engineers such as General Herman Haupt built a number of amazing trestle bridges, especially the famous "cornstalks and beanpoles" bridge over Potomac Creek in Virginia. The Koksilah River Trestle built in 1911 on the Canadian Northern Pacific Railroad in Alaska, some 614 feet long and 145 feet above the canyon, was remarkable. Later trestle bridges used iron or steel, one of them being the Kinzua Bridge over Kinzua Creek in McKean County, Pennsylvania, built in 1900 some 2,052 feet long and 301 feet above the valley, but a tornado in 2003 destroyed this stunning bridge. The Moodna Viaduct near Cornwall, New York, constructed between 1904 and 1908, was 3,200 feet long and 193 feet high. Most astounding for length was the Great Salt Lake Lucin Cutoff built from 1902 to 1904, which was some 12 miles in length. All of the great roller coasters have (or had) wooden trestle bases. Clearly, the technology for building trestles was highly developed from the country's earliest days. Building falsework for a covered bridge seems, by comparison, rather modest.

In many cases, ordinary crews built falsework. But they are unsung heroes of bridge building, sinking long, heavy poles into moving currents and unknown river bottoms. Securing the cross beams and placing the caps at an even level required strength and daring along with some help from block and tackle. With little or no safety equipment and no protection from mosquito-borne diseases, many workers became ill, were injured, or even

Left from top When the Smith Bridge Company built the bridge at Otway in 1874, one end was placed on a pier rather than an abutment because there was a long, open approach span over the flood plain. The stone masons used uniformly cut blocks, laid without mortar. (Terry E. Miller, 2011)

When the Brown Bridge in Ohio's Brown County was constructed in 1878 by the Smith Bridge Company, there were no arches, and the abutments comprised of small, flat stones. Later, when the county added gigantic laminated arches, they fashioned pedestals for the arches since the original masons had not anticipated insets for them. (Terry E. Miller, 2011)

died completing this essential process. General Herman Haupt, America's greatest builder of railroad bridges, provided perhaps the most detailed instructions on wooden bridge erection ever published. Although his book focused on the quick replacement of rail bridges destroyed by the Confederate Army but essential to the Union Army, he spoke to most of the questions about timber truss bridge—and by extension, covered bridge—construction that have vexed us. Regarding falsework, he writes: "The legs of the trestles consist of pieces of timber 6 inches square, with holes bored about 3 inches apart. Near the top, and on the sides, are bolted two pieces of plank, forming a cap. The object of this arrangement is to place the cap at such elevation that its top will be on the level of the bottom of the lower chord. These trestles, being short and light, can easily be put together on the ropes [ropes were strung from abutment to pier on which a man shimmied across to begin the process] and raised into place. Light braces, nailed on the sides, will keep them in position; . . . The whole scaffolding is light, portable, and can be used without alteration many times, in different localities and for different spans" (1864: 29–30).

The earliest bridge for which we have confirmed use of falsework was Wernwag's Colossus over the mighty Schuylkill in Philadelphia, built in 1812 with a span of 340 feet. Although the river was deep, crews clearly were able to build falsework to support this dramatically arched structure. Lee H. Nelson relates the story: "January 7, 1813: On this day, 'in the presence of the Board of Managers and an immense concours [sic] of Citizens the centres of the Bridge were struck.' Many years later, Wernwag's son John related the event as one where 'thousands' of spectators had assembled on the river banks expecting to see the bridge collapse upon removal of the blocking from between the bridge and the scaffolding. The managers must have had their own private misgivings considering the daring of the undertaking. Unbeknownst to them, Wernwag had secretly removed the blocking between the scaffolding and the arched ribs the day before. When the inspection team of managers approached the first set of blocks, the managers said, 'Well, Lewis, do you think our bridge will stand the test today?' His reply was 'Yes, gentlemen, it will.' When they discovered that all of the blocks had been removed and that the entire bridge was free and clear of the falsework, Wernwag related to his son that he never saw the countenances of men brighten up as those of the managers when he informed them that the bridge was freed from the scaffold the day before" (1990: 24–5).

Col. Stephen Long, writing in 1841, offered briefer instructions on falsework. "The scaffolding required for raising the bridge should be substantial, but need not be expensive. The ordinary trestle-work usually employed for such purposes, is amply sufficient, nothing more being required than a firm and a steady support of the truss-frames, which may always be put together in an erect position, by adding piece after piece till the frame is complete" (p. 47).

Falsework, if badly built, could result in disaster. The *Eugene City Guard* in Oregon published a letter from an observer calling himself "Zero" on October 7, 1876, detailing an unfortunate incident: "The bridge is being built by A. S. Miller & Sons, of Eugene City. It consists of two spans, one being 190 feet, the other 170. The longer span is already raised, and the false work removed. The false work for the other span was braced only to the pier, as the abutment was not finished. When the abutment was completed, and the raising of the span began, the additional bracing of the false work to the abutment was overlooked. The end of the span over the abutment was twenty inches lower than the end over the pier, which would give the whole span a tendency toward the abutment.

"At the time of the accident, the top chord on one side was up, and about one-third on the other side. No one knows just what caused the false work to give way; but, without a moment's warning, the whole span shot endways toward the abutment. Henry Kohler and John Migley [sic] were on the top chord, which was finished; Nelson Rooney [sic] and Henry Miller on the one which was unfinished, forty-four feet above water. [He then described what happened to each man. While many were hurt, none were killed.] The wreck has been cleared away and reconstruction is progressing rapidly, and without further delay will be completed by the 1st of November" (quoted in Nelson, 1960: 120–1).

Once the falsework bents and caps were in place, workers could build a platform on which to work. When the bridge consisted of multiple spans, one span at a time was constructed. When finished, the false-work was removed and salvaged for the next span. How workers managed to do this is unclear. In some cases, boats must have been used, but when the water was too shallow, bridge builders had to find other ways to move the long, heavy timbers along with the machinery used to raise them. The longer the falsework was in place, the greater the danger from sudden freshets after a heavy rain or a sudden spring thaw. Although Theodore Cooper (1839–1919) was referring to the erection of iron rail bridges in the 1880s, his concerns applied equally to wooden bridges: "The great risk involved in erecting important structures over rivers subject to sudden floods, ice jams and similar dangers, emphasizes the importance of having a style of structure which can be rapidly and surely assembled without detriment to the perfection of the workmanship or accuracy of the connections" (1889: 40).

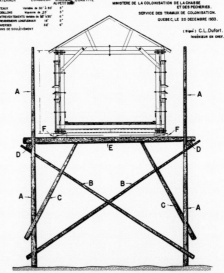

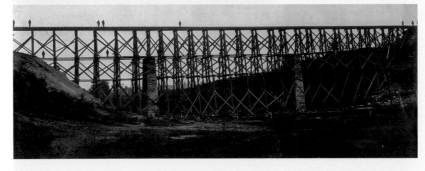

From top In 1933, when Québec was still actively building covered bridges, the "Colonisation" office (Service des travaux de colonisation) drew up these plans for false-work to support construction of a lattice (treillis) bridge. (Gérald Arbour Collection)

Construction of the Eagle Creek Bridge over the Clackamas River in Oregon in 1903. Even with the bridge 105 feet above the water, crews could build a complete set of scaffolds. (Webber and Webber, 1991: 122)

In 1862, President Lincoln engaged General Herman Haupt to manage the country's military railroads during a time of war. With bridges being destroyed continuously by both sides, this was not easy. Haupt's famous replacement trestle high over Potomac Creek on the Richmond, Fredericksburg and Potomac Railroad in Stafford County, Virginia, was constructed in record time (photo). Taken c. 1864, the photo shows the temporary bridge completed by Haupt's men. (Line drawing) When Lincoln saw this amazing 400-foot-long 100-foot-high crossing above the creek, he famously remarked "there is nothing in it but beanpoles and cornstalks!" (Photo, Library of Congress; Line drawing, Allen, 1959: 35)

Erecting the Superstructure

Perhaps the reason there are so few written instructions on erecting timber truss bridges is because there were multiple methods. In the case of short bridges using kingpost or queenpost trusses, builders could have constructed the trusses without falsework. William E. Bell in *Carpentry Made Easy* wrote: "In raising the former of these bridges [about 30 feet long], no false work or temporary supports are needed . . ." (1857: 93). He does not specify whether the trusses were to be custom built over the water or wholly built on land and hoisted into place. Considering that such trusses were light enough to be lifted by block and tackle, possibly horse powered, this was feasible.

Although Richard Sanders Allen asserted that trusses were assembled on land, rolled onto the falsework, and raised into place (1957: 24), many others are skeptical.

Above A vintage tintype photograph shows ten men and a boy finishing the second bridge at Beverly, West Virginia, in 1873, under the supervision of Lemuel Chenoweth. He also built the first bridge at the site in 1847, which was burned during the Civil War and not immediately replaced. (Randy Allan Collection)

Right African-American bridge builder Horace King completed the first bridge at Fort Gaines, Georgia, around 1870, and after a period of failed successors, including one by King, his grandson Ernest built the last covered bridge in 1913. Because the piers were so high and the river so prone to flooding, this crossing was always a problem for the state. (Georgia Division of Archives and History, Office of Secretary of State)

Right Madison County, Iowa's Cedar Bridge was originally built in 1883 by H. P. Jones near Winterset over Cedar Creek, but in 1921 it was moved overland by a steam tractor to its present location nearby. The original bridge was burned in 2002 and replaced by a replica in 2004. (Winterset, Iowa, Chamber of Commerce)

on falsework over the river. Col. Long offered clear advice on how to construct trusses on "ways," meaning a supporting framework on the ground: "The framing ways should consist of two series of parallel timbers, prolonged through a distance considerably beyond the intended length of the bridge span, firmly bonded together by transverse ties, and resting on substantial and unyielding supports or blockings. The distance between the parallel timbers should be equal to that between the strings of the intended truss-frame, in order that the latter may recline firmly upon the former during the progress of the framing.

"The parallel side pieces of the framing ways, should be perforated with mortises 3 by 5 inches, for the reception of stanchions occupying the places of the gibs and keys, and serving to keep the strings, posts, and braces in a steady and uniform position whilst the work of framing is in progress. . . .

"The ways should be perfectly straight and free from winding. The spaces between the posts should be of a uniform width, and the posts uniformly at right angles with the strings. The strings should be laid perfectly straight, and retain this position during the progress of constructing the truss-frame" (1836: 48).

That Long's recommendations were indeed practiced is affirmed by English engineer David Stevenson based on observations from a trip made in the late 1830s. He writes: "The timbers of which Town's and Long's bridges

Certainly this method was not feasible in the case of multiple-span bridges, but there is some evidence of this method's use in substantial single-span bridges. Randy Allan describes the building of the Beverly [West Virginia, then Virginia] Bridge in 1846, a 130-foot Burr truss span (2006: 23). Among the items required for construction are "2 cranes and rigging ($50)." Allan writes: "In the "raising of the bridge" with the aid of a homemade crane, large pulleys, heavy rope and teams of oxen or horses, each arch and truss is lifted into place. Superintendent Hamilton described this as quite an event. People had come from far and wide. Court was in session, but adjourned. The river bank was lined with spectators. He described the event as the most spectacular event ever witnessed in the valley. . . ."

Allan continued: "Evidently much work had been done as just 2 days later he wrote to inform the VBPW [Virginia Bureau of Public Works in Richmond, Virginia] of some good news as follows: 'The bridge is now raised with floor, and the trussels being knocked out and ready for travel once the west abutment is ready" (p. 23). How widespread this method was cannot be determined, since relatively few period writers comment on bridge erection.

There is scant evidence of how bridges were moved during the nineteenth century. While most were likely disassembled and reassembled, at least some were moved whole, as seen in Madison County, Iowa.

The preponderance of evidence supports the method of pre-cutting and assembling the trusses on land, marking and disassembling them, and re-erecting them

are composed, are fitted together on the ground previous to their erection on the piers. They are again taken asunder, and each beam is put up separately in the place which it is to occupy, by means of a scaffolding or centering of timber" (1859: 145).

Although not written until 1948 by James William Buchanan, son of Fairfield County, Ohio bridge builder J. W. Buchanan, the following is among the clearest statements on bridge construction: "Framing was usually done along the road adjacent to the bridge. . . . If possible, the floor of the old bridge was shored up and braced and used as the platform on which the new bridge was set up. Tracks, consisting of blocked-up and spiked four-by-fours were laid from the framing yard to and across the old bridge floor, if still standing, or a jerry-built platform if not, unloaded with the aid of the winch (and pinched fingers), and juggled to position. Diagonals and upright posts were inserted in their proper places and the frame assembled. Once the bridge was 'raised,' the work reverted to straight carpentry, with siding, flooring, and roofing being of more-or-less conventional type. . . . Employing only hand tools it generally took six men five or six weeks to frame, erect, and finish a 60-foot span" (quoted in Klages, 1996: 12).

Having pre-cut and fitted trusses, whether marked for precise reassembly (called "scribe rule framing") or consisting of standard parts cut uniformly (called "square rule framing") was important when there was a chance of sudden changes in the river (see *Covered Bridge Topics* 70(4): 5, 2012, for a clear description of these framing methods). Randy Allan of West Virginia described the kind of situation Cooper (above) wished to avoid: "Storm clouds began to gather about two weeks after Superintendent Hamilton had filed his progress report. On December 10–11 [1847], a very serious flood occurred over the entire length of the turnpike. With but one exception all bridges were washed out or severely damaged. In reference to the bridge on the South Fork of the Hughes River he wrote: "at the time Chenoweth had his bridge raised and when the flood came and struck the trestle and let them go out without injury to his bridge. There was some loss of lumber" (2006: 35).

Lee Nelson, writing on Oregon's bridges, related the following: "Nor were bridge builders exempt from acts of God, which not only caused loss of time and investment, but tragedy on several occasions. The Pacific Bridge Company lost the Santiam bridge at Scio, in 1881, when wind blew the construction down, killing one man and injuring three. Nels Roney's entire falsework for a Row River bridge went out in the 1883 freshet" (1960: 138).

Alfred L. Rives (1830–1903), the first American graduate of the eminent Parisian engineering school, the École Nationale des Ponts et Chaussées, described bridge building in an unpublished manuscript. Rives, later known for the 220-foot Cabin John masonry arch bridge near Washington, DC, had apparently learned how to erect Howe truss rail bridges directly from William Howe. Rives' manuscript, brought to light by Dario Gasparini and David Simmons and published in 2010, originally included drawings but these are lost. The description is too long to reproduce in full, but a few excerpts summarize the process: "In the first place, the builder should make his arrangements as to height of Truss, width of panel, dimension of timber &c.

"He should then lay out in full size one end of a truss of a sufficient length to enable him to make patterns of the principal & counter braces, bolsters, bearing blocks &c. . . .

"The builder should then make a platform to frame the chords upon, by taking the floorbeams, and laying them about 14 or 15 feet apart, and the top to be 15 or 18 inches from the ground, and perfectly level with the horizon. The builder will commence cutting & laying up the bottom chord, one plank upon the other, horizontally as in the plan so as to have them splice in every other panel. . . .

"The braces & counter braces should all be cut one length, and square at the ends, and a dowell [sic] should be used in the top end of the braces, with a hole in the bearing block so as to prevent their falling down when raising.

"In raising, a scaffold should be made in the river, or when to be constructed with the camber as required in Truss, and frame, and then the bottom chords should be laid on the work & bolted together, and the horizontal braces put in and secured with the cross bolts &c.

Below This rare photo shows the construction of the four-span Miller Bridge over the Tallapoosa River in Alabama in 1907. Using a temporary derrick and a sophisticated system of cables to move materials, the workers are building the bridge over falsework. (Horseshoe Bend National Military Park)

Bottom While building the Miller Bridge over the Talla-poosa River in Alabama in 1907, the workers lived nearby in a temporary camp. Here, the workers stand near the dining tent. The second man from the right holds a hand auger likely used to drill the thousand plus holes in the truss planks for the trunnels. (Horseshoe Bend National Military Park)

Left Workers complete a double-web Town lattice rail bridge at Hillsborough, New Hampshire, in 1904, likely left uncovered. (NSPCB Archives, R. S. Allen Collection)

"Then to make top horses of 3 x 8 in plank that will be about 4 inches short of filling up the spaces between Top & Bottom chords when raised, and with cap pieces large enough to stand outside the braces while raising— The horses should be raised on the Bottom chord and braces, and a framing block put upon the cap pieces, that will raise the top chord high enough to admit the braces to go in.

"When the top chord is raised & bolted together, the bearing blocks are then put up & spiked so as to prevent their falling down.

"The workmen may then put two men aloft upon the top chord, with ropes to haul up the top end of the braces, and commence putting in & slightly screwing the bolts" (Rives, 2010: 3–5).

Although not written until 1902, Arthur C. Striker, a bridge builder from Florence, Oregon, described the entire erection process followed there: "Bents were put on each side of the river. Heavy cedar logs were placed on level bedrock if possible, and drifted. Several holes were bored through the logs, and steel drift pins were driven in and through to the rock. The main posts were dapped into the mud sills, and dapped into the cap. Instead of sway braces, we placed diagonal [140] posts inside of end posts and main bents. The posts were leveled, and sawed off before being capped.

"After the bent was put in, the lower falsework went up, and work on the truss was started. After we placed the lower chord, we set the upper chord on the falsework directly above the lower chord, about fourteen feet. Then we placed diagonals between the two chords. At each panel we put in cross-ties on the upper chords, then dropped in rods, and tightened. A hand winch was used for raising diagonals and chords.

"The next step was to swing the truss, which meant to tighten the truss rods, first at one end, then at the other, working toward the center. Then the useable lumber was salvaged from the falsework, and the remainder broken up to float downriver" (quoted in Nelson, 1960: 139).

Covered bridges continued to be built well into the mid-twentieth century in Oregon, Québec, and New Brunswick, and uncovered Howe truss spans were built in British Columbia and elsewhere in Canada into the 1960s. Long before that, engineers were already proficient in building massive all-iron or steel bridges, including the Eads Bridge in 1874 over the Mississippi in St. Louis, Missouri, the Smithfield Street "lenticular truss" over the Monongahela in Pittsburgh in 1883, the Brooklyn Bridge in 1883, the Queensboro Bridge in New York City in 1909, and so forth. Heavy equipment, such as large-scale steam-powered cranes and derricks, was already available. Thus, engineers were working at a highly sophisticated technical level while covered bridges continued to be built. But it is also true that most covered bridges built during this period were relatively modest and often rural. Additionally, would

Inset Indiana's most famous bridge builder, Archibald McMichael Kennedy, moved to Rushville from North Carolina in 1825 and, along with his sons Emmett and Charles, built the state's most distinctive bridges, all Burr trusses. Here, the three-span bridge over the White River at Martinsville is under construction in 1873. (NSPCB Archives, R. S. Allen Collection)

Left W. W. Inman and his crew assemble unusually high Howe trusses on the Hendricks Bridge over the McKenzie River in Lane County, Oregon, in 1907. Note the temporary supports for the chords and the steel rods lying on the deck. The two spans, one an amazing 240 feet long, the other "only" 180 feet, lasted until 1925 when they were replaced. (Lane County [OR] Historical Museum)

contractors have had such machinery in places like Fairfield County, Ohio, Parke County, Indiana, rural Georgia and Alabama, and of course rural Québec, New Brunswick, and Oregon?

In 2009, Joseph Conwill interviewed Ian Sturrock, P.E., Bridge Evaluation Engineer with the British Columbia Ministry of Transportation in 2009. He, in turn, talked with Dean Barlow, an employee who helped erect open Howe truss bridges in the late 1950s. Barlow described a process that could have occurred during the nineteenth century: "The bridge was erected on pile falsework. The bottom chords and the bottom lateral bracing were erected on shims off the falsework to the proper camber. The floor system was installed on top of the bottom chords. The bottom angle blocks [were set], the braces and counter braces were then placed on top of the lower angle blocks, with extra bracing to hold the mains and counters in place. The upper angle blocks were then placed on top of the braces and counter braces. The top chord was erected leaf by leaf on top of the upper angle blocks. Rollers were used to slide the long leaf pieces onto the bridge where they were lifted into place by hand. . . . Dean recalls the vertical rods being tensioned starting at the ends and working towards the middle. The crew would alternate between each end of the bridge until they reached the middle. After the bridge was erected the piles in the falsework were cut away. I specifically asked Dean if he recalls the truss being lifted off the falsework by the tensioning of the rods and he did not remember this being the case" (Conwill, 2009a: 3).

Based on what we know, let us reconsider what was perhaps the most astounding wooden bridge erection in covered bridge history, Theodore Burr's 360-foot clear span over the Susquehanna River at McCall's Ferry, which was built from late 1814 to early 1815. Although Burr's detailed letter to fellow bridge builder Reuben Field, dated February 26, 1815, describes the process, it continues to mystify readers. Richard Sanders Allen believed that the main span was a normal covered Burr

truss, but a close reading combined with circumstantial evidence suggests it neither had a truss nor was covered. The Susquehanna River is constricted to between 348 and 609 feet (depending on water level) and up to 150 feet deep at McCall's Ferry, an area now inundated by Holtwood Dam. After noting the immense size of the abutment and pier (the latter built as far from the opposite shore as feasible), Burr writes: "The altitude or rise of the arch is 31'. The arch is double, and the two segments are combined by king-posts 7' long between the shoulders, and are united to the arch by lock-work. Between the king-posts are truss-braces and counter-acting braces" (Burr, 1815: 9). We therefore conclude that each "truss" consisted of two parallel arches with a tremendous rise made rigid by short posts, bracing, and counterbracing. Some might call this a "trussed arch" since the frame stiffens the arch.

Similar designs already existed. In 1797, Charles Willson Peale had proposed a 390-foot span with a 39-foot rise built of laminated wooden arches with bracing crossing the Schuylkill in Philadelphia where Palmer later built the Permanent Bridge (Nelson, 1990: 7). Burr himself had built such a bridge in 1802 or 1803 over the Mohawk River at Canajoharie, New York. According to Nelson Greene: "The first bridge over the Mohawk River in the middle Mohawk Valley seems to have been the one erected at Canajoharie in 1803, by Theodore Burr of Jefferson County. This was popularly called a bow bridge and consisted of a single arch 330 feet long. It fell in 1807 with a crash that was heard for miles" (1925: n.p.). A painting titled "Incomplete Bridge, Palatine" by Baroness Anne-Marguerite-Henriette Hyde de Neuville from 1808 depicts the crossing after the bridge's fall (see page 44). Enough of the structure remains to show that Burr's design resembled that of Peale, being a single arch below with truss stiffening above and the beginning of a level roadway, at least near the shore. We believe that Burr's bridge at McCall's Ferry was similar, though apparently with arches below and above the truss stiffening.

Burr and his men built these arches on a series of eight "floats" (presumably flat-bottomed boats), each having two bents (one for each set) lined up along one shore and anchored with a web of stout ropes. His intention appears to have been to float the entire structure around and somehow hoist it onto the stonework, probably with a combination of horses and humans operating block and tackle. Because their work continued into the dead of winter, the river not only froze but accumulated broken pieces of ice from upriver to a depth of 60–80 feet. After crews cleared a path through the ice—how they did that we can only speculate—the first arch and truss system was moved off the floats onto rollers and gradually swung out to the foundations and hoisted into place. The second followed.

Burr's crew was assisted by hundreds of local residents who were paid with nothing more than copious amounts of liquor. Burr, however, refers to scaffolding as well, apparently built in haste on the ice. He writes: "In the afternoon we began to cut away the scaffolding and got down 2/3 of it before dark. . . . We then set to cutting down the remaining part of the scaffolding, which was completed about half past 8 o'clock" (Burr, 1815: 11). With the trussed arches in place, workers began building the deck and lateral bracing. Just as Burr's arch over the Mohawk lasted only four or five years, McCall's Ferry only lasted three years, destroyed by an ice jam in March, 1818, but, unlike the Mohawk crossing, it was never rebuilt.

Finishing the Job

Trusses and bridge erection are no doubt the most interesting aspects of covered bridge building, but without lateral bracing, a deck, a roof, and roadway approaches, they remain incomplete. Because these subjects show much variation, and including all would produce insomnia-curing tedium, we can only summarize the main ones.

The trusses must be rigidly braced between both lower and upper chords to keep them from bowing out or bending inward. In addition, angle or knee braces must be installed between the vertical posts and the horizontal upper bracing to resist wind pressure putting the bridge out of square. Individual builders had numerous ways to accomplish this, and parts of these systems were easily replaced over time in order to correct flood damage to the lower parts, increase upper clearance, or repair damage from overly high vehicles, and so forth.

THE DECK There are basically two ways to create a deck. The more common way was to place a series of lateral beams on the lower chords, usually at the post inter-sections where the chords are strongest, but some builders placed a series of beams or planks on their sides on the chords. With fewer beams, there must be joists (planks on edge) running the length onto which a one- to two-layer floor of planking was laid. Bridges with a single layer—the boards perpendicular to the trusses—tended to be rough and produce noise, and thus builders usually added lengthwise running boards for the wheels of the vehicles. If there were, instead, a second layer, it would run parallel to the trusses.

Below Workers complete a newly built Town lattice covered bridge at Edgemont, South Dakota's city park on May 8, 2011. An Amish builder, Moses Borntreger, from Ashland Montana, built the trusses using locally available timber and shipped them to Edgemont for assembly by Kris Barker and a volunteer crew. This is South Dakota's only covered bridge. (Anne Cloyd Cassens, 2011)

Sometimes one of these layers was laid diagonally to distribute the loads across a greater number of planks. While a floor system supported on the chords was easier to build and probably stronger, it had the disadvantage of reducing clearance, since the floor level could be up to two feet above the chords.

The second way is to suspend the cross beams beneath the chords. These were usually secured by iron rods either anchored running from wood blocks on the lower chords through the beams below or from rods hung from blocks on top of the arches, or both. Less commonly, builders used iron stirrups fastened to the posts or from wood blocks on the chords to support the beams. The limitation to this method was that strength depended on the hardware not gouging into the wooden beams, but the advantage was greater overall clearance. There was also commonly a series of wooden X braces either fastened between the chords or the floor beams. These could be anchored in numerous ways, but in 1869 Robert Smith patented an iron saddle that secured the X's at a crossing of adjacent X's near the chords. Deck structure was essential, for if a bridge was to fail under a heavy load, it was more likely from deck failure than truss failure.

THE ROOF Observers looking upwards in a covered bridge will notice cross beams placed over the chords or between them, usually of wood, sometimes of iron/steel, and usually with X bracing similar to that found in the deck. Such bracing is required to keep the trusses square and to support the roof. August Borneman in Ohio developed an alternate X system using an iron ring at the cross with four rods running outwards to the beams or chords. Bridges here and there might have extra heavy bracing sets or odd patterns, such as V's instead of X's. Smith's saddle hardware is found in both decks and roofs of most Smith truss bridges. Above this are A-shaped frames for roofing. Covered bridges built in Madison County, Iowa, late in the 1880s by one particular builder used "flat" (actually, slightly convex) roofs, but elsewhere peaked roofs were the norm. Roofs were especially vulnerable, but many bridges retain their original framing. Roofs were originally covered with wood shingles, but over time these have mostly been replaced with sheets of corrugated or sheet metal, heavy roofing paper, or modern shingles.

Finally, the siding and portals completed the protection of the structure. In earlier times, horizontal siding applied to a framework of "nailers" (thin strips

Left from top The multilayered deck of Alabama's Swann Bridge, built in 1933, uses cross beams suspended from iron bolts, metal rod X bracing, a parallel line of joists, diagonal joists, and perpendicular joists, finished with floorboards running parallel to the trusses. (Terry E. Miller, 2011)

J. J. Daniels built the Mansfield Bridge in Parke County, Indiana, in 1867 using a deck with two beams per panel placed on the lower chords. (Terry E. Miller, 2011)

Québec's covered bridge decks typically placed the cross beams below the lower chords, suspended on steel plates anchored with long bolts to wood blocks above the chord, but whether this was the original plan is uncertain. (Terry E. Miller, 2012)

When Evrett [*sic*] Sherman built a series of Childs truss bridges in Preble County, Ohio, in the 1880s, he supported the decks with U-shaped iron brackets supported by two bolts attached to wood blocks on the lower chords. (Terry E. Miller, 2011)

Below While double-lane bridges were common in the early days of bridge building, today they are rare. The deck system for Indiana's Ramp Creek Bridge, built in 1838 and preserved at Brown County State Park, shows the complexity of a double deck. (Terry E. Miller, 2003)

Top Builders suspended the deck beams below the chords to gain added vertical clearance, but this also created vulnerability as the system depended on small wooden blocks and iron bolts. The system seen here is Fairfield County, Ohio's Hanaway Bridge, built in 1901. (Terry E. Miller, 2011)

Above Typical of Washington County, Pennsylvania's short bridges, the Brownlee or Stout Bridge uses cross beams suspended on long iron bolts. The beam in the background has been reinforced with an additional support. (Terry E. Miller, 2011)

of wood to which siding was nailed) was more normal, but later bridges more often had vertical siding, sometimes with battens. Many bridges had openings cut into the siding to provide light, especially when there were curves at one or both ends, a common circumstance when roads often followed creeks and cars and buggies moved slowly. Preventing the siding from being knocked off by fishermen and swimmers has long been a maintenance headache. Some counties have taken to wrapping wire around each piece of siding, and others have erected wire screens within the bridge to prevent access to the siding. Although windows may allow rain to hit some truss members, it is water *in joints* that causes the greatest harm.

THE APPROACH A complete bridge also required an approaching roadway. Where bridges had stone abutments, especially those with parapets, the roadway was filled with rock and other rubble, then covered with soil and a finish of gravel or pavement right to the floorboards. Some river banks needed to be "protected" with riprap, rocky rubble that would reduce erosion. The many bridges built on piles, especially from Illinois and Iowa west, in America's South and Northwest, and

Right The upper lateral X bracing in Québec's bridges covers a greater area than usual. Also seen is the ample angle bracing. (Terry E. Miller, 2012)

Right For panel trusses, the usual upper lateral bracing uses cross beams on the upper chords with X bracing for reinforcement, here seen in the Hannaway Bridge in Ohio. (Terry E. Miller, 2011)

Below left The upper cross bracing in Alabama's Old Easley Bridge, built in 1927, uses a lattice-like system of X's. (Terry E. Miller, 2011)

Below right Indiana's Ramp Creek Bridge, its only double-lane bridge, dating from 1838, appears to be unusually complex because each lane has its own system. In addition to the single upper chord for the middle truss, there are braces to the roof peak. (Terry E. Miller 2011)

in the Canadian provinces, were usually approached by a short open span or wooden trestle bridges. Sometimes, there was a short open wooden truss approach, usually kingpost, rarely queenpost, such as can still be seen at the Jackson's Mill Bridge in Bedford County, Pennsylvania. In the South, some bridges have trestle approaches far exceeding the length of the covered span because the approach had to cross low-lying, flood-prone flats before reaching the creek at normal water level. Even in the earliest days of bridge building, contractors already had a variety of wood treatments to retard decay in open approaches.

In the early days, when most covered bridges crossed major rivers and were in urban areas, the bridge opening was a grand affair, with bunting, speech-giving politicians, parades, bands, and mobs of happy citizens. William D. Mohr recounted the opening of Burr's double-lane Lansingburgh-Waterford Union Bridge over the Hudson (1957a: 1): "The opening of the bridge, December 4, 1804, was the occasion of a holiday. The *Lansingburgh Gazette* (Dec. 11) recounted that at noon 'a very numerous procession' was formed at Johnson & Judson's Hotel, marched to the bridge and then across to Waterford 'under the discharge of seventeen cannon.' The line of march ended at Gerardus Van Schoonhoven's hotel where a dinner was provided (at the expense of the stockholders of the bridge company) and attended by the Governor, Secretary of State, the state Comptroller and the Surveyor-General, together with other prominent persons 'and a large number of respectable gentlemen from Albany and the adjacent villages,' who 'partook in much harmony and conviviality.'"

Hazards of Construction

Building timber bridges was a dangerous occupation. Ebenezer Buckingham, builder of Ohio's famed "Y Bridge" on the National Road in Zanesville, was killed in 1832 when the superstructure under construction shifted,

throwing him into the chaos. Burr commented on this briefly in his letter concerning McCall's Ferry: "And what is still more remarkable, there was but one man that was injured; that was Augustus Stoughton. He fell 54', hit on the braces twice, then into the water. He in a few days was again at work; and no other person hurt" (1815: 11). The fact is that workers in those days were not just "on their own" but had virtually no safety equipment, no insurance, and no Worker's Compensation program, perhaps exemplifying America's early "libertarian" ideal. It is still unnerving that for photographers workers felt compelled to stand on the tops of trusses and other high structures, unaided by anything more than their balance and fearlessness of heights.

On another occasion, Burr wrote to Thomas Elder, President of the Harrisburgh Bridge Company on May 28, 1814, and described a major accident at a bridge site. This story also confirms the use of a boat [gondola] aiding in erection. "My Bridge Builders have got so sprightly that they can put up an arch in a very short time and in a masterly good manner and yesterday between 6 and 7 o'clock [in the] evening flung one down and hurt four men—one pretty bad—broke his leg—which will take some time to get well—the other 3 men I think will be able to work again in a short time—we

Top left Vinton County, Ohio's Bay or Tinker Bridge uses a double multiple kingpost truss with posts that rise well above the upper chords, but the lateral bracing is surprisingly light with thin planks for both cross beams and X's. (Terry E. Miller, 2011)

Top right Lawrence County, Pennsylvania's Banks Bridge uses a Burr truss with braces notched into the posts, angle braces anchored with mortise and tenon, and X braces secured with pegs. (Terry E. Miller, 2011)

Below Bridges that crossed streams with unusually wide flood plains, as does the Lowery Bridge in Georgia, required long, open approaches that, while vulnerable to the weather, could be easily replaced since they spanned dry land most of the year. (A. Chester Ong, 2011)

Below right Most of Oregon's bridges were constructed on free-standing pier abutments, requiring approaches, such as the Rochester Bridge in Douglas County. (A. Chester Ong, 2012)

however, Lee Nelson writes that accidents were fairly common. "In fact, early Oregon bridge-building accounts are frequently spotted with fatal accidents, usually that of a hapless carpenter falling from the trusswork, resulting in a broken neck" (1960: 122). He further writes: "With all their skills, the early bridge builders seem to have been accident-prone. Hardly a year passed without several reports of bridge construction accidents, some of them fatal. An 1867 report reads: "Last Tuesday while the new bridge on the road from Monmouth to Eola, over the Rickreal [*sic*] was being raised, Mr. Ira Mason, son of the contractor, fell backward from the top of a bent, head foremost, and struck a mud-sill fifteen feel below, instantly break his neck. . . . In 1877, a bridge being built at Monroe, in Benton County, collapsed with a number of persons, badly injuring several. . . . Nor were bridge builders exempt from acts of God, which not only caused loss of time and investment, but tragedy on several occasions. The Pacific Bridge Company lost the Santiam bridge at Scio, in 1881, when wind blew the construction down, killing one man and injuring three" (p. 138).

Few writers comment on fraud, but unfortunately honest builders constituted fewer than 100 percent. While Theodore Burr did not intend to perpetrate fraud, he is much remembered for "biting off more than he could chew," taking on far too many simultaneous projects and not being able to fulfill the terms of the agreements. As a consequence, his cash flow was often inadequate to buy building materials when he needed them, and eventually Burr went bankrupt. Lee Nelson, writing about Oregon, relates the following tale of corruption: "Some bridge builders seem to have been careless in other respects, inviting charges of fraud. A February 1, 1873, petition to the Marion County commissioners signed by twenty-two citizens including A. J. Cason, complained that the bridge on the Abiqua, north of Silverton, was fraudulently constructed. They charged that the bridge was not built according to specifications, was three feet lower at the south end and two feet lower at the north end than the old bridge had been, that the contractors used twenty-seven sticks of timber from the old bridge, and that the bridge was covered with cedar boards instead of shingles. The petition finally pointed out that the contractors 'sold the old iron to themselves for 2 cts per lb when Iron is selling from 8 to 12 cts per lb'" (1960: 139).

As with fraud, few writers mention the role of sickness related to bridge building. When workers spent long periods in the forest or around swamps, and always with water in abundance, if someone became ill, their chances for a quick recovery were low. Randy Allan's thorough study of West Virginia builder Lemuel Chenoweth provides the complete report written by Col. Josiah D. Wilson, a Clarksburg engineer on the bridges at Philippi and Fairmont: "Mr. Wilson, on page 2 of his report, wrote as follows in reference to a further

were wedging—some post under the segments of the arch next Thomas Grantz [*sic*] Esqr about 40 feet from the pier the water being pretty high and the current strong—it was with difficulty we could keep the post to stay in these places unless they were confined very hard by wedges which was done and more then [*sic*] done—it was wedged so hard as to raise the whole arch so much as to save that the end of the arch next to the abutment loose as to drop down and it dropped to the ground or bank—this stroke Broke off the segments about 30 or forty feet from the abutment end—and then all went down into the river and moved all in one majestic column about 30 rods—and the men landed—and made it fast—the arch fell across my raising gondola and sunk it" (1814: 31).

But accidents happened, perhaps more frequently than we realize, since there was no requirement of reporting them. We have previously mentioned an incident in Oregon in 1876 when a bridge under construction slipped, but no one was killed. Elsewhere,

delay in the work: 'This work was greatly retarded by sickness amongst the hands, caused by the most fatal epidemic ever experienced in that section of the country, which continued from an early period of the summer of 1851 and continued until the following fall season.' I list it here a second time because there is an article on the epidemic in the aforementioned *Centennial History*. . . . In the article E. E. Myers tells about Dr. James Edmond Reeves of Philippi who cared for the victims. He writes as follows: 'In the spring of 1851 the construction of a bridge, connecting Philippi with Georgetown, was commenced; adding about thirty to the population of this last-named village. Among the workmen, whose business required them to stand in the water, enteric fever began, from there it occurred among the workmen in stone upon the banks, and from there to the citizens generally . . . several of the workmen on the bridge, on being taken sick went home . . . until at last, during the year 1852, the work was, in consequence of it, almost suspended.' This epidemic coupled with occasional high water, engineering blunders, and consequential masonry delays prompting construction delays, makes one wonder how these two bridges were completed even within just one additional year" (2006: 59).

Conclusions

Although the documentation is spotty and sometimes circumstantial, it is nonetheless clear that there were multiple ways to erect a covered bridge. Builders freely adapted any of the methods discussed above to their own particular situation and its surroundings. For multi-span bridges, if the river depth permitted, boats could be used to bring men and materials to the span

under construction. Shorter bridges could be built directly on the abutments and longer single-span bridges could have complete trusses raised on the falsework. Clearly, though, building crews were highly skilled—whether from experience or trial and error— at building falsework in all kinds of situations. Though photographs of truss construction are relatively rare, there is enough evidence to identify the predominant method—assembling pre-cut (and probably pre-assembled/disassembled) truss members on falsework. Additionally, prescriptive documentation from designer-builders such as Col. Stephen Long, as well as descriptive material from both builders and observers, reinforce this claim.

During the nineteenth century, covered bridge building passed from being the norm to being the alternative to iron and then to losing the competition with iron. At the same time, trained engineers were perfecting the building of gigantic bridges of iron and steel over the world's major rivers using state-of-the-art construction equipment. Yet, the "traditional" methods of erecting covered bridges piecemeal on falsework apparently continued until at least the middle of the twentieth century where such bridges remained practical. In our own time, when builders have perfected replicating old bridges with all new materials, builders customarily can use the labor-saving devices of modern construction, particularly giant cranes capable of lifting entire trusses or even complete bridges onto the abutments. Just when workers began using safety equipment is uncertain, but in today's construction world they must take all required precautions, no matter how traditional they are otherwise in their "historical timber framing" practices.

Below Adpheus Fields and his crew were in the early stages of building the Worthington Bridge over the South Umpqua River near Canyonville, Oregon, in 1910 when this photo was taken. As seen, few of the Smith truss members are in place. The bridge was abandoned in the 1950s, then stripped of covering and no longer exists. (Douglas County Museum)

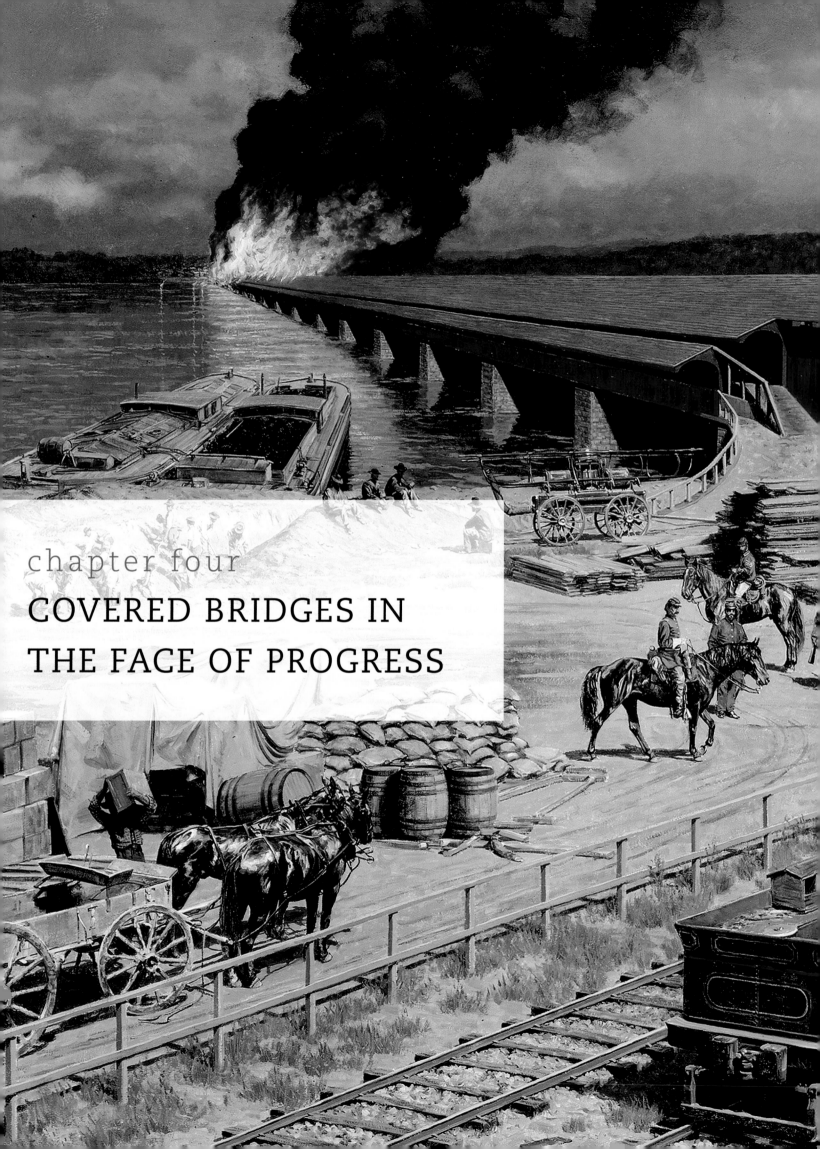

chapter four

COVERED BRIDGES IN
THE FACE OF PROGRESS

COVERED BRIDGES AS "IMPEDIMENTS TO PROGRESS"

Our perspectives on most matters change over time. From the late nineteenth century through the 1960s, covered bridges were more likely characterized as "archaic," "quaint," "obsolete," "hazardous," "inadequate," or "a nuisance" than "charming" or "valuable." Before that, a few people began to find covered bridges nostalgic, and some went so far as to advocate selective preservation, but local officials and highway authorities charged with road and bridge maintenance were far more likely to view the bridges negatively. Concerned about the accelerating losses of covered bridges, a small group of New Englanders formed the National Society for the Preservation of Covered Bridges (NSPCB) in late 1949. It was, however, not legally chartered until April 1954, when Leo Litwin, a prominent Boston pianist, became its first president, and the society began holding meetings in the [Boston] Symphony Office Building. Independently, in 1943, Richard Sanders Allen, who had been researching covered bridges for five years, created a modest newsletter called *Covered Bridge Topics*, which

became a publication of the NSPCB in 1952 and continues today on a quarterly basis currently under the editorship of Joseph D. Conwill.

A number of books began to be published that are now considered "classics" though no longer considered "authoritative." The earliest two appeared in the same year, 1931: Clara E. Wagemann's *Covered Bridges of New England* and Rosalie Wells' *Covered Bridges in America*. Next came Adelbert Jakeman's *Old Covered Bridges* in 1935 and S. Griswold Morley's *The Covered Bridges of California* in 1938. Herbert Wheaton Congdon's *The Covered Bridge* of 1941 includes 100 photographs of Vermont's bridges. Wells also includes many valuable photos of long forgotten bridges.

No other bridge books appeared until the 1950s when Eric Sloane, one of America's iconic artists, began publishing a series of hand-illustrated volumes devoted to all manner of Americana, including covered bridges. Though lightly researched, his 1954 *American Barns and Covered Bridges* became an instant classic and the starting point for many among the growing number of enthusiasts. In 1956, the National Society for the Preservation of Covered Bridges (NSPCB) published its first comprehensive list, a *Guide to Covered Bridges in the United States*, edited by Betsy and Philip Clough, which was followed in 1959 by the *World Guide to Covered Bridges,* whose 7th and most recent edition appeared in 2009.

Our understanding of covered bridges changed dramatically with the 1957 publication of Richard Sanders Allen's first book, *Covered Bridges of the Northeast: The Complete Story in Words and Pictures.* Without professional training and working as post-master of Round Lake, New York, Allen had begun photographing and studying covered bridges in 1938, collecting documents, and focusing on bridge trusses and construction. In 1959, he followed up his first work with *Covered Bridges of the Middle Atlantic States: Their Illustrated History in War and Peace.* For most readers these have long been considered not just the most comprehensive and accurate books but the place to begin. Much later, Allen continued with *Covered Bridges of the South* and *Covered Bridges of the Middle West,* both published in 1970 but reflecting less research and experience than the first two. Apparently, Allen had intended to do a book on bridges in the west until he learned of Kramer A. Adams' *Covered Bridges of the West*, in 1963, then in press.

Other societies dedicated to the study and preservation of covered bridges were founded as well, including the Ohio Covered Bridge Committee, Connecticut River Valley Covered Bridge Society, Southern Ohio Covered Bridge Association, Northern Ohio Covered Bridge Society, Theodore Burr Covered Bridge Society, and Indiana Covered Bridge Society, among others. Exceptionally, the Southern Ohio Covered Bridge Association (now the Ohio Historic Bridge Association), was specially formed in order to purchase a bypassed bridge near Zanesville, Ohio, the Salt Creek Bridge, in 1960, and it continues to hold pot-luck picnics there each July.

Most societies published newsletters or modest magazines, and books, both light and serious, proliferated as interest in the topic increased. While members of the general public were becoming more interested, those responsible for maintaining the nation's covered bridges, however, still showed far less concern. Most commissioners and engineers at both state and county levels viewed covered bridges as nuisances, if not safety hazards, with charm only matched by that of their old rusted out iron bridges. Weight limits and clearance restrictions put nearly all covered bridges in the categories of "inadequate" or "obsolete." Some officials dealt with the problem through "benign neglect." In addition to the many losses to "progress," others were lost to natural events, arson, and inundation as an increasing number of reservoirs were built.

Although once the standard type of bridge in the United States, covered bridges were becoming relatively rare by World War II and, in fact, soon disappeared completely from several states. Even as covered bridges were removed at an alarming rate and others simply disintegrated, it is ironic that builders in Oregon, Québec, and New Brunswick continued to construct covered bridges. The "Lost Bridges" project (www.lostbridges.org), spearheaded by Trish Kane and Bill Caswell, has so far documented nearly 15,000 covered bridges past and present in the United States and Canada. By 1959, there were only 1,344 covered bridges still standing in the United States, and this number declined to 852 by 1989. Figures for Canada were not

Above The Southern Ohio Covered Bridge Association was founded in 1960 specifically to own and preserve the bypassed Johnson's Mill or Salt Creek Bridge in Muskingum County. Today, the society continues as the Ohio Historic Bridge Association and continues its tradition of a pot-luck dinner at the bridge each July. (Terry E. Miller, 2009)

OFFICIAL MAGAZINE *for the* NATIONAL SOCIETY *for the* PRESERVATION *of* COVERED BRIDGES, INC.

------A NON-PROFIT EDUCATIONAL ORGANIZATION------
BOSTON, MASS.   WINTER 2013   VOL. LXXI, NO. 1

RED RUN BRIDGE was still open to traffic when Herbert Richter visited on January 18, 1959 (38-36-10). See more old photos from Lancaster County, Pennsylvania inside this magazine.

Left Founded in 1943 by Richard Sanders Allen, *Covered Bridge Topics*, the quarterly publication of the National Society for the Preservation of Covered Bridges, began as a newsletter. It continues today under the editorship of Joseph D. Conwill, one of the nation's top authorities on covered bridges. (NSPCB)

Above from left A railroad spur that led to coal mines at Goshen, Ohio, crossed the Tuscarawas River through what began as a covered three-span Howe truss bridge, but a combination of ice damage and minor vandalism caused the bridge to be stripped in 1904. During the March 1913 flood, the middle span collapsed and was swept away. The remaining two spans were later dismantled. (Terry E. Miller Collection, courtesy Ernie Gibbs)

The third Columbia-Wrightsville Bridge crossing the Susquehanna River near Harrisburg, Pennsylvania, was built after the second bridge was burned during the Civil War. Constructed by the Pennsylvania Railroad, it combined passage for both wagons and trains. On September 30, 1896, a tornado destroyed the mile-long structure within a few minutes. (NSPCB Archives, R. S. Allen Collection)

reliable until 1989 when there were 177 bridges left. Since then, the number has declined at a slower rate, but counting "authentic" bridges has now become much more problematic as historical bridges are "refurbished" to the point of replication, and a few lost bridges have actually been resurrected. The latest *World Guide* (2009) lists 814 (not including 6 in storage) for the United States and 154 for Canada.

On the Deaths of Covered Bridges

Buddhism teaches that everything about life is impermanent. Besides our own bodies, few manifestations of material existence demonstrate impermanence better than covered bridges. Houses sit safely on dry land. The oldest mission churches in the United States date to the 1520s and the oldest houses to the 1630s, but the oldest wooden covered bridge in the United States dates only to 1825 and stands near Springfield, New York, in Otsego County. The majority were built much later and often as replacements for earlier spans. Their placement could not be more vulnerable: overflowing water, carrying rail or vehicular traffic, perched on stacks of stones next to loose-soiled banks, or on piers sitting within moving water.

There are many ways for a covered bridge to die. Some are natural—flood, ice, wind/tornado, deterioration and failure, lightning strike followed by fire—and others are unnatural—dismantlement, arson, war, overloading, dynamite, and inundation, among others. Until approximately 1990, most bridges experienced something akin to "Christian death," which is final, but in recent years more and more have undergone something comparable to Buddhism's teaching of "reincarnation," that is, "birth, death, and rebirth," or, to return to the Christian metaphor, have been "born again." Some question the value of what might be called the cloning of lost bridges because this raises ethical questions concerning authenticity and historical value.

Natural Endings

FLOODS AND STORMS The greatest natural enemy of covered bridges flows beneath each and every bridge—water. Water is life-giving and humans cannot survive without it. That is why humans have preferred to settle along waterways with roads weaving across streams via various means such as fords, ferries, and bridges. Too little water results in thirst and drought but too much results in flooding. Both are hazardous to human health and life, but only the latter can be fatal to bridges, not to mention roads and nearby buildings. Flooding most commonly occurs in the spring following a winter of heavy snow followed by a sudden warming that leads to flash floods. If the river still has ice floes, these can pile up and crash into a bridge.

Some floods result from low pressure systems that park themselves over an area and dump unusual amounts of rain, which leads to flash flooding. In several famous cases, dams or levees burst, resulting in sudden massive floods and loss of life. And covered bridges are easy targets. Rarely is there anything other than gravity to keep them in place. The solidly boarded sides block the water from flowing through, turning the bridge into an unsecured dam with no resistance. As a result of several disastrous floods in the first half of the twentieth century, governments at various levels invested great sums of money in flood control systems, including both the construction of dams and reservoirs to trap the extra water, but even today flash flooding can overwhelm these systems and lead to downstream disasters. Ironically, the dams designed to prevent flooding often inundated areas with covered bridges.

Although data on the loss of covered bridges during particular floods is random, no doubt certain historical floods, particularly those in the eastern states, were devastating. Flooding was a fact of life during the nineteenth century, and bridges, some only a few years old, were routinely swept away. Many were replaced by new—or less commonly, salvaged—covered bridges.

Left First built in 1849–50 for the Claremont and Concord Railroad, the bridge at Contocook over the Contocook River was thoroughly reconstructed in 1889. The bridge was washed off its abutments twice, in 1936 (photo) and 1938, but because the rails were bolted together, it stayed put. After each disaster, engineers righted the bridge, and today it is a state landmark long retired from service. (NSPCB Archives, R. S. Allen Collection)

The most famous nineteenth-century flood was the unprecedented Johnstown Flood in southwestern Pennsylvania. On May 31, 1889, the South Fork Dam, 14 miles upriver from the city, holding back a pleasure reservoir built for Pittsburgh's rich families, burst. This unleashed a rolling and thunderous wall of water that effectively devastated the city without warning, killing 2,200 people, and spreading devastation far downstream. Virtually all bridges on the rivers and streams around Johnstown were destroyed. Jackson's Mill Bridge in Bedford County, Pennsylvania, was washed out intact and deposited about 200 yards downstream before being relocated on new abutments nearby where it sits today.

To illustrate the problem, consider the frustration experienced by the Coshocton County Commissioners in Ohio when they lost two (or perhaps even three) bridges in a single flash flood in February, 1884. E. B. Henderson had just completed building a new Howe truss bridge 164 feet long at Linton Mills in March, 1883. The *Coshocton Age* reported on February 16, 1884, that Wills Creek was 30 feet above normal and that "the bridge one mile above Linton at Jim Miskimen's Mill and the mill floated off their foundations against the new bridge at Linton and all landed in a field one mile below town" (Miller, 2009: 146).

Three Ohio floods during the first half of the twentieth century were particularly devastating for covered bridges and resulted in hundreds of losses. Perhaps the worst was the flood of March 23–27, 1913, when 6–11 inches of rain inundated extensive areas of the state, destroying most roads, thousands of bridges, and killing 467 people. Urban areas, including the major cities, were severely flooded. Reports indicate that upwards of 40,000 homes were destroyed. Fourteen square miles of Dayton were flooded by the Great Miami River, with water 10 inches deep in the streets. The Scioto River flooded Columbus, the state capital, and the Muskingum River at Zanesville was 27 feet

above flood stage, with water 20 feet deep in the city's streets. Zanesville's famous Y-Bridge, which had been a wooden covered bridge until 1900 before being replaced by a concrete bridge, entirely disappeared from view. In Akron, the normally small Cuyahoga River reached flood stage, but when seven locks on the Ohio and Erie Canal had to be dynamited to relieve pressure, the situation became a crisis. Indeed, the extensive canal system in Ohio, already losing out to railroads, was

Left The Rinard Bridge over the flood-prone Little Muskingum River in Washington County, Ohio, was built in 1876 after the first bridge from 1871 was flooded out. The present bridge was floated off its abutments in 1913, 1938, and 2004, always intact, but a second flood in 2004 wrecked the bridge. Fortunately, the trusses could be salvaged and the bridge rebuilt with original timbers. (Gregory S. Hamilton)

Below Hoosick, New York, once had two bridges, the Whitehouse Bridge over the Hoosic River [river and town spellings differ] and the Little Hoosick Bridge over an overflow area nearby. After the larger bridge was razed in 1933 when SR 7 was relocated, the Little Hoosick Bridge was abandoned. A hurricane in September 1938 floated the bridge into a nearby field. (NSPCB Archives, R. S. Allen Collection)

AS THE INDIAN MILL BRIDGE NOW LOOKS AFTER THE FLOOD OF MAR. 25-1913

destroyed, effectively ending the canal era. During this flood, bridges of all sorts—covered, open, iron, concrete—were carried away or wrecked. After this, it was usually assumed that any bridges which survived the 1913 Flood could survive just about anything. Unfortunately, that was not always true. To avoid floods of this scope in the future, the state began building a system of dams and reservoirs in western Ohio called the Miami Conservancy District. Eastern Ohio did not get this form of relief until later.

Vermont's most devastating flood began on November 2, 1927, when between 4 and 9 inches of rain began falling over several days. This amount was only a problem because October had been one of the wettest on record, with up to three times normal rainfall, leaving the soil saturated and the creeks and rivers full, though not flooded. While central Vermont was most affected, flooding occurred throughout the state. Besides destruction of innumerable houses, farm buildings, factories, roads, and commercial properties, 84 people died and some 1,285 bridges were lost, perhaps 200 of them covered. Damage to rail lines and their many wooden bridges, covered or not, was extensive.

A third major flood that destroyed numerous covered bridges occurred in Ohio and Pennsylvania starting on March 17, 1936. Known as the Pittsburgh Flood or the Great St. Patrick's Day Flood, the heavy rains coming on the heels of the wettest period in the region's history and following a sudden melting of the snow and ice, devastated cities along the Ohio River from Pittsburgh south past Cincinnati, as well as many areas on the river's tributaries. Some 150 people died and the river was 21 feet above flood stage in Pittsburgh. Following this flood, the Muskingum Conservancy District was established in eastern Ohio to build dams and reservoirs on the major tributaries of the Ohio River. Unfortunately, these reservoirs, as well as those in western Ohio, also led to the destruction of many covered bridges unluckily within the basins of the newly formed lakes.

Less common but often even more devastating have been floods brought about by hurricanes sweeping up the east coast and into the Mid-Atlantic states and even into New England. Hurricane Agnes, in June 1972, brought incredible destruction to places such as Ohio and Pennsylvania and resulted in the destruction of at least thirty covered bridges, hitting the central Pennsylvania counties of Lancaster and Dauphin especially hard. Dauphin County, which surrounds Harrisburg, then had eight covered bridges, all in top condition, but only one survived. Elsewhere, some bridges remained intact after floating off their abutments and were rebuilt. Others were completely wrecked.

Hurricane Agnes even reached into central Ohio, washing out the Doughty Creek Bridge north of Coshocton but leaving it somewhat intact on the embankment. Eventually, a local Amishman was employed to dismantle the bridge and move the parts to Roscoe Village near Coshocton, but he took his instructions to get rid of "bad timber" too seriously and discarded most of the timbers. More unusual was a flood in central Indiana in June, 1957, caused by Hurricane Audrey, which dumped seven inches of rain, destroying five covered bridges, including Indiana's longest bridge.

Tropical Storm Irene, coming during the Internet age with its instant news, devastated the entire eastern seaboard from North Carolina to Maine from August 27 to 29, 2011. The hardest hit areas with vulnerable covered bridges were in eastern New York and most of Vermont, especially the southern half. Several historical bridges were lost, including the longest single-span covered bridge in North America, at Blenheim, New York. Numerous bridges were damaged, some superficially, some significantly.

Left The Rainbow Bridge at Boscawen, New Hampshire, was built by Horace Childs in 1857 using a McCallum truss, both facts unusual because Childs had patented his own truss in 1846 and McCallum trusses were normally used only for rail bridges. All came to naught during the flood of 1907. (NSPCB Archives, R. S. Allen Collection)

Left The original Bartonsville Bridge over the William's River at Rockingham, Vermont, was built in 1870 by Sanford Granger. The video of its destruction by Hurricane Irene's flooding on August 28, 2011, was seen nationally. Subsequently, the bridge was rebuilt of all new material in 2012 using modern construction methods, including the lifting of complete trusses into position. (Susan Hammond)

Below Blenheim, New York's splendid double-lane Long truss bridge over Schoharie Creek, which was built in 1855 by Nichols M. Powers—and usually considered the longest single-span covered bridge remaining—was lost to the torrent on August 28, 2011, after the remnants of Hurricane Irene devastated parts of New York and Vermont. This photo was taken shortly before the bridge floated away and crashed against bridges downstream. (Shirley Felter)

WIND Just as the sides of a covered bridge act like a dam in the case of high water, they become like a sail in the event of straight line winds. Yet, while wind damage is far less frequent than is flooding, it is potentially devastating. One noteworthy example occurred on September 30, 1896, when a hurricane, then commonly called a cyclone, destroyed the third Columbia-Wrightsville wooden covered bridge over the Susquehanna River in Pennsylvania, the one built in

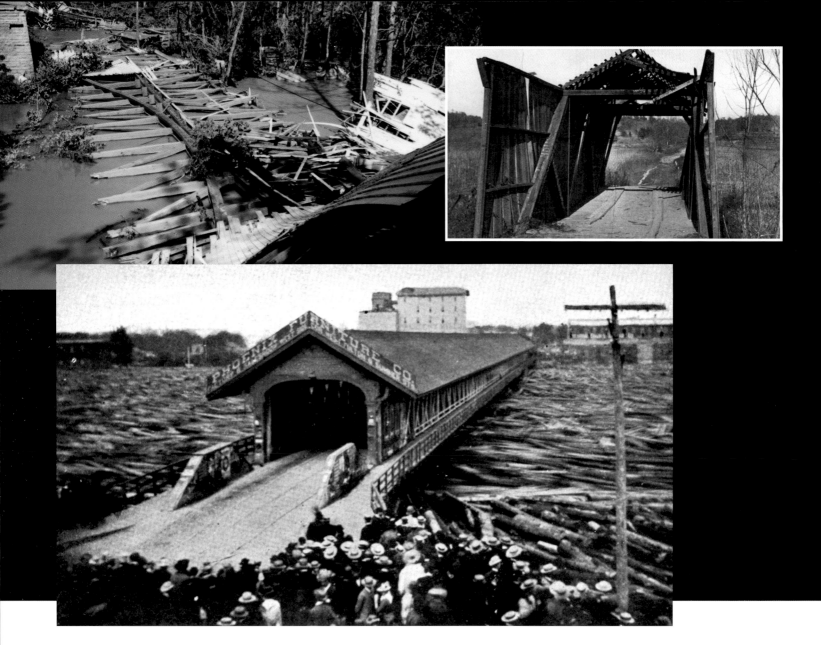

1868 to replace the second one, burned during the Civil
War. Ironically, the two iron spans built in the center as
a fire break were the only two to survive, the rest blown
to smithereens (Wilson, 1977: 4).

Tornadoes are destructive no matter how strong
the bridge is or the angle. If the vortex comes its way,
all wooden structures are helpless in the face of the
destructive funnel. Whereas straight line winds strike a
general area, tornadoes assault the unlucky, sometimes
turning one house into kindling and leaving the one
next door intact. When an EF3 tornado hit the village
of Moscow, Indiana, on June 3, 2008, it did not level
the village but destroyed only the homes of the
unfortunate. The unluckiest structure during this
weather event was the great two-span covered bridge
built by the Kennedy family in 1886. While the bridge
was torn to shreds and laid forlorn on the riverbed,
the house next to it was spared. The full story of the
resurrection of the Moscow Bridge is told later, in
Chapter 6, featuring specific bridges.

Little discussed is the relationship of covered bridges
to the environment. During the nineteenth century, the
demand for wood to build houses, furniture, ships, and
rail or highway bridges was enormous. The virgin

forests of many states from Michigan through New
England were virtually clear-cut. We cannot say with
certainty whether this clear-cutting contributed to
increased flooding, which in turn destroyed wooden
bridges that then had to be rebuilt. However, we know
that during this time many *miles* of wooden bridges
were built. Indeed, there were three covered bridges
constructed in succession over the Susquehanna
between Columbia and Wrightsville, each more than a
mile long, the first built from 1812 to 1814 and flooded
out in 1832, the second built from 1832 to 1834 and
burned during the Civil War, and the third lasting from
1868 to 1896. Hundreds of multi-span bridges crossed
the many major rivers of the east, and many had to be
rebuilt numerous times after loss to flooding or fire.

We gain some understanding of the amount of
timber being cut from Michigan's "Grand Jam of 1883,"
perhaps the worst log jam in our history. After weeks
of heavy rain during June and July, the Grand River
flooded to the point that the booms used to control
floating logs were overwhelmed, and millions of logs
broke loose jamming the river for 47 miles. The moving
wall of tree trunks destroyed numerous bridges, both
rail and highway, though it spared Saginaw's covered

bridge. It took hundreds of heroic "river hogs" (log men) the rest of the summer to sort out an estimated 28,000 miles of logs (if placed end to end). And this was just one year's timber harvest.

How will climate change resulting from global warming affect covered bridges? If predictions that rain will be more plentiful come true, then covered bridges will be even more vulnerable to flooding than in the past. The North Atlantic Oscillation (NAO), a natural phenomenon that affects weather up and down the eastern seaboard, has been in a "wet mode" since about 1970, bringing extra rain to New England. If the soil is dry when that happens, it is absorbed, but if saturated—as it was before Tropical Storm Irene in 2011—the rainwater runs off rapidly into the creeks and causes flooding. Scientists predict that global warming will maintain the wet NAO indefinitely, bringing with it continuously greater chances for severe flooding.

DETERIORATION, ABANDONMENT, AND FAILURE
Covered bridges are made of wood, an organic material subject to deterioration, particularly from moisture, insects, and the stress of being compressed or stretched. While leaving a wooden trussed bridge uncovered virtually guarantees its demise within ten years—and often sooner—covering it with a roof and siding, while beneficial and effective, only guarantees longevity up to a point. It is possible to keep out most moisture, but it is difficult to defeat the insects and impossible to avoid stress, since bridges by definition carry live loads in addition to supporting their own dead weight. While most covered bridges are fully protected with a roof and siding, there may be windows, both single or extended, to offer better lighting or permit motorists to see oncoming vehicles. Though the joints remain sheltered, wind often blows both rain and snow inside. Moreover, if the roof is not maintained, holes develop, permitting water to penetrate the interior. Many counties fight losing battles with fishermen and swimmers who knock off siding to gain access to the water. To forestall this, a few counties and towns have resorted to wrapping wire around all the siding from end to end.

Deterioration is guaranteed when a covered bridge is abandoned, either because the road has been closed or because the old bridge was bypassed. Unless the government or an organization continues maintaining the bridge, it gradually falls into disrepair, rots, and

Above Much of southeastern Ohio's Morgan County was strip mined in the 1950s, sometimes isolating now-abandoned covered bridges that once carried local traffic. Eventually, such bridges either collapsed or were destroyed when mining encompassed their locations. (Terry E. Miller, 1960)

Right upper and lower Washington County, Pennsylvania, once had a great number of modest spans of either kingpost or queenpost construction. In 1958, the state stripped the Montgomery Bridge (upper) of everything but its basic truss before removing it about 1962 (Terry E. Miller, 1961), while the Doc Hanlin Bridge, stripped of siding by vandals, simply rotted away on an abandoned road. (Terry E. Miller, 1963)

Right By the early 1960s, this unnamed bridge over Stony Creek in Somerset County, Pennsylvania, was long abandoned, stripped of siding, and dangerous to cross. Eventually it collapsed. (Terry E. Miller, 1961)

finally is either removed or collapses into the creek one dark winter night with snow weighing down what remains of the roof. Intrepid (and foolish) bridge enthusiasts have been known to risk their lives measuring, photographing, or merely walking through long abandoned bridges.

While builders came to understand stress analysis more and more during the nineteenth century, before that builders mostly learned from trial and error. Sometimes to demonstrate a new bridge's strength, they would load it with vehicles or animals. While we are not aware of stories of new bridges collapsing in such circumstances, a great many old photos attest to failures during service, particularly for rail bridges. A bridge can collapse in either of two ways: 1) failure of the deck while leaving the trusses intact, and 2) failure of the trusses. In the first case, when the deck fails and the load falls through, the bridge can usually be salvaged. In the second case, the bridge is effectively destroyed. We are reminded of how trusses make use of triangles, that triangles are rigid as long as the sides do not change, but that is exactly what happens when an overload breaks sections of the triangles.

A few examples illustrate how circumstances can lead to failure. In June, 1870, a bridge over the Miller River on the Vermont and Massachusetts Railroad at Athol, Massachusetts, was damaged when an approaching train struck a hand-car on the line, hurling it and its occupants off the track and then derailing inside the bridge, probably from hitting a tool thrown onto the tracks. The unusual stresses resulted in the locomotive falling through into the creek. A more famous accident occurred at Lebanon, New Hampshire, on the Northern Railroad of New Hampshire in 1883 when "mischievous" boys loosened the turnbuckles, a screw-like device for adjusting tension, on the rods needed to secure the bridge since it followed a curve. A passenger train initially passed through, causing the

Far left By 1993, six years before its complete restoration in 1999, the Adams Mill Bridge in Carroll County, Indiana, was in desperate condition and closed to traffic. Although on a public road, the county permitted the bridge to deteriorate and vandals knocked off the siding. (Terry E. Miller, 1993)

Left upper and lower Thanks to youthful vandalism, a train led by the freight engine Atlantic jumped the tracks inside the Chandler Railroad Bridge at Lebanon, New Hampshire, in 1890, causing the rare Childs truss span to collapse. Workers burned the remains and had a new trestle in place within eleven hours. (NSPCB Archives, R. S. Allen Collection)

bridge to shake violently, but the train made it to the station. Then a heavy freight train led by the line's biggest engine, the "Atlantic," entered the insecure bridge, and although the engine made it out the other end, the bridge broke in the middle and collapsed into the creek. After pulling the train out, the railroad burned the bridge and had a new trestle up, reportedly, within eleven hours (Allen, 1957: 45).

The *New York Times* on August 10, 1871 reported "Railway Disaster. A Train on the Maine Central Breaks Down a Bridge." On the evening of August 9, a Maine Central passenger train running late and trying to make up time passed over a covered Howe Truss deck bridge that spanned Hampden Road in Bangor, known as the Tin Bridge. Though the engine and tender along with most of the mail car made it across, the bridge collapsed under the smoking car and three passenger cars, while leaving the Pullman car at the rear on the track. Two people died and thirty were injured. Officials already knew the bridge had advanced dry rot and had brought replacement timbers to the site, but, alas, too late.

For highway bridges, the main nemesis in the past was the steam tractor, and stories abound of these monstrously heavy engines breaking through bridge decks. The two-span bridge over One Leg Creek, now Conotton Creek, at New Cumberland, Ohio, built by Jordan Hall Banks in 1870, was the scene of such an accident about 1901 when Samuel Rennecker's steam traction engine fell through the floor into the creek after the cleats clawed up the floorboards. The engineer, Jack Smith, was pinned beneath the timbers and badly hurt. To avoid such disasters in the future, Banks built a new floor laid parallel to the trusses.

During the twentieth century, covered bridges carried ever larger cars and trucks. As the century progressed, vehicles got heavier as the bridges got older and weaker. Few bridges posted weight limits over three or four tons, and drivers routinely ignored both weight limits and height restrictions. There are numerous stories of floors giving way, usually dumping a truck into the creek. In such cases, the bridge usually could be salvaged, but county engineers more commonly used the accident as an excuse to replace the entire structure. If the whole structure failed, then there was no choice.

Left "Railroad Accident at Bangor, Maine, August 9, 1871" shows a derailment that brought down at least one of the Howe truss deck spans. (A. K. Dole, in New York Public Library Digital Library G89F156 008F)

This was the case for the Blacklick Bridge east of Columbus, Ohio, in September 1977, when a construction truck carrying seventeen tons of gravel attempted to cross the old bridge, which had been posted for fewer than five tons. The trusses buckled, and the truck crashed into the shallow creek along with the bridge.

Unnatural Endings

REMOVAL Before covered bridges triumphantly became nostalgic icons, they were only utilitarian objects used to transport vehicles across rivers and simply dispensed with when they had become, at least in the eyes of the officials and engineers, obsolete, if not a menace. The Conesville Bridge in Coshocton County, Ohio, a massive structure over 400 feet in length built by the Smith Bridge Company in 1876, had become the subject of endless complaints by local residents in the 1950s because it did not meet their needs. Large trucks (including fire trucks) and school buses, for example, could not cross, and, as a consequence, local people petitioned for a new bridge. Although the old structure could easily have been bypassed, it was not—and of course, there was no one to care of it. On August 6, 1958, county employees poured 150 gallons of kerosene on the bridge and set it on fire. In just 40 minutes, the entire structure was nothing but red embers lying in the Muskingum River. Progress. Most people rejoiced at the prospects for a new bridge.

Pennsylvania still had well over 300 covered bridges in 1960. Many were owned by the state, mostly on the old five-digit "state aid" roads that served rural areas, what would be "county roads" in many other states. A booklet published in 1960 by the Pennsylvania Department of Highways titled *Pennsylvania's Challenge: Too Many Hazardous Bridges*, had on its cover a photo showing students forced to walk through an old 3.5 ton load limit covered bridge to re-enter their school bus that could not drive through with them in it.

The brief text and numerous captioned photos highlight "4439 hazardous bridges" including 118 covered bridges, virtually every such bridge owned by the state. Richard Sanders Allen, writing in 1959, warned against this trend: "Pennsylvania's vast state highway system is responsible for maintaining more than a hundred covered bridges. For these the future is bleak. The highway department sees only to repairs that are absolutely necessary, and makes no bones about desiring to tear down these spans as soon as funds are appropriated to replace them. Any bridge posted for less than 15 tons of weight and 14 feet clearance in height is already on the drafting boards to be replaced in the state's long-range plan. The target date for completing the program has been set as 1962, but it appears improbable that all the one hundred and twenty bridges owned by the state will have replacements by then. Officially, though, they are on borrowed time, and any photographer of covered bridges who plans to visit the Keystone Commonwealth would do best to corral the state bridges first" (p. 101).

Many of these bridges were still in excellent condition and capable of carrying the loads required of them automatically disqualified nonetheless. In some areas, such as in Greene County, the state simply stopped maintaining the bridges until they reached a point of deterioration that made replacement obligatory. Over the next ten or so years, the state actually did carry out these replacements, removing most state-owned covered bridges regardless of condition or degree of use.

A few counties in the United States made decisions to preserve their covered bridges as a tourist attraction early enough to save the majority of their surviving bridges. Parke County, Indiana, which today hyperbolically proclaims itself to be the "Covered Bridge Capital of the World" with its 31 remaining covered bridges, began to hold an annual covered bridge festival in 1957, the first one lasting only three days. Today, their ten-day October festival is said to be attended by some two million people. Ashtabula County, Ohio, though it lost a number of bridges during mid-century, started a festival in October, 1983. Because Ashtabula identifies itself today as Ohio's premier covered bridge county, it has continued building new covered bridges, most neo-traditional but one in historical style. In addition to self-guided driving tours with docents at some of the bridges, the festivals include parades, crafts, music, souvenirs, contests of all sorts, and food stalls, lots of food stalls. Vendors sell covered bridge memorabilia, including calendars, towels, magnets, mugs, paperweights, spoons, sweatshirts, T-shirts, aprons, among other "collectibles."

Other counties, unfortunately, made decisions that eliminated any possibility for a festival. In 1960, Noble County, Ohio, in the underdeveloped southeast quadrant of the state, had nearly 30 covered bridges, but today has not one authentic bridge remaining. A 44-foot span perched today on a hill above the fairgrounds in Caldwell consists of parts from more than one historical bridge, a pseudo-replica. Two other covered bridges, Manchester and Parrish, both in isolated areas of the county, had been safely bypassed but were then discarded, and replicas built nearby. Fairfield County, Ohio, had well over 35 bridges in 1960. Sixteen remain in the county and several were moved outside the county, but of these only four sit in their original locations, the rest having been moved to parks and private property. None is open to road traffic.

Greene County, Pennsylvania, south of Pittsburgh, had around 30 bridges in 1960. Today, there are only seven, and two of these are considered "rebuilt," meaning replacement of the majority of their original timbers. The state allowed quite of few of their covered bridges to deteriorate to the point of ruin. In some cases, roofs were deliberately removed to speed up deterioration. Perhaps the local attitude was best expressed by a county worker at a bridge visited by Miller in the 1980s: "You wouldn't be so enthusiastic about these if you had to work on them."

How do you execute a covered bridge? The easiest way is to douse it with gasoline and set it ablaze. Burning, unfortunately, leads to large sections of the bridge falling into the river, with the debris obstructing the waterway. In some cases, bulldozers simply push a bridge down into the creek where it is either burned or pulled out for wrecking and disposal. Sometimes the bridge is actually stripped of siding and roof and the trusses dismantled for salvage.

Occasionally, bridges are carefully marked and dismantled for later rebuilding. Indeed, this happened even in the nineteenth century, either to salvage the bridge for another location or return it to its original location following a flood. But sometimes failure to follow through trumped good intentions. The city of Waynesburg, Pennsylvania, once had a 32-foot long kingpost bridge on a neighborhood street. When the county decided to replace it sometime in the 1960s, the bridge was marked and dismantled for reassembly in a town park. There its parts sat for some years until they became too deteriorated for reassembly, and the bridge was simply forgotten.

The magnificent Freedom Bridge over the West Fork of the White River at Freedom, Indiana, 324 feet long from end to end in two spans, built in 1882 by

PENNSYLVANIA'S CHALLENGE

TOO MANY HAZARDOUS BRIDGES

J. J. Daniels, was recognized as an architectural gem by material-culture folklorists at Indiana University in the 1960s. The university planned to build "Hoosier Village" on the campus in Bloomington, combining numerous old homes, mills, and other structures, including the Freedom Bridge, into a "village" reflecting all of Indiana. When a crane attempted to lift the first of the spans from its abutments for movement to dry land and dismantling in 1966, the structure crumbled, falling into a pile of debris. Removal of the second span was successful, and the bridge parts were moved to the site at the university. For years they sat partially covered in a field, exposed to the elements. Because funding for Hoosier Village never materialized, the bridge parts simply rotted away, and nothing came of the project.

In 1897, Pearly Weaver, then only twenty-four, built a modest 40-foot queenpost bridge on the farm of Captain James H. Russell in Parke County, Indiana, who is said to have wanted the bridge built so his body could be carried through it—and not through the stream—

Top The Smith Bridge Company of Toledo, Ohio, built the 404-foot-long Conesville (Ohio) Bridge over the Muskingum River in 1876, and for many years it was the longest covered bridge in Ohio. On August 6, 1958, county employees doused the structure with 150 gallons of kerosene and lit a match, making way for a new bridge deemed safe for school buses. (Becky Stockum)

Above In 1960, the Pennsylvania Department of Highways published a short book detailing their plans to replace "4439 hazardous bridges," including virtually all covered bridges owned by the state. (Terry E. Miller Collection)

when he died. Later, Ralph Jordan bought the farm and bridge, and in the fall of 1970 moved the bridge to dry ground near his home where it served as a sort of barn. At some point, Jordan decided to sell the bridge for $5,000, but after someone told him the bridge was valuable, he raised the price to $55,000. No one purchased the bridge, and eventually it was torn down.

War

The Civil War (1860–5) was undoubtedly the most devastating war—physically, morally, and spiritually—in America's history. Burning bridges was a common aspect of the general devastation. Richard Sanders Allen wrote a fascinating chapter titled "Battles and Burning Bridges" in his 1959 *Covered Bridges of the Middle Atlantic States*, offering stories, among others, of the destruction of Wernwag's great covered bridge at Harpers Ferry, then between Virginia and Maryland and therefore contested territory. The Philippi Covered Bridge, still standing over the Tygart River and West Virginia's oldest covered bridge, was used by both Confederate and Union forces as barracks. While Confederate forces planned to burn the bridge, the bridge was not harmed.

The most notorious Civil War bridge burning, however, was a massive case of shooting oneself in the

foot. There had been a succession of covered bridges over the "mile wide and inch deep" Susquehanna River between Columbia and Wrightsville, Pennsylvania, each deserving the title "longest covered bridge in the world." Both George Sheldon (2006) and Scott L. Mingus Sr (2011) have researched this incident in depth. The site has had a checkered history, with a succession of six bridges built from 1812 through 1972, three of them covered. The first, built between 1812 and 1814 in 55 spans, was 5,620 feet long, more than a mile, but only lasted until 1832 when ice jams and high water destroyed it. The second bridge was built with private

funds between 1832 and 1834 in 28 spans and included a passage for carriages, a rail line, a walkway, and double-decker towpaths for canal boats. Teams of mules and horses were employed to pull rail cars across this multiple-use bridge because of the fear of fire if locomotives were used. In June of 1863, a Confederate force under Gen. John B. Gordon threatened an invasion through the bridge. Since it was feared that if the Confederate Army crossed the river through the bridge they would advance on Philadelphia, officers chose a surprising tactic. Union bridge guards under Col. J. G. Frick of the 27th Pennsylvania Volunteers retreated through the bridge, and in order to block the advancing Confederate troops decided to burn the bridge, setting fire to both ends. As the bridge burned, the Union Army celebrated what was a pyrrhic success at a devastating cost, while the citizens of the area lost their only means of travel over the great river. In spite of the Army's debatable maneuver, the owners were unsuccessful in obtaining restitution from Congress after the war. This bridge was subsequently replaced by the third bridge, also covered, in 1868. Its demise, noted earlier, resulted from a freak hurricane on September 30, 1896. Today, US 30 crosses the sixth bridge, built of concrete and steel in 1969.

Perhaps the most devastating losses in the North were inflicted by Confederate Brigadier General John Hunt Morgan and 2,460 men under his command in daring raids in Indiana and Ohio from July 8, 1863, until the last remnants surrendered on July 26 in Ohio's Columbiana County. Since his mission was to inflict damage and terrorize the population, Morgan's raiders burned great numbers of homes, businesses, and some thirty-four bridges, both rail and highway, most of them covered. While the raid was successful in causing numerous deaths and extensive damage, in the end most of the raiders were captured or killed. Morgan was taken to the Ohio Penitentiary in Columbus but escaped through a tunnel and returned to the South, resuming fighting until he was killed in battle a year later.

The most notorious campaign of the war for the South was Union General William Tecumseh Sherman's Savannah Campaign, popularly known as "Sherman's March to the Sea," which took place from November 15

to December 21, 1864. Previously Sherman's army had marched to Atlanta, not just capturing but destroying much of it as well. As Sherman's army marched towards Savannah and the coast, they pursued a "scorched earth" policy of living off the land and destroying any and all infrastructure that might contribute to the Confederate war effort. Sherman's Field Order #120 of November 9, 1864, included: "V. To army corps commanders alone is entrusted the power to destroy mills, houses, cotton-gins, &c., and for them this general principle is laid down: In districts and neighborhoods where the army is unmolested no destruction of such property should be permitted; but should guerrillas or bushwhackers molest our march, or should the inhabitants burn bridges, obstruct roads, or otherwise manifest local hostility, then army commanders should order and enforce a devastation more or less relentless according to the measure of such hostility" (1875: 651–3).

We can surmise, then, that most bridges Sherman encountered were burned, including a great number built by Georgia's famous builder, Horace King (1807–85), the only known African-American in the bridge business. Among them, Sherman burned Moore's Bridge over the Chattahoochee between Newnan and Carrollton in 1864. Later, in April, 1865, General James Wilson attacked Columbus and burned all of the many

Below In June 1863, to prevent Confederate Gen. John B. Gordon from crossing the mile-plus long Columbia-Wrightsville [PA] bridge over the Susquehanna and advancing on Philadelphia, Union officer Col. J. G. Frick ordered the bridge burned. (Bradley Schmehl)

THE UNION   versus   SECESSION,
the Union Builds Bridges.   and   Secession Destroys Them.

bridges King had built in that area. Later, when Sherman continued roaming the South and took his army to Cheraw, South Carolina, while pursuing General William J. Hardee, the latter ordered his troops to burn the great bridge over the Pee Dee River built in 1823 under the direction of Ithiel Town and with King's early involvement. Following the war, King replaced many of the bridges lost.

Long before the Civil War, a covered bridge was heavily damaged in Cleveland, (then called "Cleaveland"), Ohio's 1837 "bridge war" with Ohio City. Separated by the Cuyahoga River near its mouth, the two small towns were at first connected by only one bridge, a floating structure built in 1822. It was not until 1835 that a fixed bridge was constructed by James S. Clark, who built a two-span covered bridge on Columbus Street (now Columbus Road) just south of Detroit Avenue. Costing a total of $15,000, the privately built toll bridge was 200 feet long, 33 feet wide, and about 24 feet high. Because the navigable Cuyahoga was so important to the commerce of the city, the two spans were separated by a drawspan long enough to permit a vessel of 49 feet beam to pass through. A year later, Clark turned the bridge over to the City of Cleveland.

By 1836, the rivalry between the two villages had become heated. Clevelanders were irked because new arrivals preferred to do their trading in Ohio City, which was growing rapidly. On the other hand, Ohio City residents became angry as they saw many of their long-time residents taking their trade to Cleveland over the Columbus Street Bridge (CSB), which was now owned by Cleveland and had become free of tolls. In protest, Ohio City residents boycotted the CSB and used the old floating bridge further upstream at Main Street. The Cleveland Council, however, retaliated in 1837 by removing the eastern end of the floating bridge in spite of an injunction which came too late to prevent it.

In Ohio City the citizens were enraged at being forced to use the CSB. Under the slogan "Two bridges or none," all able-bodied men prepared for war. The Ohio City Council ruled that the CSB was a public nuisance, demanding immediate action. During the night of October 27, the marshall and his deputies tried to blow up the west pier and abutment with gunpowder. The attempted sabotage damaged but did not destroy the span. Others dug deep ditches near the approaches on either end, blocking all traffic. Under the leadership of C. L. Russell, an Ohio City attorney, and with the public blessing of a Presbyterian clergyman, a mob armed with axes, crowbars, clubs, stones, and guns descended on the bridge to destroy it.

When news of the mob reached Cleveland, Mayor Willey led the militia and a mob armed with an old 4th of July cannon to the bridge. A free-for-all soon followed during which the bridge was heavily damaged, much of its flooring ripped up, and the drawspan destroyed. Before the county sheriff and Cleveland marshal arrived to stop the battle, men on both sides were wounded, three of them seriously. The cannon could not be used because Deacon House of Ohio City bravely spiked it with an old file. On October 29, the Cleveland Council ordered the marshal to guard the dilapidated bridge against further destruction. The bridge question was finally settled in court, though it was not until 1854 that the two rival cities were joined.

Fire

Throughout history in every country, fires have often engulfed whole cities, especially during the nineteenth century and earlier when most structures—at least in the United States—were of wood. The most famous of them was the fire resulting from the San Francisco Earthquake on April 18, 1906, but San Francisco had no known covered bridges. Other cities did, and when Savannah, Georgia, burned in 1820, Fayetteville, North Carolina, in 1821, and Augusta, Georgia, in 1829, bridges were undoubtedly consumed by the flames. On April 10, 1845, a fire started in a shed in a residential section of Pittsburgh and quickly spread because of high winds throughout the entire city. Eye witnesses said the Smithfield Street Bridge over the Monongahela River, a long multi-span structure, completely burned in just ten minutes.

Unintentional fire destroyed numerous bridges along with fires set deliberately, either during war or for malicious reasons. The most common problem was sparks from steam locomotives being trapped within a covered rail bridge, setting it ablaze. Although rail bridges were covered in spite of this concern, many lines employed bridge guards armed with water to check the structure after each train passed. The covering also trapped smoke, soot, and live embers which could get into passenger coaches, since their windows were open during hot weather. As a consequence, especially in the Midwest and West, rail bridges were more often left uncovered. While this nearly eliminated the possibility of fire, it introduced rapid deterioration from rot.

Troy, New York, also suffered a devastating fire in 1862, but this time the origin was a covered bridge catching fire. An article in the *Times Union* from May 9, 2012, recounts the tragedy: "TROY—Gale force winds ripped across the city on May 10, 1862, a Saturday afternoon. A train had steamed out of the downtown Troy Union Depot and was crossing the wooden covered Green Island Bridge when sparks from the engine set the structure on fire. It wasn't long before the burning bridge's flames were whipped up by the winds and burning pieces of the bridge were flying into downtown Troy. A firestorm swept the city of wooden buildings." (http://www.timesunion.com/local/article/1862-fire-deadly-and-devastating-3546956.php#ixzz1xyOts0Qp)"

Arson

The malicious burning of covered bridges has been common since at least the mid-nineteenth century. Sorting out the motivations for covered bridge arson is better left to psychiatrists, but some are fairly obvious. We have heard tales of local builders burning a bridge with the hope of getting the replacement contract. Bridge arson reached a peak in the 1960s and 1970s, when covered bridges were still considered nuisances and before they had become beloved icons. Local farmers hated them because their trusses and roofs prevented the passage of large pieces of farm equipment. Truck drivers disliked them because their weight limits prevented the delivery of oil, the pick up of milk, or hauling heavy equipment. School districts opposed them because school buses had to avoid them by taking circuitous routes, thus costing time and money. In other cases, the bus had to offload the students on one end, drive through followed by the students, then reload. Fire companies hated them because fire trucks were usually too large or heavy for covered bridges. From a practical point of view, there were many legitimate reasons for hating covered bridges. Many of the counties lacked the financial resources to replace all these bridges in a timely manner. To force the issue, local people

Above from top "Sherman's March to the Sea," which took place from November 15 to December 21, 1864, generally enforced a "scorched earth" strategy that included the burning of many covered bridges. This scene sketched in a Civil War magazine depicts such a burning in Georgia. (Allen, 1970: 18)

In 1836, one year after James S. Clark built a two-span crossing with a mid-span drawbridge over the Cuyahoga River between Ohio City and Cleveland, rival citizen groups engaged in near warfare on and around the bridge, nearly destroying it in the process. (Wood, 1993: 121)

City fires were common in the nineteenth century when virtually all buildings and bridges were wooden. As depicted in William Coventry Wall's "View of the Great Fire of Pittsburgh," much of the city burned on April 10, 1845, including the Monongahela Bridge (Smithfield Street), which was reduced to ashes in about ten minutes. (Wikimedia)

sometimes resorted to arson to create a *fait accompli*.
In some underpopulated counties where "everybody
knows everybody and their business," local law
enforcement knew better than to prosecute the culprits.
Consequently, in many counties the arsonists were
never caught or prosecuted.

Pyromania afflicted people in the nineteenth century
as much as it does now. From Tuscarawas County, Ohio,
comes the following tale of events on the morning of
December 16, 1893. Under the title "Incendiary Fires,"
the *Tuscarawas Advocate* reported the story: "A total of
four fires were set in the vicinity of Tuscarawas [village].
At 1 AM Charles Minnich's barn at the south end of
town burned at a loss of $5,000.

"While the Minnich barn was burning, the county
bridge across the Tuscarawas River [at Trenton Station]
was also discovered in flames, and it also was entirely
consumed. We are told that a man was seen crossing
the bottom and entering the bridge with a torch in one
hand and a bundle of straw in the other, that he dropped
a portion of the straw near the west entrance, set fire to
it, and did likewise at the other end. It is supposed that
after firing the Minnich barn he burned the bridge to
prevent anyone from following him" (quoted in Miller,
1975: 43). Local residents have long believed the
arsonist was one Benedict Marti, a known pyromaniac
and animal abuser, but the $500 reward failed to pro-
duce any evidence, and no one was ever charged.

The problem was acute in 1959 when Richard
Sanders Allen wrote the following: "In recent years
Pennsylvania covered bridges have suffered from a rash
of senseless burnings that seems to be headed toward
epidemic proportions. The pattern is getting to be
shockingly familiar. There will be a small minority

ROAD CLOSED
TO
THRU TRAFFIC

of residents who want a new bridge, claiming that a perfectly sound wooden structure is 'outmoded.' State and county officials, laudably slow to spend the public's money to soothe the esthetic reactions of only a few, demur and delay. All too often of late the next step is told in big black headlines: COVERED BRIDGE BURNS—ARSON SUSPECTED. The minority, through one or two ruthless individuals, has forced the issue" (1959: 101).

Over the years, a number of important bridges were lost to arson. Virtually none had smoke detectors or had been treated with fire retardant. In July, 1969, unknown persons burned a highly unusual bridge sitting within sight of the Mississippi River. The Hamilton Bridge in Hancock County, Illinois had been built in 1881 to serve as a temporary replacement for a damaged iron span, part of a rail bridge over the Mississippi River between Keokuk, Iowa, and Hamilton, Illinois. As was common, it was left uncovered. When the new iron span was ready, the railroad moved the wooden Howe truss span to the Illinois side to span a slough on the road leading to the iron bridge, which was shared by the railroad, a trolley line, as well as wagons and pedestrians. When moved, presumably in 1881, the company covered the bridge. Since it had been built for rail use, its dimensions were exceptional: 164 feet long, 24 feet wide, and with 23.4-foot-high Howe trusses having triple iron rods. In 1955, it was bypassed and in the mid-1960s closed to all but foot traffic. Because it was so isolated, arsonists set fire to it, burning it totally. No one was ever caught and punished.

One of Pennsylvania's most scenic bridges, the Gudgeonville Bridge over Elk Creek in Erie County, although on a public road, had long been the site of nighttime drinking parties by rowdy locals and a victim of incessant vandalism. On November 8, 2008, someone burned the bridge, and, though still standing, it was declared a total loss. Its exceptionally scenic location next to a gigantic bluff might have justified reconstruction, but officials said no. Within two weeks, the arsonists were apprehended. In January 2009, the charred remains of the bridge were lifted by a crane and moved to a nearby field where it was dismantled.

In 1968, we read: "The town of Merrimack, N.H. has lost its last covered bridge. . . . The arsonists made very sure there would be nothing to save. This occurred on April 27, 1968, not quite a year, since Field's or Severn Bridge was burned by arsonists. This time too the job was very thorough. This done on June 6, 1967" (Lincoln, 1968: 8). Constructed using a Town lattice, the bridge dropped into the creek beneath as a result of the fire and was not rebuilt. Today, all that remains at the site are the abutments and a plaque that memorialize the first covered bridge built in Merrimack. An article in *Covered Bridge Topics* from January 1972, further noted: "The previous June I saw the remains of FIELD'S BRIDGE, 29-06-04, burned under similar circumstances. Failure to adequately punish the young

adults responsible after their arrest, probably doomed the nearby TURKEY HILL BRIDGE" (Bonney, 1972: 9).

A similar story from *Covered Bridge Topics* in April 1971 detailed the loss to arson of Kentucky's longest covered bridge, the Sutherland Mill Bridge, a two-span double-arch Burr truss 289 feet long. Locals, upset that the bridge had to be closed and would not be replaced for seven years, burned the bridge, hoping for a better one. Because the bridge crossed county borders, two sheriff's departments were charged with the investigation, but neither showed any interest, and nothing came of the case (Miller, 1971: 10).

Sometimes the bridges survived the fires because they burned incompletely or a local fire department could save the structure. Though the siding and roof were completely burned, the trusses remained standing, though charred.

department. Because the bridge was valuable, its timbers were wrapped in plastic for protection until the bridge could be dismantled, the truss members scraped, and the bridge reassembled in the city's park in 1991.

Not all burnings are arson, and the fire that severely damaged the double-lane bridge built in 1852 at Philippi, West Virginia, which had escaped burning during the Civil War, was accidental. On February 2, 1989, when a gasoline tanker truck was filling underground tanks at a nearby station, gasoline overflowed the tank and ran downhill into the bridge. Before the fuel could be cleaned up, a car drove through and backfired, setting the bridge ablaze. Because the bridge was in town, firemen put out the fire but the trusses were badly charred. Fortunately, the deck had been replaced with a concrete one in 1934, and the bridge did not collapse. It was decided to preserve the bridge by rebuilding its shell as it would have looked during the Civil War. In addition, a sprinkler system and smoke detectors were discretely added. Professor Emory Kemp of West Virginia State University supervised the project, and the bridge reopened on September 16, 1991.

Many bridges bear the scars of failed attempts at arson. In most cases, the failure to burn stemmed from the wood being wet, the pyromaniac not having enough accelerant, or someone noticing the fire before it engulfed the bridge. Today, more and more bridges have had flame retardant treatment, but few have fire detectors, surveillance cameras, or other devices to discourage vandalism and arson. The malicious burning of bridges by angry locals has largely ceased, partly because attitudes have changed and partly because there are fewer remaining bridges in use.

Where covered bridges are valued, such as Parke County, Indiana, however, most arsonists are caught and prosecuted. After the Dooley Station Bridge was burned in December, 1960, the culprits were caught because two nearby residents reported seeing a car with headlights off fleeing the scene of the burning bridge and called authorities. While the bridge could not be saved, the six young men responsible were caught and jailed. Four of them were eventually fined $8,000 each and sentenced to 104 days in jail.

The Meem's Bottom Bridge over the North Fork of the Shenandoah River near Mt. Jackson, Virginia, had been built in 1894 as a single-span Burr truss. On Halloween eve, October 28, 1976, unknown persons set fire to the bridge. The local fire company extinguished the blaze before the trusses had burned through. After scraping off 1.5 inches of charring and otherwise restoring the bridge at a cost of $240,000, the span reopened in 1979 with an unexpected eight ton load limit. Within a couple of years it became clear that its strength was compromised, and during the winter of 1982–3 engineers built three concrete piers and placed three lines of I-beams underneath at a cost of $140,000.

The Robert's Bridge in Preble County, Ohio, was originally built in 1829 as a double-lane bridge serving a turnpike and later the heavy traffic of US 127 south of Eaton. On August 5, 1986, unknown vandals set the bridge on fire, but as with the two bridges discussed above, the charred trusses were saved by the fire

Flood Control and Reservoirs

Bridges span creeks and rivers, but waterways also flood or jam ice into the bridges. To remedy the flooding of major rivers that repeatedly inundated urban areas, governments at various levels created flood control projects that usually required the construction of multiple dams and reservoirs on both main and tributary waterways. While the United States government has been involved in flood control since 1917, individual states also constructed systems. For example, Ohio authorized the Muskingum Watershed Conservancy District in 1933 to address flooding throughout eastern and southeastern Ohio, eventually building sixteen dams and reservoirs. While today these serve not just to control flooding but also provide vast recreational opportunities, their building had a negative impact on covered bridges and communities. In total, this system flooded around two dozen historic covered bridges; none were saved. Similar patterns involving both single and multiple reservoirs negatively impacted covered bridges throughout the nation.

In the early 1960s, the state of Indiana began planning Lake Monroe south of Bloomington, which involved damming Salt Creek, a waterway then crossed by five covered bridges. After the dam was completed in 1965 and the waters began rising, all five bridges were destroyed along with two others elsewhere in the county, leaving just one covered bridge out of eight.

In 1967, a dam was constructed north of Cambridge, Ohio, on Salt Fork, which inundated several Guernsey County covered bridges. Only the Leeper Bridge was moved to the Cambridge City Park, but a farmer wanted to save the Gunn Bridge. A second farmer challenged the first for ownership, and the issue was never resolved. In the meantime, the rising waters of the reservoir engulfed the bridge. It sat there in the water for many years, gradually deteriorating, and finally disappeared from view around 1980.

New Uses for Old Bridges

Some old bridges could retire gracefully after reaching their useful limits. Many such retirements involved moving bridges to new locations. Some now stand in fairgrounds, such as the former Rosseau Bridge moved by County Engineer Edwin Ervin to the Morgan County, Ohio, fairgrounds in 1953, an early example of compassion for outmoded covered bridges. The old bridge that stood at Vermont, Indiana, was moved to Highland Park in Kokomo in 1958, and while it still crosses Wildcat Creek like a proper bridge, it is only used for storage of picnic tables, with steel gates on each end to keep out visitors. While some continue to span water and function as bridges, others sit forlornly on blocks over dry land, such as the Buckeye Furnace Bridge in Jackson County, Ohio. Several bridges now sit on college and university campuses. The Ohio University campus in Lancaster, Ohio, placed two invaluable bridges, one covered, one all iron—both using the so-called "inverted bowstring truss" and given the twin names of John Bright #1 and #2—over Fetters Run. The Shaeffer or Campbell Bridge was moved from Fairfield County, Ohio, to the Ohio University Belmont Campus in St. Clairsville. Parke County, Indiana's Catlin Bridge has the unique honor of sitting in the midst of the Parke County Golf Course where it has spanned Big Diddle Creek since 1961.

A small homemade bridge originally built about 1925 to get a farmer's tractor over Dyes Fork in western Noble County was moved in 1965 to nearby Campsite D in an Ohio Power Company recreation area just across the line in Morgan County where it serves campsites on the other side of Brannon's Fork.

Barn bridges constitute a special category of bridge preservation, however unsatisfactory they are. Some former bridges that were bypassed and reverted to private ownership have been used to store farm equipment in situ over water. Others, however, were moved to dry land, stripped of their decks, and reused as barns, with or without the addition of doors. Some served out their last days as barns until being abandoned and either torn down or falling apart.

At least one barn-bridge achieved this status accidentally. A. M. Kennedy and Sons of Rushville, Indiana, built a 55-foot bridge over Mud Creek at Homer in Rush County in 1881, but in 1892 a flood washed the bridge downstream a short distance into a field. It was simply left there and became a barn, with the addition of a shed on one side. Visitors could only approach or enter the bridge when the farmer was not "running hogs" in and around it, but in 2009 the county dismantled and moved the bridge nearby to Caldwell Pioneer Acres, placing it over a ravine.

A number of bridges that had been converted to sheds were later converted back to being bridges when their value had risen again. One such example is the Thomas J. Malone Bridge, named after the Columbiana County, Ohio bridge enthusiast who first realized that a

Below Parke County, Indiana's Catlin Bridge has served local duffers since it was moved to the county golf course in 1961 to cross Diddle Creek. (Terry E. Miller, 1968)

Bottom Converted into a barn and moved to a field owned by Walter Fox nearby its original location, this former bridge crossed Tymochtee Creek in Wyandot County, Ohio. Over the years, the bridge was abandoned and forgotten and no longer exists. (Terry E. Miller, 1966)

county storage shed had once been a covered bridge. Originally built in the 1870s over Middle Run, at some point it could no longer carry the traffic of SR 154 and became a storage shed for Elk Run Township. Later, it was moved a second time but then forgotten until 1971 when the structure was moved to newly established Beaver Creek State Park and placed over the mill race for Gaston's Mill, the centerpiece of the park. Unfortunately, the lower part of the bridge had rotted away, and the restoration is incomplete since this part was simply cut away.

Minnesota's only remaining covered bridge, now in Covered Bridge Park in Zumbrota and again spanning the Zumbro River, was moved twice from its original location. Zumbrota's earliest crossing was a series of short, open wooden spans built in 1856 that served stage coaches as well as commercial traffic going to Redwing. In addition to rotting quickly, the spans were routinely destroyed by flash floods and ice floes nearly every year. In 1869, the authorities built a substantial bridge, hiring Evander E. L. Kingsbury, who had seen covered bridges in Massachusetts. Based on that experience, he designed a plan based on, but different in significant ways, from the Town lattice. But the

bridge was left open until 1871 when it was obvious that covering it would save the structure from the elements. The bridge served this site until 1932 when it was moved to the fairgrounds where it sat until 1997 before being moved back to the river about 1,000 feet from its original location.

Some reuses have been commercial. The former bridge at Eagleville, Ohio, in Ashtabula County, built in 1862 and 135 feet long, was sold at auction in 1972. The buyer paid $5 for the bridge, though he also had to pay for disassembly. After three years in storage, he reconstructed half in North Kingsville as Covered Bridge Pizza, and in 1977 the other half with the same name in Andover. Thus, diners can eat in an otherwise modern restaurant but amidst the original trusses. In Carroll County, New Hampshire, after the Bartlett Bridge was bypassed in 1966, the structure reverted to the nearby landowner, who built a souvenir shop within the bridge—an actual building—offering covered bridge souvenirs. The Lowell Bridge in Lane County, Oregon, after being raised to stand above the rising waters of Dexter Reservoir and bypassed, has become an interpretative display of materials related to covered bridge building in Oregon.

Other Reasons

There are other fates as well. Strip mining for coal has long plagued wide areas of West Virginia and Ohio, particularly in the eastern half. Strip mining led to the losses of a number of bridges in Morgan County, Ohio, in the 1960s when bridges were simply abandoned to the bulldozers. A few survived for a while in deteriorating states among the spoil banks until they either collapsed or were destroyed by the miners. Mining also affected bridges elsewhere, particularly in Harrison and Noble Counties in Ohio and Washington County, Pennsylvania. How many bridges were lost in West Virginia is not yet known.

Marion County, Iowa's Marysville Bridge was originally an 81-foot Town lattice, but in 1970 it was cut into two halves. One section went to the Marion County Park and the other half to the Wilcox Game

Below Perhaps Rush County, Indiana builder A. M. Kennedy's most modest bridge, this 55-foot multiple king structure started life over Mud Creek near Homer in 1881, but a flood washed it into a nearby field in 1892 where it was left. For many years the farm owner used it as a barn with added shed, but by around 2005 it had been abandoned. In 2009, the Caldwell Pioneer Engineering Club moved the bridge to their Pioneer Acres site in Rushville and began restoration, which was completed in 2010. (Larry L. Stout, Andy Rebman)

Preserve, but the latter is not accessible since it sits next to the county's shooting range. Similarly, the owners of Old Mill Village Museum near New Milford in the far northeastern corner of Pennsylvania moved an old bridge from New York State but not before chopping off the portions which were rotten. So little was left that it became a miniature bridge having no historical or structural integrity. Later, the downsized bridge was damaged by a flood and fell into ruins.

Summit County, Ohio's Everett Road Bridge was effectively destroyed in 1970 by a runaway truck, which crashed through the side. Although the bridge was extensively repaired, it was then washed off its abutments against the boulders and crushed into kindling five years later. In 1986, Cuyahoga Valley National Recreation Area officials built a replica.

Canada's Point Wolfe Bridge in Albert County, New Brunswick, within Fundy National Park and spanning a rocky gorge near the ocean, was accidentally destroyed in 1992 when road crews attempted to remove a rock outcropping near the bridge with dynamite. Huge rocks flew in all directions and destroyed the bridge along with the rock. Red-faced engineers then built a new bridge identical to the former one.

Above and left Originally built as a 135-foot bridge at Eagleville in Ashtabula County, Ohio, the Eagleville Bridge was sold at auction in 1972 for $5 to a businessman who used half the bridge for his Covered Bridge Pizza in North Kingsville in 1975 and the other in Andover in 1977. (Exterior, A. Chester Ong, 2011; Interior, Terry E. Miller, 2011)

Conclusions

The "golden age" of the covered bridge as functional conveyance ended around 1890, though Oregon, Québec, and New Brunswick continued building them until the mid twentieth century. Today, covered bridges are relatively rare and unique, and that explains part of their charm, but had we lived during the later nineteenth century, covered bridges would have had little charm since they were so ordinary. As normal crossings, citizens hardly noticed them. Road workers repairing the West Swanzey Bridge in New Hampshire told us in 2010 that even today many locals do not realize they are driving through covered bridges, because they are so familiar and normal, probably the typical response of people in the nineteenth and well into the twentieth centuries. Where modern enthusiasts marvel at photos

Left After the Bartlett Bridge in New Hampshire was bypassed in 1966, the landowner constructed a souvenir shop within, selling a variety of covered bridge items. (A. Chester Ong, 2010)

of the dramatic and superlative covered bridges of the past, people at that time likely saw them the way we see typical reinforced concrete bridges or steel truss bridges today. Before the image of the covered bridge could become a nostalgic relic of the past worth preserving, it necessarily underwent a dramatic decline, both in condition and number. As in so many cases, something is unimportant until it is about to be lost.

Attitudes change gradually, not overnight. Even as covered bridges declined rapidly in number, here and there enlightened individuals, some in official positions, began to recognize their importance in the history of civil engineering in both the United States and Canada. But these early efforts towards preservation were more often than not met with apathy or even hostility by the public in general and bridge maintenance officials in particular. Chapter 5 traces these attitudinal changes through the end of the twentieth century and into the present one as well as explores the dilemmas and controversies that come with the preservation of historical structures that must also carry modern vehicles, with all the liabilities of our increasingly legalistic society.

Left Minnesota's only covered bridge again spans the Zumbro River near where it was built in 1869 (and only covered in 1871), but it spent the years 1932–97 sitting on land in the county fairgrounds until being rebuilt 1,000 feet from its original location. (Terry E. Miller, 2012)

chapter five

FINDING A PLACE FOR COVERED BRIDGES IN THE TWENTY-FIRST CENTURY

PRESERVATION, RENEWAL, AND CONTROVERSY

Previous spread When New England College in Henniker, New Hampshire, decided to add a footbridge over the Contoocook River on campus in 1972, they hired Milton Graton and his son Arnold to build a traditional Town lattice structure 114 feet long. After constructing the trusses on land, they used oxen to pull them over falsework into place, a rarely used method from the past. (A. Chester Ong, 2010)

Below The Goodpasture Bridge, 165 feet long and built in 1938, spans the scenic McKenzie River in Lane County, Oregon. (A. Chester Ong, 2012)

When the new century began, except for Canada and Oregon, most covered bridges were between 110 and 160 years old, all constructed of wood and all originally intended for vehicles now only seen in museums. Such structures have survived profound technological and social changes in North America: the development of roads from trails and wagon tracks; the development of transportation from horses and horse-drawn conveyances to all manner of modern engine-driven vehicles; from the demographics of isolated farms and towns to large urban centers, suburbia, and exurbia all connected by modern roads; and from subsistence farming to gigantic centralized facilities for manufacturing and distribution. Considering these transformations, it is nothing less than amazing that so many "deteriorated" and "obsolete" covered bridge structures actually remain. Indeed, the majority of them continue to carry traffic on a daily basis. The early advocates for covering wooden trusses thought protecting them from the elements would extend their lives from less than ten years if left uncovered to only fifty or sixty if protected. Even the "recent" bridges of Oregon and New Brunswick now exceed that.

Before reaching their present status as revered "senior citizens" and "nostalgic icons," covered bridges suffered far less flattering descriptors, such as "outmoded," "hazardous," "unnecessary," and "impediments to modern life." Throughout the nation, many public officials charged with road and bridge maintenance wore their zeal to replace covered bridges as badges of honor. While a small minority of citizens appreciated covered bridges and began advocating for their preservation, the majority was oblivious—even apathetic—to the heavy losses of these historical structures. People wishing to rush the process of replacement sometimes burned bridges like rogue soldiers, and few of them were punished for these crimes.

An examination of covered bridges today could reasonably consider them in groups, for bridges remaining in service present far different challenges than bridges that have been retired, and bridges that have been moved take on new roles with new environments from those remaining in their original locations. The bridges remaining can be viewed in four categories:

1. Bridges remaining in service in their original location
2. Bridges no longer in service but in their original location
3. Bridges remaining in some form of service but relocated
4. Bridges no longer in service as well as relocated

Our discussion, however, will focus on matters that tend to cut across all four of these categories.

Terminology relative to covered bridges has become difficult. Putting aside the unresolvable issue of "authenticity," which is implicit in defining a "covered bridge" and was discussed in the Introduction (pages 10–14), we must address other problematic terms such as "preservation," "reconstruction," "refurbishment," "rebuilding," and "renovation." When a historical marker, sign, or website describes a particular bridge with one of these terms, we cannot know for sure whether the bridge was merely repaired and painted, whether the original trusses were disassembled for repair or completely new ones installed, or, in many cases, what percentage of the timbers were replaced.

Enthusiasts appreciate finding a covered bridge not just in its original location but still in service, conditions no longer easily met. Those responsible for maintenance and safety, usually working with limited funds, need to accomplish their goals efficiently. The traveling public is not well served by a bridge having limited clearance and width as well as a load limit that excludes many modern vehicles, such as camper vans, trucks, school buses, and fire engines. Local farmers may not be able to get their equipment through the bridge and must take lengthy detours to reach their fields. Those responsible for the bridges have responded with wide-ranging solutions, from simple strengthening to complete replication to complete replacement.

During the middle and later years of the twentieth century, engineers often chose to shore up weakened bridges with wooden or metal bents placed in the streambed. Such stopgap measures may have provided limited relief but, unfortunately, also created impediments in the waterway which snagged brush and other debris. If the bents were positioned to prevent excessive deflection alone, then the trusses continued to function as built, but when the trusses were "relaxed," the shoring usually destroyed their integrity.

A more subtle form of reinforcement involves the placement of steel I-beams beneath the deck. These might be positioned under the lower chords to reinforce

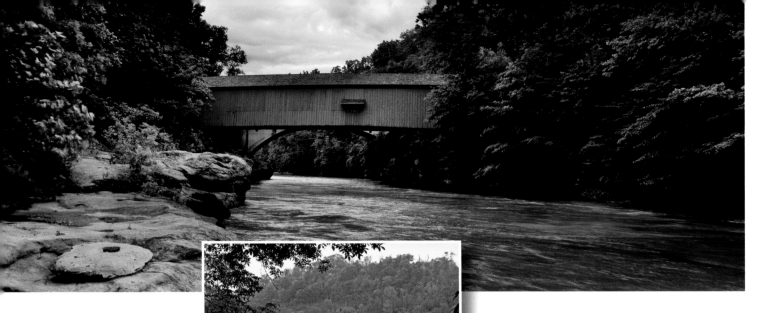

them or fashioned as a web to strengthen the entire deck. Sometimes the I-beams are visible, but sometimes the siding is extended to hide their presence. A more radical solution is to remove the deck entirely and install a new I-beam deck with a wooden floor or, in rare cases, a steel grid. Washington County, Pennsylvania, has reinforced most of its remaining road bridges with I-beam decks, which are well hidden and even have fake wooden cross beams showing below, as in the original. In these cases, the trusses only support their own weight, but the new deck supports the traffic, virtually eliminating weight restrictions. One example is the Ebenezer Church Bridge, moved to Mingo Creek

County Park in Washington County, Pennsylvania, where it was too short for its new location. Engineers placed the bridge *on* a longer deck of I-beams, making the span look a bit like a boat. Steel decks change the experience of crossing the bridge, for there is no deflection, no rattling of boards, only silence.

In a few cases, engineers removed the original deck and built a complete concrete and steel bridge beneath the trusses and roofing, which then became only an enclosed shell set atop a platform. In the case of Meems Bottom Bridge in Virginia, this was necessary since arsonists had burned the bridge, deeply charring the trusses. The same solution befell the two-lane bridge in Philippi, West Virginia, famed for its Civil War history, that carries US 250 across the Tygart River. In 1934, the highway department built a complete bridge beneath the trusses. While disappointing to those who appreciate older technology, this saved the bridge from collapse when a gasoline spill led to the bridge's burning in 1989. This restored but nonetheless wounded veteran still carries traffic, but its width and height restrictions remind motorists that it is an old bridge.

Another solution, but one that contradicts the intended stresses on the trusses, is placing extra piers under the span, creating a multiple-span bridge. Except in the case of the Town lattice, which can be cut at any point, the addition of piers may weaken rather than strengthen bridges with symmetrical panel trusses.

When a bridge is reinforced from below, its trusses need not be altered, and that at least provides visitors with the look and feel of an old and venerable bridge. Other options desire to restore the bridge to its original state—self-supporting and made completely of wood. But nearly any such plan opens a Pandora's Box of ethical and practical issues, and regardless of the decision, consensus will be difficult to achieve. The range of views might be expressed as a continuum between purists and pragmatists. The former include most "timber framers," primarily individuals who aspire to work in the manner of the past, even using antique tools. Their aim is to preserve as much original wood as possible, to copy exactly any sections that are renewed, and even to strip away reinforcements and "improvements" made over time, returning the bridge to its original state, if possible. At the opposite end of the spectrum are underfunded county engineers trying to keep their covered bridges safely in service at the lowest possible cost, along with more generously funded officials who can choose a range of options, including replication with all new materials.

Pragmatists generate most of the controversy, for their actions raise questions of authenticity and historical integrity and almost always rile purists. Can a bridge be "authentic" when 70 per cent of its timbers have been replaced? If not 70, what about 50? How much of the truss is replaced depends on the standards

used to judge the quality and condition of the original material. A pragmatist is likely to follow the maxim "if in doubt, don't," while a purist would attempt to save each and every piece, even if it meant cutting out bad spots and fitting in new material. There is no known settled terminology to describe these solutions. "Renovation" (along with many similar terms) could mean replacing only the roof, some of the siding, and some cracked floor beams, or it could mean 70 per cent of the truss timbers. Three counties can serve as case studies.

Parke County, Indiana, home to some thirty-one bridges and a long-running festival, follows a conservative approach, keeping its bridges in as close to original condition as possible. They are fortunate in that their bridges are well-built Burr trusses, some from the later period of bridge building, along with relatively light

Above left Washington King, descended from famed Georgia African-American bridge builder Horace King, built a 165-foot-long bridge over the Oconee River on College Street in Athens, Georgia, home of the University of Georgia, in 1892. By the early 1960s, the bridge could no longer handle the traffic, and in 1964 it was shortened by 11 feet and moved to Stone Mountain Park where it crosses a neck of Stone Mountain Lake. (Terry E. Miller, 1987)

Above right Originally built elsewhere as the State Line Bridge, the structure was dismantled in 1966 and re-assembled in Governor Bebb MetroPark in Ohio's Butler County in 1970. Its Burr truss design uses flared posts, giving rise to its dubious designation as a "Wernwag truss." (Terry E. Miller, 2002)

Inset The Pass Creek or Krewson Bridge's date of construction is listed as 1925, but some claim the year 1906. After being closed in 1981, the Douglas County, Oregon, span was relocated by a giant crane to a nearby park in 1987 where it serves pedestrians only. (A. Chester Ong, 2012)

traffic, since Parke County is sparsely populated and underdeveloped. Some bridges have been bypassed, leaving them in their original location and condition. However, when the Jackson Bridge was "renovated," engineers cut off the lower portion of the trusses and replaced them with new materials of "glulam" (glued laminates).

In Bucks County, Pennsylvania, just north of Philadelphia and including several affluent suburbs and exurbs, the Bucks County Covered Bridge Society promotes twelve ostensibly historic covered bridges along with a covered pony truss and a covered canal aqueduct. Van Sant's Bridge has a historical marker indicating original construction in 1875, "reconstructed" in 1955, and "rehabilitated" in 2008. The trusses are original, however, but the main deck cross beams are now steel I-beams. In this case, the terms indicate little apparent alteration of the original bridge. Sheard's Mill, Uhlerstown, and Frankenfield Bridges have their original trusses, but the decks are actually independent I-beams.

The only bridge that is original in all aspects is the South Perkasie Bridge, which was moved to Lenape Park in 1959 and today is displayed raised on blocks. The county has three other bridges that are completely new, and these will be discussed later.

Ashtabula County, Ohio, claims seventeen bridges, but five are completely modern and most of the others altered or reinforced in some way. Widely respected retired county engineer John Smolen certainly preserved his county's bridges, keeping most in service,

but those at the purist end tend to have reservations about his methods. Many of the bridges have entirely new decks built below the trusses so to provide greater overhead clearance. Several also have oversized laminated beams running through the interiors to reinforce the trusses but also reducing the width. Five have new concrete piers, and the Mechanicsville Bridge, though bypassed, was reconstructed with mostly new wood in 2004. Only two bridges have not been altered, South Denmark Road, which is bypassed, and Graham Road, which was placed on blocks in a park. Admittedly, the Warner Hollow/Windsor Mills Bridge, formerly Ohio's most scenic bridge and spanning a gorge, was long closed and in bad condition when renovation began, but it was raised, one original pier was replaced, the lower chords were replaced, and laminated beams run through the bridge. For some, the bridge has lost much of its earlier rustic charm and beauty.

These three cases exemplify the range in approaches to preservation, and parallel examples can be found throughout the nation, including even Vermont and New Hampshire. But reactions to these differing philosophies also range from the strongly negative to supportive to "so what?" For those who simply want their bridges "covered," a new deck or piers or even widening matter little. For those who focus on the details of old-time timber framing or enjoy the "feel" of original materials, the changes seen in Bucks and Ashtabula Counties are heretical and unacceptable. The counter argument is that in the past these same bridges might have been replaced with modern structures (or first burned by angry citizens). Today, few bridges are replaced simply in the name of progress. Wherever that might be tried, people, both local and distant, will raise an alarm.

However bridge enthusiasts feel about overly aggressive restoration, it is still preferable to the unquestioned replacement typical of the past. Two counties in southwestern Pennsylvania, Greene and Washington, which neglected their bridges in the past, began restoring them in recent years, though often replacing the majority of original timbers.

Above When the Lower Humbert or Faidley Bridge was constructed over Laurel Hill Creek in 1891 in Somerset County, Pennsylvania, it was a one-span Burr truss. A hundred years later, in 1991, the county reinforced the structure with I-beams and a center pier, which alters the normal stresses on the truss members. (A. Chester Ong, 2011)

Inset The South Perkasie Bridge in Bucks County, Pennsylvania, built in 1832 and the oldest of the county's twelve bridges, was moved nearby to Lenape Park in 1958 where it serves as a picnic shelter. (Terry E. Miller, 1985)

Above left and center left Ashtabula County, Ohio's Warner Hollow or Windsor Mills Bridge, originally built in 1867, sat abandoned and deteriorating for over thirty years. In 2003, the county refurbished the bridge, replacing one of its scenic piers and generally eliminating its former rustic look. (Max T. Miller, 1958; Terry E. Miller, 2012)

Left The Switzer Bridge in Franklin County, Kentucky, went through numerous renovations following its initial construction in 1855, but none as complete as that of 1998. A flood during the previous year lodged the intact bridge against a nearby bridge. Although engineers carefully dismantled the bridge, they ended up replicating rather than refurbishing the bridge. (Terry E. Miller, 2005)

Above Originally built about 1880 in two unequal spans using the multiple kingpost design, Greenup County, Kentucky's Oldtown Bridge was "renovated in 1999 to original state," another way of saying replicated. None of the old bridge remains. (Terry E. Miller, 2005)

Right The Chambers Railroad Bridge over the Coast Fork of the Willamette River in Lane County, Oregon, was first built in 1925 to carry materials to and from the nearby J. H. Chambers lumber mill, but after the mill burned in the 1950s, the line was abandoned. By 2010, the abandoned bridge was ready to fall, and the city quickly removed it and the following year erected an exact replica using the original hardware. (A. Chester Ong, 2012)

Far right Summit County, Ohio's only covered bridge, the Everett Road Bridge over scenic Furnace Run, was built by the Smith Bridge Company in 1877, but a sudden flood in 1975 crashed the bridge into the boulders. In 1986, after the area became part of the Cuyahoga Valley National Park, the bridge was replicated for foot, bicycle, and equestrian users. (A. Chester Ong, 2011)

In the mid-1980s, the Board of Commissioners of Rush County, Indiana, thought it their duty to replace four of the county's elegant Kennedy family-built bridges with their unusual scrollwork in order to provide residents with modern, safe crossings. Not only was an outcry raised, but opposing citizens put up a slate of pro-bridge candidates, and voters threw out the offending officials. All covered bridges remain today, including the Moscow Bridge that was rebuilt after being nearly destroyed by a tornado.

Replica Bridges

Before the late twentieth century, when a bridge was lost to fire, flood, or other disaster, it was lost forever. But gradually the idea of replicating lost bridges has taken hold. Although replica bridges lack the "feel" of venerable and gnarled veterans, they do provide the illusion of genuineness. At least, builders do not attempt to fake "oldness" by "stressing" the timbers as is done to some otherwise new furniture. But this solution has also become the easy way out of painstaking restoration too.

In some cases, replicas can incorporate material salvaged from the original. After Moscow, Indiana's handsome two-span Kennedy-built bridge from 1886 was torn to shreds by a tornado on June 3, 2008, the twisted trusses and arches were salvaged. When Dan R. Collom & Sons, working for J. A. Barker Engineering, completed the rebuilding of the bridge to original specifications in 2010, he was able to reuse approximately 60 percent of the original, including many of the truss members.

When the Everett Road Bridge in Summit County, Ohio, was floated off its abutments and destroyed by

Right and inset The Cedar or Casper Bridge in Madison County, Iowa, first built in 1883 by H. P. Jones using his unique flat roof style, was destroyed by arsonists in 2002, then replicated using original plans in 2004, most likely because of the bridge's importance to the county's tourism. (Terry E. Miller, 2005)

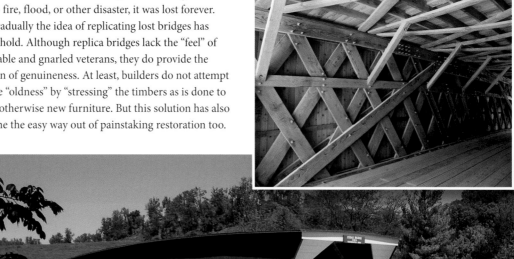

Left The Hurricane Shoals Bridge in Jackson County, Georgia, is not a replica of the c. 1870 original but a modern reconceptualization, in 2002, of the Town lattice truss. (A. Chester Ong, 2012)

a flash flood in 1975, no one attempted to salvage the timbers, but since the area had been incorporated into the Cuyahoga Valley National Park, officials replicated the bridge in 1986 with all new materials. While they rebuilt the Smith trusses accurately, it is ironic that the deck system was required to be more robust than the original even though it was designed to carry only foot traffic.

In the evening of September 3, 2002, vandals burned one of Madison County, Iowa's beloved bridges, the Cedar Bridge, also known as the Casper Bridge, which had been originally built in 1883. In 2004, the county constructed a replica which, though on a bypassed section of road, is open to traffic. Its smooth new-looking wood contrasts with the more beaten look of the other bridges, but having a replica is better than having nothing.

Two bridges in Bucks County, Pennsylvania, well illustrate the phenomenon: Mood's Bridge, destroyed by fire in June 2004 and rebuilt in 2008, and Twining Ford/Schofield Ford Bridge, also destroyed by fire in 1991 and rebuilt by local volunteers in 1997 (see pages 205–7). There are significant differences between them. Admittedly, Moods carries a high volume of traffic while Twining Ford carries only pedestrians and horses. Thus, Moods is an incomplete replica because the independent deck is entirely supported by I-beams while Twining Ford is an exact copy.

Vermont and New Hampshire have also followed the practice of replicating lost bridges. Among those replicated are the following:

Slate Bridge, Cheshire County, New Hampshire,
    lost to arson in 1993, copied in 2001
Coventry Bridge, Orleans County, Vermont,
    lost to arson in 1997, replicated in 1999
Power House Bridge, Lamoille County, Vermont,
    collapsed under heavy snow, rebuilt in 2002
North Hartland Twin Bridge, Windsor County, Vermont,
    lost in a hurricane in the 1930s, rebuilt in 2001

One of Canada's most dramatic bridge sites, Point Wolfe in Fundy National Park, now has a bridge built in 1992, long past the "normal" bridge building period even in New Brunswick. The original bridge over this rocky chasm within sight of the ocean had been built in 1910 to serve a village of woodcutters and sawmill operators. In 1991, crews attempted to dislodge large rocks near the bridge. When the crew detonated the charge, large fragments of rock struck and shattered the bridge, which thereupon fell into the river. The red-faced government crew built a replica the following year.

While the examples cited above illustrate replacements for bridges that were completely destroyed, there is another group of bridges whose originals were needlessly destroyed and replaced with replicas. Noble County, Ohio, had nearly thirty covered bridges in the late 1950s but relentlessly replaced them with generic concrete and steel spans. Only three remain, one in the fairgrounds, which actually combines parts of two

Above Admittedly, the long-bypassed Teegarden or Centennial Bridge, built in 1875 in Columbiana County, Ohio, was in poor condition, but the plan to "refurbish" the bridge led to its nearly complete replication. (Terry E. Miller, 2008)

bridges, and two in the southwest part of the county, the Manchester and Parrish Bridges. Both survived the pervasive strip mining in the area and were bypassed some years ago. Why the county tore down the originals and replaced them with pale copies is uncertain, since neither is in a park and few visit them. The most egregious examples come from Kentucky, especially Greenup County, where officials, using federal aid, in 2004 dismantled the Bennett Mill Bridge, the only remaining Wheeler truss, and replaced virtually all of the timbers, leaving a "restored" bridge that is essentially new. The same was done with the bypassed Oldtown Bridge nearby in 1999, which is described as having been returned to its original condition—that is, as a completely new covered bridge.

Perhaps the "silver lining" is that we can then experience a completely new covered bridge, with its fresh wood smell. However, there are ethical issues in posting signs suggesting that the bridges were built in earlier years.

Though Vermont is often idolized as the center of the covered bridge world, a surprising number are

replicas, some replacing bridges lost to disaster but more often to replace a deteriorating original with a copy. These are particularly disappointing to enthusiasts who had seen the originals and who knew they could have been saved. Among these bridges, often described as "completely renovated," are the following:

Henry Bridge, Bennington County, Vermont,
 1840 original, 1989 copy
Paper Mill Bridge, Bennington County, Vermont,
 1889 original, 2000 copy
Hopkins Bridge, Franklin County, Vermont,
 1875 original, 1999 copy
Fuller Bridge, Franklin County, Vermont,
 1890 original, 2000 copy
Little/Gates Bridge, Lamoille County,
 1890 original, 1995 copy
Hayward Bridge, Orange County, Vermont,
 1883 original, 2000 copy
Sanderson Bridge, Rutland County, Vermont,
 1840 original, 2003 copy
Gorham Bridge, Rutland County, Vermont,
 1842 original, 2004 copy

Other examples of such "renovation" abound and perplex those who value the old bridges. Indiana County, Pennsylvania, tore down the original Thomas Ford Bridge built in 1879 and spent a million dollars on a copy built in 1998. Jackson County, Georgia removed the c. 1870 Hurricane Shoals Bridge and built a new version in 2002. Although still a Town lattice, designers substituted all manner of modern fasteners and bracing in place of the traditional design.

Neo-Traditional Covered Bridges

The late twentieth century saw the building of many entirely new covered bridges where there were none before. These are of two types, a minority of traditional structures and a majority of innovative ones. Because none was built purely to solve a transportation problem, all were self-consciously "retro" from the start. One of

Above John Smolen, County Engineer of Ashtabula County, Ohio, designed the Smolen-Gulf Bridge, a four-span 613-foot-long modern-style Pratt truss that was built in 2008. If counted—since it is not historical—it would be the longest covered bridge in the United States. (Terry E. Miller, 2008)

Left In 1979, the Zehnder brothers, owners of the Bavarian Inn in German/Swiss-inspired Frankenmuth, Michigan, contracted with Milton and Arnold Graton to build a 239-foot three-span Town lattice bridge to modern specifications (19 feet wide) for all vehicles, costing $1.1 million. When completed on land, the finished Zehnder's Bridge was hauled over the Cass River by oxen, moving it three inches per hour. (Terry E. Miller, 2009)

Bottom left Rising phoenix-like from the ashes of the original c. 1845 structure, New Hampshire's Corbin Bridge in Sullivan County was destroyed by fire on May 24, 1993, then in the following year replicated by the state as a brand-new crossing. (Terry E. Miller, 2003)

Bottom right Although there had been a covered bridge over Conneaut Creek at this location in Ashtabula County, Ohio, from 1831 until 1898, the present bridge succeeded a non-covered span. It was designed and built by John Smolen in 1983 using a traditional Town lattice design. (Terry E. Miller, 2007)

Above and right John Smolen also designed and built the Netcher Road Bridge in Ashtabula County, Ohio, in 1999, using a large laminated arch with steel hanger rods. (Terry E. Miller, 2012)

Below Designed by the late David Fischetti and built by the Fowler Jones Beers Construction Company in 1998, the pedestrian bridge that crosses North Carolina SR 52 leading to Old Salem, a reconstructed Moravian town, uses all-wood Burr trusses whose braces and posts are doubled, enveloping a single arch. (Blue Ridge Timberwrights, Christiansburg, VA)

the earliest and most respected pioneers in this movement was Milton S. Graton (1908–94) of New Hampshire, who both restored old bridges and built entirely new ones. He was later joined by his son Arnold, and they formed what became Graton Associates, which continues today with his grandchildren. Graton's activities included numerous restorations, building replicas of deteriorated or destroyed bridges, and building completely new crossings, such as the New England College Bridge seen at the chapter beginning. He also pioneered the method of building the superstructure complete on land and pulling it on tracks into position over the river. The Graton's major projects, including replicas of lost bridges, are listed below:

REPLICAS

Turkey Jim Bridge, Grafton County, New Hampshire, 1958
Bump Bridge, Grafton County, New Hampshire, 1972
Corbin Bridge, Sullivan County, New Hampshire, 1994
Auchumpkee Creek Bridge, Upson County, Georgia, 1997

NEW CROSSINGS (TRADITIONAL)

Middle/Union Street Bridge, Windsor County, Vermont, 1969
New England College Bridge, Merrimack County, New Hampshire, 1972

NEW CROSSING (MODERNIZED TRADITIONAL)

Zehnder's Holz-Brücke [Zehnder's Bridge], Saginaw County (Frankenmuth), Michigan, 1980

Graton's work is detailed in both text and photos in his autobiography, *The Last of the Covered Bridge Builders* (1978).

Ashtabula County's State Road Bridge, unlike the county's other modern covered bridges built by John Smolen, is an entirely traditional Town lattice truss comparable to the county's other historical bridges.

Modern Covered Bridges

Some engineers now argue that a modern-style covered bridge can be not just cost-effective compared to typical reinforced concrete crossing but will outlast them as well. While this view may, in fact, be true, few such bridges are being built outside counties where covered bridge tourism is an economic factor. Engineer John Smolen of Ashtabula County, Ohio, where there is a long-running annual festival, has been a leader in designing and building modernized versions of covered bridges, using an innovative arch in the 1999 Netcher Road Bridge and Pratt trusses in both the Caine Road Bridge (1986) and the Giddings Road Bridge (1995). But his *tour-de-force* is the 613-foot four-span Smolen-Gulf Bridge, named in his honor. Built in 2008 over a deep gorge of the Ashtabula River (called locally the "Gulf"), this massive structure with its distinctive squared portals is, as the joke goes, "a covered bridge on steroids." Indeed, if the qualification "traditional" is omitted, Smolen-Gulf is now the longest covered bridge in the United States.

Another Ohio county, Union County, just northwest of Columbus, discovered the value of its four remaining antique bridges in recent years, all of these having been built around 1870 by local builder and truss designer Reuben Partridge. Using modified Pratt designs, the county has now built three new bridges, New Upper Darby and Buck Run Road in 2007, and Mill Creek, a more substantial structure, in 2010.

Professional Engineer David C. Fischetti (1946–2011) pioneered new methods and materials in constructing covered bridges. Besides his bridge restoration projects, the most famous of which was the Cornish-Windsor Bridge over the Connecticut River between Vermont and New Hampshire, he designed a new covered bridge for the Old Salem, North Carolina Moravian Museum and reimagined a semi-covered canal aqueduct in Bucks County, Pennsylvania. His work is described fully in his own book, *Structural Investigation of Historic Buildings* (2009). Spanning a highway to provide pedestrians access to the museum from a parking lot, the Old Salem Bridge, which was constructed in 1998, is a 120-foot Burr truss with doubled posts and braces. Fischetti had the bridge constructed of carefully inspected and graded recycled timber and designed a significant amount of camber for greater strength. Instead of solid wood siding, he used clear acrylic panels.

Fischetti's most imaginative project was the Tohickon Aqueduct carrying the Delaware Canal over Tohickon Creek in Point Pleasant, Pennsylvania, north of Philadelphia, which was completed in 2001. The original structure, an all-wood Town lattice, was built in 1834 and replaced in the 1890s "with an iron riveted structure containing a wood-framed trunkway. This aqueduct collapsed in 1931. After World War II, the canal was transformed into a Pennsylvania state park and the aqueduct reconstructed with steel girders supporting a cast-in-place concrete trunkway. By 1990,

the badly deteriorated concrete and steel structure needed to be replaced" (pp. 253–4). In September 1999, part of that crossing collapsed. Fischetti determined that building another Town lattice was impractical and chose the Burr truss instead. J. D. Eckman, Inc. won the contract for $2.1 million to use a combination of southern pine and glued laminated timbers (glulam), especially for the arches, these choices being necessary because the original design calling for solid wood and professional timber joinery exceeded the budget. The result is a three-span aqueduct totaling 202 feet carried by 12-foot-high trusses with the trough carrying water between them. The tops and sides of the trusses are covered except for the semi-oval portion below each arch. Fischetti's reimagined bridge is unusual in the annals of American neo-traditional engineering, but for observers concerned about "authenticity," it is also highly controversial because he made no attempt to replicate the original.

Below The original covered canal aqueduct that carried the Delaware Division of the Pennsylvania Canal over Tohickon Creek in Bucks County, Pennsylvania, was built in 1834 and lasted until the 1890s, and was then succeeded by non-wooden bridges. (Lower left) When the concrete replacement failed, David Fischetti "reimagined" the covered bridge, using double-timbered Burr trusses instead of Town lattice, and using mostly glulam beams instead of solid timber. (Below) The partially covered three-span 202-foot-long structure still cost $2.1 million. (Terry E. Miller, 2010)

"ROMANTIC SHELTERS" ("FAKE COVERED BRIDGES")

Nothing raises blood pressure among bridge enthusiasts faster than a discussion of what some call "romantic shelters" and others call "fakes" or worse. These vary from small sheds on land that resemble covered bridges to non-trussed (or "faux-trussed") sheds over water to substantial steel and concrete bridges with decorative covers. None can be described as "authentic" no matter how far you stretch the meaning. The most generous thing one can say is that they "look like" covered bridges. When they first came to notice, some hailed them as important enough to be numbered and included in the *World Guide to Covered Bridges*. Some editors of *Covered Bridge Topics* used to devote substantial space to them. More recently, they have been omitted from the *World Guide* and no longer appear in *Topics*. Nonetheless, they continue to proliferate in housing developments, in parks, and in backyards across the United States.

While most are indeed little more than large-scale kitsch, they also say something about how people feel about covered bridges. Moving a genuine bridge to a housing estate or park is expensive and almost certainly guarantees continuing maintenance costs as well. Their limited clearances and weight allowances create problems for trucks hauling campers, fire engines, school buses, and other large-scale vehicles. These problems can be minimized by building a "fake" covered bridge of outsized proportions supported on steel I-beams and concrete. Those who build this kind of structure feel they have provided a kind of atmosphere that might resonate with the charmingly English name of the estate or a broader theme of fake rusticity. The modest domestic examples on private property may express the owner's interest in covered bridges, an expression of nostalgia for the past, or an assertion of "country" individuality. They do no harm. But critics are right that listing them on an equal footing with genuine historical bridges is a mistake and only obscures the fact that the latter continue to disappear, whether to disaster or "renovation."

Some of these bridges are substantial. One of them crosses Clear Fork in Ohio's Mohican State Park and carries a complete range of cars, trucks, campers, and motor homes. It can do so because it is a steel-framed bridge with a roof and siding. Another was built just outside Walnut Creek, Ohio, in 2009. Although having all-wood trusses, it is dramatically overbuilt for any modern vehicle.

John Spargo, writing in 1953 about Bennington County, Vermont, described a scheme for building this type of bridge in a state known for its covered bridges: "Some years ago, in connection with the promotion of the silly Green Mountain Parkway scheme, to which many well-intentioned Vermonters unwisely gave their support, it was actually proposed to erect 'imitation covered wooden bridges.' For picturesque effect, and to gratify the desire of tourists to see covered wooden bridges of which they have heard, it was proposed to erect, over streams and rivers at appropriately spaced points along the 'parkway' steel bridges and to cover the steel with a concealing casing of wood! It was felt by the advocates of the scheme that it would be 'good business' for Vermont" (Spargo, 1953: 7).

New Perspectives on Covered Bridges: Bridges as Engineering History

As any collector knows, the difference between "junk" and "antiques" is in the eye of the beholder. The same could be said about covered bridges, that over time the prevalent view has shifted gradually from "nuisance bridge" to "romantic bridge" to "historical bridge." Just as apparent attic junk can later become valuable, outmoded bridges have become engineering monuments worthy of preservation, study, and respect. Increasingly, professional engineers and students of "industrial archaeology" are paying attention to covered bridges, though with a focus on truss design, joinery details, and "best practice" renovation rather than as nostalgia. In addition, historical preservationists have taken a clear position, that covered bridges are an important element in America's transportation history and need to be preserved for future generations to admire.

NATIONAL REGISTER OF HISTORIC PLACES
Thanks to the National Historic Preservation Act of 1966, the National Park Service established the National Register of Historic Places, a repository of documentation for numerous forms of "culture," including the category of "structure," which encompasses bridges. Since 1966, volunteers throughout the nation have compiled documentation to register more than a million items, and about 30,000 are added each year. Among them are—to this point—474 covered bridges. Basic data can be accessed on line, but few records with their photos have been digitized thus far. While the listing provides no protection or restriction, since 1976 there have been tax incentives for reusing extant buildings rather than building new ones. In the earlier years, some volunteers encountered downright hostility to registration because local citizens and officials thought incorrectly that designation put the structure off limits to change, improvement, or removal.

HISTORIC AMERICAN BUILDINGS SURVEY (HABS) AND HISTORIC AMERICAN ENGINEERING RECORD (HAER) Born of the Great Depression, HABS was established by the National Park Service in 1933 to create jobs for unemployed photographers, draftsmen, and architects. Part of a relatively new movement towards historic preservation, these professionals began documenting the country's

buildings, including some covered bridges. The establishment of HAER in 1969, also under the National Park Service, continued this work but on a greater scale. HAER employs teams of volunteers and paid individuals to continue documenting structures, and this has included a great number of covered bridges. The website (www.nps.gov/hdp/) allows visitors access to both photos and drawings of those bridges whose records are digitized. Fox Chapel Publishing in East Petersburg, Pennsylvania, also published a collection of excellent photos along with architect's drawings of thirteen HAER bridges in *Built in America: Covered Bridges: A Close-up Look*, edited by Pennsylvania covered bridge authority Thomas E. Walczak (2011).

INDUSTRIAL ARCHAEOLOGY First developed in the 1950s in Britain for studying the Industrial Revolution, particularly its iron and steel making centers, Industrial Archaeology has expanded in both Europe and the United States and has founded several societies (Association for Industrial Archaeology, Society for Industrial Archaeology, and International Committee for the Conservation of the Industrial Heritage) and publishes several journals (*The Journal of the Society for Industrial Archaeology* and *Industrial Archaeology Review*). Practitioners create remarkably detailed architectural drawings of structures, often having to climb into dangerous places to obtain them. The activities of industrial archaeologists coincide with the goals of HAER except that the former strive for even greater detail. They also often build highly detailed scale models of the structures under study. The American covered bridge comes under their purview, but is not yet a major thrust of their activities. In Germany, at least one industrial archaeologist focuses on European covered bridges, and a new generation of Chinese scholars is looking at China's covered bridges.

Covered Bridge Tourism: Commodified Culture

As early as the 1930s and even as many officials charged with bridge maintenance were still taking the term "covered bridge" in vain, non-partisans, particularly photographers, began taking an interest in visiting them. New England has long been a mecca for tourists photographing its scenery, quaint buildings, and the region's iconic fall foliage, and covered bridges have long been part of their promotional schemes, particularly Vermont and New Hampshire. Their bridges are favorites for picture calendars, coffee mugs, linen towels, and other memorabilia, and today they are a major draw for visitors, although oddly they have not been the focus of specific festivals in that region, perhaps because covered bridges and New England already go hand in hand. Covered bridge festivals have, instead, blossomed like spring dandelions primarily in the Middle Atlantic States, the Midwest, and to a lesser extent, the Northwest.

Since 1957, the oldest of the festivals has been held each October in Parke County, Indiana, centered in Rockville County, at the recreated Billie Creek Village comprised of vintage homes and bridges east of Rockville, and at tour headquarters at the Bridgeton mill and covered bridge. The county's thirty-one covered bridges, some among the most scenic in the Midwest, attract around two million visitors a year bringing an important economic boost to an otherwise underdeveloped and modestly populated county. Although the Mansfield covered bridge and nearby roller mill are part of that festival, they too have their own festival.

Covered bridge festivals typically offer centralized festival activities typical of any festival or county fair: food and souvenir vendors, promotional displays, exhibits, organized tours of the bridges, activities for children, and sometimes a bit of theater. Parke County's fall foliage is at its peak during the festival, but serious bridge photographers should think twice about attempting this activity during festival weekends. Even if you do not plan your own route and find yourself driving against the flow of endless campers, tour buses,

Below To enhance Walnut Creek and Ohio's Amish tourism in 2009, Holmes County Engineer Chris Young designed and built a 55-foot multiple kingpost bridge just east of town on a county highway to replace an earlier non-covered bridge. To meet modern specifications, the trusses are massive and designed to carry all loads, and the bridge's height (15 feet) and width (26 feet) allow for virtually all legal vehicles. (Terry E. Miller, 2009)

motorcycle clubs, and kayakers, you will be taking photos of bridges with crowds of people milling about. Covered bridge festivals are better for festival enthusiasts than bridge enthusiasts.

A surprising number of counties which formerly had numerous covered bridges not only failed to promote them but systematically eliminated most of them. For example, Fairfield County just east of Columbus, Ohio, had over thirty-five bridges in 1960 and could have brought extra income to many in the county with a festival, but there was already plenty of industry there, and Columbus was nearby. While counties like Fairfield never established a festival, counties like Ashtabula in Ohio's northeast, once industrialized but fallen on hard times, did capitalize on its bridges by establishing a similar bridge festival in October 1983. Ashtabula now offers not just its twelve historical bridges (though some have been modified with substantial "renovations") but also five new bridges, one of them in historical style, the others modern. As mentioned earlier, the Gulf-Smolen Bridge, at 613 feet and the longest in the United States, gives them considerable "bragging rights."

An Internet search of "covered bridge festivals" reveals at least twenty-three, including Parke and Ashtabula. Some celebrate well-known clusters of bridges, such as in Madison County, Iowa (*The Bridges of Madison County*); Washington County, Pennsylvania; Columbia and Montour Counties, Pennsylvania; Oregon State; and Blount County, Alabama. Others highlight a single bridge, such as Elizabethton, Tennessee; Roann, Indiana; Matthews, Indiana; Zumbrota, Minnesota; Terre Haute, Indiana; and Kreidersville, Pennsylvania. Do festivals help protect covered bridges and raise awareness? In counties where the festival provides a significant economic boost, the answer is yes. Officials understand the need to protect these assets. For Parke County, Indiana, this also has meant pursuing and prosecuting anyone who damages or destroys a covered bridge.

Unfortunately, modern technology has created a new hazard that leads direction-challenged and apparently illiterate truck drivers to proceed confidently through covered bridges: the GPS (Global Positioning System). Based on information "in-putted" by frail humans but seemingly transmitted from the electronic gods hovering in geo-stationary orbits above the earth, GPS devices are less than perfect. In several unlucky places, these increasingly indispensable devices are sending semi tractor-trailer drivers through covered bridges. In 2011 alone, two semi drivers, both ignoring all the warning signs regarding clearance and weight limits, attempted to pass through the recently refurbished Jackson Bridge in Parke County because their GPS devices told them to do so. Both broke numerous upper cross braces but, thanks to the engineering genius of builder J. J. Daniels (and new glulam chords), did no structural damage. Later, another driver did similar damage to the Huffman Bridge in Putnam County,

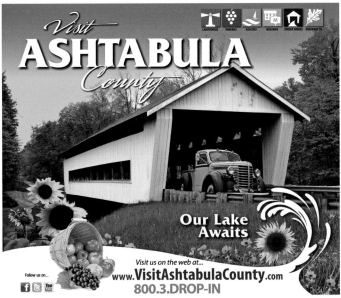

Indiana. Where some counties might have said, "we have inadequate bridges that must be replaced," these counties, because of tourism, prosecuted the drivers and quickly made the necessary repairs.

Festivals also raise the awareness of covered bridges among the general public. They attract many individuals who may enjoy festivals more than covered bridges specifically, but many do appreciate their visits to the bridges, and no one can know how this might affect their children. Author Miller's father took him to bridges when he was as young as seven simply to serve as a prop in photos. Many people realize that without the bridges there would be no festival, and with no festival, there is one fewer thing to do in your county or region. When they read that money needs to be spent to repair such bridges, they are more likely sympathetic than otherwise. Thus, whatever serious covered bridge enthusiasts may think about the festivals, they clearly have a positive effect on preserving covered bridges.

Covered bridges still have enemies, of course, and though the rate of loss has declined dramatically, their loss continues. Overloaded vehicles still attempt to cross and sometimes bring down a bridge. Unusual flooding—perhaps exacerbated by climate change—will continue to wash away or destroy bridges from time to time. There are still arsonists out there, and though some bridges have been treated with fire retardants, most have not. There is nothing to stop tornadoes like the one that wrecked Indiana's Moscow Bridge. Hurricanes and tropical storms will still affect the east coast, particularly New England, as Irene did in 2011. Here and there, unenlightened engineers or officials still prefer modernity over history. Some long-neglected bridges in areas where there are neither funds nor interest may finally fall into the river. The next generation and the one after that will still have covered bridges, but the experience will not be the same as it has been for us, both in the past or now. It is extremely important that bridge enthusiasts of all ages,

preservationists, timber framers, historians, county officials, bridge company executives, and tourism managers communicate their equally valid concerns to each other to arrive at the best possible solutions for the future of covered bridges.

Attitudes have gradually changed, but it difficult to pinpoint why. Perhaps the nation's bicentennial celebrations made us more aware of our material heritage. Increasing numbers of books have made the public increasingly aware. Here and there, officials saw the potential for tourism and began exploiting it. Where "old school" engineers only wanted to replace obsolete bridges with modern ones, a "new school" of engineers has become aware of the older traditions of timber framing and engineering. Over time, a number of them developed both interest and expertise in restoration, although what that term means remains controversial. Gradually, the perception of covered bridges has changed from nuisances to nostalgic icons of a tranquil past or the engineering marvels of our forefathers.

When today's "covered bridgers" set forth, they have a reasonable expectation that the bridge will still be there, that it will be in good condition, and that even the local residents value it. While the covered bridge will almost always still be there, however, we cannot be certain whether it is the original bridge, 70 percent of the original, 15 percent, or a replica. Historical markers and other signage usually offer little clarification beyond the year of "renovation," "rebuilding," or whatever the term used in the name of preservation. Consequently, some bridges marked "built in 18xx" have surprisingly smooth and new looking timbers, and certainly are not historical structures. Many no longer post load limits, and because the roads are paved and smooth and the decks made of tightly joined boards mounted on steel I-beams, drivers can race through them far "faster than a walk," the traditional warning still emblazoned on some covered bridge portals for the few who continue riding on or behind a horse.

Above left Ashtabula County, Ohio, established its covered bridge festival in 1983 and holds it each October when the fall colors are at their peak. This notice, published in area newspapers and on websites, highlights the Giddings Road Bridge, a non-historical Pratt truss structure designed and built by John Smolen in 1995. (Ashtabula County Convention and Visitors Bureau)

Above right This semi tractor-trailer driver apparently believed his GPS instead of his eyes when he approached the 180-foot Hunsecker Mill Bridge in Lancaster County, Pennsylvania, on May 9, 2012. Although the truck made it through without bringing the bridge down, it did serious damage to the interior bracing. Perhaps it was fortunate that the historical bridge from 1843 had been destroyed in 1972 by Hurricane Agnes, and this structure was a modern reconceived Burr truss built in 1975. (Jared Null, 2012)

chapter six
ICONIC COVERED BRIDGES OF THE UNITED STATES AND CANADA

OUTSTANDING BRIDGES ACROSS THE CONTINENT

Having gained a comprehensive understanding of the history, construction, and fate of America's covered bridges, many readers will wish to visit some of North America's remaining bridges. Thus, we offer in this chapter a series of 55 photo essays on some of the iconic covered bridges in both the United States and Canada. Each of these bridges, while intrinsically interesting in terms of structure and environment, also has a story to tell. These include stories about colorful beginnings, innovative designs, fascinating events in their history, and, in the case of some bridges, stories of death and rebirth. Sadly, two of the bridges featured—New York's Blenheim Bridge and Ohio's Geer Mill or Humpback Bridge—were lost during the writing of this book, the former to Hurricane Irene in August 2011, the latter to arson in June 2013. Another, Michigan's White's Bridge, which is discussed and illustrated on pages 86–7, was completely lost to arson in July 2013.

While it is true that the number of covered bridges remaining—under 900—is but a sliver of the approximately 15,000 that were built over time, this also makes them more special. Because they are now so rare, visitors appreciate them more, but for people living in the later nineteenth century they would have been so common and familiar as to be unnoticed. Perhaps that is why so many bridges survived only in memory but not in photos. Yet, it is fascinating that painters valued covered bridges as important motifs in their portrayal of landscapes in cities and the countryside. None of the early bridges over America's great rivers, often within cities and of daring and original designs, have survived.

The wear and tear of urban and industrial traffic wore them out, and indeed many became impediments to progress and had to be replaced. Additionally, many were lost to storms, flooding, ice jams, and failures. Of the tens of thousands of open or covered Howe truss rail bridges built, only one survives, now surrounded by thick foliage and guarded by hordes of mosquitoes along a neglected path near East Shoreham, Vermont. Fewer and fewer covered bridges continue in service, and most have been substantially "renovated," sometimes to the point of complete replication. Many others have been bypassed by new bridges or moved into parks, sometimes in scenic locations over streams or gullies, and a few just sitting on dry land.

Visiting covered bridges requires patience and perseverance. Today, visitors may program coordinates into their GPS devices and follow the artificial voice right to the bridge, but until recently travelers needed to be armed with a good set of maps with locations clearly marked. There is no consistency as to where officials might place signs along the highways indicating where to turn to visit a bridge. Sometimes old covered bridges have signs posted on their portals indicating their name and date of construction, but unmarked ones remain the rule. If you are lucky, you might find some place to park near the bridge along the road, but in other cases there is nowhere to park. When photographers wish to view the bridge from the side or the stream, they are often forced to ignore "No Trespassing" signs, risk breaking ankles in groundhog holes, snag one's clothes on barbed wire fence, and wade through waist-deep weeds hoping not to meet any critters, especially snakes. Some "bridgers" can relate tales of encounters with livestock, including the covered bridge photographer's version of the "running of the bulls." Intrepid photographers are also cautioned to recognize flora such as poison ivy, nettles, and nasty berry canes, and fauna such as spiders in gigantic webs, ant nests, skunks, and snakes.

Potential bridgers commonly ask, "How many covered bridges are there and where are they"? There is no easy answer to this because covered bridges must be seen on a continuum from undisturbed historical bridges to entirely new bridges using innovative designs. Whether each counts depends on who you are talking to. The *World Guide to Covered Bridges* was printed in 2009, and although updates are sent as inserts with *Covered Bridge Topics*, few have the time to update their *Guide*. The totals commonly given for each state may

Previous spread New Hampshire's 375-foot long Bath Bridge spans the Ammonoosuc River. The fifth bridge at this site, it was completed by 1832 with massive hewn timber trusses of unequal lengths that resulted in a one-of-a-kind structure. Once with only two piers, the bridge today has three, but there is no record of the circumstances that led to the placement of the third stone support. In 1918–19, the bridge was raised two feet to accommodate the passage beneath of taller railway engines. (A. Chester Ong, 2010)

Below Honey Run Grade Bridge, Butte County, California. (A. Chester Ong, 2012)

include debatable bridges such as brand-new ones, or may not. Many have been designated as "#2," indicating the second bridge at the site, usually post-1990. And these numbers never include the simulated ("garden") covered bridges found in some parks, estates, or on private drives put there simply for atmosphere. That is why the 2009 *World Guide* says: "Total: 814 covered bridges, 6 boxed pony bridges, 6 covered bridges in storage, 2 boxed ponies in storage, 1 mill bridge, 1 suspension bridge." Nonetheless, with this convenient handbook it is easy to know where bridges are concentrated and where they are sparse.

While New England is assumed to have the greatest concentration of covered bridges on a state-by-state basis, as the following map shows, the region cannot compete with Pennsylvania, Ohio, and Indiana, which together have more than half the covered bridges in the United States. Looking at it another way, though, New England has more bridges per square mile than anywhere else. Beyond the core of New Hampshire, Vermont, New York, Pennsylvania, Ohio, and Indiana, the numbers fall rapidly, dwindling to only fifteen distributed over three states just west of the Mississippi River (Missouri, Iowa, and Minnesota) and none to the south in Arkansas and Louisiana. There are none farther west until you reach the Pacific Ocean, where California has 10, Oregon 48, and Washington 6. Washington has only one "old" bridge, built in 1922, the rest being from 1966 to 2005. In Canada, virtually all covered bridges are in two eastern provinces, New Brunswick with 63 and Québec with 83, but there is also a single example in Ontario. Québec alone once had over a thousand covered bridges. While the *World Guide* lists a covered bridge in British Columbia, it is actually a boxed (roofless) Howe railroad bridge.

Nearly all visitors photograph covered bridges. They range in interest from those who merely step outside their cars for a quick snapshot with a cellphone to those who drag heavy cameras and tripod through brambles and swamps to get the perfect shot. Most photographers prefer sunny days, though the position of the sun may then dictate which views are best. Shooting into the sun is rarely good, and strong sunlight also produces strong contrasts between light and shade. The best views of many bridges are restricted to certain times of day— some are "morning bridges," others are "afternoon bridges." And woe to those who arrive when the sun shines on neither side, or at noon when the sun is too high to light any side surface. Skies full of large white clouds may produce so much glare that cameras have trouble sorting out the right exposure. The light of early morning and towards dusk produces challenges to color, often giving pictures a yellowish cast.

For visitors with a greater interest in structural and framing details, getting a close look is essential. Inspecting the bridge from the inside is easiest on bypassed bridges or those relocated into parks where there is no traffic. But when a bridge remains in use,

traffic can be a problem. When inspecting a lightly used bridge, especially if it is wide, cars and small trucks easily pass, but when the traffic is heavy and the lane is narrow, this can be dangerous. Even if wearing a fluorescent vest, one should not attempt to walk through the 449-foot Cornish-Windsor Bridge between Vermont and New Hampshire, where vehicles drive rapidly through the darkness. Middlebury, Vermont's Pulp Mill Bridge and West Virginia's Philippi Bridge, although double-lane, cannot be safely entered because the lanes are narrow and traffic heavy. In the old days when the original decks consisted of loose planks with or without runners, and gravel approaches were rough, cars had to slow down to cross, but now, with so many bridges on paved roads and having smooth entries and new tight decks, drivers are inclined to speed. And since many renovated bridges again carry significant loads, larger trucks, RVs, and even farm equipment may suddenly appear. In short, inspecting a bridge from within may pose dangers.

Visiting unlit and/or remote covered bridges at night is not recommended. These are sometimes attractive locations for "parking" couples, pot smokers, drunken parties, and even drug dealers. In the past, bridgers were more likely to encounter farmers enraged about trespassers, some with weapons, than today, but there are still covered bridges where nearby home-owners accuse visitors of violating their property rights. In these cases, one best apologizes and retreats to what is obviously public—the road and bridge.

Although many visitors likely fear snakes the most, we have very rarely encountered them, but especially in the South, where water moccasins and rattlesnakes are common, one is advised to wear heavy boots and proceed with caution. Insects, however, are virtually guaranteed. Mosquitoes are ubiquitous, but from southern Indiana and Ohio south, chiggers and ticks can be a problem. Such bites will remind you of your bridge trip for weeks to come. Spiders can be a problem too.

The following chapter features 55 outstanding bridges distributed over the United States and Canada. For each bridge ultimately chosen, we could have easily featured three or four more. Our choices were limited to the 200 plus bridges photographed by A. Chester Ong that were carefully selected in advance. We are certain that any knowledgeable bridge enthusiast would wish either to substitute other favorites or extend the list, but space limitations simply do not allow that.

West Union Bridge in Parke County, Indiana (A. Chester Ong, 2011)

EXISTING COVERED BRIDGES IN
THE UNITED STATES AND CANADA

Hogback Bridge, IA (ACO 2012)

Ashnola River Road Bridge, BC (BC 2006)

Gray's River Bridge, WA (BC 2006)

Earnest Bridge, OR (ACO 2012)

Felton Bridge, CA (ACO 2012)

Union Bridge, MO (TEM 1974)

ALBERTA **SASKATCHEWAN** **MAN**

BRITISH COLUMBIA

WASHINGTON **MONTANA** **NORTH DAKOT**

OREGON **IDAHO** **SOUTH DAKOT**

WYOMING **NEBRA**

USA

NEVADA **COLORADO** **KA**

UTAH

CALIFORNIA **ARIZONA** **NEW MEXICO**

TEXAS

MEXICO

State	Count	State	Count	State	Count	Province	Count
Alabama	8	Maryland	6	Oregon	48	British Columbia	1
California	10	Massachusetts [3]	10	Pennsylvania [8]	211	New Brunswick [11]	63
Connecticut [1]	5	Michigan [4]	5	South Carolina	1	Ontario	1
Delaware	3	Minnesota	1	South Dakota [9]	1	Québec [12]	86
Georgia	14	Missouri	4	Tennessee	4		
Illinois	7	New Hampshire [5]	50	Vermont [10]	99		
Indiana [2]	90	New Jersey	1	Virginia	8		
Iowa	10	New York [6]	26	Washington	6		
Kentucky	13	North Carolina	3	West Virginia	17		
Maine	9	Ohio [7]	144	Wisconsin	3		

[1] CT: 4 in *WG* + 1 new. [2] IN: 89 in *WG* + 1 new. [3] MA: 9 in *WG* + 1 new. [4] MI: 6 in *WG* – 1 lost. [5] NH: 51 in *WG* – 1 lost + 3 shared with VT.
[6] NY: 27 in *WG* – 2 lost + 1 new. [7] OH: 140 in *WG* – 2 lost + 6 new. [8] PA: 210 in *WG* – 1 lost + 1 new + 1 in storage has been reconstructed.
[9] SD: Not currently listed in the *WG*. [10] VT: 99 in *WG* – 1 lost + 1 new + 3 shared with NH.
[11] NB: 63 in *WG* – 1 lost + 1 new. [12] QC: 88 in *WG* – 2 lost.

Photo Credits: ACO, A. Chester Ong; BC, Bill Caswell; TEM, Terry E Miller

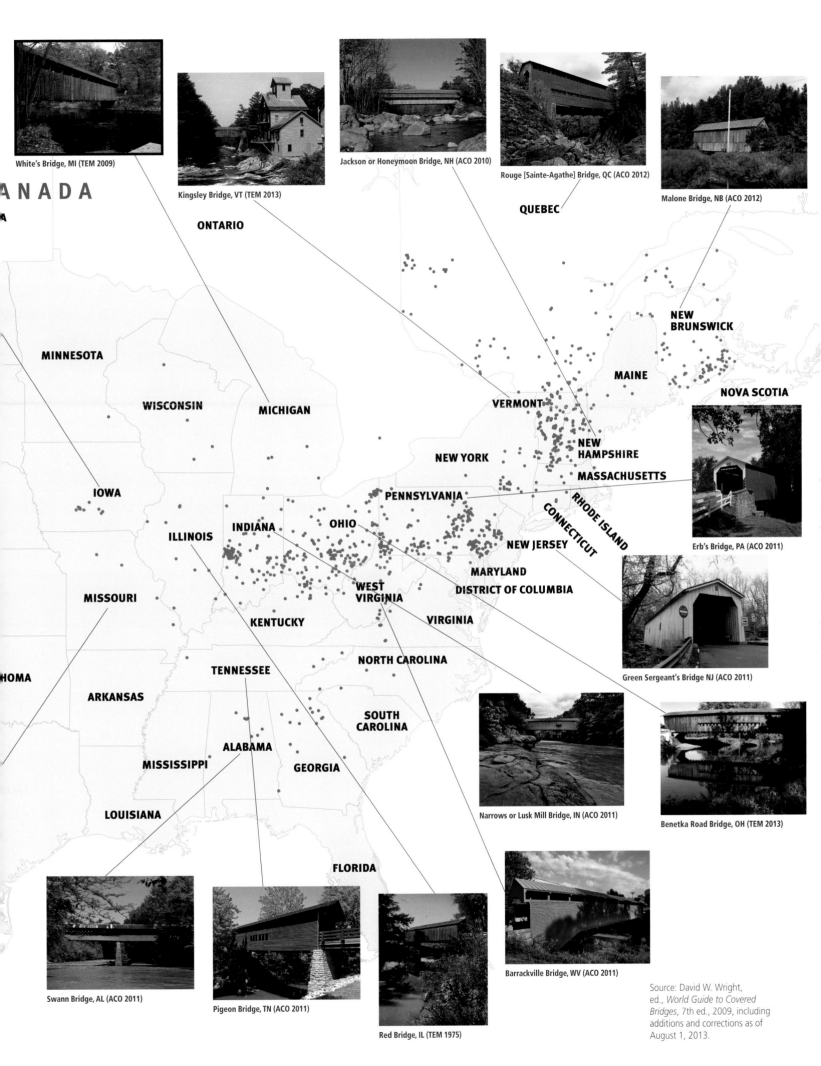

White's Bridge, MI (TEM 2009)

Kingsley Bridge, VT (TEM 2013)

Jackson or Honeymoon Bridge, NH (ACO 2010)

Rouge [Sainte-Agathe] Bridge, QC (ACO 2012)

Malone Bridge, NB (ACO 2012)

A N A D A

QUEBEC

ONTARIO

MINNESOTA

WISCONSIN

MICHIGAN

IOWA

ILLINOIS

INDIANA

OHIO

MISSOURI

KENTUCKY

TENNESSEE

ARKANSAS

ALABAMA

MISSISSIPPI

GEORGIA

LOUISIANA

HOMA

OKLAHOMA

NEW BRUNSWICK

MAINE

NOVA SCOTIA

VERMONT

NEW HAMPSHIRE

NEW YORK

MASSACHUSETTS

PENNSYLVANIA

RHODE ISLAND

CONNECTICUT

NEW JERSEY

MARYLAND

DISTRICT OF COLUMBIA

WEST VIRGINIA

VIRGINIA

NORTH CAROLINA

SOUTH CAROLINA

FLORIDA

Erb's Bridge, PA (ACO 2011)

Green Sergeant's Bridge NJ (ACO 2011)

Benetka Road Bridge, OH (TEM 2013)

Narrows or Lusk Mill Bridge, IN (ACO 2011)

Barrackville Bridge, WV (ACO 2011)

Swann Bridge, AL (ACO 2011)

Pigeon Bridge, TN (ACO 2011)

Red Bridge, IL (TEM 1975)

Source: David W. Wright, ed., *World Guide to Covered Bridges*, 7th ed., 2009, including additions and corrections as of August 1, 2013.

Ashuelot or Upper Village Bridge
CHESHIRE COUNTY, NEW HAMPSHIRE

Cheshire Co. #2, over the Ashuelot River, on Old Ashuelot Road next to SR 119 in Ashuelot Village, 169 feet, 2 spans

New Hampshire's covered bridges are well known for using Peter Paddleford's unpatented but distinctive design, but Town lattice bridges are equally prominent. Travelers on SR 119 going through the village of Ashuelot along the scenic Ashuelot River are struck by the elegance of the village's two-span covered bridge with its symmetrical covered walkways flanking the roadway and with everything—inside and out—painted white.

According to the New Hampshire Department of Transportation, the bridge was built in 1864 at a cost of $4,650, possibly by famed builder Nichols M. Powers of Vermont, to transport wood across the river for the Ashuelot Railroad's wood burners. This 24-mile-long rail line served local industries from 1850 until its abandonment in 1983. Among them were manufacturers of textiles, wooden boxes, and leather products. Today, the line has been converted to the Ashuelot Rail Trail and passes not only the Ashuelot Bridge but also the Sawyer's Crossing Bridge nearby.

With a total length of 169 feet in two spans (77 and 77.3 feet), Ashuelot's crossing is the longest among the county's six covered bridges. With the sidewalks, the total width is 28.6 feet, but even without them the interior width is greater than usual. Because the trusses themselves have no siding—their protection coming from the low-sided walkways—the play of sunlight into the bridge makes especially striking photographs. And because the interior is painted white, even night photos show the trusses clearly.

Located in the town of Winchester, New Hampshire, where it crosses the Ashuelot River, the two-span Ashuelot Bridge was constructed in 1864 to facilitate the transport of timber across the river for the wood burners of the Ashuelot Railroad. The 169-foot-long bridge today is a point of interest on a popular 23-mile-long rail trail. (A. Chester Ong, 2010)

Whether viewed during the day or at night, from inside or out, the Town lattice truss is a distinguishing characteristic of the Ashuelot Bridge. (A. Chester Ong, 2010)

Porter-Parsonsfield Bridge OXFORD COUNTY, MAINE

Oxford Co. #5 (19-09-05)/York Co. #1 (19-16-01), over the Ossipee River, just south of Porter on a bypassed section of SR 160, 160 feet, 2 spans

So-called because it links the towns of Porter and Parsonsfield, this county-line bridge is the second longest of Maine's nine remaining covered bridges. Built in 1876, it is one of five using the Paddleford truss developed, but not patented, by Peter Paddleford of neighboring New Hampshire. Nothing is known of the builder or the cost. Before it was bypassed and retired in 1960, the bridge carried relatively heavy traffic, and over the years officials made a number of "improvements" intended to strengthen it. One was the addition of gigantic laminated arches, one per truss and anchored into the abutments. These now appear to have warped and are slightly out of round. Another change was to pave the deck.

With a total length of 160 feet, it could easily have been built as a single span, but for unknown reasons two short spans of 80 feet were built. Each span uses an odd number of panels, resulting in asymmetrical arrangements of five and six panels for each.

Spanning the county-line between the towns of Porter and Parsonsfield in Maine, this 160-feet-long bridge boasts a fine Paddleford truss, which is characterized by multiple kingposts and triple chords as well as counterbraces notched into each neighboring panel. Built in 1876, the structure has undergone modification over the years to strengthen it, including, most dramatically, the addition of prominent laminated arches. (Top, Terry E. Miller, 2010; Right and below, A. Chester Ong, 2010)

When the bridge was restored in 1999, a great many truss members were replaced with new wood, and the deck was restored with wooden planks. With its two sets of oversized arches, the Porter-Parsonsfield Bridge has an especially rugged look. Separated from the new bridge by several hundred feet of woodland it remains a peaceful location where photographers might capture an attractive reflection from the creek.

With a length of only 80 feet and dating to 1852, the relatively modest yet strikingly picturesque Bridge-at-the-Green in West Arlington Vermont is one of the state's most photographed and painted sights. (A. Chester Ong, 2010)

Bridge-at-the-Green
or West Arlington Bridge BENNINGTON COUNTY, VERMONT

Bennington #1 (45-02-01), over the Battenkill River at West Arlington, 4 miles northeast of Arlington along SR 313, 80 feet

With a quintessential white New England church standing nearby and a combination of hills and classic white homes creating a backdrop, the "Bridge-at-the-Green" was made for a Norman Rockwell painting. Indeed, Rockwell (1894–1978) lived and worked nearby. Were it otherwise, this bridge would attract little notice, being a modest 80-foot Town lattice structure over a normally placid brook. Nestled in the green Vermont mountains, however, also means that when too much water flows into the

Battenkill, it rises in anger and threatens to sweep away everything in its path. Soon after the bridge was built in 1852, a spring freshet did just that, leaving the bridge on its side nearby, still spanning the creek. According to legend, locals continued using it by passing over the truss that now formed the "deck." Afterwards, the bridge was disassembled and rebuilt in its proper place but now secured with cables. Though likely replacements, these cables remain, and good thing because on August 28, 2011, during diminished Hurricane Tropical Storm Irene's fury, an uprooted tree came down the swollen river and hit the upstream side so hard that it bowed the bridge downstream. After repairs, the bridge reopened in 2012. For many years

the interior side of each truss has been covered with a thick steel mesh to protect the trusses and prevent vandals from prying off the siding, but this detracts visually and no longer allows visitors to touch the well-worn planks of the trusses.

West Cornwall Bridge LITCHFIELD COUNTY, CONNECTICUT

Litchfield Co. #2 (07-03-02), over the Housatonic River between the towns of Cornwall and Sharon, on SR 128 east of US 7 in Cornwall Township, 149 feet, 2 unequal spans, 12-foot entries

It is certain that famed American composer Charles Ives passed the West Cornwall Bridge as he traveled along the Housatonic River from his home in Danbury, CT, to vacation in the Berkshires at Stockbridge, MA, where he was inspired to compose "The Housatonic at Stockbridge," a tone poem from 1911–13 and part of his *Three Places in New England*. Besides being part of a typical New England village postcard scene, the West Cornwall Bridge is an intriguing study in structure. The first known bridge was destroyed by a flood in 1837 and replaced in 1841, but that bridge appears to have been replaced again in 1864 by the present structure, originally a simple Town lattice with no upper secondary chords.

It is assumed that this structure reused the abutments and pier from the earlier bridge, but the spans are unequal—64.1 and 81.10 feet with 3.2 feet between them—making the trussed portions 149.1 feet long, far shorter than the 173.1-foot total length when the entries are added. The 3.2 feet between, however, is defined by two upright planks and not a clear separation of spans. While it is true that the Town lattice could be supported at any point without creating load distribution problems, the placement of the pier off-center for a bridge well within the normal single-span range, seems odd. What is stranger, though, is the superimposition of a sort of queenpost truss, reportedly done in 1887, over the entire structure but with an additional set of braces, giving the appearance of kingposts within the queenpost. And to make matters more confusing, the kingposts are asymmetrical because the spans are unequal. Whatever the anomalies, the trusses have supported nothing more than themselves and the roof since 1973 when a steel I-beam floor replaced the original deck.

Considering the heavy one-lane traffic and the fact that in the 1940s a tar-laden tanker truck had crashed through the deck, this is an acceptable solution. Movie buffs may also recall this bridge's cameo appearance at the beginning of Mark Robson's 1967 film, *Valley of the Dolls*, based on Jacqueline Susann's novel.

Supported by a Town lattice truss with an additional asymmetrical queenpost frame, the West Cornwall Bridge in Connecticut comprises two unequal spans that are supported by a single mid-river pier. In 1973, steel I-beams were placed beneath this heavily traveled bridge. (A. Chester Ong, 2011)

A beautiful bridge in what is today a remote and scenic location, New Hampshire's Blacksmith Shop Bridge has its original multiple kingpost structure intact even as it has undergone careful restoration, including having been raised to mitigate the possibility of flood damage. (A. Chester Ong, 2010)

Blacksmith Shop Bridge SULLIVAN COUNTY, NEW HAMPSHIRE

Sullivan Co. #1 (29-10-01), over Mill Brook, 2 miles east of Cornish City just off Cornish City Road, 91 feet

Built in either 1881 or 1882 but long closed to traffic and now seemingly forgotten, the Blacksmith Shop Bridge stands out for its natural environment and simplicity. Although its builder, James Tasker (1826–1903) of nearby Cornish, had worked with Bela Fletcher to construct the magnificent Cornish-Windsor Bridge over the Connecticut River nearby, he also built modest bridges using not the full-timbered Town lattice design seen in his major projects but a local version of the multiple kingpost truss with closely spaced posts. This bridge, with trusses only 91 feet long and an interior width of only 11.5 feet cost a mere $873 when constructed. Multiple kingpost bridges,

otherwise rare in New England, scarce in Pennsylvania and New York, but widespread in Ohio, were common in this one area where Tasker worked. Ohio multiple kingpost designs, however, have panels measuring roughly 8–10 feet in width, while Tasker's New Hampshire bridges have panels only around 3.5 feet in width. This produces a highly rigid frame without the need for added arches.

One can only imagine how the area, then locally known as "Slab City," looked when Tasker built the bridge. Nearby stood the bridge's namesake, a blacksmith shop once operated by John Fellows (1798–1884), who would have been eighty-four at the time of construction. The stone foundations sit nearby. More than likely the area was then denuded of trees, with houses and other structures nearby forming a small hamlet. Today, all that is gone, but with the forest growth and the rocky stream below, the Blacksmith Shop Bridge is among the most scenic in a state filled with scenic covered bridges.

Though long retired, the bridge is still in excellent condition, undoubtedly stemming from continued maintenance by the town and Milton Graton's restoration in 1963. Graton raised the southern end two feet and the northern end one foot.

Cornish-Windsor Bridge

SULLIVAN COUNTY, NEW HAMPSHIRE

Sullivan Co., New Hampshire #14 (29-10-09)/Windsor Co., Vermont #9 (45-14-14), over the Connecticut River on Bridge Street, Windsor, 1.5 miles northwest of Cornish City, 449 feet, 2 spans

The Cornish-Windsor Bridge is not just the longest historical covered bridge in the United States but also one of only three remaining interstate bridges, the others also spanning the Connecticut River but at narrower points. The present bridge is the fourth at this site, the others (built in 1796, 1824, and 1828) all having been destroyed by floods. Considering that the river is still quite capable of massive floods, that the bridge carries near non-stop two-way traffic day and night, and that each span is an exceptional 204 feet, it is surprising that the bridge also carries a ten-ton load limit. This is due to the wisdom and skill of two modern bridge restoration specialists, Jan Lewandoski and the late David C. Fischetti, who returned the bridge to service in 1989 after having been closed for two years.

The present bridge is an unusually wide (24 feet overall, 19.6 feet roadway) Town lattice constructed of squared beams rather than the usual planks. The builders, Bela J. Fletcher (1811–77) of Claremont, New Hampshire, and James F. Tasker (1826–1903) of Cornish, are said to have pre-cut and assembled the trusses in a Vermont meadow northwest of the bridge site, then reassembled them over the water on falsework. Not surprisingly, such a massive bridge carrying heavy traffic deteriorated, and the owners carried out repairs in 1887, 1892, 1925, 1938, 1954–5, and 1977 (Evans and Evans, 2004: 170). The last repair resulted from flood and ice damage and cost $25,000.

After further deterioration forced the bridge's closure on July 2, 1987, authorities carried out the most extensive renovation in the bridge's history, with input from numerous individuals and governmental bodies. Engineer Fischetti has described the work in his *Structural Investigation of Historic Buildings* (2009). In order to restore the bridge's original camber, Fischetti devised three I-beam towers (on each abutment and the pier) and used massive cables to lift the bridge into the desired arch. Evans and Evans

have summarized his work based on a journal article by subcontractor Lewandoski and published by the Society for Industrial Archeology: ". . . the old bed timbers were replaced, and eleven-by-thirty-five-inch glulam timbers that cantilever out thirteen feet were placed inside of them at both the abutments and the central pier; 60 percent of the chords were dismantled; positive camber was restored to eighteen inches; new lower chords of glue-laminated material consisting of southern yellow pine were installed (most of the new chord members were 100 or 116 feet long by eight inches by eleven inches); upper chords of similar material, 88 feet long,

were replaced over the center pier" (2004: 171). Following completion of this 4.5 million dollar project, both governors attended the reopening of the bridge on December 8, 1989.

Visitors to the bridge and a former toll-house on the Vermont side see that they can take photographs from either end but must drive between them because traffic is heavy and runs two-lane, the bridge is dark, and there is no provision for pedestrians. That the bridge can continue to perform such service is a testament to the skills of the engineers and crews who renovated the bridge. The glulam chords, controversial but necessary to restore strength and camber, are not obvious, while the original truss members continue to carry the load. The cross bracing and deck are not original, but this is true of many bridges, since these parts are easily damaged or worn by the traffic. While this project was highly praised and won awards, it has also been controversial because it legitimatized the wholesale replacement of the lower chords, a "solution" that has become the "easy way out" in other restoration projects.

The longest historical covered bridge in the United States, the Cornish-Windsor Bridge crosses the Connecticut River between New Hampshire and Vermont. On a heavily traveled route with a ten-ton load limit, the bridge carries two-way traffic day and night. In addition to ongoing maintenance to its Town lattice truss, extensive repairs have been carried out periodically since it was constructed in 1866. Having been closed for two years, the bridge was returned to service in 1989 after rebuilding that included three temporary I-beam towers, one on each abutment and midstream pier, with massive cables, in order to restore the bridge's original camber. (Below left and right, A. Chester Ong, 2010; Above and center, Terry E. Miller, 2010).

Pier Railroad or Chandler Station Bridge

SULLIVAN COUNTY, NEW HAMPSHIRE

Sullivan Co. #3 (29-10-03), over Sugar River, 5 miles west of Newport along Chandler Mill Road, 217 feet, 2 spans

With only eight covered rail bridges left in the United States—five in New Hampshire, two in Vermont, and one in Oregon—out of the thousands that were built, many bridgers still have not seen one. Where highway bridges could survive into the twenty-first century because of light use, rail bridges only survived on abandoned lines. Because rail traffic was exceptionally hard on timber bridges, their life expectancy was relatively short. Though thousands of

uncovered timber bridges carried trains, the covered ones were especially vulnerable because, while the roof and siding protected the trusses, they also trapped embers that might set the bridges on fire. During the American Civil War, rail bridges were a major target. Thanks to the nation's abundant timber supply, however, rail lines routinely rebuilt their bridges as often as every 8–10 years.

The need for increasing numbers of rail bridges in the first half of the nineteenth century was a major impetus for new truss designs. The Burr truss, first designed for highway use well before railroads had

developed, was also used in rail bridges. It was engineers like Col. Stephen H. Long, William Howe, and Ithiel Town, among others, who put their minds to a solution. Today's survivors are either Town lattice or Howe trusses, but the Howe truss became the standard throughout much of the century for both covered and uncovered spans.

The New Hampshire government website (http://www.nh.gov/nhdhr/bridges/p99.html) says Pier Bridge was constructed in 1907 by the Boston and Maine Railroad, one of the nation's major lines from its founding in 1835 to its absorption into Pan Am Railways in 1964. The Newport Historical Society

Constructed during the first decade of the 1900s, the Pier Bridge crosses the Sugar River. The longest surviving covered rail bridge in the world, the Pier Bridge has two spans totaling 216.7 feet. Its doubled Town lattice trusses, lateral floor beams, structural details, as well as impressive height with a clearance of 21.1 feet, were necessary to carry trains with steam engines and heavy loads. (A. Chester Ong, 2010)

(http://www.newportnh.net/index. php?doc=3_93), however, attributes construction to the Concord & Claremont Railway in 1905–6. The engineer in charge was Jonathan Parker Snow (1848–1933), one of American history's most famous rail bridge engineers. When the B&M bought the line (whether from the Sugar River Railroad or the Concord and Claremont), it inherited an earlier bridge built here in 1871–2. While even the earlier bridges had to be unusually robust to carry a steam engine, its tender, and everything else, bridge builders throughout the nineteenth century had to deal with increasingly larger and heavier locomotives. By the middle of the twentieth century, rail bridges had to carry GE 70 ton and GE 44 ton locomotives. Their freight included paper products, fuel, timber, among other products.

The Pier Bridge, with two spans totaling 216.7 feet is the longest surviving covered rail bridge in the world. At this length, a center pier was mandatory, and that gave rise to the bridge's name. To accommodate trains,

engineers could build unusually high trusses (Pier has a clearance of 21.1 feet) that were either of massive timbers in Howe trusses or doubled webs in Town lattice trusses. Constructed with a Town lattice, Pier has extraordinary doubled trusses that tower over the pedestrians and cyclists now using the bridge. The large-scale lateral floor beams are closely spaced and suspended on iron bolts from the primary lower chord. A mile farther along the line is the Wright Railroad Bridge, 124 feet in a single span, with doubled Town trusses supported with a massive arch between the truss layers.

Although steam locomotives no longer toss live embers into the air and threaten the bridge, today's threat is would-be arsonists. To defeat them, the bridge has been treated with fire retardants and fitted with sprinkler systems. Ownership has passed to the New Hampshire Department of Resources and Economic Development, Division of Parks and Recreation, and Pier Bridge is part of the "Sugar River Rail Trail."

Scott Bridge WINDHAM COUNTY, VERMONT

Windham Co. #13 (45-13-13), over the West River, 2 miles west of Townsend next to SR 30 on a bypassed section of Back Side Road, 276 feet, 3 spans

Disastrous floods were a normal part of early American life, and the one that hit this area of Vermont in 1869 destroyed most of the bridges, including Scott Bridge's predecessor. The area's most recent flood, in August 2011 resulting from Tropical Storm Irene, caused the raging waters of the Williams River to destroy the nearby Bartonsville Bridge, a video of which "went viral." In 1870, when Harrison Chamberlin began building the present Scott Bridge,

he may have been improvising, using dry-laid stone abutments and piers to support a 166-foot covered Town lattice span over the river channel and two open wooden kingpost spans over a flood plain gully at the other end. The lattice trusses of the river span, however, lack the usual secondary upper chords. When this portion required roof maintenance in 1873, officials decided to frame and cover the two short approaches as well, resulting in what became, at 276 feet, the longest covered bridge in Vermont today.

Scott Bridge is also a heavily scarred survivor, as officials responsible for the bridge's maintenance have had to make numerous repairs over the years to address

the builder's earlier decisions. The original abutments of loose, flat river stones have been reinforced with concrete. At some point, probably early in the twentieth century, single twelve-ply laminated arches were added to each truss of the long span, adding thrust against the old stone pier, which then had to be reinforced with thick concrete braces. Later, the arch buckled, forcing closure of the bridge to traffic in 1955. To prevent the long span from collapse due to deteriorated truss members, especially the lower chords, engineers further added a concrete center pier in 1981 and, at some point, four exterior buttress braces on each side to prevent twisting.

The Scott Bridge in Windham County, Vermont, is today bypassed for vehicular traffic and passable only by pedestrians. Over the years, its structure has been modified from its original 166-foot-long Town lattice truss. Not only have the original stone abutments been reinforced with concrete, a single laminated arch was added to each truss. A concrete center pier was added in 1981. (A. Chester Ong, 2011)

Though now closed to vehicles, pedestrians walking through the bridge cannot help but be impressed with the rugged, if deformed, superstructure. The hand-hewn beams of the two kingpost spans are especially striking. Unlike normal covered kingpost bridges, these are pony trusses only two-thirds high and each has two iron rods from the apex to the lower chord as well as secondary bracing and shorter rods within. Now covered and seemingly a part of the whole, they create an odd sensation as one goes from the lattice truss to two short kingpost trusses. Where some covered bridges are highly unified in terms of both structure and style, Scott Bridge is "the sum of its parts."

Stark Bridge COÖS COUNTY, NEW HAMPSHIRE

Coös Co. #5 (29-04-05), over the Upper Ammonoosuc River in Stark village, just off SR 110, 138 feet

Of all the covered bridges in the United States, none rivals Stark for its peaceful, traditional environment—a mountain backdrop, village homes, a simple white church—the epitome of pure Americana. The bridge is endlessly depicted on calendars, especially in winter night scenes, on postcards, on tourism literature, and in picture books. These qualities are what saved the bridge from replacement in the 1950s when the

town leaders decided to replace it with a modern steel model but met with howls of protest from photographers and artists nationwide. But this picture of the perfect village belies a somewhat troubled history.

The village of Stark, with only slightly more than 500 residents, traces its history to 1774 when it was called Percy, after the First Duke of Northumberland, Hugh Percy. Only in 1832 did its name change to Stark, honoring Revolutionary War General John Stark, author of the state motto, "Live Free or Die." Sitting next to the bridge is the village's famous Stark Union Church,

built in 1853 and currently a Methodist congregation. Its simplicity of design exemplifies the austere practices of American Congregationalism that grew from Swiss theologian John Calvin (1509–64), whose plain aesthetic forms the basis for classical New England architecture.

The original design of this 134-foot-long crossing, built in 1862 probably by Charles Richardson or his son, is no longer clear. It is not known whether the symmetrical covered walkways now well integrated were added or not. According to the pattern of braces and counterbraces of the Paddleford

truss, the bridge was designed as a single span, but in the center, over the present pier, is a separation suggesting it was indeed two spans. When a flood carried off the bridge around 1890, there was already a center pier. Since the bridge snagged intact nearby, residents, aided by their oxen, returned the bridge to its abutments, but engineers removed the remains of the pier and added massive laminated arches.

Around 1942, when the Stark Bridge showed signs of failure, engineers removed the arches, built a new center pier, and installed steel I-beams, leaving the crossing as a shell over an independent, modern deck. We can offer no explanation for the self-contradictory single-span arrangement of truss members coupled with the center separation over the modern pier. Thus, photographers might see Stark as the perfect covered bridge, but structural engineering students will find it confounding.

The 138-foot-long Stark Bridge in New Hampshire is one of the most photographed and painted of New England's many beautiful bridges. Its structural transformations over recent years are reasonably well documented although it is not clear what the original design was when the bridge was built in 1862. (Top left, A. Chester Ong, 2010; Upper right and lower right, Terry E. Miller, 2010; Left and below, A. Chester Ong, 2010)

179

Taftsville Bridge WINDSOR COUNTY, VERMONT

Windsor #12 (45-14-12), over the Ottauquechee River in Taftsville village, on River Road at the intersection with US 4 in Woodstock Town, 191 feet, 2 spans

On arrival, visitors are struck by this bridge's dramatic location, just downstream from an old power plant and dam, perched on an amazingly rough looking center pier, with huge arches protruding down into the abutments and pier. Upon entering the bridge, anyone familiar with covered bridge trusses will likely furrow the brow, trying to decipher the truss design. The builder, Solomon Emmons III, grandson of his namesake and the founder of the village along with Stephen Taft in 1793, clearly understood effective truss design, though innocent of the standard truss designs of

the day. Emmons built the bridge in 1836 for $1,800, $1,050 of which was for the substantial stonework. Some writers describe the design as "mongrel"—as a mixture of trusses—but "idiosyncratic" perhaps works better. None of the elements combined here is unique—multiple kingpost, aspects of queenpost, the dramatic laminated arches with iron rod hangers—and while lacking a single name, apparently works. The elongated end panels of each span have double braces. Certain panels have horizontal braces (the

"queenpost" aspect), and the spans are unequal. The northern span is 100 feet long in eight panels and the southern span 89 feet in seven panels, the middle panel having X braces. With an outer width of 20 feet but a truss height of only 10.6 feet, the bridge has an unusually wide-proportioned portal.

As the state's third oldest bridge and subject to heavy traffic until 2011, the fact that the bridge retains so much of its original construction is amazing. That includes the lower chords consisting of 70-foot sections 18 by 16 inches with overlapping splices as long as 20 feet. Writers disagree on when the arches were added, Barna (1996: 148) speculating that Emmons himself might have added them, while Nelson (1997: 156) suggests they were added after 1900. In the 1920s, engineers corrected a noticeable lean, but the more extensive repair work carried

Constructed in 1836 to span the Ottauquechee River in the town of Woodstock, Vermont, the Taftsville Bridge has an idiosyncratic structure involving multiple kingposts, aspects of queenpost, and laminated arches with iron rod hangers. It carried traffic until recent years. (A. Chester Ong, 2010)

After the Taftsville Bridge was damaged with the passage of the remnants of Hurricane Irene in 2011, during which dozens of propane canisters struck the bridge, the State of Vermont dismantled all of the south span except the arches in preparation for restoration. (Top and bottom, A. Chester Ong, 2010; Center, Kaitlin O'Shea, 2011)

out in 1952–3 by Miller Construction of Windsor involved jacking the bridge up on the frozen river both to allow work on the chords and deck as well as permanently place the bridge above the floods; the extra cribbing on the pier is clearly visible. Other repairs have taken place on a regular basis, including protecting the rough stone pier with concrete and adding metal angle braces inside. Later, in 1993, a box truck tore out wooden parts. The siding formerly was solid, making the bridge dark inside but better for colorful advertising, but now openings on both sides admit plenty of light. Thanks to what Emmons built in 1836 and others have added, Taftsville Bridge survived Hurricane Irene in August 2011, when not only did the waters batter the bridge but large propane tanks smashed into the sides as well. However, the water undermined the south abutment, and at this writing, the south span's trusses have been disassembled, though the arches remain in place, pending reconstruction of the stonework.

Bath Bridge   GRAFTON COUNTY, NEW HAMPSHIRE

Grafton #3 (29-05-03), over the Ammonoosuc River in the town of Bath, 375 feet, 4 spans

Spanning a river full of rock outcroppings, rapids, and a dam, and framed by a classic white New England church, Bath Bridge is one of the nation's iconic covered bridges. While photographers strive to capture the bridge's rugged environment, visitors with an eye to structural matters can marvel at the idiosyncratic trusses and timber framing. Bath Bridge, dating back to 1832 and one of the nation's oldest, is a clear manifestation of Yankee ingenuity coupled with the kind of eccentricity we expect from rural New Englanders.

In the early years of the United States, bridges over wild rivers seldom lasted long, and Bath's covered bridge, being the fifth crossing, demonstrates the point. The first four bridge types, built in 1784, 1805, 1820, and 1824, are unknown but were likely pile

bridges and naturally susceptible to ice and flooding. We assume this because it was not until March 1831 that the town approved spending $1,400 to build two abutments and two piers, with an additional $400 paid in November. While the unknown masons built the abutments square to the river, they built each pier at a different angle, which greatly complicated the work of the unknown truss framers. This dry-laid stonework, however, is one of the elements giving the bridge its primeval look. One year later, in March 1832, the town approved construction of the wooden portion for $1,500. Its floor length is 374.5 feet but the spans are unequal in length, being (from east to west) 127.2, 71.10, and 175.5 feet. These are the "upstream" sides, however, for the east span's "downstream" side is two panels longer and the western span's "downstream" side is three panels shorter because of the skewed piers. As a result, the builders had to construct six trusses of different lengths.

An iconic bridge, New Hampshire's 375-foot-long Bath Bridge spans the Ammonoosuc River. The fifth bridge at this site, it was completed by 1832 with massive hewn timber trusses of unequal lengths that resulted in a one-of-a-kind structure. (A. Chester Ong, 2010)

Everything about the trusses defies classification, making this a one-of-a-kind design without a name. Rather than using large-size timbers for the chords, they joined three vertical planks for each. The rather lightweight posts are closely spaced (roughly two for the length of a normal Burr truss panel), notched between the inner two chord members, and secured with single trunnels. The "braces" are notched between the outer two chord members but cover one panel plus half of each neighboring panel. This sort of framing was the most distinctive feature of Peter Paddleford's unpatented truss commonly used in New Hampshire some years later, but there is no known connection between Bath and Paddleford. Completing the complexity are triple-planked arches carefully notched among both posts and "braces" in both the eastern and western spans but not for the short middle span, which has a low arch below the floor. The others are seated onto the lower chords and not into the stonework below. The only other surviving bridge that shows a structural similarity is Sayres Bridge over the Ompompanoosuc River at Thetford Center, Vermont, built

in 1839, but there is no evidence to connect the two. Nor is it reasonable to describe Sayres' truss as a Haupt truss, though it has some similarities to this later design otherwise unknown in New England.

Visitors cannot help but notice, however, that today Bath Bridge has *three* piers, not two, and that this addition subdivides the longest (western) span. When the third was added is unknown, but it changes the stress patterns on the truss members dramatically. Perhaps it was added in 1853 when the White Mountain Railroad built a line under the western span and ran spark-throwing steam engines just beneath this wooden bridge for many years before placing metal sheeting to protect it. During the years 1918–19, the railroad required the bridge to be raised two feet because of larger engines, and engineers also added large laminated arches on the inner side for the three eastern spans, leaving the now shortened fourth span without. Additionally, masons had to cut skewbacks into the masonry to receive these arches. As a result, a laminated arch overlaps *part* of the original western span, providing visual confusion unmatched anywhere else in the

Once with only two piers, the bridge today has three, but there is no record of the circumstances that led to the placement of the third stone support. In 1918-19, the bridge was raised two feet to accommodate the passage beneath of taller railway engines. In early 2013, the New Hampshire Department of Transportation announced that the aging Bath Bridge was being taken out of service for a year to replace floor beams, deck, metal roof, and siding. (A. Chester Ong, 2010; Right, Terry E. Miller, 2010)

covered bridge world. An exceptionally wide bridge—with an overall width of 24.6 feet—it also carries a generous load limit of six tons, though trucks are banned. Now approaching 200 years of continuous service, the Bath Bridge is not just one of the nation's most scenic but also its most eccentric structurally.

Above Moseley or Stony Brook Bridge. (A. Chester Ong, 2010)

Northfield Falls' Five Covered Bridges

WASHINGTON COUNTY, VERMONT

Washington Co. #7, #8, #9, #10, #11
(45-12-07/08/09/10/11), over Stony
Brook, Dog River, or Cox Brook
in or near the village of Northfield
Falls in the town of Northfield

Vermont well deserves its reputation as a different sort of place. With no large urban areas, an aversion to modern big-box retail developments, and a rugged individualism that matches the rocky terrain, Vermont is a place of villages, most of them along creeks and small rivers. Not surprisingly, many of the state's covered bridges are located in these picturesque locales. Founded in 1781, Northfield Falls, south of the state's modest capital of Montpelier, is part of a cluster that includes Northfield Center and South Northfield. In the past, its several waterways supplied power to numerous mills, all now gone. It was the Vermont Central Railroad, renamed the Central Vermont Railroad after 1853, that brought prosperity to the town

in the nineteenth century. Today, the area's biggest employer is Norwich University, the oldest private military college in the United States, with an enrollment of around 2,000 students. Northfield Falls still has four covered bridges, three within walking distance of each other, plus a fifth a few miles to the south.

Spanning appropriately named Stony Brook on a quiet road four miles south of the village, Moseley Bridge is a mere 36 feet long. As is true of four of the five bridges, the original deck was replaced in 1971 with steel I-beams, the stone abutments were capped with concrete, and the truss raised for added clearance. Thus, the kingpost truss, built in 1899 by John Moseley II, supports only the roof, and because it has been raised, its lower chord is exposed well above the floor line.

Its namesake is long gone but the Slaughter House Bridge spanning Dog River on the southern side of the Northfield Falls, built around 1870, preserves the original construction as well as the dry-laid stone

abutments. The wide pool just north of the span was originally a mill pond. Unlike the other bridges in Northfield Falls, the 56.6-foot-long queenpost truss actually supports the deck, built on two heavy cross beams suspended from the lower chords with steel stirrups.

Entering the village from the state highway just to the east on Cox Brook Road, visitors walk past houses and small businesses before entering the 1872 Station Bridge spanning Dog River, the first of three in close proximity. The longest, at 137 feet, this was originally a single-span Town lattice truss, but in 1963 engineers built a new deck on four lines of steel I-beams with additional support from a center pier, leaving the trusses to support only themselves and the roof.

Turning to the west, visitors see the Lower Cox Brook Bridge, also called the Second Bridge or the Newell Bridge, just across the intervening tracks of the Central New England Railroad. The name Lower Cox

Above center and right Slaughter House Bridge. (A. Chester Ong, 2010)

Above and right Third or Upper Cox Brook Bridge.
(A. Chester Ong, 2010)

Above Station or Northfield Falls Bridge.
(A. Chester Ong, 2010)

Continuing west, we quickly understand why the last bridge is called the Upper Cox Bridge, not just because it is farther up the creek but because it is physically up a hill. Before ascending the hill, you see the bridge high on the hillside above a creek that cascades down a series of rocky rapids. A low queenpost truss 51.5 feet long, again with a new I-beam deck, this bridge not only spans an exceptionally scenic brook but does so at an angle. To avoid building an unnecessarily long span, the builders placed the trusses on a skew so that the south truss is offset to the west in relation to the north truss. Although always a low "pony" truss, this bridge was covered from the time of its construction around 1872. As near as this bridge is to the other two, though, a bend in the road and trees make it impossible to see them from here.

Brook stems from its location close to where this cascading stream empties into Dog River. Like the Station Bridge, it was built in 1872, but because it is considerably shorter at 56.6 feet, its truss is a queenpost nearly identical to that of the Slaughter House Bridge, but its deck was replaced with a new one on I-beams in the 1960s.

Packsaddle or Doc Miller Bridge

SOMERSET COUNTY, PENNSYLVANIA

Somerset Co. #2 (38-56-02), over Brush Creek, 4.3 miles northwest of Fairhope on TR 407, 48 feet

Somerset County, in southwestern Pennsylvania's gentle mountains, preserves ten covered bridges, several worthy of being featured. Barronvale, an asymmetrical two-span bridge, is beautifully situated and painted bright red. The Lower Humbert Bridge spans a scenic rocky creek and offers reflection photos from the creek bed. But the Packsaddle is exceptional for the creek below that tumbles over a small precipice, creating one of the most attractive environments in the state. Viewed from the roadway, however, the bridge appears to be nothing more than a simple six-panel multiple kingpost truss bridge with a plain portal. Viewed from below the falls, however, the scene is worthy of a picture calendar. Getting there, however, is extremely difficult and somewhat dangerous, for there are no paths down the steep bank leading to the bridge.

When built in 1870, Packsaddle Bridge was probably just a run-of-the-mill project costing around $500, but after a flood in January 1996 caused considerable damage, the county faced serious expenses for repairs. The frugal commissioners decided to replace the Packsaddle with a concrete bridge, but an outcry from nearby residents resulted in restoration costing $382,263. Repairs included new concrete abutments faced with stone, steel stringers, a new timber floor, as well as

new siding and roofing. Rededicated and opened on July 18, 1998, it continues to carry a normal load of traffic.

Structurally, Packsaddle Bridge is somewhat exceptional in Pennsylvania. The vast majority of bridges are Town lattice, Burr, or kingpost/queenpost. While multiple kingpost bridges are common in Ohio, there are only six others in Pennsylvania, plus around a dozen multiple kingpost trusses with queenpost reinforcements. In the latter cases, the queenpost functions like a three-piece

polygonal arch. Considering that multiple kingpost bridges were more common in Somerset County than elsewhere, we suspect there was a preference for this design over the simple queenpost more prevalent elsewhere.

One of ten covered bridges in Somerset County, Pennsylvania, the short Packsaddle Bridge crosses Brush Creek. Constructed in 1870, this modest bridge has a six-panel multiple kingpost truss, a structure uncommon in Pennsylvania. Extensively repaired in 1996, the bridge retains its rustic charm spanning a waterfall (A. Chester Ong, 2011)

Halls Mills Bridge SULLIVAN COUNTY, NEW YORK

Sullivan Co. #1 (32-53-01), over Neversink River, 4 miles northwest of Grahamsville on an abandoned road beside CR 19, 129.9-foot truss with 5-foot portal overhangs each end

If we ignore several New York bridges that have been so extensively rebuilt that they justify being given twenty-first century building dates, then Halls Mills Bridge, along with one other in Ulster County (Forge Bridge), is among the state's youngest. For reasons unknown, the bridge was begun in 1906 but not completed until 1912. Builder David Benton, assisted by George Horbeck and James Knight, used a classic Town lattice with both primary and secondary chords but used carriage bolts instead of trunnels. For foundations, the county had a proper abutment built on the south end, but the

north end was supported by a free-standing pier, the covered bridge linked to the north bank by an open wooden approach. While picturesque, both the abutment and pier used dry-laid field stones essentially piled into a seemingly random form. Sometime in the past, officials reinforced the abutment with concrete, but the pier remained vulnerable and was undermined by the heavy rains produced by Hurricane Irene and Tropical Storm Lee in August 2011. In late 2012, local citizens raised enough money to supplement a grant from the FEMA (Federal Emergency Management Agency) to stabilize the bridge, whose collapse was imminent. At some time in the past, officials added six wooden buttresses to keep the bridge square, a practice common in New York. To do this, large beams substantially longer than the bridge is wide were bolted to the underside, and angle braces

extended from the ends to the upper chords, each buttress protected with siding.

In days past, drivers approached the bridge at a near 90-degree angle at the bottom of a steep embankment down from the main road. By 1963, Sullivan County closed the bridge to vehicles but left it open to pedestrians. Since that time, the area to the north has returned to forest, providing an exceptionally natural setting for this seemingly venerable, but vulnerable, bridge.

Begun in 1906 and completed in 1912, the Halls Mills Bridge over the Neversink River near Grahamsville, New York, was retired from vehicular traffic in 1963. A striking feature is the set of six wooden buttresses strengthened with angle braces that protrude from each side, which were added to keep the bridge square. Flooding brought about by Hurricane Irene and Tropical Storm Lee in August 2011 ravaged the stone pier, causing great concern that the bridge might fall into the stream, but fortunately this was rebuilt in 2013. (A. Chester Ong, 2011)

Jackson's Mill or Barnhart's Bridge

BEDFORD COUNTY, PENNSYLVANIA

Bedford Co. #25 (38-05-25), over Brush Creek, 2.5 miles southwest of Breezewood on TR 412 in East Providence Township, 91 feet with 3.6-foot entries

Visitors to Jackson's Mill and the covered bridge next to it can easily imagine how life might have been in nineteenth-century Bedford County when area farmers brought their grains here for milling. Originally built in 1839 and bought by M. J. Jackson in 1867, the mill operated until about 1951. Nearby are the remains of the dam, which collapsed sometime before 1980, along with various locks and channels that directed water to the mill. The bridge was constructed by brothers-in-law Adam Karns Bottenfield and Jacob Pee for $1,284, some 300 yards upstream, but following the devastating Johnstown Flood of May 31, 1889, caused by the failure of the South Fork Dam, this bridge, though far from Johnstown, floated downstream to its present location next to the mill. John G. Rohm and William B. Karns reset the bridge on new abutments there rather than move it, all for $675. A lightly framed Burr truss, it is typical of the county's bridges. Because the new location required a longer span, the builders

added two 25-foot open wood kingpost spans on each end. Locals describe these triangular-shaped spans as "grasshopper" bridges.

After being closed for some five years, the county rehabilitated the bridge in 1992 for nearly half a million dollars and reopened it to traffic. Jackson's Mill remains an isolated, peaceful place in spite of being so close to Breezewood, the "town of motels" and its endless traffic. Since Jackson is a common name, it is no surprise that Pennsylvania has two other bridges of the same name, one each in Washington and Lancaster Counties.

Originally built some 300 feet upstream, the Jackson's Mill Bridge in Bedford County, Pennsylvania, was carried downstream during the 1889 flood, where it was reconstructed and lengthened near a grist mill owned by William Jackson, which henceforth gave the bridge its name. The lightly framed Burr truss crossing, typical of Bedford County, is approached over an open wooden kingpost bridge. With its red portal and white siding, the bridge has a distinctive air next to the old mill. (A. Chester Ong, 2011)

McConnell's Mill Bridge

LAWRENCE COUNTY, PENNSYLVANIA

Lawrence Co. #1 (38-37-01), over Slippery Rock Creek, 9 miles east-southeast of New Castle, 1 mile south of US 422 in McConnell's Mill State Park, 110 feet

Situated over boulder-strewn Slippery Rock Creek in one of western Pennsylvania's most rugged gorges, the McConnell's Mill Bridge offers a scenic environment unmatched anywhere else in the state. For kayakers, the river is one of the most challenging streams as well, varying from Class II to Class IV. Just upstream stands the well-preserved mill next to a dam. Slippery Rock Creek at low water appears rather tame, but after a heavy rain when the gorge receives the runoff from the hills, it becomes a raging torrent too dangerous even for daredevils. The many gigantic boulders just downstream can be climbed when dry, but when wet exemplify the creek's name.

It is not known whether there was a bridge here in 1852 when Daniel Kennedy built the first grist mill, but the farmland is mainly above the mill side, and the steep banks of the other are a challenge even to modern cars. Kennedy's mill burned in 1868 and was rebuilt. Thomas McConnell bought the mill in 1875 and made numerous changes, converting it from waterwheel power to water turbines and replacing the original grinding stones with rollers, one of the first in the nation it is said. The mill processed local grains such as corn, oats, wheat, and buckwheat until 1928 when the owner could no longer compete

with his aging equipment. After 1942, the area was transferred to the Western Pennsylvania Conservancy, and in October, 1957 was dedicated as a state park.

Though the bridge's dramatic location over a rugged creek and near a mill and mill dam is what makes it remarkable, the bridge itself

is rather ordinary, a ten-panel Howe truss built in 1874 just before McConnell bought the property. It is still hard to imagine how horse-drawn wagons could ascend or descend the steep road on the north bank. Because the old bridge was required to carry not just visitors' cars but their campers and motor

Crossing a turbulent rock-strewn stream appropriately called Slippery Rock Creek in western Pennsylvania's Lawrence County, McConnell's Mill Bridge is located adjacent to a nineteenth-century grist mill, which shares its name. Constructed in 1874 with a Howe truss set upon stone abutments, the bridge today is reinforced with I-beams. (A. Chester Ong, 2011; Interior, Terry E. Miller, 2011)

homes, when the park opened the state added a massive I-beam frame beneath, supporting the entire bridge. At that time, the bridge was painted white, but at a later date the park had it repainted a bold, more eye-catching red.

Bogert's Bridge
LEHIGH COUNTY, PENNSYLVANIA

Lehigh Co. #1 (38-39-01), over Little
Lehigh Creek, in Little Lehigh Park
on the southwest edge of Allentown,
172 feet

Acentral feature of Allentown's Little
Lehigh Park since 1964, Bogert's Bridge
is the "poster child" for how *not* to build a
covered bridge. Granted, in 1946 and 1957,
large trucks damaged the bridge and caused
it to be closed, but it appears that Bogert's
had long been a maintenance nightmare.
The oldest of Lehigh County's six bridges,
Bogert's (along with Wehr's Bridge) dates to
1841 when stout Burr trusses were the norm
in Pennsylvania. And Bogert's appears to
be "a stout Burr truss" with the usual double
lower chords, a single upper chord, and
double arches anchored into the abutments.
But something went terribly wrong with both
bridges. Bogert's has an unremarkable truss
length of 151.4 feet plus 9.7-foot covered
openings on each end. Strength is created by
truss height and panel width. The trusses in
these two bridges are relatively low, while the
panels in Bogert's are approximately 12.6 feet
wide when 8–10 feet is normal. The bridge
is also exceptionally wide: 23.5 feet overall
with a 20.3-foot roadway width. It appears the
trusses were simply not substantial enough.
Over the years, engineers attempted to
remedy the situation with a full range of iron

rods, metal plates, wooden counterbraces,
and large beam frames within and a maze
of iron rod bracing beneath, but to no avail.
Finally, they added two masonry piers, and
today the bridge sags from one to the next.

Lehigh County's other bridges, all Burr
trusses, provide a contradictory picture.
Manassas Guth, Rex, and Geiger appear to
have been better built, similar to those found
in other Pennsylvania counties. But Schlicher's
and Wehr's show failures similar to those of
Bogert. Schlicher's, built in 1882 with a truss
length of only 90.8 feet in ten panels, failed in
such a way that produced dramatic sags near
each end, and the bridge has been closed for
many years. In 2012, it was announced that
the county plans to tear down the original
and build a replica capable of carrying traffic.
Wehr's Bridge, built the same year as Bogert's
and having panels of approximately the same
width but a truss length of only 118 feet, has
many of the same reinforcements along with
two piers, though the structure does not sag
the way Bogert's does. Even as a seeming
wheelchair patient, Bogert's provides an
attractive and useful centerpiece for Allentown's premier park.

The oldest of Lehigh County, Pennsylvania's covered
bridges, having been built in 1841, Bogert's Bridge is
supported by a flawed Burr truss which necessitated
a variety of eccentric reinforcements to be added over
the years. (A. Chester Ong, 2010)

Dreibelbis Station Bridge

BERKS COUNTY, PENNSYLVANIA

Berks Co. #7 (38-06-07), over Maiden Creek, south of Lenhartsville on Balthaser Road (also called Covered Bridge Road) beside SR 143, 190 feet

Berks County in southeastern Pennsylvania is comprised of scenic rolling farmland surrounding the city of Reading, once a great manufacturing center but now struggling with severe economic malaise. Five covered bridges survive, four open to traffic and one incorporated into a city park. Two of them (Greisemer's Mill and Kutz's Mill) stand next to old stone mills. Pleasantville has a one-of-a-kind truss, primarily two arches, one of which barely rises above the lower chords. Wertz or Red, now serving pedestrians, is one of the nation's longest single spans, with a portal length of 218 feet. We have chosen Dreibelbis Station Bridge for its scenic value and its colorful history. Though built after the Civil War in 1869, it has the air of an ancient and venerable bridge, partly from its horizontal siding and stepped false front portals similar to the state's earliest bridges now only known through photos. We are

grateful to Pennsylvania bridge historian Fred J. Moll for his detailed research on this bridge.

Records show that an early, probably uncovered, bridge was washed out here in an 1839 January freshet, with no replacement contemplated until 1869. In the meantime, Manassas Dreibelbis had bought land around the site from his father John, in April, 1846. Continuing his father's sawmill, Manassas also built a flax seed mill for producing linseed oil in 1850, which was later converted to clover milling. On January 23, 1869, Manassas, with land on the east bank, and Samuel K. Fisher, with land on the west, petitioned the Court of Quarter Sessions for a bridge estimated to cost $5,500, alleging that the fording 400 feet downriver was often dangerous. After approving the petition and sending it on to the county commissioners, the *Berks and Schuylkill Journal* published an advertisement for bids on May 29 due on June 8 at noon. The journals recorded thirteen proposals ranging from Charles Stitzel's bid of $4,987.50 to Ahrens and Co. for $7,500.00, the latter possibly for an iron or combination bridge. As was their duty, the commissioners

awarded the contract to the lowest bidder but he withdrew. The records indicate that this pattern continued through at least four other bidders. While Moll notes that the eventual builder is unknown, the HAER documentation lists payments totaling $6,000 to Simon Dreibelbis and Charles Kutz (Moll gives his name as Kurtz), who originally had submitted bids #9 and #10. In October, the bridge opened for travel, showing the efficiency of the local government—eight months from petition to opening. After the Schuylkill and Lehigh Railroad built a line along Maiden Creek in 1874, the local stop became known as Dreibelbis Station, and although all evidence of the rail line is long gone, the bridge has retained this moniker.

Dreibelbis and Kutz built a rugged sixteen-panel Burr truss with double arches measuring 190 feet portal to portal, including the covered approaches. Over the years, the bridge has suffered both deterioration and damage. In 1968, Anthony Genovese of Lancaster had to replace the ends of the rotted arches and used concrete to build new skewbacks on the abutments.

With its stepped gable portal, Dreibelbis Station Bridge in Berks County, Pennsylvania, is quite striking and only one of five covered bridges in a county that once had 51. Constructed in 1869, the bridge incorporates a sixteen-panel Burr truss with double arches measuring 172 feet from portal to portal. In September 2012, the county secured a $1.4 million dollar federal grant to restore the bridge so that it will be safe for vehicular traffic for decades to come. (A. Chester Ong, 2010)

Tropical Storm Agnes in 1972 crashed part of a bungalow against the bridge which then directed the water to shoot over its roof against the bridge. Although the bridge held, the downstream-shaped warping on the east end that resulted can still be seen. Since then, the bridge has remained open and even painted bright red. In August 2012, the National Historic Covered Bridge Preservation (NHCBP) program announced a grant of $1,440,000 to rehabilitate Dreibelbis Station Bridge with new abutments, replacement of bad truss members, new siding, and other work.

East Paden and West Paden Bridges (Twin Bridges) COLUMBIA COUNTY, PENNSYLVANIA

Columbia Co. #11 and #12 (38-19-11 and 38-19-12), over Huntington Creek, on a bypassed section of Winding Road east of Forks and SR 487, 79 feet (east) and 103 feet (west)

Here and there in both the United States and Canada there are instances of "twin bridges," that is, pairs of covered bridges in close proximity. In some cases, they stemmed from separate channels of the river, but in others they resulted from flooding that created a new or second channel. Columbia County, Pennsylvania's "twin bridges" are the only remaining pair in that state. After a flood in June 2006 caused uprooted trees and summer cottages to crash against the West Paden Bridge and destroy the span, even this pair nearly ceased to exist. Fortunately, Columbia County, which actively promotes its twenty-four covered bridges, replicated the West Paden with an entirely new structure in 2008 as part of the park's foot trail.

These two bridges, separated by only a few steps in between, typify the bridges of this hilly county of small creeks. Like the majority of the state's old bridges, East Paden is a queenpost truss and West Paden, like the rest, is a Burr truss. Spread throughout this mostly rural county, Columbia's many bridges exemplify the stereotype of a covered bridge sitting peacefully over a babbling brook. Few are striking for their length or setting, but their very modesty makes them appealing. Until 1963, drivers had to negotiate passage through both of the twins, since they were too narrow for passing, but in that year the state bypassed them and converted the surrounding areas into a park. Now visitors can enjoy picnics on the bridges.

The East Paden and West Paden Bridges spanning Huntington Creek in Pennsylvania's Columbia County are unique in Pennsylvania in that they are a set of twin bridges. East Paden is supported by a queenpost truss while West Paden utilizes a Burr truss. In 2006, West Paden was destroyed during a flood and completely rebuilt in 2008. Bypassed in 1963, today the twins rest surrounded by a pleasant park. (A. Chester Ong, 2011)

Many other Pennsylvania counties also had modest bridges similar to those of Columbia County. Perhaps because bridge tourism was slow to take hold in this far-from-New England region, many were lost. This was especially true during the period of the 1950s to the 1970s, at which time the state owned numerous covered bridges on the old five-digit state road system and instituted a policy to eliminate all "outmoded" and "inadequate" bridges. Columbia County's bridges suffered under this policy, but fortunately there were also numerous bridges on the local township roads, and most of these have survived thanks to the county's appreciation of their historical value. Considering that the twin bridges have been a major element in the county's identity, there was never much doubt that the West Paden twin would be rebuilt after succumbing to the flood.

Philippi Bridge   BARBOUR COUNTY, WEST VIRGINIA

Barbour Co. #1 (48-01-01), over the
Tygart Valley River, in the city of
Philippi on US 250, at the junction
of US 119, 304 feet, 4 spans

From the outside, the Philippi Bridge looks
impressively sharp, beautifully sided to
emphasize its massive arches, and sporting
handsome rounded portals. Beneath the
surface, however, lies a battle-scarred veteran
with a record of several "near death" experiences. Philippi, the modest county seat of
Barbour County with a population today of
around 3,000, was once an important point
on the Beverly-Fairmont Road, a turnpike
connecting the hilly interior of what was then
western Virginia to the Staunton-Parkersburg
Turnpike running from the Ohio River to
central Virginia across the Shenandoahs.
Philippi Bridge was constructed in 1852 by
West Virginia's most famous bridge builder,
Lemuel Chenoweth (1811–87) of Beverly,
along with his brother Eli, for $12,180.68
on abutments and a pier built by Emmett J.
O'Brien. The double-lane two-span bridge,

with trusses measuring 285 feet, used a form
of the Burr truss similar to that used by
Theodore Burr himself, that is, with counterbraces fitted within each panel. Today, the
Philippi Bridge is both West Virginia's oldest
covered bridge and its longest.

This bridge's first brush with death came
early in the Civil War, when Union and
Confederate troops fought skirmishes in the
Philippi area, which some call "the first land
battle of the Civil War." On June 3, 1861,
Confederate troops under Col. George
Porterfield occupied the bridge, but Union
troops under Col. Benjamin F. Kelley chased
them out. Instead of burning the bridge, the
troops used it as a barracks. In the late spring
of 1863, when Confederate Gen. William E.
Jones was ordered to burn both the Philippi
and Rowlesburg Bridges as part of a campaign
to attack the Baltimore & Ohio Railroad,
locals intervened and persuaded them to
spare the bridges.

In the twentieth century, the old bridge
found itself serving US 250, a route used by
many trucks. Besides creating restrictions

on clearance and weight, local pedestrians
took their lives into their hands to cross. In
1938, the highway department removed the
entire deck and installed a new four-span
concrete bridge beneath the no longer
functioning trusses and roof, which solved
the weight restriction problem but not the
clearance. They also built a pedestrian
walkway on the south side. The next threat
came from the great flood of November 4–5,
1985, but perhaps because of the new concrete
deck, the bridge held. However, the bridge's
most critical near-death experience came on
February 2, 1989, when gasoline spilled from
a tanker filling a nearby service station's
underground tanks and ran down the hill
into the bridge. A car's hot catalytic converter
probably set off the fire that thoroughly
charred the trusses and destroyed the siding
and roofing. In spite of this damage, Professor
Emory Kemp, Director of the Institute for
the History of Technology and Industrial
Archaeology at West Virginia University,
restored the bridge, and it reopened on
September 16, 1991.

Constructed by the renowned bridge builder Lemuel Chenoweth and his brother in 1852, the Philippi Bridge spans the Tygart Valley River as part of US 250, which was once an important segment of the turnpike between Beverly and Fairmont, West Virginia. It is the state's oldest and longest covered bridge. Skirmishes during the Civil War led to the likelihood of the bridge being burned, but local residents got involved and the bridge was spared. In 1989, some 60 percent of its timbers were destroyed when a spark set off gasoline that poured downhill from a nearby gasoline station. Two and a half years later, after extensive restoration, this historic bridge was reopened to traffic. (Opposite and above left, Terry E. Miller, 2011; Above center and right, A. Chester Ong, 2011; Drawing, Fletcher and Snow, 1934: 375; Below, Mark Withers, 2007)

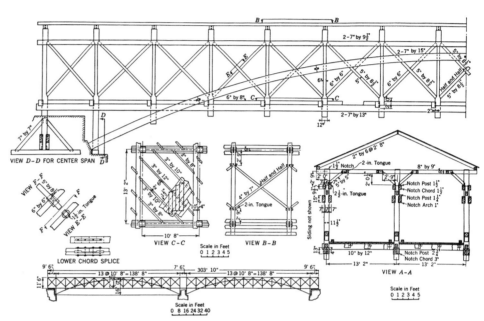

White Bridge, Lippincott Bridge, Danley Bridge, and Hughes Bridge

GREENE AND WASHINGTON COUNTIES, PENNSYLVANIA

White and Lippincott Bridges, Greene County, Danley and Hughes Bridges, Washington County

The bridges of Washington and Greene Counties in Pennsylvania's southwestern corner demonstrate how terrain influenced the kinds of bridges built. Located in the hills south of Pittsburgh, these two rugged counties have a maze of small creeks few of which require bridges of even 100 feet. As insignificant as these waterways are, they still must be bridged. As a result, both counties constructed innumerable generic, culvert-length bridges of between 30 and 75 feet, the shorter ones being kingpost trusses and most others queenpost trusses. None is particularly old: Hughes dates to 1889, White to 1919, while Danley is likely

from the 1880s. Because of the modest length and the higher cost of modern materials, covered bridges continued to be built until the 1920s. Greene County's Lippincott Bridge, only 32 feet long, is an exception, having been built later, in 1943, because of the steel shortage during World War II.

Depending on length, the trusses we see in these bridges are simple and basic or elaborated with internal bracing. Queenpost trusses longer than 60 feet were clearly more risky, and most bridges of that length and beyond sagged in later years. Until the 1960s, both counties had many more covered bridges—Greene today has only seven and Washington twenty-two—but fifty years ago there were more than thirty in each county. All those owned by the State of Pennsylvania

were removed over the years. Many county-owned bridges remained, however, but now they face a new challenge. The discovery of vast gas deposits underlying the Marcellus shale formation, especially in Washington County, has led to a dramatic rise in hydraulic fracturing ("fracking"), and this industry brings with it gigantic trucks and rigs. Thus, a number of bridges formerly on quiet country lanes have had to be moved into parks. Greene County is carrying out a program of bridge reconstruction resulting in the replacement of the majority of a given bridge's timbers, something clearly seen in the White Bridge. Still, many of Washington County's old covered bridges remain in their original location on quiet township roads surrounded by modest farms and light forest.

Greene and Washington Counties in southwestern Pennsylvania include numerous modest bridges with lengths between 30 and 75 feet, each of which has served as a critical link for rural transportation.

Above left White Bridge (Greene) (A. Chester Ong, 2011)

Above right Lippincott Bridge (Greene) (A. Chester Ong, 2011)

From far left to right Danley Bridge (Washington); Hughes Bridge (Washington); White Bridge (Greene); Hughes Bridge (Washington); detail, Danley Bridge (Washington). (A. Chester Ong, 2011)

Blenheim Bridge

SCHOHARIE COUNTY, NEW YORK

Schoharie Co. #1 (32-48-01), over Schoharie Creek, formerly at the edge of North Blenheim on a bypassed section of SR 30, 226 feet

Blenheim's long-retired span and one of the nation's most significant timber bridges was unfortunately lost to the brutal remnants of Hurricane Irene around 1 pm on August 28, 2011, when Schoharie Creek, normally little more than a trickle over a vast expanse of flat stones, rose in excess of 15 feet in a matter of hours (see page 125). The raging waters lifted the bridge from its abutments and crushed it into kindling against a bridge downstream. Because the bridge was the area's most famous attraction, local people have since collected the remains, some from 30 miles downstream. The chances

of reconstructing this bridge anytime soon appear slim because of projected costs of $2.5 million and FEMA's rejection of their application for funds. While replacement of storm-damaged operational bridges is usually covered by federal and state assistance, authorities have baulked at expending so much money for what some are calling a mere "historic artifact" at a time when many local communities are still suffering.

Although state authorization for the Blenheim Bridge Company was enacted in 1828, no action was taken until 1854 when Clarendon, Vermont, bridge builder Nichols Montgomery Powers (1817–97), repairing a covered bridge in nearby Blenheim, was asked to build one at North Blenheim. Powers agreed to do so, and in 1855 he and his crews completed a 226-foot double-lane span with

a total width of 26.3 feet which opened as a privately owned toll bridge. Powers worked for $7.00 per day and his workers $1.00 per day. Their labor, together with 94,000 board feet of white pine and white oak and 5,100 pounds of bolts and washers, came to $6,000. Although Powers normally used the Town lattice in his bridges, for Blenheim he chose Stephen H. Long's patent truss, but with an added feature: the center truss would be 24 feet high—reaching the roof peak—plus an embedded triple-layered arch within the truss. Following Long's plan, four beams comprised both upper and lower chords along with double posts and braces, and single counterbraces, the timber sizes graduated from heavier at the ends to lighter in the middle. The great arch was anchored on skewbacks in the abutments. Additionally, Powers followed Long's recommendation to "pre-stress" the bridge by jacking it up to relax the joints and placing wooden angle blocks where the counterbraces met the posts and both upper and lower chords, then letting the structure down again.

The stone masons began their work on site while the superstructure was built elsewhere. An article in the *Schenectady Union* on February 26, 1930, possibly based on interviews with eyewitnesses, described the

Constructed in 1854 over Schoharie Creek on the edge of North Blenheim, New York, the Blenheim Bridge was a venerated double-lane 232-foot structure that utilized the Long truss. Sometimes referred to as "a giant bridge" and often claimed as the longest single-span bridge in the United States, the bridge was swept away as the remnants of Hurricane Irene impacted the area in August 2011. Rebuilding, while desired by the local community, is uncertain because of the costs involved. (Terry E. Miller, 2008)

construction work. "After the giant bridge was cut and tailored back of the village, and then put together to make certain that all was right, it was taken apart and then began the difficult work of erecting it over the stream. Temporary scaffolding, called 'bents,' were set up across the river and the floor beams of the new bridge laid and leveled on this superstructure. While this work was in progress a boy was killed, when one of the tall, heavy log bents fell. Besides the ordinary carpenters necessary to put up such a high bridge, Powers hired a number of young fellows, called 'climbers' who were not afraid to work high over the fast water. And there youths put together [*sic*] and assembled, all the 'sticks' of the high work"(quoted in HABS NY, 48-BLEN, 1-).

Lola Bennett, writer of the HAER report (HAER NY-331), learned that "Scoffers said that the bridge would fall of its own weight with the removal of the falsework. When the day came, Powers climbed to the roof and said, 'If the bridge goes down, I never want to see the sun rise again!' People then said that the bridge would sag so much as to be useless. Powers replied that if this happened he would jump off. When the falsework was taken away the bridge settled only slightly, even less than Powers had calculated."

With its rare Long truss that incorporated a high central arch, the bridge had many noteworthy structural details, as these photographs show. (Terry E. Miller, 2008, except bottom, 1965)

In 1869, a freshet caused a new channel to form on the east end, this being bridged with a succession of two open wooden approaches. After the second failed under the weight of a threshing machine in 1891, the town board agreed to build an iron span, completed in 1894. The bridge had remained a private toll bridge under a succession of owners until 1891 when the company's charter expired, at which point the state became owner and made it free. The bridge also survived several accidental fires and rounds of flooding. Although the state wished to replace the bridge with a steel span in 1932, the townspeople persuaded engineers to bypass the old bridge, thereby preserving it for posterity— at least until Mother Nature had other ideas.

The Blenheim Bridge was distinct for many reasons, especially its unique structure with the high central arch. Not only was it a relatively rare Long truss but one of only six double-lane bridges in the United States. Additionally, many believed it to be the longest single-span covered bridge remaining, though others claimed that honor for Nevada County, California's Bridgeport crossing. Two factors made resolution difficult. First, the abutments for both bridges were not perfectly square with each other, meaning the upstream and downstream clear spans differed. Second, in 1997, after flooding damaged the bridge, reconstruction work enlarged Blenheim's abutments, reducing the clear span. Thus, claims asserting that Blenheim was longer depended on measurements that can no longer be verified.

Schofield Ford or Twining Ford Bridge

BUCKS COUNTY, PENNSYLVANIA

Bucks Co. #13 (38-09-13#2), over Neshaminy Creek, 3 miles west of Newtown in Tyler State Park bordering Newtown and Northampton Townships, 172.2 feet, 2 spans

The story of the Schofield Ford or Twining Ford Bridge is one of reincarnation: of its birth in 1873, its death in 1991, and its rebirth in 1997, or to shift the analogy, the resurrection of one of Pennsylvania's most scenic bridges. Even before the establishment of Tyler State Park in 1974, when the bridge sat deteriorating on the private property of George F. Tyler, the beauty of the creek at this spot—shallow water with rushes here and there—was indisputable. Today, that beauty is made even more magical with the addition of horses and riders crossing both the bridge and fording the creek. Even though the Twining Ford Bridge is a replica—albeit an exact one—it is, especially for photographers, hard to ignore or dismiss.

Until the bridge was built, travelers using the Holland Pike had to ford the creek, but during periods of high water or ice, this was impossible or at best dangerous. In 1869, citizens began petitioning for a bridge, doing so again in 1871, but neither of the townships involved could afford such a project. Only in 1873 did the county agree to build the bridge, hiring Newtown builder George Mahon and paying him a total of $7,595. Mahon used Pennsylvania hemlock and oak, and the bridge was completed early in 1874. The area had been known both as Schofield's Ford and Twining's Ford after two prominent local families, but by the beginning of the twentieth century the land was owned by a Mr Solly, and thus some called it Solly's Bridge. When George Tyler bought the land in 1917, the

Originally completed in early 1874 in Bucks County, Pennsylvania, the Schofield Ford Bridge was burned by arsonists in 1991 and completely rebuilt in 1997 by local volunteers. Today, it offers passage across the picturesque Neshaminy Creek in Tyler State Park. (A. Chester Ong, 2010)

road closed and Mr Tyler became responsible
for the bridge, which by 1932 was in poor
condition. That year he had it reinforced
with steel braces. When the state bought the
property in 1964, it would still be ten years
before the area became a state park. Six
diamond-shaped windows were added in
1979–80. In 1982, Susan Zacher listed the
structure as being in "poor condition" (1982:
80). On October 7, 1991, unknown arsonists
burned the bridge, which fell into the creek
as smoldering ruins within thirty minutes.
Local citizens almost immediately formed a
committee to rebuild the bridge. Over 800
volunteers first honed their skills by building
an old-fashioned barn. Then, using the
hemlock and white oak as in the original,
they rebuilt the bridge by hand to its original
specifications, with the bridge reopening on
September 6, 1997.

A stone pier today supports the bridge, which likely
was constructed as a single span utilizing the Town
lattice truss. While Town lattice trusses can be
reinforced with an extra pier, the queenpost reinforcement inside suggests it was originally a single
span. (A. Chester Ong, 2010)

With its stone pier located in the middle of the river, the bridge is clearly two spans. The Town lattice truss, once described as "built by the mile and cut off by the yard" (quoted in Allen, 1957: 15), can be subdivided at any point because it is a continuous pattern rather than a set of symmetrical panels. Its length of 172 feet is within the range of a single span. The feature that suggests a single span is the supplemental queenpost truss attached to the lattice by wooden dowels that reinforces the entire length much as an arch reinforces the multiple kingpost panels of a Burr truss. Although an exceptionally long queenpost, it is designed for a single span; bifurcated in two by the pier neutralizes its reinforcement abilities. We believe the pier was added to the original single span, but thus far there is no known historical documentation to support this.

Bucks County, a blend of bedroom communities for Philadelphia, rustic summer homes near the Delaware River, and open farmland farther afield, is rightly known for its twelve covered bridges. But these much-photographed and well-maintained structures present challenges to those who value the authenticity of original construction. Only one bridge, the South Perkasie Bridge, now sitting on blocks in Perkasie's Lenape Park where it was moved in 1958, has all its original timbers. The rest of the county's bridges have undergone "restoration," which could include replacement of some or most of the truss members, the substitution of an I-beam and concrete deck under the now functionless covered trusses, to replication, as is true for both Mood's Bridge, burned in 2004 and replicated in 2008, as well as the Schofield Ford Bridge. Yet, the signs on the portals

claim the original date of construction without qualification. Considering the heavy traffic using most of these bridges, they had to be made safe for modern vehicles. This is better than replacing them with generic concrete and steel spans. Purists, however, would argue that few of these bridges are "authentic" or have historical integrity, and replicas such as Schofield Ford are, for them, beyond the pale. They are correct, but considering the alternative of having *no* covered bridges, we can be grateful there still is a covered bridge at Schofield Ford. Nonetheless, we prefer to see the dates of construction qualified. With Schofield Ford, at least we know what a new covered bridge felt like in the nineteenth century, and this bridge stands as a monument to the spirit of the many volunteers who rushed to rebuild a structure that continues to be meaningful.

Doe River Bridge

CARTER COUNTY, TENNESSEE

Carter Co. #1 (42-10-01), over Doe River in Elizabethton, on Third Street, Howe truss, 136.10 feet with 9-foot hip roof entries at each end

As the centerpiece of Elizabethton's city park as well as its website icon, the Doe River Bridge is clearly important to the people of this small city of 14,200, which was founded in 1799. Easily viewed from a parallel bridge a few hundred yards downriver and framed by a small dam in the rock-strewn river, the bridge's symmetry is very striking because of its two hip roof portals extending some nine feet beyond the trusses, which were possibly added after initial construction.

Perhaps because covered bridges were relatively uncommon in eastern Tennessee, when in 1882 the city fathers saw the need to span the flood-prone Doe River they had difficulty finding a contractor. They asked local physician Dr E. E. Hunter to locate appropriate craftsmen and paid him $5 for his services as contractor. Hunter later joked that this was his "$5 bridge." Hunter hired Colonel Thomas Matson, a railroad engineer known for designing the elevated railroad tracks in New York City as well as a local narrow gauge railroad (the "Tweetsie"), to design the bridge and serve as construction chief. He, in turn, hired George Lindamood and three carpenters to build the bridge,

selecting the widely used Howe truss and securing timber from the nearby mountains—oak and white pine for the truss members, poplar for the weatherboarding, and chestnut for the shingles. The total cost for the bridge was $3,000 plus $300 for the approaches. Matson's bridge was evidently well constructed and securely anchored, for the disastrous flood of 1901, when all other Doe River bridges were swept away, failed to dislodge the span in Elizabethton in spite of its being rammed by a barn as well as by logs from a nearby lumber yard.

Since the Howe truss was widely used for railroad bridges, both in covered and uncovered bridges, and Matson was a rail line

designer, it is not surprising that he chose this design. Important for city traffic, the interior width of 16 feet could accommodate at least the smaller wagons in both directions. Until around 2000, the bridge carried car traffic (westbound only), and because of that the city marked off a pedestrian walkway with a barrier. Today, only pedestrians may cross the bridge, wise considering that it is within a city park and the focus of a week-long Elizabethton Covered Bridge Days festival each June.

Noteworthy because of its unique symmetry, with a pair of hip roof portals that extend the bridge some nine feet beyond the Howe trusses, the Doe River Bridge has stood in Elizabethton, Tennessee, since 1882. After 2000, only pedestrian traffic has been permitted to cross the bridge. (A. Chester Ong, 2011; Above, Terry E. Miller, 2011)

Bunker Hill Bridge

CATAWBA COUNTY, NORTH CAROLINA

Catawba Co. #1 (33-18-01), over Lyle Creek, 2 miles east of Claremont on an abandoned section of US 70 in Claremont Township, 80 feet with 5.5-foot canopies

Not only North Carolina's only historical trussed covered bridge, Bunker Hill Bridge is also the nation's only Haupt truss bridge, designed by Civil War General Herman Haupt (1817–1905), who oversaw military railroads for President Lincoln. Local builder Andy L. Ramsour, likely using the design seen in Haupt's 1851 *General Theory of Bridge Construction* rather than the original patent drawings from 1839 (1,445), constructed the bridge in 1895 on Island Ford Road, an old Native American trail. After

first being built as an open span, the Catawba County Commissioners voted to cover it five years later, in 1900. Because it was narrow and lightly built, the bridge was bypassed in the 1940s and eventually became part of a park. In 1994, the Catawba County Historical Association hired engineer David Fischetti of Cary, North Carolina, and timber bridge builder Arnold M. Graton of Ashland, New Hampshire, to restore the bridge.

Haupt's truss was patented as an improvement over Ithiel Town's lattice trusses based on a claim of greater efficiency in the use of timber and a greater understanding of stresses. Thus, Haupt's design used far less timber and provided greater strength. Though Haupt was famous for his tunnels and rail

Bunker Hill Bridge, which was constructed in 1895 in Catawba County, North Carolina, is the only Haupt truss covered bridge still standing in the United States. (Above left and top right, Terry E. Miller, 2011; Above center and lower, A. Chester Ong, 2011).

trestles, his truss was never widely used. Considering that the truss was patented in 1839, its use in 1895 at a time when iron bridges were usual elsewhere is surprising. And, if Haupt's truss was such an improvement, it seems odd that Southern covered bridge builders continued using the Town lattice truss well into the twentieth century when the Haupt option was known.

Humpback Bridge ALLEGHANY COUNTY, VIRGINIA

Alleghany Co. #1 (46-03-01), over
Dunlap Creek, 2 miles west of Covington just south of US 60, 100 feet

When the Kanawah Turnpike was built in the 1820s connecting the James River with the Kanawha River to open up the frontier in what is today central West Virginia, it was little more than a narrow rutted affair 208 miles and pure misery for travelers. Early on, there was a succession of three uncovered wooden bridges over Dunlap Creek Bridge just west of Covington, Virginia, near the West Virginia border. For many years, historians believed that the covered bridge had been built there in 1835 by a Mr Venable of Lewisburg (WV) and his assistant, Mr Tomas [sic] Kincaid, but later research has revealed that an unknown builder erected the present structure in 1857. Any other covered bridges on this road were lost over time to Civil War fighting and to flooding. When US 60 was built in 1929, planners necessarily bypassed the narrow covered bridge, and the Humpback Bridge sat neglected until 1954

The graceful Humpback Bridge in Alleghany County, Virginia, was constructed in 1857 to span Dunlap Creek, a tributary of the Jackson River as part of the Kanawha Turnpike. With a rise of 3.6 feet at the center, its silhouette suggests the early elegant designs of Timothy Palmer and Theodore Burr. (Above, Terry E. Miller, 2005; Others, Terry E. Miller, 2012)

when a local club led efforts to refurbish the bridge and build a small park around it. Today, the park is a popular picnic and wading spot for both locals and travelers, as well as the site for occasional baptisms by local churches, both Pentecostal and Baptist.

Though Humpback Bridge is exceptional today for its 3.6-foot rise, it reflects the earliest designs of Timothy Palmer and Theodore Burr, many of whose bridges also had arched roadways. While the truss appears to be a simple multiple kingpost, its curved chords add the arch element. Since the lower chords work in compression and exert considerable thrust against the abutments, the stonework had to be unusually robust. Later, Daniel C. McCallum would patent a truss that blended horizontal lower chords—and a flat roadway—with a curved upper chord, but Humpback's strength is considerably greater from its arched lower chords squeezed between the abutments.

Hortons Mill Bridge   BLOUNT COUNTY, ALABAMA

Blount Co. #7 (01-05-07), over Calvert Prong, north of Oneonta 5.1 miles north of the junction of US 231 and SR 75, 216 feet, 2 spans

The Hortons Mill Bridge is a 216-foot-long two-span covered bridge built in 1935 over the Calvert Prong of the Locust Fork River. With the bridge deck 70 feet above the bottom of the gorge, it is the highest covered bridge above a river in the United States. An earlier 1894 bridge accessing Thurman Horton's water mill on the west side of the gorge stood about three-quarters of a mile downstream at the foot of Sand

Mountain. The present bridge was constructed in 1934–5 by "fifteen men working from sunup to sundown for a year and a half." It is 14 feet wide and 10.5 feet high and uses the Town lattice truss. The crew was supervised by Talmedge Horton, a descendent of Thurman Horton who, along with Forrest Tidwell and his nephew Zelmer Tidwell, also built the Swann, Easley, and Nectar Bridges, all long spans which helped earn Blount County the reputation of Alabama's covered bridge capital.

The abutments of Hortons Mill Bridge rest on the rock ledges of the gorge while an intermediate pier midstream is built of

masonry and concrete. The timbers are hand-hewn oak, felled in the valley and raised to the bridge by rope. A second timber support has been added to brace the longer span. As with many covered bridges today, the original wooden shingles have been replaced with a metal roof. How the builders could construct a bridge so high over a gorge remains unclear in spite of how recent it was. Zelmer Tidwell told a reporter in the mid-1980s: "I just threw me a couple of braces across. We had to build it part of the way and then move on up and work on the other." Whether this means falsework is uncertain.

The highest covered bridge in the United States, Hortons Mill Bridge is the pride of Blount County, Alabama. Constructed in 1934–5 utilizing the Town lattice truss, the structure—with a floor length of 196 feet but a roof length of 216 feet since the trusses project out—rests on the rock ledges of the gorge while being supported midstream by a tall masonry pier. After 2007, when vandals used a cable or chain to dislodge some of the roof supports, the bridge was closed even to pedestrian traffic. Now declared structurally sound after restoration, it was reopened on March 11, 2013. (A. Chester Ong, 2011)

The first covered bridge in the South to be added to the National Register of Historic Places, Horton's Mill Bridge is now owned by the Alabama Historical Commission and was featured in a 1969 tour of covered bridges corresponding with Blount County's sesquicentennial. Subsequently, the bridge was restored in 1974 by the Alabama Historical Commission in cooperation with the Blount County Commission. Today, wood replaces the original sheet metal siding. In September 2007, vandals attempted to remove some of the roof supports from the west end of the bridge, damaging the structure, which then was deemed unsafe and closed to all traffic.

Watson Mill Bridge

MADISON/OGLETHORPE COUNTIES, GEORGIA

Madison Co. #1/Oglethorpe Co. #2 (10-97-01/10-109-02), over the South Fork of the Broad River, on Watson Mill State Park Road in the park southeast of Comer, 229 feet, 3 spans

Hot summer days, of which Georgia has many, attract plenty of visitors to the Watson Mill Bridge seven days a week. Just below the bridge is a mill dam, and below that a broad expanse of smooth, slightly rolling rock over which the shallow waters of South Fork run. There, both children and adults can safely play in the water or picnic on the banks. A stone wall on the west bank created an old wide mill race that once powered a combination grist, saw, and cotton mill built by Gabriel Watson in 1871 that succeeded an earlier mill built in 1798 about a mile downstream. Watson also operated a store and built a residence for his family. Until the bridge was built, customers living on the opposite bank had to ford the river on the rocks or later use a rope ferry.

Washington W. King (1843–1910) constructed this 229-foot structure in 1885 for $3,228 just above the dam on higher ground using the classic Town lattice truss, long the standard in Georgia. W. W. King was the eldest son of Georgia's most illustrious covered bridge builder, Horace King (1807–85), who, as an African-American freed slave, was exceptional in American bridge history. W. W. King moved first to LaGrange, then to Atlanta where he based his bridge business, which continued into the next generation of Kings. While none of Horace King's bridges remain, two other W. W. King bridges do survive, the Lowery or Euharlee Creek Bridge in Bartow County, built in 1886, and Effie's Bridge, formerly over the Oconee River within Athens, Georgia, slightly shortened and moved in 1965 to Stone Mountain State Park nearby. At Watson Mill, the nearby house burned in 1904 and after 1953 the mill was abandoned. The land was donated to form the state park in 1971, and in 1981 the bridge was restored. Today, only the mill race and foundations remain.

Unlike most other Georgia bridges, Watson Mill sits on stone abutments and piers, the former placed a few feet from the bank, thus requiring short open approaches on each end. Besides using the standard Town lattice design

with secondary chords, King also added sturdy braces from each pier to the upper chords at a slight angle from the trusses. While they give the structure greater rigidity, they also create an obstacle to traffic and reduce the usable inside width. Strangely, King's Lowry Bridge, with a much longer span of 138 feet (as opposed to the three 64-foot spans of Watson Mill), omits the upper secondary chords and appears to have had no angle bracing. Given Watson Mill's length and lack of side openings, this dark passage can create sudden surprises for the many drivers using it. John S. Lupold and Thomas L. French Jr have written a definitive study of the King family in their *Bridging Deep South Rivers: The Life and Legend of Horace King* (2004).

Constructed by Washington W. King, the son of famed African-American bridge builder Horace King, in 1885, the Watson Mill Bridge employs a classic Town lattice truss. With a length of some 229 feet, the bridge spans the South Fork of the Broad River between Georgia's Madison and Oglethorpe Counties. (Opposite, top and center right, A. Chester Ong, 2011; Center left and bottom, Terry E. Miller, 2011)

Clarkson-Legg Bridge CULLMAN COUNTY, ALABAMA

Cullman Co. #1 (01-22-01) over Crooked Creek, 9 miles west-northwest of Cullman on a bypassed section of Central Road (CR 1043) in Clarkson Covered Bridge Park, 251 feet, 4 spans

It is difficult to believe that the Clarkson-Legg Bridge remained open to traffic until 1962. When author Miller first saw the bridge in 1971, it was so deteriorated, sagging from pier to pier, leaning badly to one side, with large holes in the rotten flooring, and a thousand points of light coming through the roof, that just walking through it was foolhardy. Therefore, it is nothing short of amazing that the restoration completed

in 1975 under a grant from the American Revolution Bicentennial Project only involved straightening the trusses and putting on new siding and roofing.

The first bridge at this site was built in 1904 (some sources say 1906–7) on land owned by James W. Legg, who provided much of the timber at a cost reported to have been $1,500. Whoever built it used lightweight plank to construct an atypical Town lattice, unusual because there are no secondary chords but, instead, an added light framework of posts and braces on the insides of the trusses. The upper and lower chords consist of six planks each rather than the expected four. The trusses total 251.6 feet but there is

an additional 7.2-foot overhanging portal on each end, explaining why some sources state the bridge's length is 270 feet.

The three stone piers are unusually high, but they are contradicted by the structure. The extra multiple kingpost reinforcements define two spans, however, one 133.11 feet and the other 117.7 feet. In 1921, a flood ripped out the western half of the bridge and sent it downstream where it lodged onto land where the creek narrowed. Local people dismantled the nearly intact section and rebuilt it and the other span on higher foundations at a cost of $1,500, ironically the cost of the original construction. When Miller first visited the bridge in 1971, it was

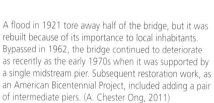

With its open-sided Town lattice truss, the 251 feet long Clarkson-Legg Bridge, which was built during the first decade of the twentieth century, is today the centerpiece of a park that includes a newly constructed grist mill and log cabin. (A. Chester Ong, 2011)

A flood in 1921 tore away half of the bridge, but it was rebuilt because of its importance to local inhabitants. Bypassed in 1962, the bridge continued to deteriorate as recently as the early 1970s when it was supported by a single midstream pier. Subsequent restoration work, as an American Bicentennial Project, included adding a pair of intermediate piers. (A. Chester Ong, 2011)

still two spans, though the eastern span was shored up with wooden poles. When the bridge was reconstructed in 1975, two new intermediate piers—obvious because they are neater than the older moss-covered central pier—were added. When the park was established, the county built a new grist mill and log cabin to simulate how the site looked when Legg's mill still existed.

Eldean Bridge MIAMI COUNTY, OHIO

Miami Co. #1 (35-55-01), over the Great Miami River, 1 mile north of Troy on a bypassed section of Eldean Road (CR 33), between Concord and Staunton Townships, 223 feet, 2 spans of 111.6 feet each with entries

Although bypassed in 1964 with a new concrete bridge, the old Eldean covered bridge remains open to drivers. Officials hoped that by doing this, vandalism would diminish, while it also provides nostalgic drivers with the sounds of rattling floor-boards and rushing waters beneath. Already a massive structure some 223 feet in length, with trusses 16 feet in height and with an interior width of 17.7 feet, the looming entrance seems even more imposing because engineers once raised the bridge 15 feet, expecting to put it out of reach of floods. Not only Ohio's second longest historical covered bridge, Eldean is also perhaps the best surviving example of Stephen H. Long's

1830 patent truss, each twelve-panel span built of double kingposts and braces and a single counterbrace, all fixed into triple upper and lower chords. Two local builders, James and William Hamilton, won the contract in 1860 to construct both abutments and superstructure. The cut stone abutments consisted of nearly 500 perches of stone at $2.73 per perch for the abutments and $2.95 per perch for the pier, totaling $1,412. Using white pine cut in Michigan and shipped to the site on the Miami and Ohio Canal, the Hamiltons received $11.75 per lineal foot, for a total of $2,632 and a grand total of $4,044 (Wood, 1993: 137–8). There is evidence that the Eldean Bridge was actually the second on the site, an earlier one having been built about 1848 to access Massachusetts native Henry Ware Allen's flour mill.

Between its heavy traffic and the elements, the Eldean Bridge has required periodic maintenance. Major repairs were undertaken in 1932, 1936, and 1980, but in 2005–6 the

Crossing the Great Miami River, the Eldean Bridge was constructed in 1860 utilizing a Long truss. Although bypassed for a half century, the bridge is still open to vehicular travel, allowing visitors to hear the nostalgic sounds of rattling floorboards. With an overall length of 223 feet, the bridge is supported with a single mid-stream cut stone pier. (Above, Max T. Miller, 1960; Others, A. Chester Ong, 2011)

James A. Barker Engineering Company of Bloomington, Indiana, thoroughly renovated the bridge, including its masonry, by raising it onto a steel frame and then taking the trusses apart wherever rotted timbers needed replacing. Though a few kingposts were completely replaced, most were salvaged by replacing the damaged ends—both lower and upper—using "Dutchman's patches." As needed, parts of the chords were also replaced. *The History Channel* featured this reconstruction work in a program called "Back to the Blueprint: Rebuilding the Eldean Bridge" in 2006. A vehicle accident on the bridge in 2011 necessitated further repairs, including replacements of damaged truss members. Being close to Interstate 75 and just north of Troy, the handsome county seat, both bridge and its park attract numerous visitors.

Smolen-Gulf Bridge

ASHTABULA COUNTY, OHIO

Ashtabula Co. #64 (35-04-64), over the Ashtabula River, 1.5 miles south of Ashtabula on State Road (CR 25), 613 feet, 4 spans

Traditionalists love to hate the Smolen-Gulf Bridge, but no one can ignore this "elephant in the room"—613 feet long in four spans, 51 feet wide, 37 feet high, and standing 93 feet above the Ashtabula River. Billed as "the longest covered bridge in the United States," there is no comparison with its vanquished but historical predecessor, the Cornish-Windsor Bridge between Vermont and New Hampshire. Smolen-Gulf is thoroughly modern and is "covered" only in the sense that it has a roof and siding. It carries semi tractor-trailers with a load limit of 40 tons, and has a life expectancy of 100 years.

Two factors led to this unprecedented bridge: first, the necessity of replacing a deteriorating iron bridge in the river gorge approached by steep inclines and sharp curves; and second, covered bridges as a major part of the county's tourism, including an October covered bridge festival. Long-time County Engineer John Smolen of Jefferson had been building neo-traditional covered bridges for decades, including State Road (1983, Town lattice), Caine Road (1986, Pratt), Giddings Road (1995, Pratt), and Netcher Road (1999, Hinged Arch). Smolen-Gulf, named in his honor and combined with the old name of the crossing, was his final project before retirement. The new bridge was dedicated on August 26, 2008.

Using Smolen's design, the bridge was built by Union Industrial Contractors and Koski Construction for a total of $7,780,000, five million of it contributed by the federal government and the rest by the county and state. Its massive truss members are all of Southern Yellow Pine glulam (glued laminated wood). The 30.9-foot roadway is flanked by two covered pedestrian ways, giving walkers a dramatic view of the river far below.

Painted "Olympus Green" and sitting on high concrete piers and abutments, this unusually shaped bridge with its rectangular portals is a reconceptualization of the American covered bridge, a completely modern design built to carry modern loads but having a cover whose purpose remains traditional—to protect the superstructure. Unlike historical covered bridges, where construction photos are rare, the building of this bridge is well documented. YouTube hosts numerous videos of the bridge, including its construction, and Ashtabula County has released a DVD, Covered Bridge Country (www.feathermultimedia.com), that includes clips of construction.

Ashtabula County, Ohio's Smolen-Gulf Bridge is a thoroughly modern 613-foot-long structure, which was dedicated in 2008. Raised high above the Ashtabula River on three concrete piers, its truss members are all fashioned out of Southern Yellow Pine glulam. In addition, the designer added two sidewalks, giving pedestrians a stunning view of the valley. (A. Chester Ong, 2011)

Cataract Falls Bridge OWEN COUNTY, INDIANA

Owen Co. #1 (14-60-01), over Mill Creek, just northeast of Cataract village within the Cataract Falls Recreation Area, 140 feet

Photographers can only dream of photographing Cataract Falls, Indiana's highest falls, along with the covered bridge. Alas, the covered bridge is just too far above the falls, and no viewing sites allow the two to be combined. Although a quiet park today, by 1820 the area was bustling with activity after Isaac Teal built a mill near the lower falls. After Teal's business declined, Theodore Jennings bought the area, including the falls, in 1841, and established multiple mills for flour, wool, and lumber and also a barrel making factory. Little is known about an earlier bridge between the upper and lower falls except that its abutments suggest a substantial span, likely covered. That bridge, along with many others in Owen County, was destroyed by a flood on August 2, 1875. Acting quickly, the county commissioners advertised for bids for a new bridge on August 19 and again on September 9, specifying that "the style, plan and finish, are to be in all respects like the covered spans of the bridge over White River, at Gosport, and known as the 'Smith Wooden Truss.'" Gosport's three-span bridge had been built just five years earlier by the Smith Bridge Company of Toledo, Ohio, and its survival during the flood impressed the commissioners. Because

Jennings' mills were above both falls, the new bridge was located there. On October 22, Smith Bridge Company received a contract for "Smith's High Double Wood Truss" at $14.35 "per linear foot of lower chord." When the bridge was completed in early December, the county paid William Baragan $1,678.84 for the abutments and Smith Bridge $2,009.00 for the covered bridge.

By that time, the population around the bridge had grown to around a hundred, and there was also a hotel. Everything except the bridge is gone now. After the county bypassed the bridge in 1988, it continued to deteriorate, but in 2000 the J. A. Barker Engineering Company of Bloomington, Indiana, with Matt Reckard supervising, placed cribbing and rails beneath the bridge, slid it onto land, and refurbished it. Today, visitors can enjoy a picnic on the bridge while listening to the roar of the nearby falls.

Constructed in 1875 in an area of Owen County, Indiana, with multiple mills, the Cataract Falls Bridge continued in service until 1988 when it was bypassed. A solidly handsome bridge, its structure incorporates a standard Smith truss as built by Smith Bridge Company of Toledo, Ohio. (Above, A. Chester Ong, 2011; Below, Terry E. Miller, 1968; Bottom, Terry E. Miller, 1971)

post trusses having two kingposts, two braces, and three upper and lower chords. The much longer Eakin Bridge, at the former village of Arbaugh, also used doubled truss members but added the pronounced camber of the Geer Mill Bridge and a single plank arch embedded between the doubled truss members seated at each end on the lower chords, not into the abutments. Geer Mill had all of these features but was built in three unequal spans, the north being four multiple kingpost panels 38.6 feet long, the middle being twelve panels with the plank arch 97.8 feet long, and the south being three panels only 28.8 feet long; the middle panel was open and lacked the horizontal beam that would have made it a queenpost. Evidently, the builders decided against a single span of 165 feet, though doable, and built the shorter spans on the banks and the longest span over the water, though this required two stone piers.

Geer Mill Bridge

VINTON COUNTY, OHIO

Vinton Co. #6 (35-82-06), over Raccoon Creek, 2.5 miles southwest of Wilkesville on a bypassed section of Geer Mill Road (TR 4W) in Wilkesville Township, 165.10 feet plus 4.8-foot entries

Unfortunately, arsonists destroyed the Geer Mill Bridge during the night of June 7, 2013, as this book was being completed. Also known as Ponn's Bridge, it was commonly called the "humpback bridge" because of its pronounced 3.5-foot camber, a deliberate arching of the trusses to provide greater strength. Located in the southeast corner of a county with only 13,000 people and one of the state's highest poverty rates, Geer Mill sat in splendid isolation and was clearly a favorite spot for both fishermen and the young, the latter having contributed colorful graffiti to virtually every interior surface. County records indicate that a predecessor, the Barnes Mill Bridge, was burned by arsonists in May, 1874. That same year, the county hired two contractors from the county seat of McArthur, Martin McGrath and Lyman Wells, to build a replacement, paying them $1,898, a great sum for a poor, underpopulated county.

The Geer Mill Bridge's trusses illustrated practices apparently peculiar to Vinton County, since they are also found in the Tinker Road Bridge (35–82–05), now sitting over a pond at the county's Junior Fairgrounds north of McArthur: building multiple king-

With its obvious camber, the Geer Mill Bridge is often called "the humpback bridge." Resting on two piers with three unequal spans, the structure of the Geer Mill Bridge includes four multiple kingpost panels on the north end, twelve panels with a plank arch in the middle, and three kingpost panels on the south end. (Top left and bottom, A. Chester Ong, 2011; Above center and right, Terry E. Miller, 1975)

Jackson Bridge PARKE COUNTY, INDIANA

Parke Co. #28 (14-61-28), over Sugar Creek, 4.1 miles northwest of Bloomingdale on CR 25 (N50W) in Penn Township, double Burr truss, 200.6 feet with 11.8-foot entries each end

Even among Parke County's many exceptional covered bridges, the 1861 Jackson Bridge stands out for its overpowering size, its elegance, and its peaceful location. To gain the strength needed for such a long span, builder J. J. Daniels constructed eighteen-panel doubled Burr trusses—three upper and lower chords, double kingposts and braces, and double arches—21.3 feet high, around 4–5 feet higher than usual. In addition to the usual cross bracing between both lower and upper chords, there are nine vertical X braces between the trusses. When, in 2011, faulty GPS devices sent two unthinking semi tractor-trailer drivers through the bridge, the trusses supported the loads without damage, but the trucks' height broke most of these extra cross braces.

Built by Indiana's most famous covered bridge craftsman, Joseph J. Daniels (b. Marietta, OH, 1826, d. Rockville, IN, 1916) and William D. Daniels, the bridge cost $8,000 provided by the county and $3,307 provided by subscription, plus $6,000 paid to Brown and Company for stonework. A cornerstone on the south abutment reads "BUILDER J. J. DANIELS 1861." The bridge has required periodic maintenance and repairs, beginning with Daniels himself tightening the bolts in 1863 and new siding and a roof following hurricane-strength storm damage during the 1913 flood. A 1977 restoration cost $75,000, but a more thorough reconstruction in 2005–6 required building a temporary bridge beneath the covered one, sliding the old bridge 200 yards north onto the road, and replacement of all deteriorated timbers, along with correcting a noticeable lean once caused by a nearby tornado. Engineers replaced the lower chords with glulam (glued laminated timber), about a third of the upper chords, as well as numerous kingposts and braces. In addition, the deck and roof systems were replaced. To avoid further rot, modern barriers were placed between the lower chords and arches and the abutments. Consequently, the 1861 date must be qualified, since the majority of the bridge's timbers are new.

A graceful yet substantial covered bridge, Parke County, Indiana's Jackson Bridge remains open to vehicular traffic. Constructed by J. J. Daniels in 1861 to cross Sugar Creek, it incorporates a double Burr truss 200.6 feet long as a single span. The bridge was restored using mostly ghulam for the lower chords and deck. (Above, Terry E. Miller, 1971; Inset, Terry E. Miller, 1968; Others, A. Chester Ong, 2011)

Bridgeton Bridge

PARKE COUNTY, INDIANA

Parke Co. #4 (14-61-04#2), over Big Raccoon Creek in the village of Bridgeton, 267 feet, 2 spans

With thirty-one sturdy covered bridges, Parke County, Indiana, well deserves the moniker "covered bridge capital of the world." Few other counties in the United States value their covered bridges more than Parke County, which has celebrated its bridges in an annual fall festival since 1957, bringing much-needed tourism revenue to an otherwise rural county. Since 1967, when the two-span Bridgeton crossing was bypassed, it has also served as a second headquarters for the festival. Even with the county's three other two-span bridges, Bridgeton remains a standout, situated just above a dam on rock-strewn Big Raccoon Creek next to a classic water-powered mill that still operates. The original 1823 sawmill added grist milling at some point, but all was destroyed in a fire in 1869. The rebuilt 1870 mill added roller milling to its water-driven system before 1900, but after a dust explosion in 1951 destroyed the water power, the mill operated on electricity until 1970 when French buhr stones were imported and water power restored.

Bridgeton was built in 1868 by Joseph J. Daniels (1826–1916), who came to Parke County from Marietta, Ohio, and was the builder of fourteen of Indiana's remaining bridges, many in Parke County. As with most bridges by Daniels, Bridgeton uses the Burr truss. Because each span is only 134 feet long, the arches rise only two-thirds the way up the trusses. On April 28, 2005, however, Jesse L. Payne, age thirty-four and a known arsonist, burned Bridgeton's much-loved crossing, whose charred remains collapsed into the creek. As had happened in the past when disaster struck, the community came together determined to rebuild an exact copy and began raising funds and receiving offers of free timber. Fortunately, one of Bridgeton's residents was Dan R. Collom, one of Indiana's premier covered bridge builders/restorers, and he supervised the reconstruction. Both spans were built whole in a nearby field from April through August 2006. Two cranes lifted the spans into place on August 28, and during September the decking, siding, and roofing were completed. The new Bridgeton covered bridge was dedicated on October 1, 2006, only eighteen months after the original burned, a testament to the determination of the people of Parke County.

Situated above Big Raccoon Creek, the Bridgeton Bridge was constructed in 1868 by J. J. Daniels as a two-span structure employing arched-shaped Burr trusses. Arson in 2005 reduced the bridge to a tangled mass of charred timbers that fell into the river. Fortunately, Indiana's premier covered bridge builder/restorer, Dan R. Collom, lived in Bridgeton and supervised its rebuilding, which was completed in only a year and a half. (Above, left, and inset, Terry E. Miller, 1968; Bottom, A. Chester Ong, 2011)

John Bright #2 Bridge FAIRFIELD COUNTY, OHIO

Fairfield Co. #10 (35-23-10), over Fetters Run on the campus of Ohio University at Lancaster, just north of the city on a footpath formerly over Poplar Creek on Bish Road, 3 miles northeast of Carroll in Liberty Township

Fairfield County's Liberty Township had thirteen covered bridges in the late 1950s. Today, it has three, and none is in its original location. Among them is John Bright #2 with the county's most unusual truss and its name being that of a local landowner. Generally classified as a "combination" truss, most observers call it an "inverted bowstring," but this term makes little sense since "bowstring" refers to an arch in compression. Bright #2, however, consists of a linked series of flat-iron segments fastened together with pins suspended from end posts held rigid by wooden upper chords. This creates, in essence, a suspension system reinforced with vertical wooden posts and crisscross iron rods within the "panels." The hardware required for connections, especially those joining the floor system to the suspension, is quite sophisticated. Based on the terminology associated with other similar trusses patented in the nineteenth century, this design is better called a "catenarian" truss. Bright #2 also has a wooden arch possibly added as a rein-forcement after 1913.

An earlier bridge over the same creek and just around the corner and called John Bright #1, apparently used the same design when it was built in 1876 by Augustus Borneman, a Lancaster contractor who, sometimes with William Black, built bridges with many types of trusses in the area, including Howe, Smith, as well as "combination." Two years later, in 1878, an unknown builder constructed the first bridge of unknown design at the Bright #2 location. After this bridge failed after only

three years, the County Commissioners' Journals recorded advertising for a new bridge to be 70 feet long on August 11, 1881, and on August 23 awarded the contract to Borneman at a cost of $13.25 per foot, rather higher than the $8.00–10.00 per foot for the standard multiple kingpost truss bridges being built elsewhere in the county. Depending on how the bridge was measured, it would have cost between $973 and $1,126, since the truss itself is 73.6 feet but there are 5.9-foot entries on both ends. Three years later, in 1884, Bright #1 failed, but Black and Borneman's replacement was an all-iron version for $2,000, or about $22.00 a foot. These two bridges, along with a similar but earlier bridge in Germantown, Ohio, are the nation's only remaining examples of the "catenarian" truss.

At the time when Fairfield County still had over thirty covered bridges and could have become Ohio's "covered bridge capital," local officials had no interest in their preservation. Over time, their number has fallen to sixteen, plus one moved outside the county. Not only do none carry traffic today but five are over "dry land" and another two over ponds. Both John Bright #1 and #2 were moved to the

Ohio University campus north of Lancaster in 1988 and placed over Fetters Run. Before taking academic retirement, Bright #2 lacked any siding and looked about as forlorn as a covered bridge can be. Today, both bridges stand firmly and exemplify one of America's singular bridge designs and the innovative work of local builder Augustus Borneman.

In its original location, the covered John Bright #2 from 1881 was near enough to the all-metal John Bright #1 from 1884 to be photographed together. Bright #2 is a rare "combination" truss misnamed "inverted bowstring." Both were moved to the Ohio University campus north of Lancaster, Ohio, in 1988. (Above left, Max T. Miller, 1959; Above right, Terry E. Miller, 1980; Below, A. Chester Ong, 2011; Bottom, reproduced from Miriam Wood, 1993: 44)

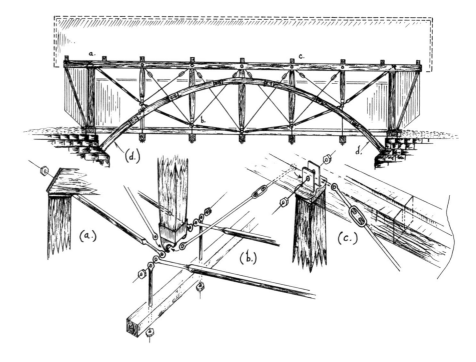

Medora Bridge

JACKSON COUNTY, INDIANA

Jackson Co. #4 (14-36-04) over the East Fork of the White River, 1 mile east of Medora on a bypassed section of SR 235, 434 feet, 3 spans

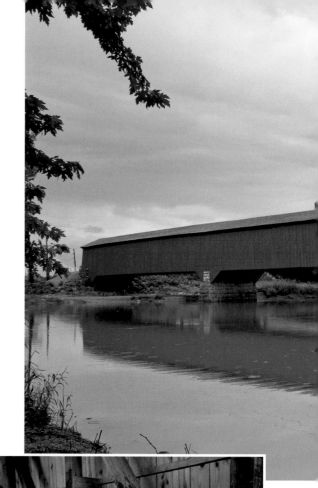

When author Miller began graduate study at Indiana University in 1967, there were four covered bridges in Jackson County, all exceptionally long and fascinating. Today, only two remain, Medora and Shieldstown. Unfortunately, one of those lost was Bell's Ford, the only covered Post truss in the United States, though the remains of one of its two spans are in storage with plans for reconstruction when funds become available. Until 1972, the Medora Bridge carried the relatively light traffic of SR 235 but was otherwise sadly neglected. Before changing their minds and bypassing the structure, however, the state announced it would remove the old bridge. Knowing this, when the author discovered a series of old advertising posters on the inside walls so caked with dirt that they were nearly invisible, he decided to save them.

End to end, Medora was thought to be the longest historical covered bridge in the United States, 459.3 feet in three spans, including the untrussed 14.1-foot entries at each end. But Cornish-Windsor over the Connecticut River between Vermont and New Hampshire is 460 feet long because the trusses extend through the overhanging entries. Medora is, nonetheless, a magnificent example of the classic Burr truss. Although Burr came from New England and worked in New York State and Pennsylvania, Indiana has some of the longest and best built such covered bridges in the country.

Medora Bridge's builder, Joseph J. Daniels (1826–1916), was born in Marietta, Ohio, and learned bridge building from his father

A rival for the claim of the longest covered bridge in the United States, Jackson County, Indiana's Medora Bridge is an outstanding example of the fabled Burr truss. Constructed by J. J. Daniels in 1875, the bridge is 434 feet in length as it spans the East Fork of the White River. (Above and below, A. Chester Ong, 2011; Right, Terry E. Miller, 2013)

Stephen. The elder Daniels was an agent for Col. Stephen H. Long and built Long's 1830 patent truss throughout southern and southwestern Ohio. J. J. Daniels continued building Long trusses in southwestern Ohio before moving to Indiana where he built the majority of his bridges using either the Howe or Burr designs. A good number of his bridges survive, including several notable ones: Bridgeton (as a replica), Jackson, Mansfield, Mecca, West Union, and Williams. Medora was one of his major projects, completed during nine months in 1875 and costing

$18,142. Daniels' last project was the Neet Bridge in Parke County, built in 1904 when he was seventy-eight, which is still standing.

Over the years following the closure of Medora Bridge, the structure continued to deteriorate—the siding was gradually disappearing, the roof was full of holes that allowed rainwater to saturate essential joints, and rotting truss members threatened collapse. In 2010, master builder Dan R. Collom and Sons of Parke County, Indiana (the home of the original builder, J. J. Daniels), began rehabilitation, preserving as much of

the original timber as possible but replacing deteriorated truss members where it was necessary. New roofing and siding, along with extensive repairs to foundations and approaches, give the appearance of a new bridge, but Medora is legitimately historical and a much-valued part of the Medora community. Though numbering only around 550 people, Medora's citizens are largely responsible for accomplishing this important preservation by raising money, securing grants, and contributing labor (http://www.medoracoveredbridge.com/).

Over the years, the bridge was generally neglected, as these early photographs show. Significant rehabilitation began in 2010 under the supervision of master builder Dan R. Collom with the replacement of rotted wooden members and the addition of new siding and roofing. (Inset, Terry E. Miller, 1967; Left and right, Terry E. Miller, 1974)

Moscow Bridge RUSH COUNTY, INDIANA

Rush Co. #7 (14-70-07), over Big Flat Rock River in Moscow village, 334 feet, 2 spans

On June 3, 2008, a tornado destroyed not only much of Moscow village but also its pride and joy, a 334-foot two-span covered bridge built in 1886 by Emmett L. Kennedy. Painted white with portals using Kennedy's signature scrollwork and carved wood ornaments reminiscent of the Victorian homes then popular, Moscow was more than just an icon of the village but one of the nation's finest covered bridges, and one of only eleven Kennedy bridges still standing out of the fifty-eight he built. Kennedy's father, Archibald M. Kennedy, was born on August 25, 1818, in Guilford County, North Carolina and moved to Rush County, Indiana, where he became the area's most prominent carpenter

and bridge builder and where the family business continued with his sons Emmett L. and Charles F., and later their sons. After a long and successful career in southeastern Indiana where he built many houses in addition to the bridges, the elder Kennedy died on June 3, 1897, ironically 111 years to the day before his son's *magnum opus*, the Moscow Bridge, was destroyed.

Though the iconic covered bridge was completely destroyed, today it stands once again, and around forty per cent of the reincarnation is original material. The fact that there is once again a Moscow Bridge also speaks to a major change of heart within Rush County, for in the 1980s the Board of County Commissioners decided to tear down four of Rush County's covered bridges (all Kennedy bridges!) and replace them with "modern" (read, plain, utilitarian) structures.

In retaliation, enraged citizens put up a slate of pro-bridge candidates and voted out the anti-bridge commissioners. Indeed, this reflects a broader change of heart about covered bridges throughout the United States, and Moscow demonstrates that when a bridge is destroyed, it can be rebuilt, either as a partial replica or out of whole cloth. When Moscow's bridge was crushed into the creek bed, state prison inmates aided in removing the bridge's broken bones from the river. Bloomington, Indiana restorer J. A. Barker contracted with Parke County framer Dan Collom in rebuilding the bridge to its original state using both salvaged materials as well as newly cut white pine and yellow poplar timber from Greene-Sullivan State Forest. Collom estimated the cost of an entirely new wooden covered bridge at $3,000,000, but with donated materials and labor, the project

cost only $540,000. The new Moscow Bridge opened in September 2010.

Indiana provides a surprising case study on covered bridge building. Pioneer bridge builder Theodore Burr worked at the beginning of the nineteenth century, and Pennsylvania, in particular, exhibits a great many sturdy Burr truss bridges, but Ohio builders preferred a variety of trusses, and today Ohio has few Burr trusses comparable to those of Pennsylvania. But Indiana's builders not only embraced the Pennsylvania Burr tradition but continued building splendid examples of this conservative type until the 1920s. Moscow is a classic Burr truss but was built only eleven years before A. M. Kennedy's death in 1897, and his sons were still going strong for two more decades.

Moscow's bridge presents a dilemma for purists. True, it is a replica but visitors can clearly see much original construction. And Collom—who himself could probably be described as a "purist"—persisted in using old-time joinery, though he did have the trusses built whole on land and lifted into place by a giant crane. Whether you accept

Moscow as "authentic" or not, most would agree that it is better to have the reincarnation than not to have it at all. And, as a local newspaper noted, had the disaster occurred forty or so years ago, officials would have cleared away the debris and built a new concrete bridge without too many regrets and called it "progress."

Constructed in 1886 by the acclaimed bridgewright Emmett L. Kennedy, the Moscow Bridge in Rush County, Indiana, is a fine example of Burr truss construction. (Terry E. Miller, 2005)

After being utterly destroyed by a tornado on June 3, 2008, the bridge lay forlorn in the Big Flatrock River before being restored by J. A. Barker and Dan C. Collom and his team, with work completed in September 2010. While the bridge today appears new, it retains some 40 percent of the original. (Left and above, A. Chester Ong, 2011; Right, Larry Stout, 2008)

Otway Bridge SCIOTO COUNTY, OHIO

Scioto Co. #15 (35-73-15), over Scioto Brush Creek in the village of Otway, on a bypassed section of SR 348, 127 feet

Residents of the village of Otway (population 87) in southern Ohio's Scioto County bordering the Ohio River have little to lure visitors other than their covered bridge. With a single city—Portsmouth—and a history of industry come and gone, Scioto County is one of Ohio's poorest and has long struggled with a declining population now stabilized thanks to its medical facilities and Shawnee State University. Otway's old bridge, though isolated and surrounded by thick foliage, typified the standardization of the bridge industry during the later part of the nineteenth century.

It was in 1874 that the Smith Bridge Company of Toledo, Ohio, built the Otway Bridge. Using Robert W. Smith's truss patented in 1867 and 1869, the company pre-cut and assembled its bridges at the factory before marking the parts and shipping them by rail and wagon to the site where Smith crews erected the bridge. Perhaps Smith's workers did not know about the hijinks of some local youths one night. Writes local historian Demia Penn: "While the bridge was under construction and the plates were put in place to support the rafters for the roof, a feat of balance and daring was performed when young Leander Smith walked the plates on stilts" (n.d.: 2).

The Otway Bridge was bypassed in 1963 after carrying a state highway for many years. Before that, engineers had attempted to strengthen the bridge several times, leaving the abandoned structure with a mishmash of add-ons. A bridge 127 feet long and meant to carry heavy traffic probably should have been designed as a triple-plane Smith, but Otway was a double-plane truss. To strengthen the bridge in 1896, engineers added pairs of six-ply laminated arches to each truss, with iron rods hung from blocks on the arches that added support to the chords. However, these

arches merely rest on the lower chords, with corbels (angle braces) immediately below anchored into the abutments. This gives the appearance of a continuous arch. Perhaps when the arches were added, engineers also reinforced the trusses with pairs of rods parallel to the "posts." The end result is a relatively plain Smith truss overlaid with both arches and enough rods to give the appearance perhaps of its having dental braces. At some point, engineers had to add a wooden approach on one end—most likely because flooding widened the original channel—but there are no known photos showing its design. The present Polygonal Warren Riveted Pony Truss approach replaced the first one. After fifty years of neglect, the main timbers are deteriorating as well, but renovation is planned. In the meantime, local residents continue to cut back the constantly encroaching jungle and maintain a small picnic area below the bridge.

Some locals remember a romantic story regarding the bridge. "A young couple by the names of Victor Howland and Laura Wintersteen were on their way to Otway to be married. While crossing the covered bridge they met Rev. Foster Wamsley. They asked him to perform the marriage ritual, and he complied with their wishes" (Penn, n.d.: 2).

While remote and set amongst lush foliage in southern Ohio's Scioto County, the Otway Bridge is still an important structure because of its age—built in 1874—and the fact that it was prefabricated by the Smith Bridge Company of Toledo, Ohio, before being shipped by rail and assembled on this site over Scioto Brush Creek. (A. Chester Ong, 2011)

Bypassed in 1963 after many efforts to strengthen it and deal with recurring flood damage along one approach, the bucolic Otway Bridge still is a favorite site for picnics and those seeking some sense of the past. (A. Chester Ong, 2011)

Roberts Bridge

PREBLE COUNTY, OHIO

Preble Co. #5 (35-68-05), over Seven Mile Creek in Crystal Lake Park in Eaton, 79 feet

Casual visitors to the Roberts Bridge, now sitting peacefully retired in an Eaton, Ohio park, might not recognize what the Roberts Bridge represents historically. First, it is one of the nation's five remaining two-lane covered bridges and the only one in Ohio. Second, it is one of the nation's oldest bridges, having been built in 1829. Third, it is a rare survivor of the early turnpike era when America's pioneering entrepreneurs began building the nation's first road network, a system that allowed for growth and prosperity, later becoming the Federal highway system, including the Interstate highway system.

In the early nineteenth century, Ohio had few roads and most of these were miserable affairs that trapped wagon wheels, broke axles, and rattled passengers. It was preferable to travel by river or canal than by road. Ohio's first great road building project was a major section of the National Road, which eventually covered 620 miles from Cumberland, Maryland, to St. Louis, Missouri. After reaching Wheeling, (West) Virginia in 1818, construction continued into Ohio during the 1820s and 1830s following Zane's Trace and other early trails across the state. Many of Ohio's earliest documented covered bridges served the National Road, and virtually all of them were double-lane bridges, usually of Burr truss construction. The four-span covered Ohio River crossing from Wheeling to Bridgeport, Ohio, which served from 1836 to 1903 and was flanked with pedestrian walkways, was one of the longest of these bridges, but Zanesville's Y-Bridge was the most noteworthy (see pages 55–6). As traffic increased both in volume and weight, wooden covered bridges gave way to more modern bridges. The National Road became US 40, which has been succeeded by I-70.

The Roberts Bridge, a typical turnpike design using two-lane Burr trusses, was built for the Camden-Eaton Turnpike Company south of Eaton on what became US 127. In

Only one of five remaining two-lane covered bridges in the United States, the Roberts Bridge formerly crossed Seven Mile Creek in Preble County, Ohio. Constructed in 1829 with a Burr truss design during a time of increasing turnpike construction, it served as an important link in the evolving national highway network. (Opposite, A. Chester Ong, 2011; Above left and right, Terry E. Miller, 1961)

those days, local governments were not yet responsible for bridge building, and thus both roads and bridges were left to private enterprise. The turnpike investors hired local landowner Orlistus Roberts to build a bridge over Seven Mile Creek, but he died before it could be completed, and James Lyman

Campbell, his seventeen-year-old apprentice, completed the work.

The bridge served the turnpike and later the new federal highway system until the 1920s when US 127 was rerouted nearby, leaving the old bridge still open to traffic but in splendid isolation among farmland. Arsonists set fire to the bridge in August 1986, and while the bridge remained standing, its roofing and siding were completely burned and its trusses charred. Because officials in Preble County valued the old bridge, they sand blasted the char, wrapped the trusses in plastic, and began planning the 1991 move to Crystal Lake Park in the county seat, Eaton, and rededicated it on September 15. Because the trusses were considerably weakened from the fire, there is added support hidden beneath, and the truss members appear to be smaller than one would expect. Today, Roberts Bridge and the Ramp Creek Bridge at Indiana's Brown County State Park, are the only survivors of the early turnpike era.

After serious damage from arson in 1986, the venerable bridge, which is Ohio's oldest covered bridge, was reconstructed and relocated to Crystal Lake Park on the south side of Eaton. (Left, A. Chester Ong, 2011; Below, Terry E. Miller, 1986)

Rock Mill Bridge **FAIRFIELD COUNTY, OHIO**

Fairfield Co. #48 (35-23-48), over the Hocking River, 7 miles west-northwest of Lancaster on a bypassed section of CR 108 in Bloom Township, 34 feet with 6-foot canopies at each end

Though diminutive in size, Rock Mill Bridge has long attracted photographers and artists because of its dramatic location over a rocky gorge and the rugged mill built into the cliff side nearby. Until 2003, when Fairfield County bought the property and created Stebelton Park, visitors were prohibited from entering the area to see the gorge, bridge, mill, and waterfalls together.

This modest queenpost truss bridge, only 34 feet in length, nonetheless spans the headwaters of the Hocking River which first flows downhill under the bridge through a narrow gorge some 40 feet deep before falling into the basin below the mill, after which the river continues through the lower gorge. Intrepid kayakers are known to have navigated this passage, dropping dangerously into the pool below.

Rock Mill is the oldest mill still standing in Ohio, having been built in 1799 and remodeled in 1824. The mill originally operated from a large overshot wheel installed in the gorge bottom at the base of the mill fed

from a mill race chiseled through the rock, 30 feet long, 18 feet deep, and 3 feet wide. In 1899, the owner installed a turbine powered by the falls, but after this failed, he converted to steam power. Efforts to save this unique six-story mill built entirely of oak dragged on for years, but restoration began only after the county purchased the property. At this writing, however, completion of the project awaits funding, but at least the park is open to visitors who are welcome to walk down a steep path to the gorge bottom.

Mills could be used for other purposes too. In 1873, a German singing society had its meetings there, and in that year Mr Fred

Straddling a chasm along the Hocking River in Ohio's Fairfield County, the Rock Mill Bridge is a reminder of how critical it was to construct bridges that would facilitate the movement of grains from nearby farms to a mill for processing. Only 34 feet long with a modest queenpost truss, this bridge was constructed in 1901, succeeding several others lost over the years. In 2003, a builder asked to "replace all bad timbers" replaced ALL of them, making it a replica. (Opposite, A. Chester Ong, 2011; Above left, Max T. Miller, 1958; Above right, Terry E. Miller, 1970; Below, Terry E. Miller, 1980)

Myers, one of the singers, lost his life when, as he entered his horse-drawn wagon parked too closely to the precipice, the horse panicked and Mr Myers lost his balance, fell into the gorge, and died two days later.

To enable farmers from both sides of the river to bring their grains to the mill, a bridge was erected in 1828. Whether covered or not, it was lost in a flood in 1846. John Slife built a covered bridge on the site in 1849, which burned in 1901. The present bridge was subsequently built by a local craftsman, Jacob Rugh Brandt (c. 1836–1911), better known as "Blue Jeans" Brandt. In addition to building bridges, Brandt designed and built churches, schools, and small bridges from 1858 onwards. Some of his larger bridges, all built after 1864, included the McCleery Bridge, the Loucks Mill Bridge, and the Peter Ety Bridge; only McCleery survives today, having been moved into the city of Lancaster. Brandt's modest bridge at Rock Mill, which carried heavy traffic until 2003, had been reinforced with I-beams. In that year, the county contracted with a local builder to refurbish the bridge for $193,000, directing him to replace only the bad timbers. However, when he returned the bridge to its original site, he decided that ALL the timbers were bad, and consequently the bridge seen today is only a replica.

Roseman Bridge

MADISON COUNTY, IOWA

Madison Co. #7 (15-61-07), over Middle River, 10 miles west-southwest of Winterset on a bypassed section of a township road, 107 feet

Nothing has ever put covered bridges into a brighter spotlight than the 1995 romantic film *The Bridges of Madison County* based on a novel of the same name by Iowa business professor and novelist Robert James Waller. In the story, photographer Robert Kincaid, played by Clint Eastwood, comes to rural Madison County to photograph its now iconic covered bridges. By chance, he stops at a farmhouse to ask directions where he meets Italian war bride Francesca Johnson, played by Meryl Streep, which then leads to a brief affair while Francesca's husband and their children are away for four days at the Illinois State Fair.

Since four of Madison County's six bridges have flat roofs, making them unique in the United States, many who have seen the film now believe that covered bridges everywhere have flat roofs. Known locally as "hogback" bridges, all were built in the 1880s by Harvey P. Jones and George K. Foster, both Ohio natives who were employees of the county. The Roseman Bridge, which dates from 1883, was bypassed in 1981 and renovated in 1992. While flat-roofed bridges occurred elsewhere from time to time, locals insist that Madison County's are actually flat while elsewhere they are roofs with a minimal peak—to most a "distinction without a difference." Why Jones chose flat (actually slightly rounded) over pitched is not known, and it appears that bridges by other builders had normal, pitched roofs. Defenders of Jones' idea claim that snow melts faster on such a roof because it receives the full effect of the sun. Perhaps the winter wind, which rarely stops blowing over the county's flat fields, more easily blows the snow off as well.

Of the six remaining bridges in Madison County—two with pitched roofs and four with flat roofs—the Roseman Bridge has become most famous because of its centrality to the film. All of the county's covered bridges are now closed to traffic, either bypassed or moved into parks, though the Cedar, also called Casper Bridge, can be driven over since it was replicated in 2004 following its destruction by arson in 2002. Roseman Bridge is located away from the others, southwest of Winterset, a classic Midwest county seat with old brickfront buildings arranged around the courthouse. Despite its isolation, the extensive graffiti on the bridge in multiple languages and writing systems attests to its attraction for tourists. Though renovated before the film was shot, director Eastwood insisted the bridge be artificially aged to make it more picturesque.

Iowa today has only nine covered bridges, though there are ten if you count the separate halves of the Marysville Bridge in Marion

The Roseman Bridge, one of Madison County Iowa's fabled "hogback" bridges, was built in the 1880s by Harvey P. Jones and George K. Foster. It is said by locals that the nearly flat roofs encourage snow melt, and winter winds blow the snow off as well. It is this bridge that was the centerpiece for the 1995 film *The Bridges of Madison County*. With a Town lattice truss reinforced with long "queenpost" frames, the bridge is supported today by pairs of cylindrical metal tubes, which replaced the original wooden bents. (A. Chester Ong, 2012)

County, one in a park, the other at a game preserve. Since six are in Madison County, they have the state's only covered bridge festival, which began in 1970. Seven of Iowa's bridges use the Town lattice truss and two use Howe. Those built by Jones are otherwise typical except that he used two sets of nuts and bolts at each intersection instead of wooden trunnels. Jones also reinforced most of his bridge trusses with long "queenpost" frames, but the exterior wire braces from extended floor beams to the upper chords, meant to stabilize the bridges, were probably later additions. Visitors looking up at the overhead structure also see the roof only inches above the cross beams and X bracing. Because Iowa's rivers are muddy and subject to overflow, the Madison bridges were originally built on wooden bents later replaced with pairs of cylindrical metal tubes, giving them the appearance of being perched precariously on poles. Adding to this effect are the open wooden approaches.

If many Americans think all covered bridges look like those of Madison County, people worldwide may also, as a result of Eastwood's film. This included China where at least some of the millions who saw it were aware of China's long tradition of spectacular and very different covered wooden bridges.

Harpersfield Bridge

ASHTABULA COUNTY, OHIO

Ashtabula Co. #19 (35-04-19), over the
Grand River, 1/4 mile south of Harpersfield on an old section of SR 534 in
Harpersfield Township, 2 spans (115.2
and 114.10 feet) totaling 238.7 feet
with entries

Bypassed in 1959 but open to local traffic, the Harpersfield Bridge is surrounded by parkland on both river banks. The broad but shallow river allows visitors, even children, to play in the water among the many rock outcroppings. Fishermen try their luck in the deeper pools above the old dam just east of the bridge. But something is odd—a steel truss span 135 feet long on the northern end. After the disastrous flood of March, 1913 cut a new channel on the north side of the river, perhaps saving the covered bridge by spreading out the flood waters, the highway department was forced to build a new steel truss span and rebuild the north abutment. The covered bridge itself was built in 1868 after a flood

destroyed an unknown predecessor bridge along with what remained of John Ransom's mill complex that had closed in 1864.

The bridge consists of two Howe truss spans. Perhaps because of its length, its interior width of 16 feet—24 feet wider than normal—allowed wagons and buggies to pass. Newspaper records indicate the bridge was completed on December 30, 1868 and accepted by the county on January 7, 1869, when commissioners estimated the cost at $8,000. The abutments and pier were built by Mr Patrick Sullivan (b. Waterford, Ireland, 1839, d. Ashtabula County, Ohio, 1910, of "stone cutters disease" [probably silicosis]), but the bridge builder's name is only known as Mr Potter, since county records failed to mention him. A flood in December 1873 threatened the bridge but did not dislodge it. In 1910, Mr Ralph Wright attempted to drive a steam tractor from the Wright Brother's Basket Factory in Saybrook through the bridge. About halfway through the first span,

Constructed in 1868, the Harpersfield Bridge over the Grand River in Ohio's Ashtabula County originally stood alone as a two-span covered structure. It is Ohio's longest *historical* covered bridge. After the 1913 flood widened the channel of the river, a steel truss span was attached to the north abutment. (Opposite and above, A. Chester Ong, 2011)

the deck gave way, dumping tractor and driver into the shallow river. After the 1913 flood, which destroyed a 1908 wooden dam 50 feet upriver from the bridge, the state built a new concrete dam. In 1957, because it still carried the heavy traffic of SR 534, engineers added a number of metal supports to reinforce the deteriorated lower chords and correct the bridge's noticeable sag. In 1990, the county began major renovations that included replacement of much of the lower chords and iron rods, rebuilding the deck on glulam beams, new siding, new asphalt shingles, and the addition of a pedestrian walkway to the western side After the Conesville Bridge in Coshocton County was burned in 1958, the Harpersfield Bridge held—and still holds—the distinction of being Ohio's longest *historical* covered bridge.

Over the years, engineers supplemented the wooden trusses with metal supports, later replacing the lowers chords and rebuilding the deck on glulam beams. More recently, new siding, asphalt shingles, and a pedestrian walkway were added. (Left, A. Chester Ong; Above, historical flood photo, source unknown, 1913)

Whitewater Canal Aqueduct

FRANKLIN COUNTY, METAMORA, INDIANA

Franklin Co. #11 (14-24-11), over Duck Creek, at the east end of Metamora, on the north side of Main Street on the Whitewater Canal, 60 feet

America's early canal system, inaugurated by the Erie Canal in New York State in 1825, quickly spread into the Midwest, including Ohio, Indiana, and Illinois, where the lack of good roads made the movement of farm products, forest products, and coal difficult, if not otherwise impossible. Canals, like roads, had to cross creeks and rivers.

While stone aqueducts would be sturdiest, they were costly and time-consuming to build. The second choice was wood, and for all but the smallest streams this required the strength of wooden trusses, which because they quickly deteriorated when exposed to the elements had to be covered.

Trussed canal aqueducts were of two types: deck trusses, where the canal trough ran *between* the trusses, and through trusses, where the trough was positioned below the trusses. Deck trusses could be covered with siding boards and did not require a roof,

but through trusses required both sides and roof, similar to a highway bridge. Because the canals began failing with the spread of railroads around the middle of the century, and—at least in Ohio—what remained was destroyed by the great flood of 1913, neither canals nor their aqueducts were likely to survive, that is, all except one, the fully covered Duck Creek Aqueduct on the Whitewater Canal at Metamora, Indiana. It would be more appropriate to say "barely survived." Bryan Ketcham's 1949 *Covered Bridges on the Byways of Indiana* pictures

the aqueduct still carrying water but obviously in disrepair, with diagonal bracing inside helping to resist total collapse. Thankfully, work done in 1947 (Ketcham's photo was taken earlier) stabilized the bridge, and today, following further restoration, the aqueduct again carries canal boats loaded with Metamora's many visitors.

In order to transport farm goods and livestock to Cincinnati from the Whitewater River valley in eastern Indiana, the state legislature approved the Mammoth Internal Improvement Act of 1836 to construct a canal stretching 76 miles from Nettle Creek near Hagerstown through Connersville, Brookville, into Harrison, Ohio, and back to Lawrence-burg, Indiana, on the Ohio River. Because the terrain dropped the canal 491 feet over a short distance and required 56 locks and 3 dams, it was outrageously expensive, costing the state $1,400,000, a sum so large that in 1839 the

A fine example of a covered canal bridge, the Whitewater Canal Aqueduct at Metamora, Indiana, spans Duck Creek. Constructed as part of a network of canals to transport farm goods and raw materials to market, the Burr truss structure naturally also carries the weight of water, which is displaced as a vessel passes through it. (A. Chester Ong, 2011; Drawing, Library of Congress, HAER Collection)

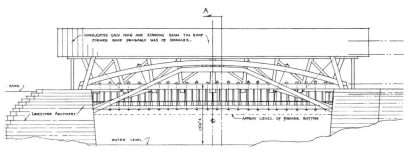

Metamora, once a sleepy village after the decline of the canal age, has become a tourist destination with horse-drawn boat rides through the covered wooden aqueduct bridge, a working grist mill, carriage rides, an old-time railroad, among other activities, in addition to restaurants and shops. (A. Chester Ong, 2011)

State of Indiana declared bankruptcy. Even though work resumed in 1842 when the state transferred ownership to the White Water Valley Canal Company, completing some sections dragged on for years. The first boats ran in 1843 and only reached Connersville in 1845. At the same time, the terminus changed from Lawrenceburg when Ohio interests built a new section from Harrison to Cincinnati. A great flood in November 1847 damaged or destroyed many sections of the canal, some of which were then abandoned. It appears that the section of the canal running through Metamora, although still open, was little used and finally closed in 1862 when part of the towpath became a railroad right of way.

Considering this checkered history, it is amazing that the Duck Creek Aqueduct was even built. Although one source claims an earlier aqueduct was built in 1843 and destroyed in a flood in August 1846, HAER IN-108 records indicate 1847 as the surviving aqueduct's date of construction, with "subsequent work" in 1868, 1901, and 1947, because the canal was still used to transport water to mills and hydro-electric facilities long after boats ceased running. Most recently, the Indiana Department of Natural Resources contracted with J. A. Barker Engineering Co. of Bloomington, Indiana, to "design repairs to correct a severe lean of bridge, structural cracks in main timbers, strengthen arch-to-truss connections, and create reliable waterproof joints between suspended flume and abutments" (http://www.jabarkerengineering.wordpress.com).

Because the Duck Creek Aqueduct is the only surviving historical specimen in North America—the 201-foot Tohickon (deck-style) Aqueduct on the Delaware Division of the Pennsylvania Canal in Bucks County, Pennsylvania, was reimagined and constructed in 2001 using modern materials—we can learn much from its structure. Its 60-foot span is supported by two eight-panel trusses that most describe as "Burr" but which, by virtue of their flared kingposts, have erroneously been called Wernwag trusses. The trusses' main function is to support the trough that carries the massive weight of the water; a boat does not add weight because it displaces water equal to its own weight. Because the canal must remain at the same level throughout, the aqueduct is necessarily close to the creek bed, with the clearance between the trough and the water only about five feet; this makes it vulnerable to flooding and floating debris. To gain maximum height, the two trusses sit on top of the abutments, with the arches attached to the lower chords with iron bolts. The upper cross bracing is unusually robust, consisting of four double X's. The builder used 24 wood blocks on the lower chords with rods running

below to support sub-lower chords several feet below the main ones. Numerous large joists sit on these sub-chords, with the board trough built on them and rising on the sides to contain the water. Four overflow troughs allow excess water to drain into the creek.

We suspect that the sidewalk running along the north side is a recent addition because old photos do not show it. Perhaps this walkway accommodates the horses that pull the reconstructed canal boats through today, since the original towpath on the south side is now occupied by a railroad. Because there is no interior towpath, we presume the teams were unhooked at one end and reconnected at the other end after the boat floated through on its own momentum.

The sleepy village of Metamora, whose short-lived canal-based prosperity declined generations ago, escaped modernization by being forgotten. In recent years, however, property owners have converted the village into a tasteful tourist attraction, offering lodging, restaurants and shops, a working mill and horse-drawn boat rides.

Pengra Bridge LANE COUNTY, OREGON

Lane Co. #15 (37-20-15), over Fall Creek, 8.5 miles southeast of Eugene, 5 miles northwest of Lowell on Place Road, 120 feet

Photographing Oregon's covered bridges can be surprisingly daunting. Shots taken from the stream are unusually difficult because of the thick foliage, coupled with a near lack of fishermen's paths. Pengra Bridge, otherwise mostly typical of the state's standardized design, stands out on two accounts, one obvious, one hidden. A visitor peering through one of the bridges "picture window" openings would notice rocky outcroppings along the south bank. Getting there provides the kind of stream-scene photo one would expect in a place like Oregon. The present wooded appearance, however, has come about since the bridge was built in 1938, because older photos show a bridge sitting in a barren, somewhat denuded environment.

The second factor is hidden. The truss is a typical "Western Howe" with eight panels, the three on each end having a single brace, the two in the center having two braces forming X's along with the usual steel rod "posts." As is typical in Oregon, the upper chord is shorter than the lower one since it extends through only six of the panels, giving the truss a trapezoidal shape. What is remarkable is that the lower chords are single timbers each measuring 16 by 18 inches by 126 feet, the longest timbers ever cut for a bridge in the state. While Oregon bridge engineers preferred single-piece chords for their strength, handling them was extremely challenging. Not only was transport tricky—they used a truck and trailer to pull these timbers—but sawmills could not process them. The Douglas fir "sticks" in Pengra were cut from the Booth-Kelly timber holdings east of Springfield, partially hewn in the forest, then hand-hewn at the bridge site. The upper chords were also single pieces, but only 98 feet long.

Located southeast of Eugene, Oregon, the Pengra Bridge is a 120-foot long Western Howe truss structure with a total of eight panels. Constructed in 1938, it replaced one 192 feet long that had been built in 1904, the residual distance being filled in by long open approaches. (A. Chester Ong, 2012; Historical photograph, Mrs Arthur C. Striker Collection, in Adams, 1963: 39)

The present bridge replaced an earlier one 192 feet long built in 1904, spanning both the creek and bank areas. Typical in Oregon, later designers placed concrete piers out from the shore to minimize the covered span's length, which reduced the 1938 span to 120 feet but required long open approaches. Deterioration caused Pengra Bridge to be bypassed, then closed in 1979. With the aid of a grant from the Oregon Covered Bridge Program, the bridge was repaired and reopened in 1995.

Bridgeport Bridge

NEVADA COUNTY, CALIFORNIA

Nevada Co. #1 (05-29-01), over the South Fork Yuba River in the former village of Bridgeport, now South Yuba State Park, on a bypassed section of Pleasant Valley Road, 233 feet

Until 1848, California was a distant, desert-like territory of the United States with relatively few settlers. While San Francisco's population was only 200 before 1848, by the mid-1850s it had risen to 36,000. When James W. Marshall discovered gold near Sutter's Mill at Coloma on January 24, 1848, some 300,000 optimistic, if not wild-eyed, prospectors came by sea from Latin America, Hawaii, and China, and by land from Oregon and the distant east seeking fortune. The "forty-niners" of the Gold Rush, few of whom actually became rich, also brought environmental devastation, and conflicts with Native Americans that led to thousands of deaths. After California became a state in Fall 1850, the new government began developing roads and transportation, including authorizing, in 1853, the creation of toll roads by private companies. One of them was the Virginia Turnpike Company, which was founded in 1856 to service the Northern Mines and the Nevada Comstock Lode. Covered bridges similar to ones back east became part of this transportation system after John T. Little from Castine, Maine, built the state's first such bridge at Salmon Falls in 1850.

The tiny settlement that formed Bridgeport along the South Fork of the Yuba River was at the heart of the Gold Rush, with reports of

up to 100 wagons crossing each day. After the Virginia Turnpike Company was formed in 1856, this 10-mile-long route came to include a crossing at Bridgeport. The early structures were likely insubstantial uncovered bridges, and the new toll bridge built in 1858 was flooded out during the winter of 1861–2. At that point, the company decided to erect a large-scale fully covered bridge and hired David Ingefield Wood (other sources say David Isaac John Wood or David Issac Johnwood) to build a 233-foot single-span Howe truss structure reinforced with two pairs of laminated arches. The Douglas fir truss timbers are said to have come from Plum Valley in Sierra County. Today, the bridge is still covered with wooden shingles that outline the arches, as was the original.

When turnpike owner David Wood died in 1876, his son Samuel continued to operate the company, but as railroads developed, road traffic declined, and in 1901 Wood sold the bridge to Nevada County. Although documented in 1934 by the Historic American Buildings Survey (HABS) and designated a California Historical Landmark in 1948, authorities decided to replace the bridge with a modern structure in 1962. Efforts to keep the bridge in place succeeded, and after repairs the bridge continued in service until 1973 when it was bypassed just upstream. A flood on October 20, 1997, however, nearly destroyed the bridge, but the state made the necessary repairs and kept the bridge open to casual drivers until 2010. When serious

Spanning the South Fork of the Yuba River, the Bridgeport Covered Bridge is one of ten remaining in California. Constructed in 1862 as a component of a needed road system in a rapidly developing area, this striking single-span bridge, 233 feet long, uses a 24-panel Howe truss structure reinforced by two pairs of laminated arches whose shape is outlined by the shingled exterior. The clear span is 210 feet on one side and 208 feet on the other. (A. Chester Ong, 2012)

deficiencies subsequently were discovered, the bridge was closed even to pedestrians in 2011 and remains so at the time of writing. In August 2012, the National Historic Covered Bridge Preservation Program announced a grant of $545,000 for repairs.

Bridgeport's builder was apparently well experienced, for his 24-panel Howe truss carries a clear span of 210 feet (at least as measured on one side since the abutments are not perfectly square; the other side measures only 208 feet). Until the destruction of New York's Blenheim Bridge in 2011, bridge enthusiasts argued whether that or Bridgeport was the longest single-span covered bridge. Today, Bridgeport has the undisputed honor.

Honey Run Bridge BUTTE COUNTY, CALIFORNIA

Butte Co. #1 (05-04-01), over Butte Creek, 6 miles east-southeast of Chico, just off Honey Run Road, 230 feet, 3 spans

Perched on large cylindrical tubes and spanning a peaceful rocky river with a high bluff forming the backdrop, California's Honey Run Bridge is visually attractive by any standard, but what creates the greatest curiosity is its roofline in three levels. This resulted from there being three spans of different heights, a short one only 30 feet long on the west, the main span of 130 feet, and an 80-foot span on the east, those at each end having a roof several feet lower than the main span. When visitors attuned to structural details enter on the west (the eastern end is closed by wire mesh), they are also struck by the odd conglomeration of trusses. The first and shortest span is a pony-sized kingpost,

with two vertical iron rods supporting the chords below and a pair of external angle braces assuring rigidity. The middle and eastern spans are "combination" wood and iron Pratt trusses.

Honey Run Bridge was an indirect result of the Gold Rush, which extended to nearby Paradise in 1859. Though the Gold Rush was over by the time Honey Run Bridge was built, it had brought with it extensive settlement, and as time went on the residents demanded more and more infrastructure. In 1883, the citizens of Paradise and Magalia (formerly Dogtown, site of the 1859 discovery of a 54 pound gold nugget) petitioned for a road, and by 1885 what was then called Carr Hill Road (now Honey Run Road) had been completed, but travelers still had to ford Butte Creek. In September 1886, the Butte County Board of Supervisors published a "Notice to Contractors" requesting bids for a two-

span bridge 240 feet long, 16 feet wide, and preferably of Howe truss design. Eventually, the American Bridge Company of San Francisco won the contract to build a Pratt "iron combination bridge" for $4,295 along with a second bridge at Rock Creek for $2,050. Honey Run was to have mortared stone abutments and two pairs of riveted steel cylinders filled with concrete. Carr Hill was completed by January 3, 1887, when Superintendent George Miller reported the bridge acceptable. At that time, the bridge remained uncovered, but the builders had protected the exposed wooden frame with metal sheathing, remains of which can be seen today. In 1901, George Miller petitioned the Board of Supervisors to authorize housing the bridge for about $560 because exposure had already required the replacement of the entire floor system. Because the housing conformed to the differing heights of the

Honey Run Bridge, a triple-span structure over rocky Butte Creek in northern California, is 230 feet long. The bridge has a unique profile because of its stepped roofline in three levels, which resulted from the fact that the bridge consists of three spans of different heights and lengths. Trusses also vary from the shortest, being a pony-sized kingpost, while the middle and eastern spans are "combination" wood and iron Pratt trusses that differ in details. (A. Chester Ong, 2012)

three spans, the bridge then attained its unusual outline.

Although the two main spans are described as having Pratt trusses, they differ in details from Thomas and Caleb Pratt's 1844 patent, which was true of other known "combination Pratts" as well. The trapezoidal wooden frame, with smaller wooden posts marking off six panels in the longer and five in the shorter span, all work in compression, while the crisscross iron rods within panels act in tension. The most complex parts are those connecting the metal rods to wooden posts or chords, fittings which were probably prefabricated at a foundry in San Francisco.

The bridge carried traffic until April 12, 1965 when a truck struck a corner of the eastern span, causing it to collapse into a twisted pile of debris. Officials decided to replace the entire bridge with a new one nearby, as well as demolish the remains of the old covered bridge, until local citizens formed the Honey Run Covered Bridge Association to raise money for reconstruction of the ruined span. Their efforts paid off, and in 1972 the bridge reopened for pedestrian use within a peaceful park setting.

Although constructed in 1887, the bridge was not covered until 1901. Severely damaged by an out-of-control truck in 1965, the bridge was reopened only to pedestrian traffic in a park-like setting once restoration was completed in 1972. (A. Chester Ong, 2012)

247

Knight's Ferry Bridge
STANISLAUS COUNTY, CALIFORNIA

**Stanislaus Co. #1 (05-50-01), over the
Stanislaus River, on the south edge
of Knight's Ferry on Old Sonora Road,
330 feet, 4 spans**

For most Americans, California was just a distant territory until 1849 when gold was discovered, triggering a sudden influx of eager but often undisciplined people from many countries and backgrounds. Among the early pioneers to the foothills of the Sierra Nevada 40 miles east of present day Modesto was Dr William Knight who, with partner James Vantine, established a ferry in 1848 across the clear, cold, mountain-fed water of the Stanislaus River using an old whaling ship. Although Knight's name lives on today, he soon lost his life when, on November 9, 1849, he was either shot on the street during an argument or stabbed sleeping in his bed. Knight's ferry business passed into the hands of several successor owners, and David Locke built both saw and grist mills there in 1854. Three years later, Locke built an open wooden truss bridge near his mills which, when it opened, ended ferry operations. Bridge tolls were far less than ferry tolls, and crossing was always reliable. During the late winter of 1862, a sudden melt coupled with heavy rain quickly brought the river to 35 feet above low water. While the open-truss bridge would allow the torrent to pass through, a nearby bridge at Two-Mile Bar floated off its abutments and crashed against Locke's bridge, destroying it.

After re-establishing the ferry and constructing a footbridge, Locke and his partners at the Stanislaus Bridge and Ferry Company began constructing a new covered bridge of native fir, pine, and oak eight feet higher. The bridge opened in 1863 but was not fully completed until May 1864. The builder used what was then the best known and most modern truss, that of William Howe, which had become widely known throughout the United States by the 1860s and was especially common in rail bridges, including many uncovered examples throughout the West. Fully covered bridges in the West, however, were rare before Knight's Ferry, making this crossing one of California's (as well as the West's) earliest. Although a bridge of 379 feet could have been built in two or three spans, Knight's Ferry Bridge has four unequal spans, the longest over the main river channel.

The town of Knight's Ferry began declining soon thereafter as Modesto became more important and the newly constructed railroad bypassed the area. Nonetheless, the mill

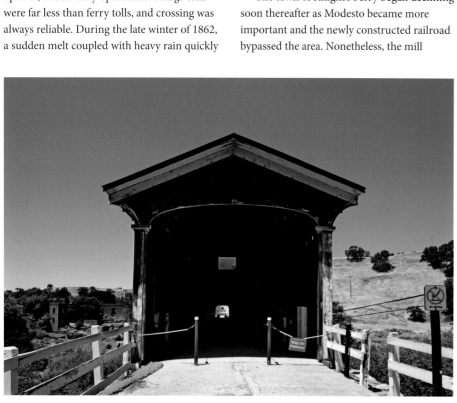

owners added a water-powered single turbo generator that produced electricity until 1920. After the citizens demanded a free bridge, on November 12, 1884, the county paid $7,000 for the bridge and dispensed with tolls. With minimal repairs, the bridge remained open to traffic until 1981 when engineers discovered damage to the trusses. Since then, the bridge and the surrounding area have come under the Sacramento District Corps of Engineers, which established a park and boat access. Today, families spend their Sundays eating in the shade (temperatures can reach past 100 degrees F) while their children play in the cool waters of the river nearby. Visitors can walk through the covered bridge to see the ruins of the old mills and the electrical generating equipment on the northern bank.

Constructed of locally sourced fir, pine, and oak, the bridge uses a classic Howe truss, a design widely employed in building railroad bridges at the time. (A. Chester Ong, 2012; Below right, Terry E. Miller, 2012)

Nestled over the Stanislaus River to the west of the Sierra Nevada range in central California, at 330 feet in length the Knights Ferry Bridge is the longest covered bridge west of the Mississippi River. A successor to a ferry established by the pioneer Dr William Knight in 1848 and continued by business associates after his death in 1849, the covered bridge was completed in 1864. (A. Chester Ong, 2012)

Lowell Bridge LANE COUNTY, OREGON

Lane Co. #2 (37-20-18), over the Middle Fork of the Willamette River, now part of Dexter Reservoir, 13 miles southeast of Eugene, just south of Lowell on Pioneer Road, 165 feet

When drivers traveling from Eugene on Oregon 58 southeast towards Klamath Falls first come to Dexter Reservoir, one of two large lakes created by damming the Middle Fork of the Willamette River, they may be surprised to see what appears to be a covered bridge sitting in the middle of the lake. When conditions are right, low hanging clouds or fog just above the bridge give it a surreal appearance. Coming closer, you see the near perfect reflections of the bridge in the still water and confirm that the bridge is, indeed, sitting in the lake, with a new road crossing just beyond.

After the town of Lowell was founded along the river in 1874, pioneer Amos Hyland operated a ferry until 1907 when Smith Bridge agent Nels Roney built the first covered bridge, a 201-foot span using an unusually high Smith truss, for $6,295. Because a truck accident on the bridge left the trusses out of alignment and weakened, Lane County Bridge Supervisor Walt Sorensen built an open 165-foot-long, 24-foot-wide "Western Howe" replacement in 1945 to accommodate the many logging trucks passing over the river. Constructed for $25,473, it was later covered with siding and roof in 1947. In 1953, in

anticipation of the rising waters of Dexter Reservoir, the county raised the bridge around seven feet, leaving it safely two feet above the lake level. Although the bridge ably continued to carry exceptionally heavy trucks, a dump truck driver, blithely unaware that his bed was partially raised, tore into the bridge, doing extensive damage in 1981. As a result, the county built a new bridge parallel to the covered one. Now the area just north of the bridge has become a park and the bridge itself a museum devoted to Oregon covered bridge building. Visitors cannot but be impressed with the massive beams of this structure, built with large-scale triple upper and lower chords and a series of triple-braced panels and triple steel rods. Its unusual width permitted cars to

pass within and could accommodate heavy logging trucks with ease. One can fairly describe the Lowell Bridge as both fully modern and fully traditional, since it uses a form of the Howe truss developed in Oregon.

Lee H. Nelson relates the following amusing story from 1953 when Lowell Bridge was to be flooded (1960: 182):

"Construction of Dexter Dam necessitated raising the bridge seven feet to accommodate filling of the reservoir. In reporting this, the *Eugene Register Guard* announced that the bridge had been 'razed,' a typographical error. An alert reader, in a letter to the editor, set things right as follows:

The reporter must surely be dazed,
Who reported the Lowell bridge razed.
Should he visit the scene
It would surely be seen
that the bridge was not razed
But was r-a-i-s-e-d."

Constructed over the Middle Fork of the Willamette River in Oregon, to accommodate logging trucks, the first covered bridge at the site dates to 1907 but was replaced by the current covered bridge in 1945, then was raised seven feet in 1953 as part of the Dexter Reservoir project. When the covered bridge was by-passed in 1981 with the construction of a modern bridge, it was seemingly marooned in the water. Approached via a connecting causeway, the structure was repurposed as the Lowell Bridge Interpretive Center, highlighting Lane County's covered bridges, four of which are located within a 10-mile radius. (A. Chester Ong, 2012; Above right, Terry E. Miller, 2005)

Point Wolfe Bridge

ALBERT COUNTY, NEW BRUNSWICK, CANADA

Albert Co. #5 (55-01-05 #2), over the Point Wolfe River, 4.7 miles south of the entrance to Fundy National Park on a park road

Situated at the tide-influenced mouth of the Point Wolfe River within sight of the Bay of Fundy on the Atlantic coast, the Point Wolfe Bridge is also among the most dramatic, spanning a deep, boulder-filled chasm where the river is squeezed between two cliffs before emptying into the sea. In the 1820s, a village occupied by timbermen grew up on the river bank, complete with houses, a store, a boarding house, and a sawmill that

was later steam-powered. The first bridge, an improvised suspension bridge, was succeeded by a sturdier one, but after its collapse in 1908 residents petitioned the provincial highway department for a substantial bridge. A contract signed in 1909 for a bridge costing $1,456 failed to materialize, and it was not until 1910 that A. E. Smye completed the job, building a 98-foot standard Howe truss. Like many other highway bridges in New Brunswick, this was left open, but in 1911 the authorities wisely covered it with roof and siding. Within the next few years, however, the village declined and was abandoned. None of the buildings remain today, but the area

has been incorporated into Fundy National Park. In 1991, when a crew attempted to blast rock from a massive outcropping close to the southeast corner of the bridge, one of the severed boulders glanced off the lower chord, which shook the bridge so badly that it collapsed into the river. The Albert County community convinced the highway department to rebuild a copy of the 1910 bridge. The replica was constructed by the Callahan Contracting of Moncton for $545,602. It was first assembled at their headquarters, then dismantled and sent for pressure treatment, and finally reassembled at the site in 1992.

Perched above the Point Wolfe River within sight of the Bay of Fundy in New Brunswick, Canada, this bridge was first built in 1910 using an open standard Howe truss. A year later, it was covered and remained even as the nearby village, once prosperous, declined. Destroyed in 1991 due to nearby blasting, the bridge was rebuilt as a replica the following year, which is the accurate date responsibly shown on the sign under the gable.
(A. Chester Ong, 2012)

Perrault Bridge MRC DE BEAUCE-SARTIGAN, QUÉBEC, CANADA

MRC de Beauce-Sartigan #1 (61-06-01), over Rivière Chaudière, 8 miles north-northwest of Saint-Georges in the village of Notre-Dame-des-Pins, bypassed in a park, 495 feet, 4 spans

Twice the size of Texas, parts of Québec remain virtually unpopulated and undeveloped even today. Most of the province's eight million people live in the southern portion bordering the states of Maine, New York, and Vermont, and thus it is not surprising that when provincial authorities began actively building covered bridges (*ponts couverts*) around 1840, they adopted American designs. Although some of the province's remaining 86 covered bridges (there were around 250 in 1958) use multiple kingpost, Howe, and in one case McCallum trusses, the vast majority are Town lattice, the pre-eminent design in nearby Vermont as well. Covered bridge building exploded after 1890 when the newly created Ministry of Colonization, Mining, and Fisheries was charged with expanding the province's

infrastructure into newly settled areas, allowing people to develop farming and mining. Since many were built on orders of the Ministry, these are often called "colonization bridges," though "settlement bridges" would be a better translation.

Some of the earlier Town lattice bridges follow the American pattern, with both primary and secondary upper and lower chords, and use trunnels to pin the lattice planks. Colonization bridges used a modified form with only primary upper and lower chords, a lighter weight lattice work than in American bridges, and a series of vertical posts on the insides of each truss. Instead of trunnels, builders after 1900 used metal hardware.

The Perrault Bridge, built in 1928–9 and named for then Minister of Colonization Jean-Édouard Perrault, is claimed as the province's longest bridge. Counterclaims that the Pont Félix-Gabriel-Marchand de Mansfield-et-Pontegract in MRC de Pontiac is four feet longer requires including semi-structural entries. The present bridge,

however, is actually the second on this site, its slightly shorter predecessor in only three spans having survived only months before being flooded out in April 1928. The Ministry's planners had pointedly ignored local warnings about the river's ferocity during flooding and built the first crossing too close to the high water mark as well as too short, causing the abutments to constrict the river during high water. Completed in 1927, the first bridge of otherwise similar design succumbed in less than a year. When officials planned the second bridge, which was started almost immediately, they heeded local advice, building a four-span crossing on concrete piers substantially above the river.

Because of increasing traffic, officials bypassed the bridge in 1969. Over the years, as bridge tourism began developing, substantial funds were expended for the bridge's upkeep. Major repairs took place in 2002 when the Canada-Québec Infrastructures Programme together with the municipality invested one million dollars in the bridge, making it one of the province's premier tourist attractions.

The first bridge at this site, seen under construction, was built in 1927 and had only three spans, leaving too narrow a passage for the river. The following April it was flooded out and came to rest against a bridge downriver. The present four-span bridge was completed in 1929. (Collection Alice Bourque)

With its four spans stretching 495 feet across Rivière Chaudière in Québec, Canada, the imposing Perrault Bridge was constructed in 1928-9 employing the Town lattice truss. Bypassed in 1969, the Perrault Bridge, as part of a multipurpose park, is an accessible and heavily visited attraction. (A. Chester Ong, 2012)

Florenceville Bridge

CARLETON COUNTY, NEW BRUNSWICK, CANADA

Carleton Co. #6 (55-02-06), over the St. John River in Florenceville, on Old Florenceville Bridge Road, 154 feet

On the face of it, the *World Guide*'s entry for Florenceville makes no sense: a bridge 154 feet long over the same river as Hartland's "longest in the world" span just six miles away. Visitors quickly notice that the covered span is only one of five, the other four being steel trusses. There must be a logical explanation for this. Understanding this complex history has been made possible by Gérald Arbour of Québec and Gregory Campbell of New Brunswick.

The Florenceville crossing was a ferry until 1882. An article in the *Carleton Sentinel* on April 4, 1882, discussed plans for a new bridge with a roadway length of 1,060 feet, with "three" [should have been four] spans of 175 feet and one of 150 feet. The chief engineer, Mr Beckwith, planned a wooden Burr truss bridge "the same as the bridge across the Meduxnekeag here." Before the bridge could be completed, an "ice freshet" carried off three of the five spans. According to the *Carleton Sentinel* of June 5, 1886, which had celebrated the bridge's opening on June 1, the government had already expended $15,000 on that bridge. Following the flood, they contracted with "Mr. Albert Brewer [from Carleton], who, on the 20th September, 1885, with David Jackson as head framer, and Andrew Ellis in charge of the pier construction began the work of rebuilding. . . . " The finished structure,

costing $14,500, consisted of five open spans as noted above, using New Brunswick's standard highway Burr truss, the multiple kingpost portion having flared posts and a set of arches, all built on wooden piers with protective ramparts facing upriver and covered in boiler plate. The bridge, 37.7 feet above the low water mark, was 20 feet wide with a roadway of 17 feet. Each end had open wooden kingpost approaches 32 feet long. An old postcard shows the arches of the four longer spans rising well above the upper chords. The trusses appear to have been painted white and the arches either painted black or protected with creosote.

Something happened to the two end spans. In 1907, officials had to replace the western-most span with a covered Howe truss, and

How the Florenceville covered bridge in New Brunswick, Canada, stands at one end of a much longer bridge comprised of four steel trusses segments cannot be explained easily in a caption. Its complex history is explained in the accompanying text. (Below and upper right, Terry E. Miller, 2000; Bottom, A. Chester Ong, 2012; Postcard, c. 1887–1907)

in 1908, the easternmost span, also with a covered Howe truss. An undated newspaper clipping from around 1911 indicated that the remaining middle spans, which had already been strengthened with additional sets of non-concentric arches below the originals, needed to be replaced. New steel truss spans were then built by the William P. McNeil Company of New Glasgow, Nova Scotia, but using the original wooden piers. The old wooden piers had to be replaced in 1917, but, as in the case of the Hartland Bridge, the contractor built new concrete piers next to the old ones and moved the entire bridge over. Within a year or so, the open kingpost approaches were replaced with steel girder spans. A few days before August 26, 1932, Alonzo Shaw's house on the west end caught fire, and the flames tragically spread to the covered span. "One wooden covered span on the western end was completely destroyed, the flooring burned or removed from most of one steel span. . . ." The burning bridge collapsed into the river around 1.30 pm. After that, the westernmost span was replaced with a new steel span similar to the middle three but built by the Saint John Dry Dock and Shipbuilding Co. Thus, today's Florenceville Bridge carries traffic across the easternmost covered wooden span and four steel truss spans.

Irish River and Hardscrabble Bridges

SAINT JOHN COUNTY, NEW BRUNSWICK, CANADA

Saint John Co. #4 and #5 (55-11-05 and 55-11-06), over Vaughan Creek, 26 miles east of Saint John at St. Martins, both 78 feet

When two covered bridges can be photographed together, they are often called "twin bridges" even though they are more like "twin cities" than human twins. In the past, two bridges (or even three) in proximity were relatively common, but today few twins remain. In some cases, their proximity resulted from the river cutting one of more new channels during flooding, requiring the construction of an additional bridge, as is the case with Columbia County, Pennsylvania's famous Paden twins near Forks (pages 196–7). The Vaughan Creek twins at

St. Martins, New Brunswick's answer to Nova Scotia's tourist-heavy Peggy's Cove, both cross the same creek but on different roads. Vaughan Creek #1, also known as the Irish River Bridge, was built in 1935 using the standard New Brunswick Howe truss, that is, having a trapezoidal frame ending in braces but with X's in all other panels. Vaughan Creek #2, about a quarter mile away, also known as the Hardscrabble Bridge, is the same length as its twin but #2 was built in 1946. The latter bridge has the distinction of being located within sight of the Bay of Fundy as well as next to colorful fishing boats, lobster traps, and piles of plastic floats. The waters of Irish Creek rise and fall with the tides. Since the late 1980s, both bridges have had exterior walkways added.

All of New Brunswick's sixty-plus surviving covered bridges date from the post-1900 period. Although a history of earlier bridges remains to be written, they certainly existed, but the first known covered bridge, from 1827, was only partially in New Brunswick because it crossed the St. Croix River from Calais, Maine, to St. Stephen, New Brunswick. The oldest surviving bridge is Nelson Hollow in Northumberland County, built in 1900, and the youngest, not counting Point Wolfe, is the Quisilbis River #2 Bridge in Madawaska County, dating from 1952. New Brunswick's covered bridges depend on context for interest, since virtually all are tightly closed with unpainted wood and square portals, and all but a few have nearly identical Howe trusses.

Within walking distance of one other, as shown in the photograph on the left, the Hardscrabble Bridge is in the background. Known as the Vaughan Creek twins in New Brunswick, Canada, they both cross the same water body but on different roads. Left unpainted to weather naturally, the Irish River Bridge was completed in 1935 and the Hardscrabble Bridge in 1946, with exterior walkways added to both in the late 1980s. (A. Chester Ong, 2012)

Powerscourt or Percy Bridge

MRC DU HAUT-SAINT-LAURENT, QUÉBEC, CANADA

MRC du Haut-Saint-Laurent #1 (61-27-01), over Rivière Châteauguay, 5 miles south of Huntingdon on Chemin de la premère-Concession (road) in the village of Powerscourt, 180 feet, 2 spans

Just over a mile north of Québec's border with New York, the Powerscourt Bridge is exceptional for several reasons. First, it is the oldest covered bridge in Canada, having been built in 1861. Unless one counts the heavily restored Victoria Bridge in Montreal, which is slightly older, then Powerscourt is also the oldest bridge of any type in Canada. Engineering historians value it as the only wooden McCallum truss remaining in the world.

Born in Scotland, Daniel C. McCallum (1815–78) came to New York State in 1822, and after limited training in carpentry became General Superintendent of the New York and Erie Railroad in 1855 by virtue of building successful open wooden rail bridges using his own designs. McCallum obtained two patents, in 1851 and 1857, both for different versions of his "Inflexible Arched Truss," which was essentially a Long truss with a curved ("arched") upper chord and two angle braces at each end that cross from the ends of the lower chords and run across two panels to the upper chord. Since all of McCallum's bridges were for railroads, and these were ephemeral by nature, none has survived. Secretary of War Stanton appointed McCallum Military Director and Superintendent of the Union railroads during the Civil War, and by war's end he had risen to the rank of Brigadier General. Seeing that the days of all-wood bridges were numbered, however, he sold his patent rights to a Canadian builder, Robert Graham, who built the Powerscourt Bridge

Known as the Percy Bridge as well as the Powerscourt Bridge, this remarkable structure is the sole surviving wooden McCallum truss— an "Inflexible Arched Truss"—found anywhere in the world. Located just one mile north of Québec's border with New York State and crossing Rivière Châteauguay, this double-span bridge echoes McCallum truss railroad bridges built earlier in the United States. (A. Chester Ong, 2012)

in 1861 for $1,675 to replace an earlier bridge from 1857. While Graham used the abutments and pier from the earlier bridge, these had to be rebuilt in 1903.

Powerscourt is unusual because it is a highway bridge, and it is uncertain whether McCallum ever built highway bridges in the United States. It is also uncertain whether Graham built others in Canada. With a length of only 180 feet, it could have been built as a single span, and McCallum's truss was certainly capable of spanning that distance. Graham, however, simplified McCallum's patent by using only a single strut at each end rather than two as specified in the patent. The result is basically a Long truss with curved upper chords. Canada recognized the importance of the bridge and designated it a National Historic Site of Canada in 1984. The bridge was fully restored by local timber framers in 2009.

Hartland Bridge

CARLETON COUNTY, NEW BRUNSWICK, CANADA

Carleton County #7 (55-02-07), over St. John River at Hartland, on Hartland Bridge Hill Road, 1,282 feet, 7 spans

Not only is Hartland's bridge "the longest covered bridge in the world," but it is twice as long as the second and third longest (both in Québec). With seven spans averaging 183 feet each, as well as a covered sidewalk on the southern side, just walking across the bridge requires time and energy. But "in the old days" (that is, the nineteenth century), bridges of this length were common in the eastern United States over such rivers as the Connecticut, Potomac, Merrimack, and especially the Susquehanna, that approached or exceeded a mile. Between ice jams, floods, progress, and the Civil War, all of these bridges are long gone, leaving us only one place with such a monumental bridge. Because of its relatively recent date of construction, its history is well documented, especially by John Glass and Doris Kennedy in *The Bridge in Hartland, New Brunswick* (1990), whose account is summarized here.

Hartland was settled in 1797 by a family from New York State, and grew thanks to the nearby agricultural lands as well as the lumber industry, which floated logs down the wide St. John River flowing through the town. Today, the population of around 1,000 is served by two bridges, one covered, one modern, but until 1901 travelers had to depend on cable ferries driven by the currents in the summer or ice bridges in the winter, neither being reliable. As early as 1870, citizens began talking about a bridge, but their request to provincial authorities in 1890 was rejected. Over the next few years, citizens petitioned for a bridge, expressing a preference for an eight-span steel crossing, but the province could not afford the nearly $80,000 required for a modern bridge. A group of prominent citizens headed by Charles A. McCormack thus proposed the Hartland Bridge Co., which was subsequently authorized by provincial authorities in 1899 with McCormack as both President and Superintendent of Construction, the latter because he was an experienced builder.

Following a period of debate concerning the location, provincial authorities chose a site just south of the ferry crossing. Knowing that a wooden bridge was affordable, on December 13, 1899, Provincial Engineer Wetmore awarded the contract to Albert Brewer of Woodstock, NB, for $27,945.00, giving him eighteen months to complete the work. The company sold government-backed bonds to raise funds and set tolls intended to recoup their investment. The tollhouse was located on the northeast corner of the bridge, and the toll master was to charge $.03 per person, $.06 for a single rig, $.12 for a double team, $.001/2 per head of sheep, and $.03 per head of cattle, all tolls being "each way."

The seven spans used the Howe truss originally patented by William Howe in 1840 but slightly modified for use in New Brunswick. Wood was readily available and cheap, whereas steel was both difficult to obtain and expensive. Building uncovered Howe truss rail bridges had long been customary in both Canada and the United States even though the elements often severely

From whatever angle one regards the Hartland Bridge in New Brunswick, Canada, its length of 1,282 feet confirms that it is "the longest covered bridge in the world." Indeed, it is two times longer than the second and third longest historical covered bridges in North America, both in Québec. (A. Chester Ong, 2011)

Built using Howe trusses, which are visible in this 1901 photograph, and supported by massive wooden piers, the uncovered bridge replaced a cable ferry, thus providing a reliable crossing over the St. John River. The bridge was only covered in 1919 after substantial deterioration of the wooden members led to replacement of much of the original structure. (Doris Kennedy Collection)

Viewed from the pedestrian walkway, which was added in 1945, the Howe trusses are protected by metal guide rails. Vehicular traffic through the bridge is only one direction at a time, and passage requires the cooperation of drivers. (A. Chester Ong, 2011)

degraded them within a few years. Open wooden highway bridges, however, were little known outside New Brunswick, but the people of Hartland preferred it that way. Additionally, the Hartland Bridge was built on wooden piers with wing walls to deflect debris and logs coming downstream. Though the official opening took place on July 4, 1901, the bridge opened unofficially on May 13 at 9 pm when a local doctor needed to make an emergency call on the other side. The opening celebration brought distinguished provincial authorities to the town. A burst of fireworks finished the day.

While happy to have the bridge, the town's citizens were less keen on paying the tolls needed to pay for it. In March 1903, the directors conceded reductions for funerals, and after May 1, 1906, toll collection ceased. At the same time, the bridge began deteriorating because the rain and snow led to rot, while the piers needed stones around them for protection. With little money, the company and the citizens began clamoring for the province to take possession of the bridge. Some suggested covering the bridge, but most people objected, fearing it would become a haven for unsavory characters waiting in the

darkness to molest or rob those crossing the bridge alone. A fire on July 15, 1907 resulted in severe damage to the village, but firemen managed to prevent the bridge from being destroyed. By 1913, the bridge had deteriorated to the point that some wanted to replace it, either with new Howe trusses or by the long-desired steel bridge. But World War I intervened, making replacement impossible, even as the condition of the bridge became worse and worse. By the end of the war, it was clear that a new bridge must be built. But doing so meant returning to a ferry crossing during replacement, something the citizens

did not want. By January 23, 1919, it was decided to cover the bridge as well as repair it, the latter taking place during the winter months when the ice allowed the structure to be raised in order to replace major parts such as chords. The bridge was to reopen for traffic on April 6, 1920.

Disaster, however, was lurking. During that afternoon, rain began, and soon ice floes choked the river. During the night, the ice carried off two spans on the western end, along with a pier, leaving the town again without a bridge and people stranded without an operating ferry. Within weeks, officials decided that the bridge must have concrete piers and the two missing spans had to be rebuilt. When the bridge finally reopened, on March 3, 1921, it had not just two new spans but extensive repairs to the rest. Simultaneously, workers began constructing new concrete abutments and piers.

The final stage of rebuilding involved two steps, one major, one less so: raising the entire bridge 30 inches and moving it 20 feet downstream onto the new piers. This unusual feat, not described by Glass and Kennedy, was completed by October 20, 1921, when the last span was successfully moved. Amazingly, throughout the process, the bridge remained open, though people using the bridge had to pass through a narrowed gap where the spans were still offset.

The second matter was covering the entire structure with siding and roofing for

protection from further deterioration. But the cover also made the bridge extremely dark, and at night citizens feared using it. Soon electric lights were installed. The final change to its appearance and function occurred in 1945 when the covered sidewalk was added to the southern side.

The local view of the span has changed from early disappointment at not getting a steel bridge, to anger over its being covered, to today's celebration of it as the town's most valuable attraction, "the longest covered bridge in the world."

The quiet eastern end of the Hartland Bridge, which includes a park adjacent to the commercial core of the town, contrasts with the steep incline on the western side that leads up to a bluff overlooking the river valley. The eastern end includes convenient parking and a visitor center (A. Chester Ong, 2011)

In spite of openings along the side where there is an enclosed pedestrian walkway and interior lighting at night, driving through the bridge is likened by some to passing through a long elevated tunnel. (A. Chester Ong, 2011)

ACKNOWLEDGMENTS

Few authors write in a vacuum. Even the best informed are wise to consult with associates and friends who may in fact know much more and often save such authors from embarrassment. This adage has been particularly true in the case of *America's Covered Bridges*. A great many individuals have contributed knowledge, corrections, photographs, and helpful suggestions. Although we risk inadvertently leaving someone out, we nonetheless wish to acknowledge the immense help we have gotten from so many individuals.

We are particularly grateful to Joseph D. Conwill of Rangeley, Maine, a noted author of books and articles on covered bridges, a skilled photographer, and the long-time editor of *Covered Bridge Topics*. Conwill's knowledge of bridges is exceptional, and he willingly shared this with us. In addition, he read much of the draft, making essential corrections. Nonetheless, any errors that have survived the editorial process remain our responsibility.

Bill Caswell, co-creator of www.lostbridges. com and an engineer living in Hillsboro, New Hampshire, made several trips on our behalf to the Archives of the National Society for the Preservation of Covered Bridges in Vermont to scan needed photos and other materials from the Richard Sanders Allen Collection. Without Bill's GPS locational data, the map of existing covered bridges on pages 164–5 could not have been produced. We are grateful also for his confirming both location and numbers of all covered bridges in the United States and Canada as of August 1, 2013.

We also appreciate our many consultations with two long-time Ohio colleagues, Miriam F. Wood, a founding member of the Ohio Historic Bridge Association and also its Historian, and David A. Simmons of the Ohio Historical Society and President of the Ohio Historic Bridge Association.

In addition, we wish to acknowledge the generosity of the following individuals and institutions for their responsiveness to our requests for information and images. If we have inadvertently omitted anyone, please accept our apologies for this unintended oversight.

Alabama Department of Archives and History, Montgomery, Alabama
Alaska State Library, Juneau, Alaska
Randy Allan, historian, Beverly, West Virginia
Gérald Arbour, researcher and author on Québec's covered bridges, Montreal, Québec, Canada
Ashtabula County Convention & Visitors Bureau
Myrtle Auvill, bridge historian, West Virginia
Debra Basham, West Virginia State Archives, Charleston, West Virginia
Pierre Bégin, Mayor, Notre-Dame-des-Pins, Québec, Canada
Beverly, Massachusetts Historical Society
Bibliothèque et Archives Nationales Québec, Canada

Billie Creek Village, Rockville, Indiana
Blue Ridge Timberwrights, Christiansburg, Virginia
Patricia Boulos, Boston Athenaeum, Boston, Massachusetts
Brian Bollinger, Belmont, New Hampshire
Karen Bratton, Douglas County Museum, Roseburg, Oregon
The Bridgeman Art Library, New York, New York
The British Museum, London, United Kingdom
Gregory Campbell, librarian, Woodstock, New Brunswick, Canada
Carnegie Museum of Art, Pittsburgh, Pennsylvania
Anne Cloyd Cassens, photographer, Edgemont, South Dakota
Philip S. C. Caston, specialist in German covered bridges, Neubrandenburg, Germany
John H. Diehl, founder of the Ohio Covered Bridge Committee, Cincinnati, Ohio
Gerald Dyck, Assonet, Massachusetts
Encore Editions, New Hope, Pennsylvania
Steven Engerrand, Georgia Archives, Morrow, Georgia
Shirley Felter, photographer, Blenheim, New York
Martha Capwell Fox, National Canal Museum, Easton, Pennsylvania
Paul Giguere, Maine Department of Transportation
James R. Gnagy Jr, covered bridge photographer, Canton, Ohio
Jennie Munger Gregory Memorial Museum, Ashtabula, Ohio
Martha Haithcock, Randolph County Public Library, Asheboro, North Carolina
Gregory S. Hamilton, photographer, Hebron, Ohio
Michelle Hammer, Harpers Ferry National Historic Park Library, West Virginia
Susan Hammond, photographer, Chester, Vermont
Hawaii State Archives, Honolulu, Hawaii
Historic American Engineering Record (HAER), Washington, DC
Michele Houston, Pioneer Engineers Club of Indiana, Rushville, Indiana
Ove Jensen, Park Ranger, Historian, Horseshoe Bend National Military Park, Daviston, Alabama
Claire Dunne Johnson, St. Johnsbury, Vermont (posthumous)
Trish Kane, Collections Curator, Theodore Burr Covered Bridge Resource Center, Oxford, New York and co-founder of www.lostbridges.com
Doris Kennedy, historian, Hartland, New Brunswick, Canada
Lafayette County, Mississippi Genealogy and History Network
Lancaster [Pennsylvania] Online
Robert W. M. Laughlin, historian, covered bridges of Kentucky, Louisville, Kentucky
The Library Company of Philadelphia, Pennsylvania
Library of Congress, Prints and Photographs Division, Washington, DC

Jane Lightner, Preble County Historical Society, Eaton, Ohio
Christopher Marston, Historic American Engineering Record (HAER), Washington, DC
Marianne Martin, Colonial Williamsburg Foundation, Virginia
Michael P. Miller, American Philosophical Society, Philadelphia, Pennsylvania
Laurel Mitchell, Carnegie Museum of Art, Pittsburgh, Pennsylvania
Fred J. Moll, Historian of the Theodore Burr Covered Bridge Society, Fleetwood, Pennsylvania
Monroe County Historical Society, Missouri
Byllye Montalto, Klyne Esopus Historical Society Museum, Ulster Park, New York
National Society for the Preservation of Covered Bridges Archives, Westminster, Vermont
New York Historical Society, New York, New York
New York Public Library, New York, New York
Melanie Norton and Nancy Spencer, Sullivan County Historical Society and Museum, Laporte, Pennsylvania
Jared Null, Cochranville, Pennsylvania
Ohio Historical Society, Columbus, Ohio
Kaitlin O'Shea, photographer, Montpelier, Vermont
Randolph County Public Library, North Carolina
Theresa E. Rea, Senator John Heinz History Center, Pittsburgh, Pennsylvania
Andy Rebman, photographer, Greenwood, Indiana
Cheryl Roffe, Lane County Historical Society, Eugene, Oregon
Ross County Historical Society, Chillicothe, Ohio
Bradley Schmehl, artist, York, Pennsylvania
Becky Stockum, Coshocton, Ohio
Larry Stout, photographer, Rushville, Indiana
United States Department of Transportation, Washington, DC
United States Patent Office, Washington, DC
Marianne Vanden Bout, Resident Docent/ Caretaker, Faith Trumbull DAR Chapter House and Museum, Norwich, Connecticut
Miriam and Ira D. Wallach Division of Arts, Prints, and Photographs, The New York Public Library, New York, New York
Warner Brothers, Hollywood, California
Becky Webb, great-granddaughter of bridge builder Emmett L. Kennedy, Rushville, Indiana
Wikipedia Commons
Winterset, Iowa, Chamber of Commerce
Mark Withers, photographer, Bethesda, Maryland
Yale University Art Gallery, New Haven, Connecticut

REFERENCES

Adams, Kramer. 1963. *Covered Bridges of the West: A History and Illustrated Guide.* Berkeley: Howell-North.

Allan, Randy. 2006. *Lemuel Chenoweth, 1811–1887: Bridging the Gaps.* Parsons, WV: McClain Printing.

Allen, Richard Sanders. 1957. *Covered Bridges of the Northeast: The Complete Story in Words and Pictures.* Brattleboro, VT: Stephen Greene Press.

_____. 1959. *Covered Bridges of the Middle Atlantic States: Their Illustrated History in War and Peace.* Brattleboro, VT: Stephen Greene Press.

_____. 1970a. *Covered Bridges of the Middle West.* Brattleboro, VT: Stephen Greene Press.

_____. 1970b. *Covered Bridges of the South.* Brattleboro, VT: Stephen Greene Press.

_____. 1983. *Old North Country Bridges Upstate New York.* Utica, NY: North Country Books.

_____. 1991. "Lemuel Cox, American Bridge Builder (1736–1806)." *Covered Bridge Topics* 49(2): 11–14.

_____. 1995. "Simeon S. Post's Patent Truss Bridge." *Covered Bridge Topics* 53(3): 5–9.

Annual Report of the Commissioner of Railroads and Telegraphs in Ohio. 1867 ff. Columbus: State of Ohio.

Arbour, Gérald. 2005. *Les ponts couverts au Québec.* Government of Québec.

Auvil, Myrtle. 1973. *Covered Bridges of West Virginia: Past and Present.* 2nd ed. Parsons, WV: McClain Printing.

Barna, Ed. 1996. *Covered Bridges of Vermont.* Woodstock, VT: Countryman Press.

Bell, William E. 1857. *Carpentry Made Easy; or, The Science and Art of Framing on a New and Improved System.* Philadelphia: Ferguson Bros. & Co. 2nd ed, Philadelphia: Ferguson Bros. & Co., 1887.

Biddle, Owen. 1805. *The Young Carpenter's Assistant; or A System of Architecture Adapted to the Style of Building in the United States.* Philadelphia: Benjamin Johnson, 1805. Reprinted New York: Dover, 2006.

Bonney, Richard P. 1972. "Arson and Covered Bridges." *Covered Bridge Topics* 29(4): 9.

Burr, Theodore. 1814. Letter to Thomas Elder, May 28. Reprinted in *Theodore Burr Covered Bridge Society of Pennsylvania: 50th Anniversary Book.* Harrisburg: Theodore Burr Covered Bridge Society, 2009.

_____. 1815. "Theodore Burr on the Challenges of Building McCall's Ferry Bridge." Reprinted in *Covered Bridge Topics* 67(1): 9–11.

Caulkins, Frances Manwaring. 1874. *History of Norwich, Connecticut.* Norwich, CT: Friends of the Author.

Cockrell, Bill. 2008. *Oregon's Covered Bridges.* Charleston, SC: Arcadia Publishing.

The Columbian Magazine. 1787. Philadelphia, January, p. 245.

Congdon, Herbert Wheaton (photographer Edmund Homer Royce). 1959. *The Covered Bridge: 100 Photographs of Vermont Covered Bridges.* Middlebury, VT: Vermont Books.

Conwill, Joseph D. 1977. "Early History of the Howe Truss." *Covered Bridge Topics* 35(1): 10–12.

_____. 1993. "Wheeler Truss Discovered in Kentucky." *Covered Bridge Topics* 51(2): 10–11.

_____. 1996. "Town Lattice Trusses by the Master Himself." *Covered Bridge Topics* 54(1): 3–4.

_____. 2003. *Maine's Covered Bridges.* Charleston, SC: Arcadia Publishing.

_____. 2004a. *Covered Bridges Across North America.* St. Paul, MN: MBI Publishing.

_____. 2004.b *Vermont Covered Bridges.* Charleston, SC: Arcadia Publishing.

_____. 2005. "More on Long Truss Prestressing: Conversations with Wayne Perry." *Covered Bridge Topics* 63(2): 3–4.

_____. 2009a. "Building a Howe Truss Bridge: Correspondence with Ian Sturrock, P.E." *Covered Bridge Topics* 67(3): 3.

_____. 2009b. "Long Truss Bridge Framing." *Covered Bridge Topics* 67(2): 4–7.

_____. 2012. "Scribe Rule and Square Rule." *Covered Bridge Topics* 70(4): 5.

Cooper, Theodore. 1889. "American Railroad Bridges." *Transactions of the American Society of Civil Engineers*, 211(418): 1–58, and *Engineering News*, July 6, 1889. Reprinted Nabu Public Domain Reprints, n.d.

Corts, Thomas E., ed. 2003. *Bliss and Tragedy: The Ashtabula Railway-Bridge Accident of 1876 and the Loss of P. P. Bliss.* Birmingham, AL: Sherman Oak Books and Samford University Press.

Cummings, Hubertis M. 1956. "Theodore Burr and His Bridges Across the Susquehanna." *Pennsylvania History* 23(4): 476–86.

Derrick, Franklin. 1928. Quoted in http://dianneandpaul.net/DianneGenealogy/d0006/g0000072.html

Dreicer, Gregory K. 1993. "The Long Span. Intercultural Exchange in Building Technology: Development and Industrialization of the Framed Beam in Western Europe and the United States, 1820–1870." Doctoral dissertation, Cornell University.

_____. 2010. "Building Bridge and Boundaries: The Lattice and the Tube, 1820–1860." *Technology and Culture* 51(1): 126–63.

Dwight, Timothy. 1821–2. *Travels in New-England and New-York.* 4 vols. New Haven: Self-published.

Evans, Benjamin D. and June R. Evans. 2004. *New England's Covered Bridges: A Complete Guide.* Hanover, NH: University Press of New England.

Fischetti, David C. 2009. *Structural Investigation of Historic Buildings: A Case Study Guide to Preservation Technology for Buildings, Bridges, Towers, and Mills.* Hoboken, NJ: John Wiley & Sons.

Fletcher, Robert and J. P. Snow. 1934. "A History of the Development of Wooden Bridges." *Proceedings: American Society of Civil Engineers.* No. 99. Also Vol. 60, No. 8, Part 2: 314–408.

Glass, John and Doris Kennedy. 1990. *The Bridge in Hartland, New Brunswick.* Fredericton, NB: New Ireland Press.

Graton, Milton S. 1978. *The Last of the Covered Bridge Builders.* Plymouth, NH: Clifford-Nicol.

Greene, Nelson, ed. 1925. *History of the Mohawk Valley: Gateway to the West 1614–1925.* Chicago: S. J. Clarke. Ch. 83, "Mohawk River Bridges" reproduced at www.schenectadyhistory.org/resources/mvgw/history/083.html

Griggs, Francis E., Jr. 2009. "Timothy Palmer and the Permanent Bridge." *Journal of Bridge Engineering of the American Society of Civil Engineering* November/December: 507–17.

Guise, David. 2009. "Abstracts & Chronology of American Truss Bridge Patents, 1817–1900." Society for Industrial Archeology, Occasional Electronic Publication No. 1.

Haupt, General Herman. 1851. *General Theory of Bridge Construction.* 2nd ed. New York: D. Appleton, 1865. Reprinted Nabu Public Domain Reprints, n.d.

_____. 1864. *Military Bridges: With Suggestions of New Expedients and Constructions for Crossing Streams and Chasms. Including, Also, Designs for Trestle and Truss Bridges for Military Railroads.* New York: D. Van Nostrand.

_____. 1901. *Reminiscences of General Herman Haupt; Giving Hitherto Unpublished Official Orders, Personal Narratives of Important Military Operations, and Interviews with President Lincoln &c....* Milwaukee, WI: Self-published. Reprinted Nabu Public Domain Reprints, n.d.

Hayner, Frank B. 1967. "Union Bridge in Waterford, New York." *Covered Bridge Topics* 25(2): 7.

Historic Highway Bridges in Pennsylvania. 1986. Harrisburg: Commonwealth of Pennsylvania, Pennsylvania Historical and Museum Commission, Pennsylvania Department of Transportation.

Jakeman, Adelbert M. 1935. *Old Covered Bridges: The Story of Covered Bridges in General.* Brattleboro, VT: Stephen Daye Press. 2nd ed. Brattleboro, VT: Stephen Daye Press, 1961.

James, J. G. 1982. "The Evolution of Wooden Bridge Trusses to 1850." *Journal of the Institute of Wood Science* 9(3/4): 116–35, 168–92. Reprinted in *Covered Bridge Topics* 55(1)–56(2), 1997–8.

Johnson, Claire Dunne. 1996. *St. Johnsbury.* Charleston, SC: Acadia.

Kemp, Emory L., ed. 2005. *American Bridge Patents: The First Century, 1790–1890.* Morgantown: West Virginia University Press.

Ketcham, Bryan E. 1949. *Covered Bridges on the Byways of Indiana.* Cincinnati: Self-published.

Klages, John W. 1996. *Covered Bridges of Fairfield County, Ohio.* Lancaster, OH: Fairfield Heritage Association.

Knapp, Ronald G. (photographer A. Chester Ong). 2008. *Chinese Bridges: Living Architecture From China's Past.* Singapore: Tuttle.

La Rochefoucauld-Liancourt, François Alexandre Frédéric de, and Henry Neuman. 1799. *Travels Through the United States of North America, the Country of the Iroquois, and Upper Canada, in the Years 1795, 1796, and 1797: With an Authentic Account of Lower Canada.* London: Printed for R. Phillip.

Latrobe, Benjamin Henry. 1905. *The Journal of Latrobe.* New York: D. Appleton & Co.

Laughlin, Robert W. M. and Melissa C. Jurgensen. 2007. *Kentucky's Covered Bridges.* Charleston, SC: Arcadia Publishing.

[Lincoln, Mrs. Orrin H.] 1968. "Turkey Hill Covered Bridge, Merrimack, N.H." *Connecticut River Valley Covered Bridge Society Bulletin* 15(1): 8.

Litwin, Leo, ed. 1964. "The Covered Bridges of Bellows Falls, Vermont." *Covered Bridge Topics* 22(2): 13–17.

Long, Col. Stephen H. 1836. *Col. S. H. Long's Bridges, Together with a Series of Directions to Bridge Builders.* Concord, NH: John F. Brown. 2nd ed. Philadelphia: Wm. F. Geddes, 1841.

Lupold, John S. and Thomas L. French, Jr. 2004. *Bridging Deep South Rivers: The Life and Legend of Horace King.* Athens: University of Georgia Press.

Massachusetts Magazine. May 1793. 5(5).

Miller, Terry E. 1971. "Longest Covered Bridge in Kentucky—Destroyed by Arson." *Covered Bridge Topics* 29(1): 10.

_____. 1975. *The Covered Bridges of Tuscarawas County, Ohio.* Dover, OH: Self-published.

_____. 2009. *The Covered Bridges of Coshocton County, Ohio: A History.* Kent, OH: Self-published.

Mingus, Scott L., Sr. 2011. *Flames Beyond Gettysburg: The Confederate Expedition to the Susquehanna River, June 1863.* New York: Savas Beatie.

Mohr, William D. 1957a. "The Hudson River Lansingburgh-Waterford Union Bridge." *Covered Bridge Topics* 15(2): 1–2.

_____. 1957b. "The Story of the Mohawk Bridge." *Covered Bridge Topics* 14(4): 5–6.

Moll, Fred J. 2012. *Pennsylvania's Covered Bridges.* Charleston, SC: Arcadia Publishing.

Morley, S. Griswold. 1938. *The Covered Bridges of California.* Berkeley: University of California.

Mort, Mike. 2008. *A Bridge Worth Saving: A Community Guide to Historic Bridge Preservation.* East Lansing: Michigan State University Press.

Mosse, James Robert. 1863. "American Timber Bridges." *Proceedings of the Institution of the Civil Engineers.* Vol. 22, Paper 1,063: 305–26.

Neff, Eldon M. 1963. "Highlights in the Life of Robert W. Smith." *Connecticut River Valley Covered Bridge Society Bulletin* 9(4): 4–5.

Nelson, Joseph C. 1997. *Spanning Time: Vermont's Covered Bridges.* Shelburne, VT: New England Press.

Nelson, Lee H. 1960. *A Century of Oregon Covered Bridges: 1851–1952.* Portland: Oregon Historical Society.

_____. 1990. *The Colossus of 1812: An American Engineering Superlative.* New York: American Society of Civil Engineers.

Palladio, Andrea. 1738. *The Four Books of Architecture.* English translation. London: Isaac Ware. Reprinted New York: Dover, 1965.

Parrott, Paul. 2005. *Chasing Covered Bridges and How to Find Them.* Nashville: Turner.

Peale, Charles Willson. 1797. *An Essay on Building Wooden Bridges.* Philadelphia: Self-published.

Penn, Demia. n.d. "The Story of the Otway Bridge." Mimeograped. Otway, Ohio.

Pennsylvania Department of Highways. 1960. *Pennsylvania's Challege: Too Many Hazardous Bridges.* Harrisburg: Pennsylvania Department of Highways.

Perry, Wayne. 1985. "Sketches of the Childs Truss." *Covered Bridge Topics* 43(3): 8–11.

[Peters, Richard]. 1806. "A Statistical Account of the Schuylkill Permanent Bridge, Communicated to the Philadelphia Society of Agriculture, 1806." Reprinted in *Memoirs of the Philadelphia Society for Promoting Agriculture*, Vol. 1. Philadelphia: Johnson & Warner, 1815: 1–88.

Pierce, Phillip C. et al. 2005. *Covered Bridge Manual.* McLean, VA: United States Department of Transportation, Federal Highway Administration Publication No. FHWA-HRT-04-098.

Pope, Thomas. 1811. *A Treatise on Bridge Architecture; in which the Superior Advantages of the Flying Pendent Lever Bridge are fully proved.* Reprint of plain text edition, Memphis, TN: General Books, 2010; Facsimile edition by Gale/Sabin Americana/Print Editions 1500–1926, n.d.

Rathnell, James K., Jr. 1963. "Charles Dickins Description of a Covered Bridge." *Covered Bridge Topics* 21(1): 1, 4–5.

Rives, Albert L. 2010. "Description of Howe's Bridge, 1853." *Covered Bridge Topics* 68(1): 3–7.

Schneider, Norris F. 1958. *The Famous Y Bridge at Zanesville, Ohio.* Zanesville: Self-published. Reprinted Southern Ohio Covered Bridge Association, 1971.

Shank, William H. 1966. *Historic Bridges of Pennsylvania.* Harrisburg: Buchart-Horn, Consulting Engineers.

Sheldon, George. 2006. *Fire on the River: The Defense of the World's Longest Covered Bridge and How It Changed the Battle of Gettysburg.* Lancaster, PA: Quaker Hills Press.

Sherman, William Tecumseh. 1875. *Memoirs of General William T. Sherman.* Vol. 2. New York.

Shiller, Eli. 1979. *The First Photographs of the Holy Land.* Jerusalem: Ariel Publishing House.

Simmons, David A. 1987. "A Remarkable Story of Preservation." *Ohio County Engineers News* November: 18.

_____. 1991a. "Unusual Patent History Represented by Franklin County Bridge." *Ohio County Engineers News* Winter: 14-15.

_____. 1991b. "Unique Covered Bridge in Delaware County." *Ohio County Engineers News* Spring: 10–11.

Sloane, Eric. 1954. *American Barns and Covered Bridges.* New York: Wilfred Funk. Reprinted Mineola, NY: Dover, 1982.

Spargo, John. 1953. *Covered Wooden Bridges of Bennington County: Historical and Descriptive Account.* Bennington: Bennington Historical Museum and Art Gallery.

Stevenson, David. 1859. *Sketch of the Civil Engineering of North America.* 2nd ed. London: John Weale.

Times Union (Troy, New York). May 9, 2012. www.timesunion.com/local/article/1862-fire-deadly-and-devastating-3546956. php#ixzz1xyOts0Qp

Town, Ithiel. 1839. *A Description of Ithiel Town's Improvement in the Principle, Construction, and Practical Execution of Bridges, for Roads, Railroads, and Aqueducts, whether built entirely of wood, or of cast or wrought iron.* 2nd ed. New York: Self-published.

Tredgold, Thomas. 1871. *Elementary Principles of Carpentry.* London: E. & F. N. Spon.

Truax, William. 2011. "Tag Archives: Simeon S. Post." *Bridgewright* (bridgewright.wordpress.com). December 9.

Van Tassel, Charles Sumner. 1901. *Book of Ohio.* 3 vols. Bowling Green, OH: Self-published.

Wagemann, Clara E. 1931. *Covered Bridges of New England.* Rev. ed. Rutland, VT: Charles E. Tuttle, 1952.

Walczak, Thomas E., ed. 2011. *Built in America: Covered Bridges: A Close-up Look.* East Petersburg, PA: Fox Chapel Publishing.

Weale, John, ed. 1843. *Bridges in Theory, Practice, and Architecture.* 2 vols. London.

Webber, Bert and Margie Webber. 1991. *Oregon Covered Bridges: An Oregon Documentary in Pictures.* Medford, OR: Pacific Northwest Books.

Wells, Rosalie. 1931. *Covered Bridges in America.* New York: William Edwin Rudge.

Whipple, S[quire]. 1847. *A Work of Bridge Building: Consisting of Two Essays, The One Elementary and General, The Other Giving Original Plans, and Practical Details for Iron and Wooden Bridges.* Utica, NY: H. H. Curtiss. Reprinted Ann Arbor: University of Michigan Library, 2011.

_____. 1883. *An Elementary and Practical Treatise on Bridge Building.* New York: D. Van Nostrand.

Wilson, Dick. 1977. "Covered Bridge Disasters." *Bulletin, Connecticut River Valley Covered Bridge Society* 23(3): 4.

Wilson, Raymond E. 1967. "The Story of the Smith Truss." *Covered Bridge Topics* 25(1): 3–5.

Wood, De Volson. 1883. *Treatise on the Theory of the Construction of Bridges and Roofs.* 2nd ed. New York: John Wiley & Sons.

Wood, Miriam. 1993. *The Covered Bridges of Ohio: An Atlas and History.* Columbus, OH: Self-published.

Wright, David W., ed. 2009. *World Guide to Covered Bridges (2009 Edition).* 7th ed. National Society for the Preservation of Covered Bridges.

Zacher, Susan M. 1994. *The Covered Bridges of Pennsylvania: A Guide.* 2nd ed. Harrisburg: Pennsylvania Historical and Museum Commission.

THE TUTTLE STORY
"BOOKS TO SPAN THE EAST AND WEST"

Many people are surprised to learn that the world's largest publisher of books on Asia had its humble beginnings in the tiny American state of Vermont. The company's founder, Charles E. Tuttle, belonged to a New England family steeped in publishing.

Tuttle's father was a noted antiquarian dealer in Rutland, Vermont. Young Charles honed his knowledge of the trade working in the family bookstore, and later in the rare books section of Columbia University Library. His passion for beautiful books—old and new—never wavered throughout his long career as a bookseller and publisher.

After graduating from Harvard, Tuttle enlisted in the military and in 1945 was sent to Tokyo to work on General Douglas MacArthur's staff. He was tasked with helping to revive the Japanese publishing industry, which had been utterly devastated by the war. When his tour of duty was completed, he left the military, married a talented and beautiful singer, Reiko Chiba, and in 1948 began several successful business ventures.

To his astonishment, Tuttle discovered that postwar Tokyo was actually a book-lover's paradise. He befriended dealers in the Kanda district and began supplying rare Japanese editions to American libraries. He also imported American books to sell to the thousands of GIs stationed in Japan. By 1949, Tuttle's business was thriving, and he opened Tokyo's very first English-language bookstore in the Takashimaya Department Store in Ginza, to great success. Two years later, he began publishing books to fulfill the growing interest of foreigners in all things Asian.

Though a westerner, Tuttle was hugely instrumental in bringing a knowledge of Japan and Asia to a world hungry for information about the East. By the time of his death in 1993, he had published over 6,000 books on Asian culture, history and art—a legacy honored by Emperor Hirohito in 1983 with the "Order of the Sacred Treasure," the highest honor Japan can bestow upon a non-Japanese.

The Tuttle company today maintains an active backlist of some 1,500 titles, many of which have been continuously in print since the 1950s and 1960s—a great testament to Charles Tuttle's skill as a publisher. More than 60 years after its founding, Tuttle Publishing is more active today than at any time in its history, still inspired by Charles Tuttle's core mission—to publish fine books to span the East and West and provide a greater understanding of each.